Advanced Graphics with the IBM Personal Computer

Advanced Graphics
with the
IBM Personal Computer

Ian O. Angell

Department of Computer Science
University College
University of London

A HALSTED PRESS BOOK

JOHN WILEY & SONS
New York

First published 1985

Published by
Higher and Further Education Division
MACMILLAN PUBLISHERS LTD
Houndmills, Basingstoke, Hampshire RG21 2XS
and London

Published in the U.S.A.
by Halsted Press, a Division of
John Wiley & Sons, Inc., New York

Printed in Great Britain

Library of Congress Cataloging in Publication Data
Angell, Ian O.
    Advanced graphics with the IBM personal computer.

    1. Computer graphics. 2. IBM Personal Computer—
Programming. I. Title. II. Title: Advanced graphics
with the I.B.M. personal computer.
T385.A518 1984   001.64'43   84-25180
ISBN 0-470-20134-7

To Florence

Contents

deal with the general case of a perspective view of a stored three-dimensional scene that has no special properties

Preface

With the rapid advance of computer technology has come a substantial reduction in the price of computer hardware. In the coming years the price of peripheral devices will also tumble. This means that users with a limited budget, who previously had access to only the most elementary computing devices, can now afford sophisticated computers like the IBM Personal Computer. They are able to escape from the limitation of tabular numerical output and buy inexpensive special-purpose colour graphics devices to produce hardcopy, or simply photograph the screen. Software, however, does not appear to be getting cheaper.

Because of the enormous capital expenditure that was required to set up graphical output in the past, both for machines and for software, the subject of computer graphics has so far been the preserve of large research groups. This inaccessibility has led to a *mystique* growing up around the subject and it has achieved a false reputation for difficulty. This book is an attempt to lay the ghost of complexity; it will also show that complicated (and hence expensive) software packages, which are naturally of great value in research organisations, need not frighten away the average business or scientific computer user. For most purposes these packages are unnecessary. This book, as well as being an introduction to computer graphics, may be considered also as a (very inexpensive) software package: it is a lot cheaper than commercially available packages!

Naturally, because of this fundamental approach, users have to achieve a reasonable understanding of the graphics potential of the IBM Personal Computer before pictures, other than those provided, can be drawn. This need not be a disadvantage; the amount of groundwork required will be seen to be very limited and, as a direct result, the users' knowledge grows along with the package and they are far less likely to misinterpret any of the graphical routines. References and relevant further reading material are also recommended in order to expand the reader's horizons in the subject.

In explaining some of the techniques of computer graphics it is assumed that the reader has an elementary knowledge of Cartesian coordinate geometry (the author recommends the books by Cohn (1961), Coxeter (1974) and McCrae (1953) — see References and Further Reading at the end of the book), and also of the BASIC programming language on the IBM Personal Computer. The program listings, however, are written in such a way that complete beginners can run them and produce useful displays without having any knowledge in either of the aforementioned areas. Many interesting programming exercises are proposed, and these should raise the standard of readers' BASIC expertise. BASIC is a universally popular language that is available (in various guises) on all types of microcomputer, so the programs may be easily adjusted to run on micros other than the IBM: it is also a good medium for transmitting the algorithms used in computer graphics, enabling readers to translate these ideas readily into any other computer language of their choice.

The concepts necessary for the study of computer graphics are organised as a combination of theory and worked examples; these are introduced as and when they are needed in the natural progression of the subject. Program listings that form part of the examples may be considered not only as algorithms for describing solutions to fundamental graphical problems, but also as a computer graphics software package in BASIC, or just as programs to draw patterns. Alongside the examples are a series of exercises which expand on these ideas. The practical problems that are implicit in programming the various concepts of computer graphics are often more a source of difficulty to the user than the concepts themselves. Therefore it is essential that readers implement many of the program listings given in the book in order to understand the algorithms, as well as attempt a large number of the exercises. As an extra learning aid, a companion diskette is available, which contains all of the program listings that are given in this book. If readers are frightened by the mathematics they should run the programs first before studying the theory.

This approach to the subject has been used with great success in teaching computer graphics to undergraduates and postgraduates at the University of London, as well as in commercial tutorials and seminars. Quickly producing apparently complex pictures results in the positive feedback of enthusiastic interest. The ability to construct pictures on line-drawing and colour interactive graphics VDUs makes a long-lasting impression on students; and the step by step approach brings them quickly to the level of very sophisticated computer graphics. That level is outside the scope of this book, but where necessary readers will find relevant references to guide them into the more advanced topics (see Newman and Sproull (1979), Foley and van Dam (1982), Harrington (1983)).

This book is aimed in general at those who are competent BASIC pragrammers but who are complete beginners in graphics. It starts with a general introduction to the graphics features of the IBM Personal Computer. Then follows the section on high-resolution graphics; this contains the elemntary ideas and basic information about pixel and two-dimensional graphics, which must be mastered before the more involved ideas of three-dimensional graphics are attempted.

Some of these ideas are then used in a section on low-resolution graphics, which relates to the construction and use of characters and blocks of pixels, and which includes a short excursion into recursive programs. This in turn leads to a chapter on the display of data (in line drawings and colour) — histograms, pie-charts etc. — probably the most important non-specialised, commercial use of computer graphics.

The reader is then introduced to the geometry of three-dimensional space, and to a variety of projections of this space onto the two-dimensional space of graphics devices. The related problems of hidden lines and hidden surfaces, as well as the construction of complex three-dimensional objects, are dealt with in detail. Finally, text-only graphics and the construction of a screen editor and video animation are discussed.

Graphics is one of the most rapidly expanding areas of computer science. It is being used more and more in the fields of Computer Aided Design (C.A.D.), Computer Assisted Management (C.A.M.) and Computer Assisted Learning (C.A.L.). At one time it was only the big corporations such as aircraft and automobile manufacturers who used these techniques, but now most companies are realising the potential and financial savings of these ideas. What is more, not only is computer graphics profitable, it is fun! The IBM Personal Computer is an ideal machine on which to learn and use the basics of computer graphics, and an excellent springboard up to the most sophisticated (and expensive) graphics devices.

It is hoped that this book will display some of the excitement and enthusiasm for computer graphics experienced by myself, my colleagues and students. To demonstrate just how useful computer drawings are for illustrating books and pamphlets, all but three of the pictures in the following chapters were drawn on the IBM Personal Computer specifically for this book.

University College   IAN O. ANGELL
London

Acknowledgements

I should like to thank IBM (UK) for their loan of an IBM Personal Computer during the production of this book. I am particularly grateful to Benn Goulding and Leslie Banks for all their advice, help and encouragement.

Introduction

This book may be read at a number of different levels. Firstly, it can be considered as a recipe book of graphics programs for those who simply want to draw complex pictures with their IBM Personal Computer. Naturally it is hoped that the reader, having drawn these figures, will be inspired to delve more deeply into the book in order to understand how and why the programs were constructed. Secondly, some of the programs can be used as a package to produce and to label data diagrams (pie-charts, histograms and graphs) for business and laboratory purposes. Finally, and the main objective in writing the book, it is an introductory text to computer graphics that leads the reader from the elementary notions of the subject through to such advanced topics as character graphics, construction of three-dimensional objects and hidden surface (and line) algorithms.

The complex programs given later in the book are much too involved to be given as single listings. Furthermore there is a great deal of repetition in the use of elementary algorithms. Therefore the *top down* or *modular* approach is used in writing and explaining programs. The solution to each major graphics problem is conceived as a series of solutions to subproblems. These subproblems may be further broken down into a set of problems to be solved (*modules*). Such modules are programmed in the form of BASIC subroutines. Each is given an identifier (in lower case characters and referred to in the text inside quotes, such as 'scene3') and will solve a particular subtask. Then the submodules are combined to solve the required graphics problem. The program listings present the algorithms that are needed for the solution of these subtasks, and the naming of procedures in this way makes the understanding of the algorithms easier. Lower case characters are used solely for comments and routine identifiers (and groupings of routines in the text): all other program variables are in upper case to avoid confusion.

To aid the more serious readers, a companion diskette to this book is available. This contains all the listings in the book, as well as the data for pixel blocks and character sets used in later programs (which would otherwise have to be constructed by the readers themselves — a rather time-consuming job).

For those who merely want to run these programs, a complete list of programs is given at the end of each chapter, together with suitable data values. In fact it is a good idea for everyone, including the more serious readers, to LOAD and/or MERGE the relevant listings from diskettes and run the programs before approaching the text of each chapter.

There are plenty of REMarks in the program listings. However, some of the programs approach the storage limits of the IBM Personal Computer; in these cases you should delete the REMarks before resaving the programs on another disk. A REMark is placed before each routine (on program lines with numbers ending in 0) so that it indicates the start of the routine: all other REMarks are on program lines with numbers not ending in zero. Most of these REMarks are on lines ending in 9, with two major exceptions. Because subroutines do not have input and output parameters, program lines ending in 1 are reserved for **in** REMarks which give a list of all input parameters needed by the subroutine that are not generated as output parameters from internal calls to other routines. Program lines ending in 2 are reserved for **out** REMarks which give a list of all output parameters from a subroutine. You may find that all these REMarks take up too much store and slow down the execution time of the program, in which case you should strip them away with the help of listing I.1. All programs except listing I.1 begin at program lines not less than 100. So MERG(E)ing listing I.1 into an existing program listing will place this program at the front of the code. Running the combined program will delete every line with line number not ending in zero from the original program (all the REMarks) and request the name of a disk file where the deREMed program, minus listing I.1, can be stored for future use. You will have to know how BASIC programs are stored on the Personal Computer before you will understand listing I.1. Note that locations &H30 and &H31 of the BASIC segment hold the low and high bytes of the address of the start of the BASIC program.

Listing I.1

```
1  'MERGE this program to the front of a target program which
      contains REMarks to be deleted. All target lines with numbers
      ending in zero's are executable. The rest are REMarks.
2  DEF SEG
3  'INPUT the name of the file which will hold the deREMed listing.
4  PRINT " Type name of disk file for deREMed listing ";
      "e.g.  B:NOREMS.BAS " : INPUT FILE$
5  'locations PTR% and PTR%+1 of the BASIC segment hold the lo- and hi-
      byte values of the location of a program line. Initially the
      first program line. Store these two bytes.
6  PTR%=&H30 : STO1%=PEEK(PTR%+1) : STO0%=PEEK(PTR%)
7  '129 signifies the END of the derem program in the memory.
      Program lines that follow are from the target program.
8  IF PEEK(PTR%+4)<>129
      THEN PTR%=PEEK(PTR%+1)*&H100+PEEK(PTR%) : GOTO 8
9  PTR%=PEEK(PTR%+1)*&H100+PEEK(PTR%)
10 'TARGETPTR% and TARGETPTR%+1 hold the start of target program.
      PROGPTR% (and +1) will be used to over-write the target program
      locations, with program lines that are not REMarks.
11 PROGPTR%=PTR% : TARGETPTR%=PTR%
12 'PTR% (and +1) point to the present line under consideration,
      NEXTPTR% (and +1) point to the next program line.
13 NEXTPTR%=PEEK(PTR%+1)*&H100+PEEK(PTR%)
14 'NEXTPTR% is zero at the end of target program.
15 IF NEXTPTR%=0 THEN GOTO 36
16 'find the line number of the program line being considered.
17 LINENUM%=PEEK(PTR%+3)*&H100+PEEK(PTR%+2)
18 PRINT "considering line number";LINENUM%
19 'if LINENUM% doesn't end in a zero it is a REMark.
20 IF LINENUM% MOD 10 <> 0 THEN GOTO 33
```

```
21 'program lines are moved up the memory, over-writing other
   lines of the target program that have already been checked.
22 LINESIZE%=NEXTPTR%-PTR%
23 'store the address of the next program line. That is add the
   size of the program line to the present address.
24 POKE PROGPTR%,(PROGPTR%+LINESIZE%) MOD &H100
25 POKE PROGPTR%+1,INT((PROGPTR%+LINESIZE%)/&H100)
26 'move up the locations holding program line.
27 FOR I%=2 TO LINESIZE%-1
28 POKE PROGPTR%+I%,PEEK(PTR%+I%)
29 NEXT I%
30 'go on to next line in deREMed program.
31 PROGPTR%=PROGPTR%+LINESIZE%
32 'go on to next line in the target program.
33 PTR%=NEXTPTR%
34 GOTO 13
35 'mark the end of the program with two zeros.
36 POKE PROGPTR%,0
37 POKE PROGPTR%+1,0
38 'the start of program pointers show the deREMed program.
39 POKE &H30,TARGETPTR% MOD &H100
40 POKE &H31,INT(TARGETPTR%/&H100)
41 'save the deREMed program.
42 SAVE FILE$
43 'reset the start of program pointers.
44 POKE &H30,STO0% : POKE &H31,STO1%
45 END
```

The variable names in the programs will sometimes be rather long-winded, and therefore inefficient. Also the programs themselves may seem over-explicit in the number of routines involved. This is because the programs are meant to convey the ideas behind an algorithm, and the speed of execution is of secondary concern. The statements themselves are generously spaced out to aid clarity. Readers who wish to use the programs on a regular basis are advised to slim down the variable names and reduce the number of spaces, and also cannibalise the programs to make them more efficient. For example, calls to small subroutines (for example, 'lineto') can be replaced by explicit lines of code in the programs.

Listing I.2 is given as an example of what graphics to expect after reading this book. This listing is used to draw figure I.1, a drawing of a wire-body of revolution – in this case a goblet.

The program requires listings 1.1 ('colour' and 'monochrome' display routines, usually called 'lib0'), 2.1 ('start', two functions FN X and FN Y), 2.2 ('setorigin'), 2.3 ('moveto'), 3.3 ('lineto' and 'clip') and 3.4 ('angle'). If you have release 2.0 of Advanced BASIC then the four listings 2.1, 2.2, 2.3 and 3.3 may be replaced by the more efficient equivalent listings 2.1a, 2.2a, 2.3a and 2.4a. This combination of routines is part of a second library, called 'lib1', which was designed for drawing lines and areas on the colour monitor.

Listings 8.1 ('mult3' and 'idR3'), 8.2 ('tran3'), 8.3 ('scale3'), 8.4 ('rot3') and 9.1 ('look3') must also be MERGEd into the program. These routines form the 'lib3' library, which is used for transforming and observing objects in three-dimensional space.

The program also needs listing 9.9 ('revbod') to be MERGEd into the 'scene3' main program given in listing I.2.

Figure I.1

Listing I.2

```
100 'scene3 / goblet
110 GOSUB 9700 'start
120 DIM X(24),Y(24),XD(12),YD(12)
130 DIM A(4,4),B(4,4),R(4,4)
140 DATA  0,-8,  4,-8,  4,-7.5,  0.5,-7.5,  0.5,-1,  3,-0.5,
          4,1,   7,7,   6.5,7,   3.5,1,     2.5,0,   0,0
150 RESTORE 140
159 'generate definition set.
160 NUMV%=11 : N1%=NUMV%+1
170 INPUT "Type number of horizontal lines ",NUMH%
180 INPUT "Type initial angle ",PHI
190 FOR I%=1 TO N1%
200 READ XD(I%),YD(I%)
210 NEXT I%
220 GOSUB 9300 'idR3
230 GOSUB 8200 'look3
240 GOSUB 60000 'colour monitor
250 XMOVE=HORIZ/2 : YMOVE=VERT/2
260 GOSUB 9600 'setorigin
270 GOSUB 6500 'revbod
280 GOSUB 60100 'monochrome monitor
290 END
```

To run on the colour monitor the program needs variable MODE%, PALETTE%, BACKGROUND%, FOREGROUND% and PAPER%. Try 1, 1, 0, 0, 3 respectively. The production of figure I.1 requires the further data HORIZ = 36, EX = 1, EY = 2, EZ = 3, DX = 0, DY = 0, DZ = 0, 'number of horizontal lines' = NUMH% = 16 and 'initial rotation' = PHI = 0. Each value has to be typed in individually on request by the machine. Run the program with different data values: what happens if HORIZ = 60 and the other values stay the same? Set HORIZ = 16, EX = 1, EY = −2, EZ = 3, DX = 1, DY = 0 and DZ = 0. Try NUMH% = 20, PHI = 0.1. Also run with

MODE% = 2 and PAPER% = 1. You will have to read up to and including chapter 9 to understand the details of what is happening.

This example illustrates the reasoning behind the layout of this book. Assuming you are a fast typist, or you have bought the accompanying diskette, then a relatively complex three-dimensional picture can be constructed very quickly with a minimum of fuss. Even one-finger typists (like the author) will have little difficulty in implementing this and the other programs, before they go on to study the book in detail.

It is hoped that this example will inspire you to implement *all* the programs in this book, to try most of the examples, and then to go on to draw your very own complex computer graphics pictures.

Now you can go on and read the rest of this book, and I wish you many happy hours with your IBM Personal Computer.

1 Graphics Commands on the IBM Personal Computer

It will be assumed throughout the course of this book that the reader is reasonably familiar with the BASICA interpreter on the IBM Personal Computer (or IBM PC as it will be referred to). This understood, the best first approach to graphics on this or any new machine is to write small programs in order to get used to the graphical capabilities and any limitations of that machine. This first chapter, therefore, will look at some of the BASIC commands on the IBM PC that are concerned wholly or partly with graphics. The graphics statements will not be described in detail, you can get that information from the manual, but particularly useful applications of certain statements will be expanded upon. The display potential of the IBM PC is explored with a series of example programs and simple exercises. In the following chapters this knowledge will be used to develop a sound understanding, both practical and mathematical, of computer graphics in general. This book will concentrate on graphics and so not too much effort is spent in making the programs 'idiot proof' (or more politely 'robust'). The code necessary to prevent nonsensical input from killing programs would confuse the underlying graphics theory: and anyway it is assumed that all readers of this book are very sensible people! It is a good exercise, however, to take the programs from the book and add the required robust code. Furthermore, machine code and assembler programs have been deliberately ignored, in the belief that the IBM PC user will program mostly in BASIC. Machine code implementations of algorithms do speed up execution times but they are of no value for transferring the ideas behind those graphics algorithms and, after all, the main purpose of this book is to explain these methods. If readers require speedier execution times then they must either hand-compile their programs or, even better, purchase an Advanced BASIC compiler.

The hardware and software facilities available for producing pictures on the IBM PC are considered first. It is assumed that the reader has a BASICA interpreter in order to produce coloured pictures on a colour monitor. It is necessary to switch between the colour monitor and the standard monochrome display at various times in the programs, so the two subroutines of listing 1.1 are introduced. These are collectively called 'lib0' throughout this book and will be incorporated in *every* program. You will notice that they are a variation on the routines given in Appendix A of the BASIC manual. The details of the commands they use (such as SCREEN, WIDTH etc.) will be explained later in this chapter. Also note the 'soft-key menu' at the base of both the monochrome display and colour monitor screens. This is a nuisance when drawing graphics pictures, so the menu is deleted with a KEY OFF command.

Listing 1.1

```
60000 'switch to colour monitor
60001 '**in ** from MODE%,PALETTE%,BORDER%,
                    BACKGROUND%,FOREGROUND%,PAPER%
60002 '**out** WYDTH%
60010 DEF SEG=0 : KEY OFF
60020 IF MODE%=0 THEN INPUT "WIDTH ",WYDTH% ELSE WYDTH%=40*MODE%
60030 POKE &H410,(PEEK(&H410) AND &HCF) OR &H10
60040 SCREEN 1,0,0,0 : SCREEN 0 : WIDTH WYDTH%
60050 LOCATE ,,1,6,7
60060 SCREEN MODE%,0
60070 IF MODE%=0 THEN COLOR FOREGROUND%,BACKGROUND%,BORDER%
               ELSE IF MODE%=1 THEN COLOR BACKGROUND%,PALETTE%
60080 IF MODE%<>0 THEN LINE (0,0)-(320*MODE%-1,199),PAPER%,BF
60090 RETURN

60100 'switch to monochrome display
60110 DEF SEG=0
60120 POKE &H410,(PEEK(&H410) OR &H30)
60130 SCREEN 0
60140 WIDTH 40
60150 WIDTH 80
60160 LOCATE ,,1,12,13
60170 RETURN
```

In all but the most elementary machines, it is possible to set up these plotting routines or their equivalents (and many more as your knowledge increases) in a library file on backing store. Then there is no need to explicitly retype them into each new program. Files can be stored on disk in a special format by the IBM PC (SAVE"filename.BAS", A : the A implies the file is saved in ASCII format) and they can be MERGEd into other programs (MERGE"filename.BAS") when required. On the companion diskette to this book you will find the two routines of listing 1.1 in the 'lib0' library.

There are three modes for picture generation on the IBM PC, labelled 0 (*text-only*), 1 (*medium-resolution*) and 2 (*high-resolution*). A mode is specified by a SCREEN command (see later), and the current mode will be stored in the integer variable MODE%. All the modes produce television pictures using *raster scan* technology. This is also true of most of the newer commercial mini and mainframe computers. An area of memory 16 K(ilo)bytes long (1 Kbyte = 2^{10} bytes = 1024 bytes: called 1K for short), and known as the *screen buffer*, is reserved out of the available RAM (Random Access Memory, the area available for programming use) to hold the display information for the screen. This memory is examined, bit by bit, as the electron beam of the television/monitor sweeps across the raster screen. The display is composed of dots or *pixels* (from picture-cells) each of which corresponds in the simplest case of mode 2 to a single bit (one-eighth of a byte) in the memory: a binary on/off (1/0) switch. Whenever a binary on (1) is detected during the raster scan, the beam is switched on for a short period and so produces a dot of light on the screen. In mode 1 two bits correspond to each pixel: mode 0 is more complicated (see later). The screen can be considered in two ways, either as a grid of individual points which are addressed by a *graphics* command, or as a grid of blocks, each being capable of holding one *character*, which may be placed there by a *text* command.

Available Colours

The colour monitor has a maximum of thirty-two available colours, numbered 0 to 31 (in hex: &H0 to &H1F). These are called the *actual colours* of the IBM PC. The colours can therefore be considered as a five-bit binary number: bit 0 being on the right (least significant) and bit 4 on the left (most significant). The value (0 or 1) of these bits uniquely describes the colour that appears on the screen as follows.

Bit 0 (0/1): colour (does not contain/contains) blue
Bit 1 (0/1): colour (does not contain/contains) green
Bit 2 (0/1): colour (does not contain/contains) red
Bit 3 (0/1): colour (low/high) intensity
Bit 4 (0/1): colour (not flashing/flashing)

Thus, for example, colour 27 = &H1B = 11011 (binary) is flashing, of high intensity, and contains blue and green but not red. The combination blue with green is called cyan. Similarly no colours give black, blue and red give magenta, and green and red give brown (high-intensity brown is yellow), and blue, green and red give white. Note that not all of these 32 actual colours/effects are available with every colour monitor. Also the number of colours available at any one time is mode-dependent.

Text Output

Text output (that is, characters) is available in all three modes. The colour monitor screen is assumed to be 25 rows deep by 40 (or 80) columns wide. The choice of width of the screen is specified by a WIDTH statement and the present width value is stored in the integer variable WYDTH%. You will have noticed that the graphics area does not fill the screen, but forms a rectangle inside a 'border'. This ensures that any curvature of the screen does not distort the final picture ('pin-cushion distortion').

Characters and numeric values may be PRINTed on the screen, to specify the start position of the text, by

LOCATE row, column

Starting at the specified row and column, the text string is printed from left to right, following a flashing text-cursor across the screen. If the string hits the end of a row then it continues at the first column of the next row below. PRINTing in column 40 (or 80) of either row 24 or 25 will cause the screen to *scroll* upwards. This can be rather inconvenient, so to avoid scrolling you may have to POKE characters into those positions (see chapter 13). Figure 1.1 shows the character positions for a mode 1 screen of WIDTH 40.

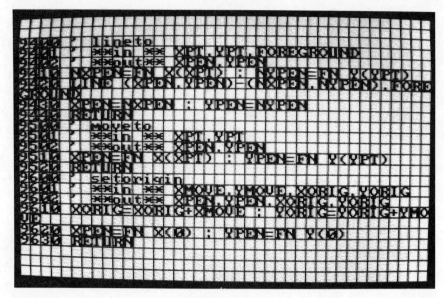

Figure 1.1

A useful variation of the LOCATE statement is

LOCATE row, column, 0

which enables you to position the text-cursor without it flashing on the screen — an irritation when using a graphical display.

Example 1.1

Listing 1.2 uses LOCATE and PRINT to show the colours available on the colour monitor. Before RUNning this program in mode 0 you should first MERGE in 'lib0'. Then give it WIDTH 40.

Listing 1.2

```
100 MODE%=0 : BORDER%=0
110 BACKGROUND%=7 : FOREGROUND%=0
120 GOSUB 60000 'colour monitor
130 LOCATE 4,11 : PRINT " AVAILABLE COLOURS "
140 ROW%=10 : COLUMN%=2
150 FOR I%=0 TO 31
160 IF I% MOD 8=0 THEN COLOR I%,7,1 ELSE COLOR I%,0,1
170 LOCATE ROW%,COLUMN%,0 : PRINT I%
180 COLUMN%=COLUMN%+5
190 IF COLUMN%>40 THEN COLUMN%=2 : ROW%=ROW%+2
200 NEXT I%
210 COLOR 0,7 : GOSUB 60100 'monochrome display
220 END
```

A character is written in a foreground colour on a background colour, inside a given border. The definitions of foreground, background and border colours are mode-dependent. Throughout this book the present values of these colours are stored in integer variables FOREGROUND%, BACKGROUND% and BORDER%. It is, therefore, now necessary to look at the use of text in the three modes.

The Text-Only Mode: Mode 0

Mode 0 is initiated by a SCREEN command

    SCREEN 0 [,[burst] [,[apage] [,vpage]]]

Note the use of the square-bracket notation, used in the BASIC manual for showing parts of a statement that can be suppressed.
[burst] : a zero value makes all images black and white, a non-zero value (the
          default) enables colour to be used.
In this mode it is possible to have up to 8 separate pages (numbered 0 to 7) of text
[apage] : specifies the page that is active (that is, printing goes on this page)
[vpage] : specifies the page that is visible.
This means that it is possible to PRINT on one page, while looking at another (much more of this in chapter 13).

    Mode 0 allows all 32 actual colours/effects in the foreground, but only 8 colours in the background (actual colours 0 to 7), and 16 colours in the border (actual 0 to 15). The colours are specified by the COLOR statement

    COLOR [foreground] [,[background] [,border]]

The screen can be cleared in the background colour with a CLS statement.

Example 1.2

Each character to be printed will have a unique numerical code number between 0 and 255: the ASCII code (American Standard Code for Information Interchange), see Appendix G of the BASIC manual. The ASCII code for a given character C$ say is ASC(C$), and the character corresponding to a given code I is CHR$(I). The following program (listing 1.3 and 'lib0': from now on 'lib0' will be taken for granted) randomly PRINTs characters, in a variety of foreground, background and border colours, on two pages of a mode 0 screen (pages 0 and 1), bringing the active page into view with each PRINT. Also note the use of the SOUND statement. For more about switching between pages see chapter 13.

    Also you should note that when writing text in the graphics modes, only characters with ASCII codes of less than 128 are immediately available. If you need any characters with codes greater than 127 then you must load GRAFTABL (see the BASIC manual) before entering the BASICA interpreter.

Listing 1.3

```
100 MODE%=0 : BORDER%=0
110 BACKGROUND%=0 : FOREGROUND%=1
120 GOSUB 60000 'colour monitor
129 'print 1000 characters and make noises.
130 FOR I%=1 TO 1000
140 FOREGROUND%=INT(RND*32) : BACKGROUND%=INT(RND*8)
150 BORDER%=INT(RND*16) : CHAR%=32+INT(RND*96)
160 COLUMN%=INT(RND*WYDTH%)+1 : ROW%=INT(RND*25)+1
170 FREQ%=100+RND*1000 : DUR%=RND*8
180 COLOR FOREGROUND%,BACKGROUND%,BORDER%
190 PAGE%=INT(RND*2) : SCREEN ,,PAGE%,PAGE%
200 LOCATE ROW%,COLUMN% : PRINT CHR$(CHAR%);
210 SOUND FREQ%,DUR%
220 NEXT I%
230 GOSUB 60100 'monochrome display
240 END
```

It is possible to have 16 background colours if you give up a flashing foreground (see Appendix I of the BASIC manual)

> type OUT &H3D8,8　for width 40
> or　OUT &H3D8,9　for width 80

The Medium-Resolution Mode: Mode 1

Mode 1 allows 40 column or 80 column width text, and is initiated by another SCREEN statement

> SCREEN 1 [,[burst]]

[burst] : as above

This mode allows the use of four colours at any one time. These are called the *logical colours*, numbered 0 to 3. The border colour (one of the actual colours 0 to 15) is identified with the BACKGROUND% colour, defined to be logical colour 0, and the remaining logical colours (numbered 1 to 3) are taken from one of two available palettes as shown below.

Logical colour	Palette 0 Actual colour/number	Palette 1 Actual colour/number
1	green/2	cyan/3
2	red/4	magenta/5
3	brown/6	white/7

Thus the non-border logical colour i from palette j is actual colour $2 * i + j$. The BACKGROUND% (= border) and palette (stored as variable PALETTE%) are initialised by a COLOR statement

> COLOR [background] [,[palette]]

This allows you to draw in any FOREGROUND% colour chosen from logical colours 0 to 3. It is also possible to fill the screen in any colour (called the paper colour, stored in variable PAPER%).

Example 1.3

Text, however, is normally logical colour 3 on a logical 0 background. The foreground colour can be changed to a non-zero logical colour by typing

DEF SEG: POKE &H4E,logical colour (1, 2 or 3)

Listing 1.4 is an interactive program that will enable you to try all logical colour and palette combinations. You should see the labelling program in chapter 6 (listing 6.2) for a method of writing text characters in logical colour 0 on an arbitrary background.

Listing 1.4

```
100 MODE%=1
110 GOSUB 60000 'colour monitor
120 LOCATE 4,6 : INPUT " actual colour of background ",BACKGROUND%
130 LOCATE 6,6 : INPUT " palette ",PALETTE%
140 LOCATE 8,6 : INPUT " logical colour of foreground ",FOREGROUND%
150 IF FOREGROUND%=0 THEN GOTO 140
160 COLOR BACKGROUND%,PALETTE%
170 DEF SEG : POKE &H4E,FOREGROUND%
180 LOCATE 10,12 : PRINT "What's up DOC?"
190 GOSUB 60100 'monochrome monitor
200 END
```

The High-Resolution Mode: Mode 2

Mode 2 is initiated by another SCREEN statement

SCREEN 2

This mode allows the use of two colours only: a black (logical zero) BACKGROUND% in 40 or 80 column widths and a black or white (logical 1) FOREGROUND%. The graphics area can, of course, be totally filled in a PAPER% colour (0 or 1) before drawing.

Graphics Output

Graphics output is available only in modes 1 and 2, the medium-resolution and high-resolution modes respectively. Before plotting, the graphics area can be filled in a given PAPER% colour (defaulting to the BACKGROUND% colour). For the time being the screen is considered to be a matrix of dots (or pixels): 320 (in mode 1) or 640 (in mode 2) across, by 200 (in both modes) down (later WINDOW and VIEW will be used to alter this simplified interpretation). Thus a pixel on the screen may be uniquely identified by a pair of integers (X, Y) called a pixel vector. X is the number of dots across counting from left to right starting at zero, and Y is the number of dots down starting at zero. Thus the top left-hand corner is (0, 0) and the bottom right-hand corner is (319, 199). Note that in the pixel vector the column (across) comes before the row (down) which is opposite to the LOCATE statement which puts row before column, and also that the pixels start at (0, 0) whereas character positions start at row 1, column 1. These graphics modes are initiated in the same way (SCREEN) as described in the Text-Only Mode section of this chapter, as are the colour properties of each mode (COLOR). The IBM PC has a number of operations that manipulate pixels. They will now be considered.

PSET and PRESET

These statements allow the user to print dots of a specified [color] at a pixel vector (X, Y). The formats of these statements are

PSET (X, Y)[,color]　　and　　PRESET (X, Y)[,color]

The only difference between the statements is in the default option, when [color] is not specified. PSET chooses the foreground colour whereas PRESET chooses the background.

Example 1.4
PSET is used to place dots of random colours at random pixel vectors (listing 1.5) on PAPER% = 1. Also note again the use of SOUND, and of RND for generating pseudo-random numbers.

Listing 1.5

```
100 CLS : INPUT "MODE ",MODE%
110 IF MODE%=0 THEN GOTO 100
120 PALETTE%=1 : PAPER%=1
130 FOREGROUND%=2 : BACKGROUND%=0
140 GOSUB 60000 ´colour monitor
150 FOR I%=1 TO 1000
159 ´place a dot, colour COLOR, at (X%,Y%)
160 COLOR%=INT(RND*(4/MODE%))
170 X%=INT(RND*320*MODE%) : Y%=INT(RND*200)
180 PSET (X%,Y%),COLOR%
189 ´make a SOUND
190 FREQ%=100+RND*1000 : DUR%=RND*2
200 SOUND FREQ%,DUR%
210 NEXT I%
220 GOSUB 60100 ´monochrome display
230 END
```

Example 1.5
One use of PSET is to draw fractals (see Mandelbrot, 1977).

　　The following method is used to draw a simple type of fractal. Imagine a square with sides of length 4^n. This may be divided into 16 smaller squares, each with sides of length 4^{n-1}, which are numbered 1 to 16 as in figure 1.2. Four of these smaller squares, numbers 2, 8, 9 and 15, are rearranged to produce figure 1.3.

Each of the squares in the pattern is now split up into 16 even smaller squares in the same way and these are similarly rearranged. This process is repeated until only squares with sides of length 1 remain. The resulting fractal pattern consists entirely of unit squares which are PSET as single pixels. The mode 1 program in listing 1.6 starts from a square with sides of length 64, which is 4^3, thus in the program there

1
2
3
4
5
6
7
8
9
10
11
12
13
14
15
16

Figure 1.2

2
1
3
4
9
5
6
7
10
11
12
8
13
14
16
15

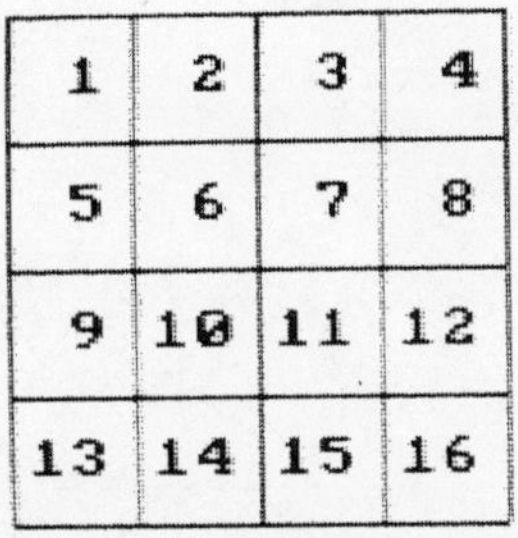

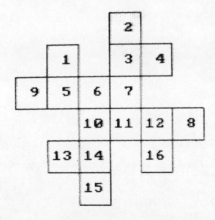

Figure 1.3

Figure 1.4

must be three FOR. . .NEXT loops nested inside each other. The final picture produced is shown in figure 1.4. Note the use of the OPTION BASE 1 command which implies that the indices of all arrays start at 1 rather than 0.

Listing 1.6

```
100 MODE%=1 : PALETTE%=0
110 BACKGROUND%=1 : FOREGROUND%=2
120 GOSUB 60000 'colour monitor
130 OPTION BASE 1
140 DIM X%(16),Y%(16)
149 'assign an x and y coordinate to each square.
150 FOR I%=1 TO 4
160 FOR J%=1 TO 4
170 K%=4*I%+J%-4
180 X%(K%)=J%-3 : Y%(K%)=I%-3
190 NEXT J% : NEXT I%
199 'move squares 2,8,9 and 15.
200 X%(2)=0 : Y%(2)=-3
210 X%(8)=2 : Y%(8)=0
220 X%(9)=-3 : Y%(9)=-1
230 X%(15)=-1 : Y%(15)=2
239 'plot each square inside a square inside a square as one pixel.
240 FOR I%=1 TO 16
250 FOR J%=1 TO 16
260 FOR K%=1 TO 16
270 XX%=160+16*X%(I%)+4*X%(J%)+X%(K%)
280 YY%=100+16*Y%(I%)+4*Y%(J%)+Y%(K%)
290 PSET (XX%,YY%),2
300 NEXT K% : NEXT J% : NEXT I%
310 GOSUB 60100 'monochrome display
320 END
```

Exercise 1.1

If you know how to write *recursive programs* or you understand how the 'Eight Queens Problem' in chapter 5 was written, then you should try to give a recursive program for drawing figure 1.4.

How the Screen is Organised

It was noted that a part of RAM is designated as the screen buffer. This is 16K (&H4000 in hex) memory locations long and starts at address &HB8000. By setting DEF SEG = &HB800 (remember the last zero of an address is dropped in a DEF SEG command!) the screen buffer may be considered to be offset locations &H0 to &H3FFF of this memory segment. Offset locations 0 to 7999 (&H0 to &H1F3F) represent 'even' pixel rows 0, 2, 4, . . ., 198, and locations 8192 to 16191 (&H2000 to &H3F3F) the 'odd' pixel rows 1, 3, . . ., 199. Each pixel row consists of 80 locations (bytes), so that is why 8000 (= 80 × 100) bytes are needed for the even lines on the screen, and similarly for the odd. In mode 2 each 8-bit byte represents 8 pixels on the screen: a bit set (= 1) is coloured white, and not set (= 0) is coloured black. This allows 640 (= 80 × 8) pixels in each row for mode 2. In mode 1 each byte represents 4 pixels. The 8 bits are divided into 4 2-bit binary numbers (each with a value between 0 and 3), and these numbers specify which of the four logical colours is displayed at the corresponding pixel on the screen. Two examples are given to demonstrate how this works (listings 1.7 and 1.8). Note that parts of the screen buffer are not used: locations 8000 to 8191 (&H1F40 to &H1FFF) and 16192 to 16383 (&H3F40 to &H3FFF).

Example 1.6

Listing 1.7 gives a program that POKEs the hexadecimal value &H1B into all the bytes corresponding to 'even' lines on the screen (that is, offset locations &H0 to &H1FFF). You should note the different effects brought about by running the program in both modes 1 and 2. &H1B = 00011011 binary, so in mode 1 there are four pixels with logical colours 0 (00 binary), 1 (01), 2 (10) and 3 (11) respectively, while in mode 2 there are 8 pixels with logical colours 0, 0, 0, 1, 1, 0, 1, 1 from left to right.

Listing 1.7

```
100 CLS : INPUT "MODE ",MODE%
110 IF MODE%<>1 AND MODE%<>2 THEN GOTO 100
120 IF MODE%=1 THEN PALETTE%=1 : BACKGROUND%=1
130 GOSUB 60000 ´colour monitor
140 DEF SEG=&HB800 : CLS
150 FOR OFFSET%=0 TO 7999
160 POKE OFFSET%,&H1B
170 NEXT OFFSET%
180 GOSUB 60100 ´monochrome display
190 END
```

Listing 1.8

```
100 CLS : INPUT "MODE ",MODE%
110 IF MODE%<>1 AND MODE%<>2 THEN GOTO 100
120 IF MODE%=1 THEN PALETTE%=1 : BACKGROUND%=1
130 GOSUB 60000 'colour monitor
140 DEF SEG=&HB800
150 CLS : LOCATE 10,14
160 PRINT"in mode ";MODE%
170 LOCATE 12,1
180 INPUT"type in a value between 0 and 255 ";V%
190 IF V%<0 OR V%>255 THEN GOTO 150
200 POKE 0,V%
210 LOCATE 14,9 : PRINT"which in hex is :- &H";HEX$(V%);
220 LOCATE 2,3 : PRINT 4*MODE%;"pixels in top left corner :-";
230 FOR I%=0 TO 4*MODE%-1
240 COLOR%=POINT(I%,0)
250 IF COLOR%=0 THEN BACK%=3 ELSE BACK%=0
260 LINE (269+10*I%,7)-(278+10*I%,16),BACK%,BF
270 LINE (270+10*I%,8)-(277+10*I%,15),COLOR%,BF
280 NEXT I%
290 LOCATE 20,8 : PRINT "press any key to continue";
300 KB$=INKEY$ : IF KB$="" THEN GOTO 300 ELSE GOTO 150
310 END
```

Example 1.7: POINT and LINE

Listing 1.8 gives a program which POKEs a number between 0 and 255 (that is, one that can be represented as an 8-bit binary number) into location &HB8000 (that is, DEF SEG = &HB800 and offset 0). It then uses the POINT command to find the colour of the 4 (mode 1) or 8 (mode 2) pixels corresponding to this binary value at the beginning of the top row of the screen. Note that the format of the POINT command

$$COL = POINT(X, Y)$$

gives the colour of the pixel in column X and row Y of the screen.

The program also uses the LINE command for drawing coloured boxes corresponding to the top left-hand corner pixels. The format for LINE is

$$LINE [(x1, y1)] - (x2, y2)[,[color] [,B[F]] [,style]]$$

Option B means a hollow rectangle with opposite corners (x1, y1) and (x2, y2) constructed in a given [color]. Option BF means the rectangle is filled in. If these options are not specified a straight line segment is drawn between the two points. If (x1, y1) is not explicit then it is assumed that the user means the last point referenced by a graphics operation.

The style parameter (only available in BASIC release 2.0) must be a 16-bit integer mask. Listing 1.9 gives a simple example of its operation, drawing 200 horizontal lines, each with a different integer mask. The integer is used to draw dotted rather than solid lines. The sixteen bits in the mask are used to create a sequence of 1s (foreground colour) and 0s (background), used repeatedly between the end points of the line. When drawing horizontally, the colour corresponding to the least significant bit is placed to the left and the most significant bit to the right (opposite to the normal way a binary number is considered) — see listing 1.9. With vertical lines, the colour for the least significant bit comes below that of the most significant bit. You should write a program, similar to listing 1.9, for drawing 320 vertical lines.

Listing 1.9

```
100 MODE%=1
110 GOSUB 60000 'colour monitor
120 FOR Y%=0 TO 199
130 LINE (0,Y%)-(319,Y%),1+Y% MOD 3,,Y%
140 NEXT Y%
150 GOSUB 60100 'monochrome monitor
160 END
```

Having created a picture on the colour monitor screen and returned program control to the monochrome display, it is essential to know how to store the picture for future display. For example, typing

DEF SEG = &HB800: BSAVE "A:FIG.PIC",0,&H3FFF

will store the complete screen buffer on disk A as file FIG.PIC. Then typing

DEF SEG = &HB800: BLOAD "A:FIG.PIC"

will reload the file into the screen buffer (and hence display it on the screen) for successive programs.

Exercise 1.2
Store the fractal picture of example 1.5, and reload it into a program that can interchange the logical colour values of the pixels using POINT and PSET. Also write another program that loads in a stored picture and then XORs each location in the screen buffer with &HFF.

Example 1.8
Two more example programs are now given to illustrate the use of LINE. The first (listing 1.10) draws random coloured lines all over the screen, so creating a 'Jackson Pollock' type picture. Note how the complete graphics frame is coloured in the PAPER% colour by the call to

LINE (0, 0) — (319, 199),PAPER%,BF

in the colour monitor routine from 'lib0'.

The second program (listing 1.11) mixes text with graphics to print 'What's up Doc?' inside a multicoloured boundary created by calls to LINE with the BF option.

Listing 1.10

```
100 MODE%=1 : PALETTE%=0 : PAPER%=1
110 FOREGROUND%=3 : BACKGROUND%=0
120 GOSUB 60000 'colour monitor
130 X%=0 : Y%=0
140 FOR I%=1 TO 1000
150 OLDX%=X% : OLDY%=Y%
160 X%=INT(RND*320) : Y%=INT(RND*200)
170 LINE (OLDX%,OLDY%)-(X%,Y%),INT(RND*4)
180 NEXT I%
190 GOSUB 60100 'monochrome display
200 END
```

Listing 1.11

```
100 MODE%=1 : PALETTE%=1
110 FOREGROUND%=0 : BACKGROUND%=1
120 GOSUB 60000 'colour monitor
130 FOR L%=0 TO 95 STEP 5
140 FOREGROUND%=(FOREGROUND%+1) MOD 4
150 LINE (L%,L%)-(319-L%,199-L%),FOREGROUND%,BF
160 NEXT L%
170 LOCATE 13,14 : PRINT"What's up Doc ?";
180 GOSUB 60100 'monochrome display
190 END
```

DRAW

The next graphics instruction considered is DRAW, with format

> DRAW string

The string is composed of a sequence of instructions from a *graphics definition language*, which enables a 'graphics pen' to move around the screen. This statement has limited use in the type of graphics considered in this book, so a small example only is given for completeness (listing 1.12). This animates a line drawing of a 'spaceship' moving diagonally across the screen. You should consult the manual for the complete description of the very powerful graphics definition language. The example uses BM330, 6 to move the ship to its initial position, and a string variable SHIP$ to DRAW the ship. SHIP$ uses E (move diagonally up and right), R (move right), M−20, 12 (relative move by 20 left and 12 down), D (move down) and C0 or C1 (for setting the colour). Over-drawing a shape in the background colour deletes a previous image, so that a loop which incorporates this idea with moving the initial point of reference of the ship down the screen creates the effect of downward diagonal movement.

Listing 1.12

```
100 MODE%=1
110 GOSUB 60000 'colour monitor
120 SCREEN 1 : COLOR 0,0
129 'small delay
130 FOR I%=1 TO 1000 : NEXT I%
```

```
139 'create ship string
140 SHIP$="E16 R8 M-20,12 M+12,-20 D8"
149 'move to start position
150 DRAW"BM300,6"
159 'movie of ship travelling down screen
160 FOR I%=1 TO 88
170 DRAW"C1;BM-18,18;XSHIP$;"
180 DRAW"C0;BM-16,16;XSHIP$;"
190 NEXT I%
200 GOSUB 60100 'monochrome display
210 END
```

PAINT

This is an extremely useful command for graphics modes. Format

   PAINT (x, y)[[,paint] [,boundary] [,background]]

allows you to start at pixel (x, y) and move in any direction, painting the pixels
met in colour [paint] and stopping at pixels of colours [boundary] and [paint].
There are some limitations to its use however. If you draw an outline that includes
a very acute angle, then the limited resolution of the screen may mean that two
edges of the outline will touch at points other than a vertex of the outline, which
in turn could isolate pixels of a background colour and so leave them totally
surrounded by pixels of the edge colour. In this situation the PAINT operation will
fail to colour these isolated pixels and 'holes' will appear in your design. Also if you
draw an outline of a figure (such as a triangle) in the [boundary] colour on top of a
partially completed picture, then this triangle may contain some areas already
drawn in the [boundary] colour. This may mean that PAINTing will stop before
the triangle is properly filled-in. Listing 1.13 demonstrates these problems. It draws
random triangles on the screen and fills them with random colours. Observe the
operations carefully and you will note the occurrence of the two separate types of
problem.

Listing 1.13

```
100 MODE%=1 : PALETTE%=0
110 FOREGROUND%=1 : BACKGROUND%=1
120 GOSUB 60000 'colour monitor
129 'draw 1000 triangles.
130 FOR I%=1 TO 1000
140 X1=RND*319 : X2=RND*319 : X3=RND*319
150 Y1=RND*199 : Y2=RND*199 : Y3=RND*199
160 EDGECOL%=INT(RND*4)
170 LINE (X1,Y1)-(X2,Y2),EDGECOL%
180 LINE (X2,Y2)-(X3,Y3),EDGECOL%
190 LINE (X3,Y3)-(X1,Y1),EDGECOL%
199 'find the median of the triangle.
200 XMED=(X1+X2+X3)/3 : YMED=(Y1+Y2+Y3)/3
209 'PAINT the triangle.
210 PAINT (XMED,YMED),EDGECOL%,EDGECOL%
220 NEXT I%
230 GOSUB 60100 'monochrome display
240 END
```

The second type of problem can be eliminated by limiting the final picture to three colours in mode 1 (see listing 1.14). Suppose the logical colour 0 is kept for drawing triangles and also PAINTing them in. Then outline the same triangle in a different (non-zero) logical colour and also fill the triangle with this new colour. There can be no problems because now the first PAINT instruction using logical colour 0 will meet only logical colours 1, 2 or 3 in the required area, and the second PAINT using a non-zero logical colour will meet only logical colour zero. Note that the first problem of acute angles still occurs.

Listing 1.14

```
100 MODE%=1 : PALETTE%=0
110 FOREGROUND%=1 : BACKGROUND%=1
120 GOSUB 60000 'colour adapter
130 LINE (0,0)-(319,199),1,BF
139 '1000 triangles.
140 FOR I%=1 TO 1000
150 X1=RND*319 : X2=RND*319 : X3=RND*319
160 Y1=RND*199 : Y2=RND*199 : Y3=RND*199
170 EDGECOL%=1+INT(RND*3)
179 'draw triangle in background colour.
180 LINE (X1,Y1)-(X2,Y2),0
190 LINE (X2,Y2)-(X3,Y3),0
200 LINE (X3,Y3)-(X1,Y1),0
209 'calculate median.
210 XMED=(X1+X2+X3)/3 : YMED=(Y1+Y2+Y3)/3
219 'PAINT triangle in background colour.
220 PAINT (XMED,YMED),0,0
229 'draw triangle in required colour.
230 LINE (X1,Y1)-(X2,Y2),EDGECOL%
240 LINE (X2,Y2)-(X3,Y3),EDGECOL%
250 LINE (X3,Y3)-(X1,Y1),EDGECOL%
259 'PAINT triangle in required colour.
260 PAINT (XMED,YMED),EDGECOL%,EDGECOL%
270 NEXT I%
280 GOSUB 60100 'monochrome display
290 END
```

Release 2.0 of BASICA allows the filling-in of areas with *tiles* rather than pure colours. The [paint] parameter is given as a string expression (see listing 1.20), which is interpreted as a sequence of (n say) 8-bit numbers. Each number is treated as four colours (4 sets of two bits, from left to right) in mode 1, or 2 colours in mode 2 (8 sets of 1-bit numbers, also from left to right). A tile is created by stacking these n groups of colours one below the other. This process can be imagined to start at the top left hand corner of the screen, moving horizontally in steps of 4 (mode 1) or 8 (mode 2) and vertically in steps of n until the whole screen is filled. In this way each pixel on the screen has its colour uniquely defined by a tile. If a subarea of the screen bounded by colour [boundary] is tile-PAINTed, then each pixel in that area will be changed to the colour it would have had if the whole screen were filled. The termination of tile-PAINTing is more complex than ordinary PAINTing. If an attempt is made to tile-PAINT an area already filled with tiles, then the machine may find the path blocked by a line of the old tile equal to one in the new tile. This termination can be avoided (if unwanted) by adding the [background] parameter, which is a character equivalent to the 8-bit number that is the problem line in the tile. You must be careful, however, to ensure that (with repetition) no more than two consecutive lines of the new tile are the same as the [background] or you will obtain an *Illegal function* error.

CIRCLE

CIRCLE (x, y),r[,color[,start,end[,aspect]]]

enables you to draw a circle or part-circle of radius r centred at pixel (x, y) in a given colour [color]. Part-circles (or arcs) are specified by [start] and [end] which are angles given in radians (see the manual).

The [aspect] value requires further consideration. It has been noted that a monitor screen is defined by a rectangular matrix of dots or pixels. The shape of an individual pixel need not be a square. In mode 1 the screen is 320 by 200 pixels, however the real dimensions of the screen will not necessarily be in the same ratio. For example, the so-called *aspect ratio* of the screen may be 4:3 and not 320:200 (8:5). It is the [aspect] value that compensates for this apparent inconsistency. So if your screen has aspect ratio 4:3 then the [aspect] value you choose should be $(4/3)/(8/5) = 5/6$. If your screen aspect ratio is 8:5 then naturally [aspect] would be 1. Arbitrarily choosing a different [aspect] will create an ellipse on the screen. Note that in mode 2 the screen is 640:200, in which case the [aspect] will be 5/12 or 1/2 respectively for the two cases mentioned above.

Listing 1.15 draws random arcs on the screen. Note how RANDOMIZE is used to change the sequence of pseudo-random numbers.

Listing 1.15

```
100 MODE%=1 : PALETTE%=1
110 FOREGROUND=1 : BACKGROUND%=1 : ASPECT%=5/6
120 CLS : RANDOMIZE
130 GOSUB 60000 'colour monitor
140 FOR RAD%=95 TO 5 STEP -1
150 FOREGROUND%=1+INT(RND*3) : PI=3.141593
160 START=-2*PI+RND*4*PI : ENND=-2*PI+RND*4*PI
170 CIRCLE (160,100),RAD%,FOREGROUND%,START,ENND,ASPECT%
180 NEXT RAD%
190 GOSUB 60100 'monochrome display
200 END
```

GET and PUT

These are two very powerful operations.

GET (x1, y1) − (x2, y2),arrayname

allows you to store in an array all the information relating to the pixels in a rectangle on the screen, where the rectangle is defined by pixels (x1, y1) and (x2, y2) (see the LINE operation).

　　　PUT (x, y),arrayname[,action]

allows you to put the information previously created by GET back on the screen at pixel (x, y). The [action] value relates to one of five options:

PSET: places the data back on the screen in the original form

PRESET: inverts the data before putting it on the screen, that is, swaps logical colours 0 and 3, and 1 and 2

OR: places the data on the screen where the logical colour of each pixel depends on the colour of the pixel from the array and that already on the screen, according to the following truth table:

		Logical colour in array			
		0	1	2	3
	0	0	1	2	3
Screen	1	1	1	3	3
colour	2	2	3	2	3
	3	3	3	3	3

AND: places the data on the screen according to the following truth table:

		Logical colour in array			
		0	1	2	3
	0	0	0	0	0
Screen	1	0	1	0	1
colour	2	0	0	2	2
	3	0	1	2	3

XOR: places the data on the screen according to the following truth table:

		Logical colour in array			
		0	1	2	3
	0	0	1	2	3
Screen	1	1	0	3	2
colour	2	2	3	0	1
	3	3	2	1	0

Note that the last four operations are equivalent to the standard four logical operations NOT, OR, AND and XOR operating on the logical colours, each colour being considered as two separate binary bits.

The size and type of array used to store the screen values have to be explained. Two bytes are needed to describe the x-dimension of the rectangle and two for the y-dimension. Then the pixel data of the rectangle has to be stored. Mode 1 requires 2 bits-per-pixel whereas mode 2 needs only 1. The number of complete bytes that cover one row of the rectangle (the x-dimension) must be repeated for each row (the y-dimension) of the rectangle. The total is therefore

$$4 + INT((x * \text{bits-per-pixel} + 7)/8) * y$$

where x and y are the horizontal and vertical lengths of the rectangle. If this is stored in an integer array (the identifier name ends in a % sign) then each array element is two bytes. So, for example, to store the whole mode 1 screen (320 × 200) would require

$$4 + INT((320 * 2 + 7)/8) * 200 \text{ bytes} = 16004 \text{ bytes} = 8002 \text{ integers}$$

Example 1.9

The GET and PUT operations are used to create moiré patterns. These 'lace-curtain' type effects are created by drawing a dense set of lines all over the screen. If the lines go through a pixel an odd number of times then that pixel is set to the line colour, but for an even number it is set to the background colour. The effect is achieved on the IBM PC by repeatedly GETting the whole screen, drawing lines on a blank screen, and then PUTting the old screen back using XOR. Figure 1.5 is created with this method using listing 1.16, by drawing either one or two pairs of lines on the screen, where each pair joins points on opposite edges of the screen.

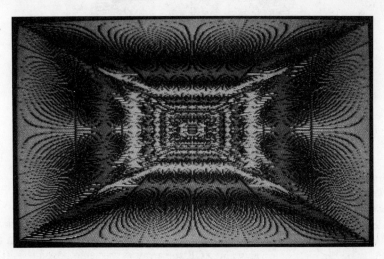

Figure 1.5

Listing 1.16

```
100 MODE%=1 : PALETTE%=0
110 BACKGROUND%=1 : FOREGROUND%=2
120 GOSUB 60000 'colour monitor
130 DIM SKREEN%(8002)
140 GET (0,0)-(319,199),SKREEN%
150 FOR I%=0 TO 159
159 'draw line sequence on clear screen.
160 CLS
170 LINE (I%,0)-(319-I%,199),3
180 LINE (319-I%,0)-(I%,199),3
190 IF I%>99 THEN GOTO 220
200 LINE (0,I%)-(319,199-I%),3
210 LINE (319,I%)-(0,199-I%),3
219 'XOR on previous screen.
220 PUT (0,0),SKREEN%,XOR
229 'save screen.
230 GET (0,0)-(319,199),SKREEN%
240 NEXT I%
250 GOSUB 60100 'monochrome display
260 END
```

Exercise 1.3

Use GET and PUT to draw the circular moiré pattern of figure 1.6.

Figure 1.6

Example 1.10

Animation can be produced with a technique similar to that used by the 'ship'
routine of listing 1.12. The method is to create a picture with graphics commands
and GET it into an array. Then XOR the array back onto the screen at a given point,
thus PUTting the picture in view, and XOR the array at the same position which
will totally obliterate it, thus leaving the original background in view and unchanged.

The movie is achieved by repeatedly changing the position of the rectangle on the screen. Note that XORing onto a non-blank (not logical 0) background may discolour the object being drawn. This idea is included in listing 1.17, where the original object is a two-colour character (logical 3 foreground on logical 0 background) with lines of logical colours 1 and 2 added. The 'bug' is made to fly around the screen bouncing off the sides.

This method of animation will be used to construct a movable cursor-cross that is essential for the CHARACTER and PIXEL BLOCK GENERATOR programs of chapter 5 and the DATA DIAGRAM program of chapter 6.

Listing 1.17

```
100 MODE%=1 : PALETTE%=0
110 FOREGROUND%=1 : BACKGROUND%=1
120 GOSUB 60000   'colour monitor
130 DIM A%(10)
139 'draw character in logical colour 3 and add lines in logical
      colours 1 ( horizontal ) and 2 (vertical ).
140 PRINT CHR$(15)
150 LINE (0,3)-(7,3),2
160 LINE (0,4)-(7,4),2
170 LINE (3,0)-(3,7),1
180 LINE (4,0)-(4,7),1
189 'store shape and delete with XOR.
190 GET (0,0)-(7,7),A%
200 PUT (0,0),A%,XOR
209 'initialise movie data.
210 SPEED%=4 : X%=2 : Y%=2
220 XADD%=SPEED% : YADD%=SPEED%
230 LINE (0,0)-(319,199),2,B
240 PUT (X%,Y%),A%,XOR
249 'movie loop.
250 OLDX%=X% : OLDY%=Y%
260 X%=X%+XADD%
270 IF X%>312-SPEED% OR X%<SPEED% THEN XADD%=-XADD% : SOUND 400,1
280 Y%=Y%+YADD%
290 IF Y%>192-SPEED% OR Y%<SPEED% THEN YADD%=-YADD% : SOUND 100,1
299 'get rid of shape from old position.
300 PUT (OLDX%,OLDY%),A%,XOR
309 'put in next position.
310 PUT (X%,Y%),A%,XOR
320 GOTO 250
```

Exercise 1.4

Use the GET/PUT animation method to draw a picture of a solid and multicoloured spaceship taking off from the bottom of the screen and flying vertically to the top. Try to get flickering flames coming from the base of the rocket.

Example 1.11

A program that draws the Borromean Rings (figure 1.7) is used to demonstrate PUT options other than XOR. This diagram is of three rings that are interconnected and cannot be separated, yet if any one is deleted then the rings do not intertwine. The idea is to draw rings in the centre of the screen and GET them into memory (5 different rings are used, some on background 0 and others on background 3), and

then PUT them back onto the screen with a variety of AND, OR and XOR options.
Listing 1.18 shows how nine different PUTs are used to construct the figure. Note
that this is not the smallest number possible: it can be done in five PUTs, but the
dynamic effect of the nine PUTs is more pleasing than the other more efficient
method.

Listing 1.18

```
100  ´            BORROMEAN´s Rings
109  ´set background (logical colour 0) to blue (actual colour 1)
110  MODE%=1 : PALETTE%=0
120  BACKGROUND%=1 : FOREGROUND%=1 : ASPECT%=1
129  ´1877 allows 1878 locations =(4+INT((121*2)+7)/8)*121)/2
        so we can have a 121x121 pixel block
130  DIM A%(1877),B%(1877),C%(1877),D%(1877),E%(1877)
140  GOSUB 60000 ´colour monitor
150  GOSUB 1000 ´create arrays of rings : A%,B%,C%,D%,E%
160  GOSUB 3000 ´plot rings in correct sequence
170  GOSUB 60100 ´monochrome display
180  END

1000 ´create the arrays of rings
1002 ´**out** A%,B%,C%,D%,E%
1010 FOREGROUND%=1 : BASE%=0 : GOSUB 2000 ´ring A%
1019 ´green (1) on a blue(0) background
1020 GET (100,40)-(220,160),A%
1030 FOREGROUND%=2 : BASE%=0 : GOSUB 2000 ´ring B%
1039 ´red (2) on a blue(0) background
1040 GET (100,40)-(220,160),B%
1050 FOREGROUND%=3 : BASE%=0 : GOSUB 2000 ´ring C%
1059 ´brown(3) on a blue(0) background
1060 GET (100,40)-(220,160),C%
1070 FOREGROUND%=1 : BASE%=3 : GOSUB 2000 ´ring D%
1079 ´green(1) on a brown(3) background
1080 GET (100,40)-(220,160),D%
1090 FOREGROUND%=2 : BASE%=3 : GOSUB 2000 ´ring E%
1099 ´red(2) on a brown(3) background
1100 GET (100,40)-(220,160),E%
1110 RETURN

2000 ´construct ring in logical colour FOREGROUND% on a
        background which is logical colour BASE%
2001 ´**in ** FOREGROUND%,BASE%,ASPECT%
2010 CLS : PAINT (0,0),BASE%
2020 CIRCLE (160,100),60,FOREGROUND%,,,ASPECT%
2030 PAINT (160,100),FOREGROUND%,FOREGROUND%
2040 CIRCLE (160,100),50,BASE%,,,ASPECT%
2050 PAINT (160,100),BASE%,BASE%
2060 RETURN

3000 ´construct BORROMEAN´s Rings
3001 ´**in ** A%,B%,C%,D%,E%
3008 ´green rings placed at (100,10), red rings at (65,70)
        and brown at (135,75)
3009 ´ Use the five rings as follows :-
3010 CLS : PUT (100,10),A%
3020 PUT (65,70),B%
3030 PUT (135,70),C%
3040 PUT (100,10),D%,AND
3050 PUT (65,70),E%,AND
3060 PUT (100,10),A%,OR
3070 PUT (135,70),C%,OR
3080 PUT (65,70),E%,AND
3090 PUT (100,10),A%,OR
3100 RETURN
```

Figure 1.7

Exercise 1.5

Produce a picture of the Olympic symbol, five intersecting rings, using the ideas of the Borromean Ring program, and tile-PAINTing to create five colours.

WINDOW

The powerful WINDOW facility available with release 2.0 of BASICA enables the screen to be considered in terms of *real-world coordinates* rather than a rectangular matrix of pixels (320 by 200 or 640 by 200) — the *physical coordinates* of the screen. The statement has the form

WINDOW [[SCREEN] (x1, y1) − (x2, y2)]

The computer first sorts x/y parameters so that x1 < x2 and y1 < y2 (note that equality is not allowed). These two points define a real-world window onto two-dimensional space. If SCREEN is set, then (x1, y1) is identified with the top left-hand corner of the screen and (x2, y2) with the bottom right, whereas if SCREEN is not included (x1, y1) is identified with the bottom left-hand corner and (x2, y2) with top right (the normal Cartesian representation of space). All other points in space used by graphics commands are then scaled according to this rectangle, and any line is *clipped* so that the correct segment of line lying in the window is drawn on the screen. See chapter 3 for more on clipping. Note that the scaling in the x-direction need not be the same as in the y-direction.

An example of this statement is given in listing 1.19, which repeatedly draws the same circle (PAINTed) inside an expanding window. This deliberate movement of the bottom left-hand corner of the window to (2, 3) demonstrates that it need not always be the origin. Note that defining a new WINDOW does not clear the screen. If the screen was cleared each time, then the effect of *pan*ning out from the circle is achieved, and reversing the order of WINDOW construction would give a *zoom*ing effect. A peculiar y-scale was deliberately chosen in order to demonstrate a particular property of the CIRCLE command. Once it has centred the circle, calculated the radius measured along the x-direction and fixed the ASPECT, the CIRCLE command works in terms of screen pixels, so that the peculiar y-scaling does not affect the shape of the circle. RUN, SCREEN and WINDOW with no parameters disable the present WINDOW settings and return you to the 320 (or 640) by 200 physical coordinates. You must check your manual to see how the other graphics commands (for example, POINT, GET) are affected by WINDOW and then write small program segments similar to listing 1.19 to check them out. Also study the PMAP command that enables you to relate real-world coordinates to the equivalent physical (pixel) coordinates and vice-versa — also see listings 3.5 and 3.6.

Listing 1.19

```
100 MODE%=1 : GOSUB 60000 ´colour monitor
110 XOFF=2 : YOFF=3
120 FOR X=1 TO 8 STEP .1
130 Y=X*.2 : RAD=.5
140 FILL%=INT(RND*4) : BOUND%=3-FILL%
150 WINDOW (XOFF,YOFF)-(X+XOFF,Y+YOFF)
160 XC=XOFF+RAD : YC=YOFF+Y/2
170 LINE (XOFF,YOFF)-(XOFF+X,YOFF+Y),BOUND%,B
180 CIRCLE (XC,YC),RAD,BOUND%,,,1
190 PAINT (XC,YC),FILL%,BOUND%
200 NEXT X
210 GOSUB 60100 ´monochrome display
220 END
```

VIEW

Release 2.0 also has the VIEW facility. The statement is of the form

VIEW [[SCREEN] [(x1, y1) − (x2, y2)[,[color] [,[boundary]]]]]

The meanings of (x1, y1) and (x2, y2) are the same as for WINDOW. The statement allows you to restrict the use of graphics commands to a rectangular subarea of the screen called a *viewport*, an area defined by (x1, y1) and (x2, y2). The command clears the viewport in colour [color], and places a rectangle of colour [boundary] around it. Graphics commands then affect only the pixels inside the viewport. Pixels inside this area must be given in absolute terms if SCREEN is specified, but relative to the bottom left-hand corner of the viewport if it is not. Only one viewport is active at any given time. RUN and SCREEN disable the viewport, and VIEW with no parameters identifies a viewport with the whole screen. Listing 1.20 is an example which randomly defines viewports, drawing and tile-PAINTing a circle inside each one. Note that colour byte A2 in the program cannot be zero: a multiple zero entry in a tile would cause an error.

Listing 1.20

```
100 MODE%=1 : GOSUB 60000 'colour monitor
110 X1=INT(RND*320) : Y1=INT(RND*200)
120 X2=INT(RND*320) : Y2=INT(RND*200)
130 IF X1=X2 OR Y1=Y2 THEN GOTO 120
140 COL%=INT(RND*4) : BOUND%=3-COL%
150 VIEW (X1,Y1)-(X2,Y2),COL%,BOUND%
160 XC=INT(RND*ABS(X1-X2)) : YC=INT(RND*ABS(Y1-Y2))
170 RAD=RND*ABS(X1-X2)
180 CIRCLE (XC,YC),RAD,BOUND%,,,1
190 A1=INT(RND*16) : A2=INT(RND*15)+1
200 TILE$=CHR$(A1)+STRING$(4,CHR$(A2))
210 PAINT (XC,YC),TILE$,BOUND%
220 GOTO 110
```

If you are running DOS 2.0, you have the option of printing the graphics screen on your printer. You must type GRAPHICS before you enter the BASICA interpreter and then, after your picture is complete on the graphics monitor and before you return to the monochrome display, you must type Prt Sc (Print Screen, that is, shift *) on the keyboard. The computer will wait until the printing is finished before continuing.

Having now dealt with most of the useful graphics commands, we shall move on in the next chapter to the study of two-dimensional real-world graphics.

Complete Programs

All the programs from this chapter require that listing 1.1 (from now on called the 'lib0' library) be MERGEd in with the specified listings.

    I. Listing 1.2 ('available colours in text'). Data required: WIDTH, try 40 or 80.
   II. Listing 1.3 ('mode 0 characters'). WIDTH required: try 40.
  III. Listing 1.4 ('PRINT text in graphics mode'). Data required: actual colour of background (0 to 15), palette (0 or 1) and logical colour of foreground (1, 2 or 3).
  IV. Listing 1.5 ('random dots'). Requires MODE% (1 or 2).
   V. Listing 1.6 ('fractal'). No data required.
  VI. Listing 1.7 ('fill the *even line locations*'). Requires MODE% (1 or 2).
 VII. Listing 1.8 ('equivalence of pixels and bytes'). Data required: MODE% (1 or 2) and a set of numbers between 0 and 255.
VIII. Listing 1.9 ('LINE demonstration'). No data required.
  IX. Listing 1.10 ('random coloured lines'). No data required.
   X. Listing 1.11 ('LINE block example'). No data required.

2 *From Real Coodinates to Pixels*

Character graphics apart, computer graphics should deal with objects (points, lines, areas, volumes) from a continuous two-dimensional or three-dimensional Euclidean space. Objects are measured in real units (inches, miles or even light-years) and not as an integral number of pixels. This is the reason why WINDOW was introduced in release 2.0 of the Advanced BASIC interpreter. This chapter considers the methods used for mapping real-world objects (such as lines, points, circles etc.), defined in terms of such real measurement, onto the screen matrix of pixels.

In order to understand how WINDOW works, it is best to start by resorting to the original interpretation of the SCREEN, imagining it as a *graphics frame* consisting of a mode-dependent rectangular matrix of *pixels*. These pixels are stacked in NXPIX% (say) vertical columns and NYPIX% (say) horizontal rows. If MODE% = 1 (medium-resolution) then NXPIX% = 320, and if MODE% = 2 (high-resolution) NXPIX% = 640: NYPIX% = 200 in both modes. Individuals from the set of NXPIX% by NYPIX% pixels can be uniquely identified by a bracketed pair of integers – sometimes called a pixel vector (I, J), where $0 \leqslant I \leqslant NXPIX\%-1$ and $0 \leqslant J \leqslant NYPIX\%-1$. The vector specifies the position of the pixel in the Ith column and J^{th} row: the vector $(0, 0)$ identifies the *top left-hand corner* pixel of the frame – remember that this is different from the normal mathematical way of numbering rows, where $(0, 0)$ is usually the *bottom left-hand corner*. The IBM PC has its own set of BASIC instructions which enables users to operate on the matrix of pixels, treating them as points of light that can be switched off or on in different colours. This allows the operator to approximate lines, or polygons and other special types of area, with a series of coloured dots (the pixels).

The following chapters of this book may be considered as taking the reader some way towards generating a medium and high-resolution two-dimensional and three-dimensional graphics package for the IBM PC: the programs are given in BASIC and rely (with a few exceptions) on a small number of *primitive* routines given in this chapter.

Primitives that Map Continuous Space onto the Graphics Frame

The definition of objects by using only discrete pairs of integers is very rare in most practical applications and, since WINDOW is not being used at present, it is necessary to consider ways of plotting views of objects on a graphics screen where positions are measured in real units, as well as the relationship between two-dimensional real space and screen pixels. Before attempting this step, however, ways must be found of representing two-dimensional space using Cartesian coordinate geometry.

Two-dimensional space can be imagined as the plane of this page extending to infinity in all directions. This description of coordinate geometry starts by arbitrarily choosing a fixed point in this space, called the *coordinate origin*. Through the origin is drawn a line which stretches to infinity in both directions – this is the *x-axis*. The normal convention is to place this line left to right on the page (the horizontal). Another two-way infinite line, the *y-axis*, is drawn through the origin perpendicular to the *x*-axis, hence conventionally this is placed from the top to the bottom of the page (the vertical). A scale is fixed along both axes: unit distances need not be the same on both axes, but this is normally the case (see figure 2.1). The values on the *x*-axis are assumed positive to the right of the origin and negative to the left: values on the *y*-axis are positive above the origin and negative below.

Taking any point **p** (figure 2.1) in space, its position can now be uniquely fixed by specifying its *coordinates*. The *x-coordinate*, X say, is that distance along the *x*-axis (positive to the right of the axis and negative to the left) at which a line perpendicular to the *x*-axis passing through **p** cuts the *x*-axis. The *y-coordinate*, Y say, is correspondingly defined using the *y*-axis. These two values, called a *coordinate pair* or *two-dimensional vector*, are normally written in brackets thus, (X, Y), the *x*-coordinate coming before the *y*-coordinate. Such a bracketing of numbers is usually referred to as a vector: the dimension of the vector (in this case 2) will be understood from the context in which the term is used. A vector, as well as defining a point (X, Y) in two-dimensional space, may also be used to specify a direction, namely that direction which is parallel to the line joining the origin to the point (X, Y) – but more of this (and other objects such as lines, curves and polygonal areas) in chapter 3.

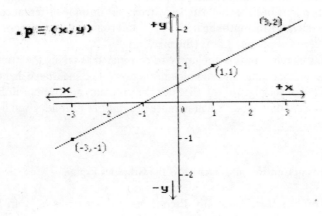

Figure 2.1

It is now possible to devise means (the aforementioned primitive routines) for mapping such geometrical concepts onto the two-dimensional discrete rectangular matrix of pixels that forms the graphics frame.

This chapter concentrates on two-dimensional space: an extension into three-dimensional space is dealt with starting at chapter 7. In both cases, a method of mapping a rectangular area of two-dimensional Cartesian space onto the graphics frame is needed. Remember that the graphics frame may be in MODE% = 1 or MODE% = 2. Furthermore the aspect ratio of the monitor must be taken into account (see chapter 1): the aspect value is stored in the variable ASPECT. ASPECT is mode-dependent, so it is the mode 1 value that is equated with ASPECT in listing 2.1 — in this case 1; the equivalent mode 2 value of ASPECT is then calculated by the program if necessary. Make sure you know if your monitor or television set has ASPECT = 1 or 5/6 in mode 1. For simplicity, this area will initially have its edges parallel to the *x* and *y* axes of Cartesian space. It is assumed that this rectangular area of space has its *bottom left-hand corner* identified with the coordinate origin (0.0, 0.0), and that the length of the horizontal edge is HORIZ (and the corresponding vertical edge VERT). The origin is first identified with the bottom left-hand corner pixel (0, 199) of the frame (note the 'upside-down' vertical numbering of the pixels, which need not be the case with WINDOW), and then the rectangular area is scaled so that it fits into the frame; naturally the area exactly fits the frame when the ratios HORIZ: VERT and NXPIX% * ASPECT: NYPIX% are equal (that is, 320 * ASPECT:200). A scaling factor, XYSCALE, is chosen which maps the point (HORIZ, VERT) onto the top right-hand corner pixel.

This rectangle is a *window* onto Cartesian space (hence WINDOW of release 2.0); being no longer anchored to the coordinate origin, the window may wander about space viewing rectangular areas of the same size as the original, although the edges of the areas must be parallel to the original coordinate axes.

At any time during the execution of the program the coordinate origin may move from its original position at the bottom left-hand corner of the frame. Its position relative to the first origin will be stored as XORIG and YORIG; the *x* and *y* components respectively. Initially (XORIG, YORIG) is identified with (0.0, 0.0). Hence any point in Cartesian space with coordinates (XPT, YPT), a pair of reals, maps into a pixel with horizontal component

INT((XORIG + XPT) * XYSCALE + 0.5)

and vertical component

200—INT((YORIG + YPT) * XYSCALE * ASPECT + 0.5)

INT is the BASIC function that truncates the fractional part of a decimal number and returns an integer. These two components are stored as functions FN X and FN Y (see listing 2.1): they must be placed in the program in such a position that they are executed before any other statement that uses them. During the construction of a picture, an imaginary *plot pen*, in value a pair of integers, moves about the graphics frame; initially it is placed at (0, 0), and in general it is the (XPEN, YPEN) pixel. The values ASPECT, MODE%, NXPIX%, NYPIX%, XYSCALE, XPEN, YPEN, XORIG and YORIG must be available at all times to the plotting routines that follow, so these names must not be used for any other purpose. The routines were written specifically for the IBM PC but the general principles of constructing similar routines for other graphical devices are also discussed. For example, to start with, the values of NXPIX% and NYPIX% would be changed to fit the specification of a different machine, and it is possible that variables such as MODE% and ASPECT are unnecessary.

The first routine 'start' reads in the MODE% and any other necessary mode-dependent information such as PALETTE%, BORDER%, PAPER%, BACKGROUND% or FOREGROUND% colours. It then initialises the required variables in readiness for a call to the 'colour monitor' routine and subsequent plotting. For completeness this routine can be used in all three modes, however it is used almost exclusively for the graphics modes. In MODE% 1, BACKGROUND% (0 to 15) is any of the 16 possible colours: colour zero is then defined to be this colour, and naturally colours one, two and three are PALETTE%-dependent (value 0 or 1). The FOREGROUND% colour may be any of the four colours. In MODE% 2 the background is black and there are only two FOREGROUND% colours — black (colour 0) and white (colour 1). PALETTE% and BORDER% are not required. Subsequently changes of colour used for construction (such as FOREGROUND%) are achieved by an assignment statement that changes this variable value. A LINE call within the monitor routine enables the graphics area to be filled initially in the PAPER% colour in both modes. Listing 2.1 is an example 'start' routine for the IBM PC. Note the use of OPTION BASE 1 so that in all the two-dimensional and three-dimensional programs all array indices start at 1 and not 0.

Listing 2.1

```
9700 ´start
9702 ´**out** MODE%,PALETTE%,BORDER%,BACKGROUND%,FOREGROUND%,
             ASPECT,PAPER%,NXPIX%,NYPIX%,
             XORIG,YORIG,HORIZ,VERT,XYSCALE,XPEN,YPEN
9710 CLS : OPTION BASE 1
9720 INPUT "MODE ",MODE%
9730 IF MODE%=1 THEN INPUT "PALETTE ",PALETTE%
9740 IF MODE%=0 THEN INPUT "BORDER ",BORDER%
9750 IF MODE%<>2
     THEN INPUT "BACKGROUND and FOREGROUND ",BACKGROUND%,FOREGROUND%
9760 IF MODE%=0 THEN RETURN
9770 ASPECT=1
9780 XORIG=0 : YORIG=0
9790 XPEN=0 : YPEN=0
9800 NXPIX%=320*MODE% : NYPIX%=200
9810 INPUT"HORIZ and PAPER ",HORIZ,PAPER%
9820 IF MODE%=2 THEN FOREGROUND%=1-PAPER% : ASPECT=ASPECT/2
9830 XYSCALE=NXPIX%/HORIZ
9840 VERT=NYPIX%/(XYSCALE*ASPECT)
9850 DEF FN X(Z)=INT((XORIG+Z)*XYSCALE+.5)
9860 DEF FN Y(Z)=200-INT((YORIG+Z)*XYSCALE*ASPECT+.5)
9870 RETURN
```

This routine can be rewritten for a different micro by simply replacing the statements containing the IBM PC BASIC graphics instructions with the equivalent routines for the new micro. Most of the other routines in this book are independent of the structure of the IBM PC graphics statements.

In many of the routines that follow it is necessary to transform the x/y coordinates of a point into their pixel equivalents, so the two functions FN X and FN Y are included in the 'start' routine.

The next primitive routine is 'setorigin' (listing 2.2); this moves the coordinate origin by an amount XMOVE horizontally and YMOVE vertically (distances in the scale of the coordinate system), thence adjusting the (XORIG, YORIG) values. After such a move the plot pen moves to the pixel that is equivalent to the new origin.

Listing 2.2

```
9600 ´setorigin
9601 ´**in ** XMOVE,YMOVE,XORIG,YORIG
9602 ´**out** XPEN,YPEN,XORIG,YORIG
9610 XORIG=XORIG+XMOVE : YORIG=YORIG+YMOVE
9620 XPEN=FN X(0) : YPEN=FN Y(0)
9630 RETURN
```

It will be possible to draw straight lines after two further routines have been produced: 'moveto' which moves the plot pen to a pixel equivalent of the point in coordinate space at one end of the line, and 'lineto' which draws the line in the present FOREGROUND% colour by moving the plot pen from its present position (set by a previous call to 'setorigin', 'moveto' or 'lineto') to the pixel equivalent of the point on the other end of the line. Listings 2.3 and 2.4 show 'moveto' and 'lineto' routines designed specifically for the IBM PC. The 'lineto' routine includes statements that initiate the machine-dependent BASIC pixel instructions for drawing a line whereas the 'moveto' routine is machine-independent. Hence if you wish to implement these routines on a different micro you need only alter the 'lineto' routine.

Listing 2.3

```
9500 ´moveto
9501 ´**in ** XPT,YPT
9502 ´**out** XPEN,YPEN
9510 XPEN=FN X(XPT) : YPEN=FN Y(YPT)
9520 RETURN
```

Listing 2.4

```
9400 ´lineto
9401 ´**in ** XPT,YPT,FOREGROUND%
9402 ´**out** XPEN,YPEN
9410 NXPEN=FN X(XPT) : NYPEN=FN Y(YPT)
9420 LINE (XPEN,YPEN)-(NXPEN,NYPEN),FOREGROUND%
9430 XPEN=NXPEN : YPEN=NYPEN
9440 RETURN
```

Primitives using WINDOW

Solutions to many of the problems found in the previous section are already implicit in BASICA by using WINDOW. There is no need to use functions FN X and FN Y for mapping real coordinates into pixels. Furthermore, leaving out the SCREEN option in WINDOW places coordinates in the correct mathematical orientation with lower *y*-values at the bottom of screen and higher at the top. However, it is still necessary to prepare the rectangular screen for plotting by defining its real dimensions to be in the ratio 320 * ASPECT: 200 (a new 'start'), changing origin (that is, creating a new WINDOW — a new 'setorigin' which can be called only when control is with the colour monitor and not with the monochrome display —) and also having new 'moveto' and 'lineto' routines. Of course there must be an initial call to WINDOW before any of these routines is valid — achieved on the first call to 'setorigin'. Without a call to 'setorigin' the screen will have the default pixel dimension 320 * MODE% by 200, and the coordinates will be 'upside-down'. These new routines, see listings 2.1a, 2.2a, 2.3a and 2.4a, will be used to replace their equivalent routines in 'lib1'.

For the rest of this book it will be assumed that the more efficient new routines are used for 'lib1', however it is a useful exercise to use the more explicit old routines now and again. Although the old routines may run correctly with many of the programs that follow, some programs are incompatible and will fail. Therefore it will be necessary to change certain statements of these programs. To help you initially, the necessary changes are included in the first few programs by following each problem statement with a REMark containing the changes inside curly brackets { } .

Listing 2.1a

```
9700 ´start
9702 ´**out** MODE%,PALETTE%,BORDER%,BACKGROUND%,FOREGROUND%,
             ASPECT,PAPER%,NXPIX%,NYPIX%,
             XORIG,YORIG,HORIZ,VERT,XPEN,YPEN
9710 CLS : OPTION BASE 1
9720 INPUT "MODE ",MODE%
9730 IF MODE%=1 THEN INPUT "PALETTE ",PALETTE%
9740 IF MODE%=0 THEN INPUT "BORDER ",BORDER%
9750 IF MODE%<>2
     THEN INPUT "BACKGROUND and FOREGROUND ",BACKGROUND%,FOREGROUND%
9760 IF MODE%=0 THEN RETURN
9770 ASPECT=1
9780 XORIG=0 : YORIG=0
9790 XPEN=0 : YPEN=0
9800 NXPIX%=320*MODE% : NYPIX%=200
9810 INPUT"HORIZ and PAPER ",HORIZ,PAPER%
9820 IF MODE%=2 THEN FOREGROUND%=1-PAPER% : ASPECT=ASPECT/2
9830 VERT=(NYPIX%/NXPIX%)*HORIZ/ASPECT
9840 RETURN
```

Listing 2.2a

```
9600 ´setorigin
9601 ´**in ** XMOVE,YMOVE,XORIG,YORIG,HORIZ,VERT
9602 ´**out** XPEN,YPEN,XORIG,YORIG
9610 XORIG=XORIG+XMOVE : YORIG=YORIG+YMOVE
9620 XPEN=0 : YPEN=0
9630 WINDOW (-XORIG,-YORIG)-(HORIZ-XORIG,VERT-YORIG)
9640 RETURN
```

Listing 2.3a

```
9500 ´moveto
9501 ´**in ** XPT,YPT
9502 ´**out** XPEN,YPEN
9510 XPEN=XPT : YPEN=YPT
9520 RETURN
```

Listing 2.4a

```
9400 ´lineto
9401 ´**in ** XPEN,YPEN,XPT,YPT,FOREGROUND%
9402 ´**out** XPEN,XPEN
9410 LINE (XPEN,YPEN)-(XPT,YPT),FOREGROUND%
9420 XPEN=XPT : YPEN=YPT
9430 RETURN
```

Example 2.1
Identify a rectangle in Cartesian space, 30 units wide, with the graphics frame of the
IBM PC in MODE% = 1 (what are VERT etc.?) and set PALETTE% to 0, BACK-
GROUND% to 7 (white), FOREGROUND% to 2 (red) and PAPER% to 1 (green).
Then draw a square of side 15 units, centred in the rectangle (figure 2.2a). The

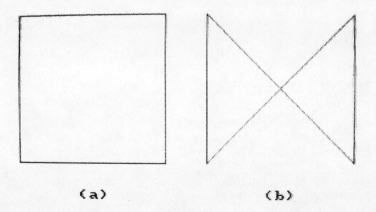

(a)   (b)

Figure 2.2

square is centred by moving the origin to (HORIZ/2, VERT/2) and thus the corners
of the square are (±7.5, ±7.5). Try the same program (listing 2.5) again in MODE%
= 2, with PAPER% = 0 and FOREGROUND% = 1. What are VERT etc. now? In
this MODE% variable PALETTE% is not needed. Invert the colours by setting
PAPER% to 1 (white) with FOREGROUND% colour 0 (black). Experiment with
different graphics modes and colours.

It is as well to note at this juncture that the order in which the points are joined
is critical. For example, if the coordinates of the second and third corners of the
square are interchanged then figure 2.2b will be drawn.

Listing 2.5

```
100 ´drawing a square.
110 GOSUB 9700 ´start
120 GOSUB 60000 ´colour monitor
130 XMOVE=HORIZ*.5 : YMOVE=VERT*.5
140 GOSUB 9600 ´ setorigin
149 ´join corners of the square in order.
150 XPT= 7.5 : YPT= 7.5 : GOSUB 9500 ´moveto
160 XPT=-7.5 : YPT= 7.5 : GOSUB 9400 ´lineto
170 XPT=-7.5 : YPT=-7.5 : GOSUB 9400 ´lineto
180 XPT= 7.5 : YPT=-7.5 : GOSUB 9400 ´lineto
190 XPT= 7.5 : YPT= 7.5 : GOSUB 9400 ´lineto
200 GOSUB 60100 ´monochrome display
210 END
```

A primitive routine 'polygon' is given next (listing 2.6) which uses the IBM PC
line-drawing instruction to draw polygons in the FOREGROUND% colour. The
routine requires the NPOL% vertices of the polygon as arrays X and Y (the *x* and *y*
coordinates). The listing includes an example main program that calls this routine.

Listing 2.6

```
100 ´example to draw a polygon.
110 GOSUB 9700 ´start
120 INPUT "type in number of vertices of polygon ",NPOL%
130 DIM X(NPOL%),Y(NPOL%)
140 FOR I%=1 TO NPOL%
150 PRINT "type X("+STR$(I%)+")  and  Y("+STR$(I%)+")"
160 INPUT X(I%),Y(I%)
170 NEXT I%
180 GOSUB 60000 ´colour monitor
190 XMOVE=HORIZ*.5 : YMOVE=VERT*.5
200 GOSUB 9600 ´setorigin
210 GOSUB 300 ´polygon
220 GOSUB 60100 ´monochrome display
230 END

300 ´polygon subroutine
301 ´**in ** NPOL%,X(NPOL%),Y(NPOL%)
309 ´move to last vertex in polygon.
310 XPT=X(NPOL%) : YPT=Y(NPOL%) : GOSUB 9500 ´moveto
319 ´join polygon vertices in order.
320 FOR I%=1 TO NPOL%
330 XPT=X(I%) : YPT=Y(I%) : GOSUB 9400 ´lineto
340 NEXT I%
350 RETURN
```

Exercise 2.1
In all the plotting routines above, both old and new, the scale of the mapping is fixed once and for all, and the horizontal and vertical scaling factors are identical (taking into account the ASPECT). There is no need to heed this convention: write a routine 'factor' which alters the horizontal scale by FX and the vertical by FY. Naturally this implies that two separate scales must be defined in the old routines (XSCALE and YSCALE say), and you would have to change FN X and FN Y. In the new routines simply call the correct WINDOW (also see chapter 6).

Exercise 2.2
There is no reason for the x-axis and y-axis to be identified with the horizontal and vertical respectively. In fact they need not even be mutually perpendicular. Experiment with these ideas, which necessarily involves changing all the plotting routines 'start', 'moveto' etc.

Some simple patterns are now drawn to demonstrate the use of these plotting routines. There are those who think that the construction of patterns is a frivolous waste of time. Others, including the author, consider it to be a very useful first stage in understanding the techniques of computer graphics. Often patterns of an apparently sophisticated design are the result of very simple programs. Quickly producing such graphical output is an immediate boost to morale, and gives a lot of confidence to the beginner. Furthermore, new designs are always in demand: geometrical art is used for the covers of books and pamphlets and in advertising literature. It can do no harm at all to initiate artistic ideas which will be of great use in the pictorial display of data. Patterns are also an ideal way of introducing some of the basic concepts of computer graphics in a very palatable way. Take the next example which looks at the important role of trigonometric functions (sine and cosine), and of angular measurement in radians. Remember that π radians is the same angular measure as 180 degrees.

Example 2.2
Figure 2.3, a very popular design, is constructed by joining each vertex of a regular N-sided polygon (an N-gon) to every other. N (integer variable N%) should not be greater than 20.

The origin is set at the centre of the design, and all the vertices at a unit distance from the centre: the size of HORIZ = 4 is chosen so that the design fits neatly onto the screen. If one of these vertices lies on the positive x-axis (the horizontal), then the N vertices are all of the form (COS(ALPHA), SIN(ALPHA)), where ALPHA is an angle of $2\pi I/N$ and I is chosen from 1, 2, . . ., or N. Here, for the first time, the point coordinates are calculated by the program and not explicitly typed in, as in listing 2.5. Furthermore, since the program uses these values over and over again, it is sensible to store them in arrays and access them when required by specifying the

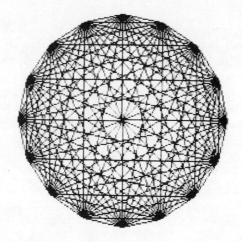

Figure 2.3

correct array index. Note that in listing 2.7, if $1 \leqslant I < J \leqslant N$; if $J \leqslant I$ then the Jth point is not joined to the Ith point, as the line will have already been drawn in the opposite direction.

Listing 2.7

```
100 ´joining the vertices of a regular N-gon.
110 GOSUB 9700 ´start
120 INPUT "type in value of N ",N%
130 DIM X(N%),Y(N%)
139 ´setup vertices of a regular ·N-gon in arrays X and Y.
140 ALPHA=0 : ADIF=3.141593*2/N%
150 FOR I%=1 TO N%
160 X(I%)=COS(ALPHA) : Y(I%)=SIN(ALPHA)
170 ALPHA=ALPHA+ADIF
180 NEXT I%
190 GOSUB 60000 ´colour monitor
200 XMOVE=HORIZ*.5 : YMOVE=VERT*.5
210 GOSUB 9600 ´setorigin
219 ´join point I to point J : 1<=I<J<=N.
220 FOR I%=1 TO N%-1
230 FOR J%=I%+1 TO N%
240 XPT=X(I%) : YPT=Y(I%) : GOSUB 9500 ´moveto
250 XPT=X(J%) : YPT=Y(J%) : GOSUB 9400 ´lineto
260 NEXT J% : NEXT I%
270 GOSUB 60100 ´monochrome display
280 END
```

Example 2.3

Figure 2.4 is constructed by listing 2.8 in a similar manner. M sets of N points on regular N-gons and one set of N coincident points are given by the following formula:

the Ith point in the Jth set, $1 \leqslant I \leqslant N$ and $0 \leqslant J \leqslant M$, is $(Rcos\ \theta, Rsin\ \theta)$ where R and θ are given by

$$R = (M-J)/M$$

$$\theta = 2\pi I/N + \alpha$$

where $\alpha = 0$ if I MOD 2 is zero, and π/N otherwise.

Triangles are then formed by joining every pair of neighbouring points on all but the inner N-gon to the nearest point inside them with lines of logical colour FORE-GROUND%, and finally PAINTing in logical colour 1.

Figure 2.4

Listing 2.8

```
100 ´Rose pattern
110 GOSUB 9700  ´start
120 INPUT "type in N and M ",N%,M%
130 GOSUB 60000 ´colour monitor
140 XMOVE=HORIZ*.5 : YMOVE=VERT*.5
150 GOSUB 9600  ´setorigin
160 DIM X(N%),Y(N%),XD(N%),YD(N%)
170 AD=3.141593/N% : AD2=2*AD : RD=1/M%
179 ´setup outer regular N-gon of unit radius.
180 R=1 : AS=0 : A=AS
190 FOR I%=1 TO N%
200 X(I%)=COS(A) : Y(I%)=SIN(A)
210 A=A+AD2
220 NEXT I%
229 ´loop through M inner N-gons.
230 FOR J%=1 TO M%
240 R=R-RD : AS=AS+AD : A=AS
249 ´setup inner N-gon of radius 1/M smaller than outer N-gon.
250 FOR I%=1 TO N%
260 XD(I%)=R*COS(A) : YD(I%)=R*SIN(A)
```

```
270 A=A+AD2
280 NEXT I%
289 ´draw triangles with points from inner and outer N%-gons.
290 FOR I%=1 TO N%
300 NI%=(I% MOD N%)+1
310 XPT=X(I%)   : YPT=Y(I%)   : GOSUB 9500 ´moveto
320 XPT=XD(I%)  : YPT=YD(I%)  : GOSUB 9400 ´lineto
330 XPT=X(NI%)  : YPT=Y(NI%)  : GOSUB 9400 ´lineto
340 XPT=X(I%)   : YPT=Y(I%)   : GOSUB 9400 ´lineto
349 ´find median of triangle and PAINT.
350 XMED=(X(I%)+XD(I%)+X(NI%))/3 : YMED=(Y(I%)+YD(I%)+Y(NI%))/3
360 PAINT (XMED,YMED),1,FOREGROUND%
369 ´{ or PAINT (FNX(XMED),FNY(YMED)),1,FOREGROUND% }
370 NEXT I%
379 ´reset inner to outer N-gon.
380 FOR I%=1 TO N%
390 X(I%)=XD(I%) : Y(I%)=YD(I%)
400 NEXT I%
410 NEXT J%
420 GOSUB 60100 ´monochrome display
430 END
```

There are two immediate observations to be made from these very simple examples. The first concerns *resolution*. Because the graphics frame is a discrete matrix, then *straight lines* must be approximated by a sequence of pixels. Unfortunately the resolution of the IBM PC, like most microcomputer graphics systems, is low (that is, NXPIX% and NYPIX% are the order of hundreds) so the lines appear jagged.

The second observation is that, as N increases in listings 2.7 and 2.8, the outline of the figure (the N-gon) closely approximates to a circle. This idea is incorporated in a routine 'circle1' (listing 2.9) which draws a circle with radius R about the centre (XCENT, YCENT) to give a picture similar to figure 2.5: the circle is made into a

Figure 2.5

solid disk by PAINTing at the centre of the circle. Note that angles are measured in radians (that is, an increment of $3 * HORIZ/(R * NXPIX\%)$ is made each time through the loop) — a value that depends on the radius and produces a reasonable circle without waste of effort. Also note that the vertices of the N-gon are needed only once, so the values are not stored but calculated as and when required. Again the limitation in resolution of the screen is apparent on the circumference of the circle.

Listing 2.9

```
100 'examples of circles.
110 GOSUB 9700 'start
120 INPUT " centre and radius ",XCENT,YCENT,R
130 GOSUB 60000 'colour monitor
140 GOSUB 200 'circle1
150 INPUT " centre and radius ",XCENT,YCENT,R
160 GOSUB 300 'circle2
170 PAINT (0,0),FOREGROUND%,FOREGROUND%
179 '{ or PAINT (FN X(0),FN Y(0)),FOREGROUND%,FOREGROUND% }
180 GOSUB 60100 'monochrome display
190 END

200 'circle 1
201 '**in ** XCENT,YCENT,R,HORIZ,NXPIX%{,XYSCALE}
210 XMOVE=XCENT : YMOVE=YCENT : GOSUB 9600 'setorigin
220 ADIF=3*HORIZ/(R*NXPIX%)
228 '{ or ADIF=3/(R*XYSCALE) }
229 'calculate and join points (XPT,YPT) around circle.
230 XPT=R : YPT=0 : GOSUB 9500 'moveto
240 FOR A=ADIF TO 2*3.141593+ADIF STEP ADIF
250 XPT=R*COS(A) : YPT=R*SIN(A) : GOSUB 9400 'lineto
260 NEXT A
270 RETURN

300 'circle 2
301 '**in ** XCENT,YCENT,R,XYSCALE,FOREGROUND%,ASPECT
310 CIRCLE (XCENT,YCENT),R,FOREGROUND%,,,ASPECT
319 '{ or CIRCLE (FN X(XCENT),FN Y(YCENT)),INT(R*XYSCALE),
              FOREGROUND%,,,ASPECT }
320 RETURN
```

The IBM PC already has a BASIC function CIRCLE which will draw circles. This is incorporated in a primitive routine 'circle2' (also in listing 2.9) for drawing a circle, one which is necessarily more efficient than 'circle1'. Remember that the ASPECT must be taken into consideration when using the CIRCLE function. A main program that calls these routines and PAINTs part of the screen is also given.

There may be the possibility of *side effects* when using these routines; for instance, the origin or plot head may have been moved by the routine. For example, 'circle1' changes the position of both the origin and plot pen, whereas listing 'circle2' does not. It would therefore be sensible to add the following line to the 'circle1' routine:

265 LET XMOVE = −XCENT: LET YMOVE = −YCENT:
      GO SUB 9600 'setorigin

Exercise 2.3

Write two routines to draw an ellipse of major axis A units (horizontal) and minor axis B units (vertical). The first, similar to 'circle 1', should use the fact that a typical point on this ellipse has coordinates (Acos α, Bsin α) where $0 \leqslant \alpha \leqslant 2\pi$. However it must be remembered that, unlike the circle, α is not the angle made by a radius through the point with the positive x-axis. It is simply a descriptive parameter. The second routine, similar to 'circle2', must use the CIRCLE function with the ASPECT value changed.

Incorporate either of these routines in a program that draws a diagram similar to figure 2.6. Here are two things to note: (1) there is no need for A to be greater than B, and (2) observe the optical illusion of the two apparent white diagonal lines. Another illusion may be seen in figure 2.6 — dark circles radiating out from the centre of the pattern. The study of optical illusions is fascinating (see Tolansky, 1964) and it is a never-ending fount of ideas for patterns. This exercise was introduced because it leads the way to the general technique of drawing curves — see chapters 3 and 6.

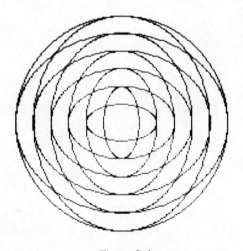

Figure 2.6

Example 2.4

An extension of this idea, the natural next step, is the construction of a spiral (figure 2.7a). Again the general form of the curve about the origin is (Rcos α, Rsin α) but now α varies between angles β to $\beta + 2N\pi$, where β (the parameter BETA) is the initial angle that the normal to the spiral makes with the positive x-axis, and N is the number of turns in the spiral (integer variable N%). The radius R is no longer a constant value but varies with the value of α: if RMAX is the outer radius of the spiral then R is given by the formula

$$R = RMAX(\alpha - \beta)/2N\pi$$

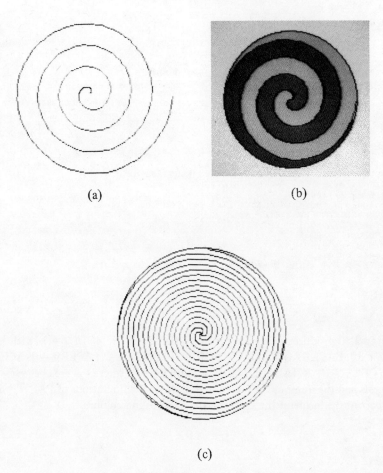

(a)   (b)

(c)

Figure 2.7

Note that this routine, which centres the spiral at (XCENT, YCENT), causes no side effects because the origin is reset back to its original position before leaving the routine. This routine is used in a main program which uses the PAINT facility of the IBM PC to draw figure 2.7b.

Listing 2.10

```
100 'Example of spirals.
110 GOSUB 9700 'start
120 INPUT " centre,radius,number of turns and angle ",
            XCENT,YCENT,RMAX,N%,BETA
130 GOSUB 60000 'colour monitor
139 'draw first spiral.
140 GOSUB 500 'spiral
150 BETA=3.141593+BETA
159 'draw second spiral.
160 GOSUB 500 'spiral
```

```
169 ´draw outer circle.
170 CIRCLE(XCENT,YCENT),RMAX,FOREGROUND%,,,ASPECT
178 ´{ or CIRCLE(FN X(XCENT),FN Y(YCENT)),RMAX*XYSCALE,
                    FOREGROUND%,,,ASPECT }
179 ´PAINT in the two areas.
180 PAINT (XCENT,YCENT+RMAX/N%),2,FOREGROUND%
189 ´{ or PAINT (FN X(XCENT),FN Y(YCENT+RMAX/N%)),2,FOREGROUND%}
190 PAINT (XCENT,YCENT-RMAX/N%),1,FOREGROUND%
199 ´{ or PAINT (FN X(XCENT),FN Y(YCENT-RMAX/N%)),1,FOREGROUND%}
200 GOSUB 60100 ´monochrome display
210 END

500 ´spiral
501 ´**in ** XCENT,YCENT,RMAX,N%,BETA
509 ´move origin to centre of spiral.
510 XMOVE=XCENT : YMOVE=YCENT : GOSUB 9600 ´setorigin
520 ADIF=3.141593/50 : ALPHA=BETA
530 RDIF=RMAX/(100*N%)
539 ´calculate and join points (XPT,YPT) on the spiral.
540 FOR R=RDIF TO RMAX STEP RDIF
550 XPT=R*COS(ALPHA) : YPT=R*SIN(ALPHA) : GOSUB 9400 ´lineto
560 ALPHA=ALPHA+ADIF
570 NEXT R
579 ´reset origin.
580 XMOVE=-XCENT : YMOVE=-YCENT : GOSUB 9600 ´setorigin
590 RETURN
```

Listing 2.10 produces a diagram similar to figure 2.7b in MODE% = 1 (with HORIZ = 30, BACKGROUND% = 7, FOREGROUND% = 3, PAPER% = 0, XCENT = 15, YCENT = 10, RMAX = 8, N% = 2 and BETA = 0) where the area between the two spirals and the outer circle is coloured in. Note the limitations of PAINT, which leaves part of the inside of the spirals in the background colour.

Exercise 2.4
Use the routine in a program that generates figure 2.7c. Again note the optical illusion when the observer's head is moved in a circle in front of the diagram, keeping the horizontal (and hence also the vertical) direction parallel to the original direction. The spirals appear to rotate about the centre!

Example 2.5
Write a routine (listing 2.11) that draws diagrams similar to figure 2.8. Here the concept of an *envelope* is introduced. Instead of drawing a curve by a sequence of small line segments (as in the circle of listing 2.9), a sequence of lines is drawn, each of which is tangential to the curve. For example, figure 2.8 shows four rectangular hyperbolas placed in the *quarters* of the plane.

N (variable N% in the program) points are placed on each of the four arms (of unit length) that divide the plane into the four quarters. The 4N points are therefore $(\pm I/N, 0.0)$ and $(0.0, \pm I/N)$ where $I = 1, 2, \ldots, N$.

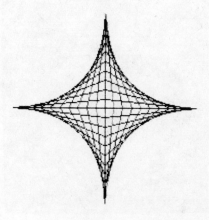

Figure 2.8

Listing 2.11

```
100 'Example of an envelope.
110 GOSUB 9700 'start
120 INPUT "type in N ",N%
130 GOSUB 60000 'colour monitor
140 XMOVE=HORIZ*.5 : YMOVE=VERT*.5
150 GOSUB 9600 'setorigin
159 'draw unit axes.
160 XPT= 1 : YPT= 0 : GOSUB 9500 'moveto
170 XPT=-1 : YPT= 0 : GOSUB 9400 'lineto
180 XPT= 0 : YPT= 1 : GOSUB 9500 'moveto
190 XPT= 0 : YPT=-1 : GOSUB 9400 'lineto
199 'produce N sets each of four points, one on each axis.
    Join the points of each set in order.
200 FOR I%=1 TO N%
210 ID1=I%/N% : ID2=(N%+1-I%)/N%
220 XPT= ID1 : YPT=   0 : GOSUB 9500 'moveto
230 XPT=   0 : YPT= ID2 : GOSUB 9400 'lineto
240 XPT=-ID1 : YPT=   0 : GOSUB 9400 'lineto
250 XPT=   0 : YPT=-ID2 : GOSUB 9400 'lineto
260 XPT= ID1 : YPT=   0 : GOSUB 9400 'lineto
270 NEXT I%
280 GOSUB 60100 'monochrome display
290 END
```

Exercise 2.5
Generalise this routine so that there are a variable number of arms, M, stretching out from the origin and dividing the plane into equal segments.

Exercise 2.6
Draw a diagram similar to figure 2.9; the routine will have an integer parameter N. It will calculate 4N points $\{P(I): I = 1, 2, \ldots, 4N\}$ around the edges of a square of

Figure 2.9

unit side, starting at a corner. There is one point at each corner and the points are placed so that the distance between consecutive points is 1/N. Then pairs of points are joined according to the following rule: P(I) is joined to P(J) for all positive I and J less than or equal to 4N, such that J—I (subtraction modulo 4N) belongs to the sequence 1, 1 + 2, 1 + 2 + 3, ... For example, if N is 10 then P(20) is joined to P(21), P(23), P(26), P(30), P(35), P(1), P(8) and P(16).

Example 2.6
Emulate a Spirograph, in order to produce diagrams similar to figure 2.10.

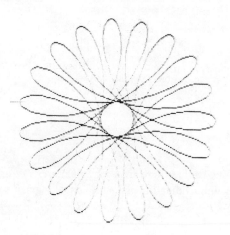

Figure 2.10

A Spirograph consists of a cogged disk inside a cogged circle, which is placed on a piece of paper. Let the outer circle have integer radius A and the disk integer radius B. The disk is always in contact with the circle. There is a small hole in the disk at a distance D (also an integer) from the centre of the disk, through which is placed a sharp pencil point. These values are stored as integer variables A%, B%, D%. The disk is moved around the circle in an anticlockwise manner, but it must always touch the outer circle; the cogs ensure that there is no slipping. The pencil point traces out a pattern, which is complete when the pencil returns to its original position.

It is initially assumed that the centres of the disk and the circle and also the hole all lie on the positive x-axis, the centre of the circle being the coordinate origin. In order to emulate the Spirograph it is necessary to specify a general point on the track of the pencil point. Let α be the angle made with the positive x-axis by the line joining the origin to the point where the circle and disk touch. The point of contact is therefore ($A\cos\alpha$, $A\sin\alpha$) and the centre of the disk is (($A-B)\cos\alpha$, $(A-B)\sin\alpha$). Letting β be the angle that the line joining the hole to the centre of the disk makes with the x-direction, then the coordinates of the hole are

$$((A-B)\cos\alpha + D\cos\beta, (A-B)\sin\alpha + D\sin\beta)$$

The point of contact between the disk and circle will have moved through a distance $A\alpha$ around the circle, and a distance $-B\beta$ around the disk (the minus sign is because α and β have opposite orientation). Since there is no slipping these distances must be equal, hence the equation $\beta = -(A/B)\alpha$. The pencil returns to its original position when both α and β are integer multiples of 2π. When $\alpha = 2N\pi$ then $\beta = -N(A/B)2\pi$, the pencil point hence returns to its original position for the first time when $N(A/B)$ becomes an integer for the first time; that is, when N is equal to B divided by the highest common factor of B and A. The routine 'Euclid' given in listing 2.12 uses Euclid's algorithm (see Davenport, 1952) to calculate the highest common factor (integer HCF%) of two positive integers A% and B%.

This function is used in the routine 'Spirograph' (listing 2.12) which calculates the value of N and then varies α (ALPHA) between 0 and $2N\pi$ in steps of $\pi/100$; for each α, the value of β (BETA) is calculated and then the general track is drawn. Figure 2.10 was drawn by a call to 'Spirograph' in MODE% = 2 on PAPER% = 3, with A% = 13, B% = 6 and D% = 5. The size of HORIZ must be chosen so that the figure fits on the screen, in this case HORIZ = 40.

Listing 2.12

```
100 'Spirograph example.
110 GOSUB 9700 'start
120 INPUT "type in A,B,D ",A%,B%,D%
130 GOSUB 60000 'colour monitor
140 XMOVE=HORIZ*.5 : YMOVE=VERT*.5
150 GOSUB 9600 'setorigin
160 GOSUB 300 'Spirograph
170 GOSUB 60100 'monochrome display
180 END
```

```
200 ´Euclid
201 ´**in ** A%,B%
202 ´**out** HCF%
210 I%=A% : HCF%=B%
220 IF A%<B% THEN I%=B% : HCF%=A%
230 J%=I% MOD HCF%
240 IF J%=0 THEN RETURN
250 I%=HCF% : HCF%=J% : GOTO 230

300 ´Spirograph
301 ´**in ** A%,B%,D%
310 RAB%=A%-B% : ALPHA=0 : ADIF=3.141593/50 : AOB=A%/B%
320 GOSUB 200 ´Euclid
330 N%=B%/HCF% : NO%=100*N%
339 ´calculate and join points (XPY,YPT) on path of Spirograph.
340 XPT=RAB%+D% : YPT=0 : GOSUB 9500 ´moveto
350 FOR I%=1 TO NO%
360 ALPHA=ALPHA+ADIF
370 BETA=ALPHA*AOB
380 XPT=RAB%*COS(ALPHA)+D%*COS(BETA)
390 YPT=RAB%*SIN(ALPHA)-D%*SIN(BETA)
400 GOSUB 9400 ´lineto
410 NEXT I%
420 RETURN
```

It is evident from this example that drawing patterns is not as straightforward as it first appears. Even such a simple picture as figure 2.10 requires the mathematical back-up of Euclid. Progressing through computer graphics, you will discover more and more that it is essential to have at least an elementary knowledge of not only coordinate geometry but also calculus, algebra, Euclidean geometry and number theory. Be prepared to scour your local library (or pester your friendly neighbourhood mathematician) for the necessary information.

Complete Programs

At this stage listing 1.1 is defined to be the 'lib0' library, and listings 2.1 ('start' and the two functions FN X and FN Y), 2.2 ('setorigin'), 2.3 ('moveto') and 2.4 ('lineto'), or their equivalent listings 2.1a, 2.2a, 2.3a and 2.4a, are the 'lib1' library. Later, if using the old routines, listing 2.4 will be replaced by listing 3.3 ('clip' and a new version of 'lineto'). Listings 3.4 ('angle') and 3.5 ('filler') are also included in 'lib1'. The two libraries 'lib0' and 'lib1' must be MERGEd with the programs below, and complete programs may be run in MODE% = 1 with PALETTE% = 1, BACKGROUND% = 0, FOREGROUND% = 2 and PAPER% = 3.

    I. Listing 2.5 ('drawing a square'). Data required: HORIZ, try 30.

   II. Listing 2.6 ('main program' and 'polygon'). Data required: HORIZ, the number of vertices on a polygon, and their X/Y coordinates in pairs: these must fit on the screen. Try 30, 3 and (8, 8), (−8, 8), (0, −8).

  III. Listing 2.7 ('joining vertices of regular N-gon'). Data required: HORIZ = 4 and an integer $3 \leqslant N\% \leqslant 20$.

  IV. Listing 2.8 ('rose'). Data required: the values of HORIZ, M% and N%.

HORIZ = 4, N% ⩽ 30 and for the best results set 3 ⩽ M% ⩽ N% ⩽ 15.

V. Listing 2.9 (main program and routines 'circle1' and 'circle2'). Each routine requires the centre (XCENT, YCENT) and radius R. Choose these values so that the figure is consistent with your value of HORIZ (for example, 30). For 'circle1' try centre (15, 10) with radius 5, and for 'circle2' try centre (3, 0) with radius 6.

VI. Listings 2.10 (main program and 'spiral'). Each routine requires the centre (XCENT, YCENT), maximum radius RMAX, the number of turns in the spiral N% and an angle BETA. Choose these values so that the figure is consistent with your value of HORIZ (for example, 30). For example, call 'spiral' with centre (15, 10), RMAX = 8, N% = 3 and BETA = 1.

VII. Listing 2.11 ('envelope'). Data required: HORIZ (try 4) and an integer N%, 2 ⩽ N% ⩽ 20.

VIII. Listing 2.12 (main program, 'Euclid' and 'Spirograph'). Data required: three integers A%, B% and D%, where A% > B% > D%. Choose HORIZ so that the diagram fits on the screen: set HORIZ so that the value of VERT is greater than 2 * (A%−B% + D%). Try HORIZ = 40, A% = 12, B% = 7 and D% = 5. Also try in MODE% = 2.

3 Two-Dimensional Coordinate Geometry

Chapter 2 introduced the concept of the two-dimensional rectangular coordinate system and defined points in space as vectors, whence line segments between pairs of points could be drawn. To be strictly accurate, a *straight line* (or *line* for short) in two-dimensional space is not a finite segment, but stretches off to infinity in both directions. So it is necessary to introduce ways of representing a general point on such a line.

It is well known that the equation of a straight line is $y = mx + c$. This gives the relationship between the x and y coordinates of a general point on the line, where m is the tangent of the angle that the line makes with the positive x-axis, and c is the point of intersection of the line with the y-axis; hence when $x = 0$ then $y = c$. This formula may be well known, but it is not very useful. What happens if the line is vertical? m is infinite! A far better formula is

$$ay = bx + c$$

This allows for all possible lines: if the line is vertical, then a is 0. (b/a) is now the tangent of the angle that the line makes with the positive x-axis, and the line cuts the y-axis at (c/a) provided that a is not zero, and the x-axis at $(-c/b)$ provided that b is not zero. The line is parallel to the y-axis if a is zero, and to the x-axis if b is zero.

This formulation of a line will be used frequently in the following pages, although another, possibly more useful, method is introduced. Before describing this new method, two operations on vectors must be defined — scalar multiple and vector addition. Another operation, the absolute value of a vector, is also required. Suppose there are two vectors $p_1 \equiv (x_1, y_1)$ and $p_2 \equiv (x_2, y_2)$, then

scalar multiple: $kp_1 = (k{\times}x_1, k{\times}y_1)$, multiply the individual coordinates by some scalar value (that is, real) k.

vector addition: $p_1 + p_2 = (x_1 + x_2, y_1 + y_2)$, add the x-coordinates together, and the y-coordinates together.

absolute value: $|p_1| = \sqrt{(x_1^2 + y_1^2)}$ is the distance of the point p_1 from the origin (this is also called the length of the vector).

In order to define a line, first any two points on the line are chosen — again they are called $p_1 \equiv (x_1, y_1)$ and $p_2 \equiv (x_2, y_2)$. A general point $p(\mu) \equiv (x, y)$ is given by the combination of scalar multiples and vector addition

$$(1 - \mu)p_1 + \mu p_2 \quad \text{for some real value of } \mu$$

that is, the vector $((1 - \mu)\times x_1 + \mu\times x_2, (1 - \mu)\times y_1 + \mu\times y_2)$. The μ is placed in brackets after $\boldsymbol{p}$ to show the dependence of the vector on the value of μ. Later when the relationship is understood more fully, the (μ) will be deleted. If $0 \leqslant \mu \leqslant 1$ then $\boldsymbol{p}(\mu)$ lies on the line somewhere between $\boldsymbol{p}_1$ and $\boldsymbol{p}_2$. For any specified point $\boldsymbol{p}(\mu)$, the value of μ is given by the ratio

$$\frac{\text{distance of } \boldsymbol{p}(\mu) \text{ from } \boldsymbol{p}_1}{\text{distance of } \boldsymbol{p}_2 \text{ from } \boldsymbol{p}_1}$$

where the measure of distance is positive if $\boldsymbol{p}(\mu)$ is on the same side of $\boldsymbol{p}_1$ as $\boldsymbol{p}_2$, and negative otherwise. The positive distance between any two vector points $\boldsymbol{p}_1$ and $\boldsymbol{p}_2$ is given by (Pythagoras)

$$|\boldsymbol{p}_2 - \boldsymbol{p}_1| = \sqrt{((x_1 - x_2)^2 + (y_1 - y_2)^2)}$$

See figure 2.1, which shows a line segment between points $(-3, -1) \equiv \boldsymbol{p}(0)$ and $(3, 2) \equiv \boldsymbol{p}(1)$: the point $(1, 1)$ lies on the line as $\boldsymbol{p}(2/3)$. Note that $(3, 2)$ is at a distance of $3\sqrt{5}$ from $(-3, -1)$ whereas $(1, 1)$ is at a distance of $2\sqrt{5}$. From now on, the (μ) will be omitted from the point vector representation.

Example 3.1
This idea is further illustrated by drawing the pattern shown in figure 3.1. At first sight it looks complicated, but on closer inspection it is seen to be simply a square, outside a square, outside a square etc. The squares are getting successively smaller and they are rotating through a constant angle. In order to draw the diagram a technique is needed, which, when given a general square, draws a smaller internal square rotated through this fixed angle. Suppose the general square has four corners

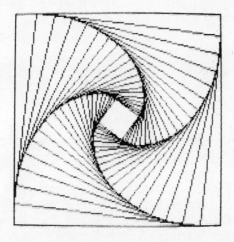

Figure 3.1

$\{(x_i, y_i) | i = 1, 2, 3, 4\}$ and the ith side of the square is the line joining (x_i, y_i) to (x_{i+1}, y_{i+1}) — assuming additions of subscripts are modulo 4, that is $4 + 1 = 1$. A general point on this side of the square, (x'_i, y'_i), is given by

$$((1 - \mu) \times x_i + \mu \times x_{i+1}, (1 - \mu) \times y_i + \mu \times y_{i+1}) \text{ where } 0 \leqslant \mu \leqslant 1$$

In fact $\mu : 1 - \mu$ is the ratio in which the side is bisected. If μ is fixed and the four points $\{(x'_i, y'_i) | i = 1, 2, 3, 4\}$ are calculated in the above manner, then the sides of the new square make an angle $\alpha = \tan^{-1}[\mu/(1 - \mu)]$ with the corresponding side of the outer square. So by keeping μ fixed for each new square, the angle between consecutive squares remains a constant α. In listing 3.1, which generated figure 3.1 (HORIZ = 4), there are 21 squares and $\mu = 0.1$.

Listing 3.1

```
100 'square outside square etc.
110 GOSUB 9700 'start
120 GOSUB 60000 'colour monitor
130 XMOVE=HORIZ*.5 : YMOVE=VERT*.5
140 GOSUB 9600 'setorigin
150 DIM X(4),Y(4),XD(4),YD(4)
160 DATA 1,1,1,-1,-1,-1,-1,1
169 'initialise first square.
170 FOR I%=1 TO 4
180 READ X(I%),Y(I%)
190 NEXT I%
199 'set MU value and draw 20 squares.
200 MU=.1 : UM=1-MU
210 FOR I%=1 TO 21
219 'join four vertices of square i.e. (X(J),Y(J)) : J=1:4.
    Calculate next four vertices i.e. (XD(J),YD(J)) : J=1:4.
220 XPT=X(4) : YPT=Y(4) : GOSUB 9500 'moveto
230 FOR J%=1 TO 4
240 XPT=X(J%) : YPT=Y(J%) : GOSUB 9400 'lineto
250 NJ%=(J% MOD 4)+1
260 XD(J%)=UM*X(J%)+MU*X(NJ%) : YD(J%)=UM*Y(J%)+MU*Y(NJ%)
270 NEXT J%
279 'copy arrays XD and YD into X and Y respectively.
280 FOR J%=1 TO 4
290 X(J%)=XD(J%) : Y(J%)=YD(J%)
300 NEXT J%
310 NEXT I%
320 GOSUB 60100 'monochrome display
330 END
```

It is useful to note that the vector combination form of a line can be reorganised into

$$p_1 + \mu(p_2 - p_1)$$

When given in this new representation the vector p_1 may be called a *base vector*, and $(p_2 - p_1)$ called the *directional vector*. In fact any point on the line can stand as a base vector, it simply acts as a point to anchor a line that is parallel to the directional vector. This concept of a vector acting as a direction needs some further explanation. It has already been noted that a vector pair (x, y) say, may represent a point; a line joining the coordinate origin to this point may be thought of as specifying a direction — any line in space that is parallel to this line is defined to have the same directional vector. A line that goes from the origin O towards (x, y) has so-called positive *sense*; a line from (x, y) towards the origin has negative sense.

The Intersection of Two Lines

This base and direction representation is also very useful for calculating the point of intersection of two lines, a problem that frequently crops up in two-dimensional graphics. For suppose that there are two lines $p + \mu q$ and $r + \lambda s$, where $p \equiv (x_1, y_1)$, $q \equiv (x_2, y_2)$, $r \equiv (x_3, y_3)$ and $s \equiv (x_4, y_4)$ for $-\infty < \mu, \lambda < \infty$. The point of intersection is defined by unique values of μ and λ that satisfy the vector equation

$$p + \mu q = r + \lambda s$$

that is, a point common to both lines. This vector equation can be written as two separate equations:

$$x_1 + \mu \times x_2 = x_3 + \lambda \times x_4 \tag{3.1}$$

$$y_1 + \mu \times y_2 = y_3 + \lambda \times y_4 \tag{3.2}$$

Rewriting these equations:

$$\mu \times x_2 - \lambda \times x_4 = x_3 - x_1 \tag{3.3}$$

$$\mu \times y_2 - \lambda \times y_4 = y_3 - y_1 \tag{3.4}$$

Multiplying equation (3.3) by y_4, equation (3.4) by x_4 and subtracting:

$$\mu \times (x_2 \times y_4 - y_2 \times x_4) = (x_3 - x_1) \times y_4 - (y_3 - y_1) \times x_4$$

If $(x_2 \times y_4 - y_2 \times x_4) = 0$ then the lines are parallel and there is no point of intersection (μ does not exist), otherwise

$$\mu = \frac{(x_3 - x_1) \times y_4 - (y_3 - y_1) \times x_4}{(x_2 \times y_4 - y_2 \times x_4)} \tag{3.5}$$

and similarly

$$\lambda = \frac{(x_3 - x_1) \times y_2 - (y_3 - y_1) \times x_2}{(x_2 \times y_4 - y_2 \times x_4)} \tag{3.6}$$

Naturally if both lines are parallel then the denominator in these equations becomes zero and an infinite result is produced, because the two parallel lines cannot intersect.

The solution becomes even simpler if one of the lines is parallel to a coordinate axis. Suppose this line is $x = d$, then $r \equiv (d, 0)$ and $s \equiv (0, 1)$, which when substituted in equation (3.5) gives

$$\mu = (d - x_1)/x_2$$

and similarly if the line is $y = d$

$$\mu = (d - y_1)/y_2$$

Example 3.2

Find the point of intersection of the two lines (a) joining $(1, -1)$ to $(-1, -3)$ and (b) joining $(1, 2)$ to $(3, -2)$.

The lines may be written

$$(1 - \mu)(1, -1) + \mu(-1, -3) \quad -\infty < \mu < \infty \tag{3.7}$$

$$(1 - \lambda)(1, 2) + \lambda(3, -2) \quad -\infty < \lambda < \infty \tag{3.8}$$

or when placed in the base/directional vector form

$$(1, -1) + \mu(-2, -2) \tag{3.9}$$

$$(1, 2) + \lambda(2, -4) \tag{3.10}$$

Substituting these values in equation (3.5) gives

$$\mu = \frac{(1 - 1)\times -4 - (2 + 1)\times 2}{(-2\times -4 - (-2)\times 2)} = -1/2$$

whence the point of intersection is $(1, -1) - 1/2(-2, -2) \equiv (2, 0)$.

The general case is solved by the program given in listing 3.2.

Listing 3.2

```
100 'intersection of two lines in 2-D space.
110 DIM X(4),Y(4)
120 CLS
130 LOCATE 3,12
140 PRINT "INTERSECTION of LINES"
150 LOCATE 5,5
160 PRINT "Line A from (X(1),Y(1)) to (X(2),Y(2))"
170 LOCATE 6,5
180 PRINT "Line B from (X(3),Y(3)) to (X(4),Y(4))"
189 'INPUT the vertices of lines A and B.
190 LOCATE 8,1
200 FOR I%=1 TO 4
210 LOCATE 10+I%,5
220 PRINT "( X(";I%;") , Y(";I%;") ) ";
230 INPUT X(I%),Y(I%)
240 NEXT I%
250 CLS
259 'PRINT information about lines.
260 LOCATE 3,12
270 PRINT "INTERSECTION of LINES"
280 LOCATE 5,5
290 PRINT
    "Line A goes from (";X(1);",";Y(1);") to (";X(2);",";Y(2);")"
300 LOCATE 8,5
310 PRINT
    "Line B goes from (";X(3);",";Y(3);") to (";X(4);",";Y(4);")"
319 'calculate (XINT,YINT), their point of intersection (if any).
320 X(2)=X(2)-X(1) : Y(2)=Y(2)-Y(1)
330 X(4)=X(4)-X(3) : Y(4)=Y(4)-Y(3)
340 DET=X(2)*Y(4)-X(4)*Y(2)
350 LOCATE 12,5
360 PRINT "Point of Intersection ";
```

```
370 IF ABS(DET)<.000001 THEN PRINT "does not exist" : GOTO 410
380 MU=((X(3)-X(1))*Y(4)-(Y(3)-Y(1))*X(4))/DET
390 XINT=X(1)+MU*X(2) : YINT=Y(1)+MU*Y(2)
400 PRINT " is   (";XINT;",";YINT;")"
410 LOCATE 20,1
420 END
```

Exercise 3.1

Experiment with this concept of vector representation of two-dimensional space.
You can make up your own questions: it is easy to check that your answers are
correct. Consider example 3.2. (2, 0) lies on the first line because the value $\mu = -1/2$
was used in its calculation: the answer is correct if the point also lies on the second
line — which it does with $\lambda = 1/2$.

Exercise 3.2

Write a program that reads in data about two straight lines in the form of equations
and then calculates their point of intersection (if any).

Clipping

If you had run the program containing listing 3.1 and 'lib1' with HORIZ = 1 on
releases of BASICA before 2.0, or on some other microcomputers, you would have
noticed that the lines going off the screen were being drawn in a peculiar (but
predictable?) way. In such cases it is impossible to draw a correct line to or from a
point (x, y) outside the graphics area, and thus there is a limitation $0 \leqslant x \leqslant 320 *$
MODE% $-$ 1 and $0 \leqslant y \leqslant 199$. It is very easy in such cases to inadvertently stray
outside this area. In fact when drawing two-dimensional and three-dimensional
scenes it is commonplace to define scenes that cover an area greater than that
allocated to the graphics frame. So it is necessary to find an algorithm that will
clip off all exterior line segments without losing any that should be drawn. Release
2.0 of BASICA does the clipping automatically for you, nevertheless it is useful to
understand an algorithm for achieving such clipping. If desired, those with release
2.0 of BASICA can ignore the following section.

The problem reduces to calculating which part (if any) of a line segment joining
pixel point (XA, YA) to pixel point (XB, YB) lies within the area. In order to
simplify matters the pixel coordinate system is redefined to let the centre of the
screen be the origin, and the pixels are vertically inverted so that they are in the
normal mathematical orientation. It is assumed that the centre of the screen in the
original system is given by the (non-pixel) point (XMID, 199/2), where XMID =
(320 * MODE% $-$ 1)/2, and so the change of origin and vertical inversion means
that the four corners of the graphics area are (XMID $\pm$ XMID, 99.5 $\pm$ 99.5) with
the top right-hand corner now (XMID, 99.5).

The sides of the rectangle are extended, thus dividing space into nine sectors, see
figure 3.2 which also shows the graphics area and the border. In this diagram a

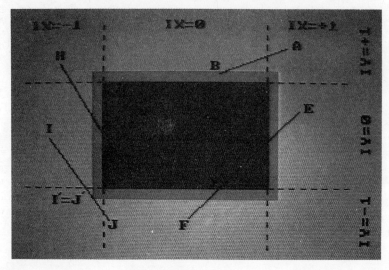

Figure 3.2

number of different line segments have been drawn to aid the explanation of the algorithm. Each point in space may now be classified by two parameters IX and IY where

(1) IX = −1, 0 or +1 depending on whether the x-coordinate value of the point lies to the left, on or to the right of the graphics area.

(2) IY = −1, 0 or +1 depending on whether the y-coordinate of the point lies below, on or above the graphics rectangle.

These values are calculated, when needed, inside the algorithm program.

If the two points at the ends of the line segment — that is. (XA. YA) and (XB, YB) — have parameters IXA,IYA and IXB,IYB respectively, then there are a number of possibilities to consider.

(i) If IXA = IXB ≠ 0 or IYA = IYB ≠ 0, then the whole line segment is outside the rectangle and hence may be safely ignored (for example, line AB in figure 3.2).

(ii) If IXA = IYA = IXB = IYB = 0, then the whole line segment lies in the graphics area and so the complete line must be drawn (for example, line CD).

(iii) The remaining case must be considered in detail. If IXA ≠ 0 and/or IYA ≠ 0 then the point (XA, YA) lies outside the rectangle and so new values for XA and YA must be found — to avoid confusion these are called XA' and YA'. (XA', YA') is the point on the line segment nearer to (XA, YA) where the line cuts the graphics area. The formula for this calculation was considered above (the intersection of a line with another line parallel to a coordinate axis). If the line misses the rectangle, then (XA', YA') is defined to be that point where the line cuts one of the extended vertical edges. If IXA = IYA = 0 then (XA', YA') ≡ (XA, YA). The point (XB', YB') is calculated in a similar manner. See the algorithm given by routine 'clip' in listing 3.3. The required clipped line is that joining (XA', YA') to (XB', YB'). If the original line misses the rectangle then the algorithm ensures that (XA', YA') = (XB', YB') and the new line segment degenerates to a point and is ignored. For example, EF is clipped to E'F', GH is clipped to GH' (G = G') and IJ degenerates to a point I' = J'.

Thus 'clip' takes the two pixel end-points of the line, (XA, YA) and (XB, YB), and transforms them into the centred system. It then discovers which of the above three possibilities is relevant and deals with it thus: (i) exit the routine immediately, (ii) join the two points or (iii) calculate the 'dashed' points and join them with a line segment.

Listing 3.3 also includes a new version of the 'lineto' routine which calls 'clip' instead of LINE, thus enabling it to cope with the problem of joining lines anywhere in space. From now on always use 'clip' and this new version of 'lineto' in library 'lib1' if you do not have release 2.0 of BASICA. It will prove invaluable, especially in the later study of three-dimensional objects.

Listing 3.3

```
9400 'lineto
9401 '**in ** XPEN,YPEN,XPT,YPT
9402 '**out** XA,YA,XB,YB
9410 XA=XPEN : YA=YPEN
9420 XPEN=FNX(XPT) : YPEN=FNY(YPT)
9430 XB=XPEN : YB=YPEN
9440 GOSUB 10000 'clip
9450 RETURN

10000 'clip routine
10001 '**in ** MODE%,XA,YA,XB,YB,FOREGROUND%
10009 'change coordinate system.
10010 XMID=(320*MODE%-1)/2
10020 XA=XA-XMID : YA=99.5-YA
10030 XB=XB-XMID : YB=99.5-YB
10039 'find the sector values of two points (XA,YA) and (XB,YB).
10040 IXA=0 : IF ABS(XA) > XMID THEN IXA=SGN(XA)
10050 IYA=0 : IF ABS(YA) > 99.5 THEN IYA=SGN(YA)
10060 IXB=0 : IF ABS(XB) > XMID THEN IXB=SGN(XB)
10070 IYB=0 : IF ABS(YB) > 99.5 THEN IYB=SGN(YB)
10079 'points in same off-screen sector so RETURN.
10080 IF (IXA*IXB=1) OR (IYA*IYB=1) THEN RETURN
10090 IF IXA=0 THEN GOTO 10120
10099 'move 1'st point to nearer x-edge.
10100 XX=XMID*IXA : YA=YA+(YB-YA)*(XX-XA)/(XB-XA) : XA=XX
10110 IYA=0 : IF ABS(YA) > 99.5 THEN IYA=SGN(YA)
10120 IF IYA=0 THEN GOTO 10140
10129 'move 1'st point to nearer y-edge.
10130 YY=99.5*IYA : XA=XA+(XB-XA)*(YY-YA)/(YB-YA) : YA=YY
10140 IF ABS(XA-XB)<.000001 AND ABS(YA-YB)<.000001 THEN RETURN
10150 IF IXB=0 THEN GOTO 10180
10159 'move 2'nd point to nearer x-edge.
10160 XX=XMID*IXB : YB=YA+(YB-YA)*(XX-XA)/(XB-XA) : XB=XX
10170 IYB=0 : IF ABS(YB) > 99.5 THEN IYB=SGN(YB)
10180 IF IYB=0 THEN GOTO 10200
10189 'move 2'nd point to nearer y-edge.
10190 YY=99.5*IYB : XB=XA+(XB-XA)*(YY-YA)/(YB-YA) : YB=YY
10200 IF ABS(XA-XB)<.000001 AND ABS(YA-YB)<.000001 THEN RETURN
10209 'join non-coincident points.
10210 XA=INT(XA+XMID+.5) : YA=INT(100-YA)
10220 XB=INT(XB+XMID+.5) : YB=INT(100-YB)
10230 LINE (XA,YA)-(XB,YB),FOREGROUND%
10240 RETURN
```

Exercise 3.3

Use this altered routine in the programs of chapter 2. Choose the value of HORIZ in such a way that some lines in the diagrams go outside the graphics area.

Note that from now on the new 'lib1' will be used exclusively, and no further reference will be made to the old library. It is left to the users to make all necessary changes if they do not have release 2.0 of BASICA.

Returning to the use of a vector ($q \equiv (x, y) \neq (0, 0)$, say) representing a direction, note that any positive scalar multiple kq, for $k > 0$, represents the *same direction and sense* as q. (If k is negative then the direction has its sense inverted.) In particular, setting $k = 1/|q|$ produces a vector ($x/\sqrt{(x^2 + y^2)}, y/\sqrt{(x^2 + y^2)}$) with unit absolute value.

Thus a general point on a line, $p + \mu q$, is a distance $|\mu q|$ from the base point p, and if $|q| = 1$ (a unit vector) then the point is a distance $|\mu|$ from p.

Now consider the angles made by directional vectors with various fixed directions. Suppose that α is the angle between the line joining O (the origin) to $q \equiv (x, y)$, and the positive x-axis. Then $x = |q| \times \cos \alpha$ and $y = |q| \times \sin \alpha$ — see figure 3.3: there are similar figures for the three other quadrants.

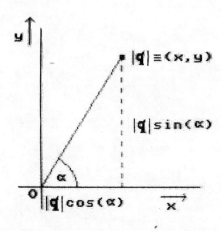

Figure 3.3

If q is a unit vector (that is, if $|q| = 1$) then $q \equiv (\cos \alpha, \sin \alpha)$. Note that $\sin \alpha = \cos(\alpha - \pi/2)$ for all values of α. Thus q may be rewritten as $(\cos \alpha, \cos(\alpha - \pi/2))$. But $\alpha - \pi/2$ is the angle that the vector makes with the positive y-axis. Hence the coordinates of a unit directional vector are called its *direction cosines*, since they are the cosines of the angles that the vector makes with the corresponding positive axes.

Before continuing, the trigonometric functions available in BASIC must be considered: SIN and COS. and the inverse function ATN. SIN and COS are functions with one parameter (an angle given in radians) and one result (a value between −1 and +1). The ATN function takes any value and calculates the angle in radians (in the so-called *principal range* between −π/2 and +π/2) whose tangent is that value.

This leads on to the problem of finding the angle that a general direction $q \equiv (x, y)$ makes with the positive x-axis, and which is solved by routine 'angle' given in listing 3.4. 'angle' will be of great use in later chapters when considering two and three-dimensional space, and so it is added to the library 'lib1'.

Listing 3.4

```
8800 'angle
8801 '**in ** AX,AY
8802 '**out** THETA
8809 'THETA is the angle that the line from origin to (AX,AY)
     makes with positive x-axis.
8810 IF ABS(AX)>.000001 THEN GOTO 8860
8819 'line is vertical.
8820 THETA=3.141593/2
8830 IF AY<0 THEN THETA=THETA+3.141593
8840 IF ABS(AY)<.000001 THEN THETA=0
8850 RETURN
8859 'line is not vertical so it has a finite tangent.
8860 THETA=ATN(AY/AX)
8870 IF AX<0 THEN THETA=THETA+3.141593
8880 RETURN
```

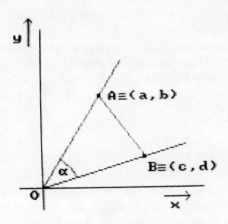

Figure 3.4

Now suppose that there are two directional vectors (a, b) and (c, d) — for simplicity both are assumed to be unit vectors and to go through the origin (see figure 3.4). The acute angle, α, between these lines is required. From the figure it is seen that $OA = \sqrt{(a^2 + b^2)} = 1$ and $OB = \sqrt{(c^2 + d^2)} = 1$. So by the Cosine Rule

$$AB^2 = OA^2 + OB^2 - 2 \times OA \times OB \times \cos \alpha = 2 \times (1 - \cos \alpha)$$

But also by Pythagoras

$$AB^2 = (a - c)^2 + (b - d)^2 = (a^2 + b^2) + (c^2 + d^2) - 2(a{\times}c + b{\times}d)$$

$$= 2 - 2(a{\times}c + b{\times}d)$$

Thus $a{\times}c + b{\times}d = \cos\alpha$. It is possible that $a{\times}c + b{\times}d$ is negative, in which case $\cos^{-1}(a{\times}c + b{\times}d)$ is obtuse and the required acute angle is $\pi - \alpha$. Since $\cos(\pi - \alpha) = -\cos\alpha$, then the acute angle is given immediately by $\cos^{-1}(|a{\times}c + b{\times}d|)$. For example, given the two lines with direction cosines $(\sqrt{3}/2, 1/2)$ and $(-1/2, -\sqrt{3}/2)$, then $a{\times}c + b{\times}d = -\sqrt{3}/2$ and thus $\alpha = \cos^{-1}(\sqrt{3}/2) = \pi/6$. This simple example was given in order to introduce the concept of a *scalar product* $\cdot$ of two vectors $(a, b) \cdot (c, d) = a{\times}c + b{\times}d$. Scalar product is extendable into higher-dimensional space (see chapter 7 for a three-dimensional example) and it always has the property that it gives the cosine of the angle between any pair of lines with directions defined by the two vectors.

Curves: Functional Representation versus Parametric Forms

A curve in two-dimensional space can be considered as a relationship between x and y coordinate values, the so-called *functional relationship*. Alternatively the coordinates can be individually specified in terms of other variables or parameters, the *parametric form*.

It has already been seen that a line (a circular arc of infinite radius) may be expressed as $ay = bx + c$. If the equation is rearranged so that one side is zero, that is, $ay - bx - c = 0$, then the algebraic expression on the left-hand side of the equation is called a functional representation of the line and written as

$$f(x, y) \equiv ay - bx - c$$

All, and only, those points with the property $f(x, y) = 0$ lie on the curve. This representation divides all the points in two-dimensional space into three sets: $f(x, y) = 0$ (the zero set), $f(x, y) > 0$ (the positive set) and $f(x, y) < 0$ (the negative set). If the function divides space into the curve and two other *connected areas* only (that is, any two points in a connected area may be joined by a curvilinear line that does not cross the curve), then these areas may be identified with the positive and negative sets defined by f. However, be wary, there are many elementary functions (such as $g(x, y) = \cos(y) - \sin(x)$) that define not one but a series of curves and hence divide space into possibly an infinite number of connected areas. (Note that $g(x, y) = g(x + 2m\pi, y + 2n\pi)$ for all integers m and n.) So it is possible that two disconnected areas can both belong to the positive set.

Note also that the functional representation need not be unique. The line can be put in the equivalent form

$$f'(x, y) \equiv bx + c - ay$$

in which case the positive set of this function is the negative set of the original, and vice versa.

The case where the curve does divide space into two connected areas is very useful in computer graphics, as will be seen in the study of two-dimensional and (especially) three-dimensional graphics algorithms. For example take the straight line

$$f(x, y) \equiv ay - bc - c$$

A point (x_1, y_1) is on the same side of the line as (x_2, y_2) if and only if $f(x_1, y_1)$ has the same non-zero sign as $f(x_2, y_2)$. The functional representation tells more about a point (x_1, y_1) than just the side of a line on which it lies — it also enables the distance of the point from the line to be calculated.

Consider the above line; its direction vector is (a, b). A line perpendicular to this will have direction vector $(-b, a)$ (why? because the product of the tangents of two mutually perpendicular lines is -1: see McCrae, 1953). So the point q on the line closest to the point $p \equiv (x_1, y_1)$ is of the form

$$q \equiv (x_1, y_1) + \mu(-b, a)$$

that is, a new line joining p to q is perpendicular to the original line. Since q lies on this original line:

$$f(q) \equiv f((x_1, y_1) + \mu(-b, a)) = 0$$

that is

$$a \times (y_1 + \mu \times a) - b \times (x_1 - \mu \times b) - c = f(x_1 . y_1) + \mu(a^2 + b^2) = 0$$

Hence $\mu = -f(x_1, y_1)/(a^2 + b^2)$. The point q is a distance $|\mu(-b, a)|$ from (x_1, y_1) which naturally means that the distance of (x_1, y_1) from the line is $\mu \times \sqrt{(a^2 + b^2)} = -f(x_1, y_1)/\sqrt{(a^2 + b^2)}$: the sign denotes on which side of the line the point is lying. If $a^2 + b^2 = 1$ then $|f(x_1, y_1)|$ gives the distance of the point (x_1, y_1) from the line.

This idea leads straight to a way of implementing *convex areas*, that is, an area with the property that a straight-line segment joining any two points within the area lies totally inside the area. Only convex polygons are considered in this book, however it is obvious that any convex area may be approximated by a polygon, provided that it has enough sides.

Consider the convex polygon with n vertices $\left\{ p_i \equiv (x_i, y_i) | i = 1, 2, \ldots, n \right\}$ taken in order around the polygon (either clockwise or anticlockwise). Such a description of a convex polygon is called an *oriented convex set* of vertices. The problem of finding whether such a set is clockwise or anticlockwise is considered in chapter 7. The n boundary edges of the polygon are segments of the lines

$$f_i(x, y) \equiv (x_{i+1} - x_i) . (y - y_i) - (y_{i+1} - y_i) \times (x - x_i)$$

where $i = 1, \ldots, n$, and the addition in the subscripts is modulo n (that is, $n + j \equiv j$ for $1 \leqslant j \leqslant n$). Try to explain why these formulae do actually describe the line segments!

The functional representation of a given line segment, say the one joining p_i to p_{i+1} for some i, is calculated in the above way in order to take advantage of an interesting property of this formulation. If you imagine yourself astride the line looking from p_i towards p_{i+1}, then the positive side of the line is to the left and the negative side to the right.

If a convex polygon is oriented anticlockwise, then the *inside* of the polygon is classified by the set

$$\{(x, y) \mid f_i(x, y) > 0 \text{ for all } i, \ 1 \leqslant i \leqslant n\}$$

A point on the *boundary* is given by

$$\{(x, y) \mid f_i(x, y) \geqslant 0 \text{ for all } i, \ 1 \leqslant i \leqslant n, \text{ and }$$
$$\text{there is at least one } i \text{ such that } f_i(x, y) = 0\}$$

The *outside* of the polygon is defined by

$$\{(x, y) \mid f_i(x, y) < 0 \text{ for at least one } i, \ 1 \leqslant i \leqslant n\}$$

This technique of 'inside and outside' is fundamental to the calculation of the intersection of two polygons (see below) and the hidden surface algorithm of chapter 12.

Example 3.3
Consider the convex polygon with vertices $(1, 0)$, $(5, 2)$, $(4, 4)$ and $(-2, 1)$: see figure 3.5. In this order the vertices obviously have an anticlockwise orientation.

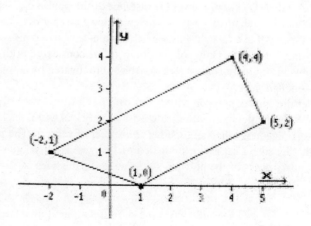

Figure 3.5

Are the points $(3, 2), (1, 4), (3, 1)$ inside, outside or on the boundary of the polygon? What is the distance of $(4, 4)$ from the first line?

$$f_1(x, y) \equiv (5 - 1) \times (y - 0) - (2 - 0) \times (x - 1) \quad \equiv 4y - 2x + 2$$

$$f_2(x, y) \equiv (4 - 5) \times (y - 2) - (4 - 2) \times (x - 5) \quad \equiv -y - 2x + 12$$

$$f_3(x, y) \equiv (-2 - 4) \times (y - 4) - (1 - 4) \times (x - 4) \equiv -6y + 3x + 12$$

$$f_4(x, y) \equiv (1 + 2) \times (y - 1) - (0 - 1) \times (x + 2) \quad \equiv 3y + x - 1$$

Hence point $(3, 2)$ is inside the body because $f_1(3, 2) = 4$, $f_2(3, 2) = 4$, $f_3(3, 2) = 9$ and $f_4(3, 2) = 8$: all have positive signs.

Point $(1, 4)$ is outside the body because $f_3(1, 4) = -9$ (negative).

Point $(3, 1)$ is on the boundary because $f_1(3, 1) = 0$, and the values $f_2(3, 1) = 5$, $f_3(3, 1) = 15$ and $f_4(3, 1) = 5$ are all positive.

$(4, 4)$ is a distance $f_1(4, 4)/\sqrt{(4^2 + 2^2)} = 10/\sqrt{20} = \sqrt{5}$ from the first line.

Intersection of Two Convex Polygons

Imagine two convex polygons that intersect one another. The area of intersection is either null or another convex polygon. The methods mentioned in this chapter are used to draw both polygons, calculate the vertices of the new polygon (if it exists) and colour it in.

Before this problem can be solved, the limitations of the PAINT operation must be noted: (a) you cannot initiate PAINTing at a point outside the screen area, and (b) an area defined by a curvilinear boundary may have certain internal pixels isolated by that boundary, so these pixels cannot be PAINTed. To get round these problems, a routine 'polygon filler' ('filler' for short) is introduced in listing 3.5, which enables a convex polygon defined by NC% vectors XC(1. . .NC%) and YC(1. . .NC%) to be filled in colour COLFAC%, with the edges of the polygon coloured in the present FOREGROUND% colour. This routine will also be very useful in later work so it is added to the 'lib1' library. As with most of the programs in this book, the listings are given in BASIC so that they are readily understandable as algorithms, however since their execution is necessarily slow it is essential for serious work that you should either write an equivalent machine code routine or compile the program.

The method first transforms the vectors $(XC(i), YC(i))$, $1 \leqslant i \leqslant NC\%$, into the equivalent pixel vectors on the screen, $(PX(i), PY(i))$: the scaling is achieved by WINDOW. It then finds the maximum (YMAX) and minimum (YMIN) y-value of the pixel vectors that are both in the polygon and on the screen (that is, the polygon is clipped onto the screen). Then taking each y-pixel line in turn, the x-pixel value of the intersection of this line with each of the NC% edges of the polygon is calculated. The MU value of the intersection is found, and if it lies between zero and one it is known to be a proper intersection with the polygon. Obtaining the

maximum (XMAX) and minimum (XMIN) *x*-values that lie on the screen, after
clipping-off pixels outside the screen area, enables a horizontal line to be drawn on
the screen in colour COLFAC% for each *y*-pixel line. This fills in the area, and the
outline of the polygon is finally drawn in colour FOREGROUND%.

Listing 3.5

```
4000 ´polygon filler
4001 ´**in ** NC%,XC(NC%),YC(NC%),COLFAC%,FOREGROUND%,MODE%
4009 ´find the Y-extremes of the polygon.
4010 DIM PX(NC%),PY(NC%)
4020 YMAX=-1 : YMIN=200
4030 FOR V%=1 TO NC%
4039 ´pixel vector (PX(V%),PY(V%)) equivalent to (XC(V%),YC(V%))
4040 PX(V%)=PMAP(XC(V%),0) : PY(V%)=PMAP(YC(V%),1)
4050 IF PY(V%)<YMIN THEN YMIN=PY(V%)
4060 IF PY(V%)>YMAX THEN YMAX=PY(V%)
4070 NEXT V%
4080 IF YMIN<0 THEN YMIN=0
4090 IF YMAX>199 THEN YMAX=199
4100 IF YMAX<YMIN THEN GOTO 4310
4109 ´look at each pixel Y-line in turn.
4110 FOR Y=YMIN TO YMAX
4119 ´find the X-extremes of the polygon on this Y-line.
4120 XMAX=-1 : XMIN=320*MODE%
4129 ´for each edge of the polygon, a line segment joining
       (PX(V%),PY(V%)) to (PX(NV%),PY(NV%)), find its point
       of intersection (X,Y) (if any) with the Y-line.
4130 FOR V%=1 TO NC%
4140 NV%=(V% MOD NC%)+1
4150 IF (PY(V%)-PY(NV%))=0 THEN GOTO 4210
4160 MU=(Y-PY(V%))/(PY(NV%)-PY(V%))
4170 IF MU<0 OR MU>1 THEN GOTO 4210
4180 X=PX(V%)+INT(MU*(PX(NV%)-PX(V%))+.5)
4190 IF X<XMIN THEN XMIN=X
4200 IF X>XMAX THEN XMAX=X
4210 NEXT V%
4220 IF XMIN<0 THEN XMIN=0
4230 IF XMAX>= 320*MODE% THEN XMAX=320*MODE%-1
4240 IF XMAX<XMIN THEN GOTO 4260
4249 ´draw the Y line in colour COLFAC%.
4250 LINE (PMAP(XMIN,2),PMAP(Y,3))-(PMAP(XMAX,2),PMAP(Y,3)),COLFAC%
4260 NEXT Y
4269 ´draw the outer edge of polygon in colour FOREGROUND%.
4270 FOR V%=1 TO NC%
4280 NV%=(V% MOD NC%)+1
4290 LINE (XC(V%),YC(V%))-(XC(NV%),YC(NV%)),FOREGROUND%
4300 NEXT V%
4310 ERASE PX,PY
4320 RETURN
```

Now that we have the ability to fill in areas, the next problem to consider is a
method for finding the convex polygon of intersection of two convex polygons.
Because the 'inside and outside' method mentioned above will be used, it is necessary that all polygons are given in anticlockwise orientation. (You should read
chapter 7 to find a method for testing the orientation of a triangle in two-
dimensional space.) Suppose the polygons A and B are placed as NA% vertices in
arrays XA and YA, and NB% vertices in arrays XB and YB respectively, and that the
resulting polygon of intersection has NC% vertices placed in arrays XC and YC.

The method is to take each extended line segment of polygon B in turn and slice off pieces from polygon A that lie outside these lines. Two two-dimensional arrays XF and YF are needed to implement this method. Polygon A is copied into XF(P1%, . .) and YF(P1%, . .) . P1% is originally 1 – and the first line taken from polygon B and the outside vertices sliced off A: all inside vertices and vertices of intersection are added to XF(P2%, . .) and YF(P2%, . .) in the correct order . P2% is originally 2. NC% vertices are left in these arrays after each slice. By switching the values of P1% and P2% it is possible to slice off areas outside the second line (and then the third, fourth etc.) until eventually just the polygon of intersection remains, and this is finally copied into arrays XC and YC, which can be entered immediately into 'filler'. If at any time NC% becomes less than 3, then naturally there is no intersection. This routine 'overlap' and a main program (which also uses 'filler') are given in listing 3.6. This method will be used again in chapter 12 as part of a general hidden surface algorithm.

Listing 3.6

```
100  'To demonstrate intersection of two convex polygons.
110  GOSUB 9700 'start
119  'INPUT information on two anticlockwise oriented polygons
        given by vertices (XA(i),YA(i))  i=1...NA%
        and (XB(i),YB(i))  i=1...NB%.
120  INPUT " number of vertices in first polygon ",NA%
130  DIM XA(NA%),YA(NA%)
140  FOR I%=1 TO NA%
150  PRINT " type in XA(";I%;")  and  YA(";I%;")  ";
160  INPUT XA(I%),YA(I%)
170  NEXT I%
180  INPUT " number of vertices in second polygon ",NB%
190  DIM XB(NB%),YB(NB%)
200  FOR I%=1 TO NB%
210  PRINT " type in XB(";I%;")  and  YB(";I%;")  ";
220  INPUT XB(I%),YB(I%)
230  NEXT I%
240  GOSUB 60000 'colour monitor
250  XMOVE=HORIZ/2 : YMOVE=VERT/2 : GOSUB 9600 'setorigin
259  'draw outline of two polygons.
260  XPT=XA(NA%) : YPT=YA(NA%) : GOSUB 9500 'moveto
270  FOR I%=1 TO NA%
280  XPT=XA(I%)  : YPT=YA(I%)   : GOSUB 9400 'lineto
290  NEXT I%
300  XPT=XB(NB%) : YPT=YB(NB%) : GOSUB 9500 'moveto
310  FOR I%=1 TO NB%
320  XPT=XB(I%)  : YPT=YB(I%)   : GOSUB 9400 'lineto
330  NEXT I%
339  'calculate polygon of intersection  given by vertices
        (XC(i),YC(i))    i=1...NC% ( NC%<=NA%+NB% ).
340  DIM XC(NA%+NB%),YC(NA%+NB%)
350  GOSUB 5000 'overlap
360  IF NC%<3 THEN GOTO 390
369  'fill the interection polygon in colour COLFAC%
        and colour the edges FOREGROUND%.
370  COLFAC%=1 : FOREGROUND%=2
380  GOSUB 4000 'polygon filler
390  GOSUB 60100 'monochrome display
400  END

5000 'overlap of polygon A and polygon B
5001 '**in ** NA%,XA(NA%),YA(NA%),NB%,XB(NB%),YB(NB%)
5002 '**out** NC%,XC(NC%),YC(NC%)
```

```
5008 'the NA% vertices of polygon A in arrays XA and YA
      and the NB% vertices of polygon B in XB and YB.
5009 'polygons stored in anticlockwise orientation.
5010 DIM XF(2,NA%+NB%),YF(2,NA%+NB%)
5019 'P1% ( and P2%=3-P1% ) alternate between values 1 and 2.
5020 P1%=1 : NF%=NA%
5029 'place vertices (V%) of polygon A in XF(1,...) and YF(1,...).
5030 FOR V%=1 TO NA%
5040 XF(1,V%)=XA(V%) : YF(1,V%)=YA(V%)
5050 NEXT V%
5059 'use each edge-line (E%) of polygon B to slice off part of
      the polygon remaining in XF(P1%,..) and YF(P1%,...).
5060 X1=XB(NB%) : Y1=YB(NB%)
5070 FOR E%=1 TO NB%
5080 X2=XB(E%) : Y2=YB(E%)
5089 'the E%'th edge-line is CA.y+CB.x+CC=0.
5090 CA=X2-X1 : CB=Y1-Y2 : CC=-X1*CB-Y1*CA
5100 P2%=3-P1% : XI1=XF(P1%,NF%) : YI1=YF(P1%,NF%)
5110 VAL1=CA*YI1+CB*XI1+CC : A1=ABS(VAL1) : NC%=0
5120 IF A1<.000001 THEN S1%=0 ELSE S1%=SGN(VAL1)
5128 'go thru the NF% vertices in arrays XF(P1%,...) and YF(P1%,...).
      If they are positive relative to the edge-line (VALs>0) then
      add them to the XF(P2%,...) and YF(P2%,...) arrays.
5129 'if they are negative then ignore them. Add any intersection
      to XF(P2%,..) and YF(P2%,...). At any one time there will
      be NC% elements in each of these arrays.
5130 FOR V%=1 TO NF%
5140 XI2=XF(P1%,V%) : YI2=YF(P1%,V%)
5150 VAL2=CA*YI2+CB*XI2+CC : A2=ABS(VAL2)
5160 IF A2<.000001 THEN S2%=0 ELSE S2%=SGN(VAL2)
5170 IF S1%>=0 THEN NC%=NC%+1 : XF(P2%,NC%)=XI1 : YF(P2%,NC%)=YI1 :
                 IF S1%=0 THEN GOTO 5210
5180 IF S1%=S2% OR S2%=0 THEN GOTO 5210
5189 'calculate point of intersection and add to arrays XF(P2%,...)
      and YF(P2%,...). Increment NC%.
5190 MU=A1 : UM=A2 : DENOM=A1+A2 : NC%=NC%+1
5200 XF(P2%,NC%)=(UM*XI1+MU*XI2)/DENOM :
      YF(P2%,NC%)=(UM*YI1+MU*YI2)/DENOM
5210 VAL1=VAL2 : S1%=S2% : A1=A2 : XI1=XI2 : YI1=YI2
5220 NEXT V%
5229 'if NC%<3 then polygons do not overlap.
5230 IF NC%<3 THEN RETURN
5239 'interchange P1% and P2% and repeat process.
5240 NF%=NC% : P1%=P2% : X1=X2 : Y1=Y2
5250 NEXT E%
5259 'copy intersection polygon C into arrays XC and YC.
5260 FOR V%=1 TO NC%
5270 XC(V%)=XF(P1%,V%) : YC(V%)=YF(P1%,V%)
5280 NEXT V%
5290 RETURN
```

Having dealt with the functional representation of a line, what about the parametric form? It was noted that this form is one where the x and y coordinates of a general point on the curve are given in terms of parameter(s) (which could be the x or y values themselves), together with a range for the parameter. A parametric form of a line has already been considered, it is simply the base and directional representation:

$$b + \mu d \equiv (x_1, y_1) + \mu(x_2, y_2)$$

$$\equiv (x_1 + \mu_x x_2, y_1 + \mu_x y_2) \text{ where } -\infty < \mu < \infty$$

μ is the parameter, and $x_1 + \mu_x x_2$ and $y_1 + \mu_x y_2$ are the respective x and y values, which depend only on variable μ.

Functional representations and parametric forms can be produced for most well-behaved curves. For example, a sine curve is given by $f(x, y) \equiv y - \sin(x)$ in functional representation, and by $(x, \sin(x))$ with $-\infty < x < \infty$ in its parametric form. The general conic section (ellipse, parabola and hyperbola) is represented by the general function

$$f(x, y) \equiv a{\times}x^2 + b{\times}y^2 + h{\times}x{\times}y + f{\times}x + g{\times}y + c$$

Coefficients a, b, c, f, g, h uniquely identify a curve. A circle centred at the origin of radius r has $a = b = 1, f = g = h = 0$ and $c = -r^2$, whence $f(x, y) \equiv x^2 + y^2 - r^2$. All the points (x, y) on the circle are such that $f(x, y) = 0$, the inside of the circle has $f(x, y) < 0$, and the outside of the circle $f(x, y) > 0$. The parametric form of this circle is $(r\cos\alpha, r\sin\alpha)$ where $0 \leqslant \alpha \leqslant 2\pi$. (The parametric forms of a circle, ellipse and spiral were met in chapter 2.)

It is very useful to experiment with these (and other) concepts in two-dimensional geometry. There will be many occasions when it is necessary to include these ideas in programs, as well as the ever-present need when generating coordinate data for diagrams.

Example 3.4
Draw figure 3.6. A circular ball (radius r) disappears down an elliptical hole (major axis a, minor axis b). Parts of both the ellipse and circle are obscured.

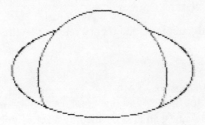

Figure 3.6

Let the ellipse be centred on the origin with the major axis horizontal, and the centre of the circle be a distance d vertically above the origin. The ellipse has functional representation

$$f_e(x, y) \equiv x^2/a^2 + y^2/b^2 - 1$$

and in parametric form $(a.\cos\alpha, b.\sin\alpha)$ with $0 \leqslant \alpha \leqslant 2\pi$.
For the circle

$$f_c(x, y) \equiv x^2 + (y - d)^2 - r^2$$

and in parametric form $(r_x\cos\lambda, d + r_x\sin\lambda)$ where $0 \leqslant \lambda \leqslant 2\pi$.
In order to generate the picture, the points (x, y) common to the circle and ellipse
(if any) must be calculated. As a useful demonstration, the representations are
mixed in the search for a solution, using the functional representation for the circle
and the parametric form of the ellipse. The problem is to find points $(x, y) \equiv$
$(a_x\cos\alpha, b_x\sin\alpha)$ on the ellipse, which also satisfy $f_c(x, y) = 0$. That is

$$a^2 \times\cos^2\alpha + (b_x\sin\alpha - d)^2 - r^2 = 0$$

or, expanding this expression

$$a^2 \times\cos^2\alpha + b^2 \times\sin^2\alpha - 2\times b\times d\times\sin\alpha + a^2 - r^2 = 0$$

and since $\cos^2\alpha = 1 - \sin^2\alpha$

$$(b^2 - a^2)\times\sin^2\alpha - 2\times b\times d\times\sin\alpha + d^2 - r^2 = 0$$

This is a simple quadratic equation in the unknown $\sin\alpha$, which is easily solved (the
quadratic equation $Ax^2 + Bx + C = 0$ has two roots $(-B \pm \sqrt{(B^2 - 4\times A\times C)})/(2\times A)$).
For each value of $\sin\alpha$ it is possible to find values for α with $0 \leqslant \alpha \leqslant 2\pi$ (if they
exist) and then calculate the points of intersection $(a_x\cos\alpha, b_x\sin\alpha)$.

There is no hard and fast rule regarding which representation to use in any given
situation — a *feel* for the method is required and that only comes with experience.

Exercise 3.4
Write a program that will draw figure 3.6.

The remainder of this chapter is the theory relevant to the solution of a large
exercise.

Exercise 3.5: Hatching Polygons
One of the most useful routines in any line-graphics package is that which *hatches*,
using equi-spaced parallel lines, an area defined by a set of polygons. Write such a
routine which hatches an area defined by n vertices $p_1, p_2, \ldots, p_n$. The x and y
coordinates of these vertices are stored in arrays PX(1..n) and PY(1..n). It is
assumed that the n vertices are on the edges of m different polygons. Array
TOP(1..m) will partition the n vertices into m groups; that is, the first polygon is
defined by vertices 1 to TOP(1), the second by TOP(1) + 1 to TOP(2) etc. It is
assumed that the last vertex in a partition is joined back to the first. To help you
write the program the following theory is presented.

Without loss of generality it may be assumed that there is only one polygon and
just one set of parallel hatching lines. For multiple polygons the only changes to

the following theory will be in the definition of subscripts (TOP must be considered), and for combinations of sets of hatching lines the following theory is repeated for each set in turn.

Suppose that the direction of the parallel lines is given by vector $d \equiv (DX, DY)$, that is parallel to the line joining the origin to d. The distance between the hatching lines is defined to be DIST. This still leaves an infinite number of possible sets of parallel lines! To uniquely define one set it is still necessary to specify a *base point*, $b \equiv (BX, BY)$, on any one of the lines from the set.

Note that a line with direction d which passes through b has the general vector form in the base/directional vector notation

$$b + \mu d \quad \text{where} \quad -\infty < \mu < \infty$$

Another and more common way of defining a straight line is by the coordinate equation

$$a_{\times} y = b_{\times} x + c$$

It may also be given in a functional notation

$$f(x, y) \equiv a_{\times} y - b_{\times} x - c$$

whence a general point $x \equiv (x, y)$ on the line is given by the equation $f(x) = 0$.

Since a hatching line has direction vector d, then $a = DX$ and $b = DY$, and so a line is given by

$$DX_{\times} y = DY_{\times} x + c$$

Each hatching line is defined by a unique 'c-value'. The line that passes through b has the 'c-value' CMID given by

$$CMID = DX_{\times} BY - DY_{\times} BX$$

It is possible to calculate all the 'c-values' for lines with direction d (not necessarily in the set of hatching lines) that pass through each of the n vertices stored in arrays PX and PY, and then find the extreme values CMAX and CMIN thus:

$$CMAX = \max_{1 \leqslant I \leqslant n} \left\{ DX_{\times} PY(I) - DY_{\times} PX(I) \right\}$$

and

$$CMIN = \min_{1 \leqslant I \leqslant n} \left\{ DX_{\times} PY(I) - DY_{\times} PX(I) \right\}$$

This means that the polygon lies totally between the two lines

$$DX_{\times} y = DY_{\times} x + CMIN \quad \text{and} \quad DX_{\times} y = DY_{\times} x + CMAX$$

In order to hatch the given polygon with lines parallel to d, then naturally only lines with 'c-values' between these extremes need be considered from the set. It should be noted that even though vector b is used to 'anchor' the set of parallel lines with inter-line distance DIST, there is no need for the line that passes through b to intersect the polygons.

For ease of calculation it is sensible to resort to the vector notation for lines. Note that the hatching lines are all in the form

$$q + \mu d \quad \text{where} \quad -\infty < \mu < \infty$$

Here q represents a base point on a general hatching line. So it is necessary to find a vector q for each of the hatching lines that cuts the polygon. The q values are defined to be the points of intersection of this set of hatching lines with the line through b with direction d' (which is perpendicular to d, that is, to the hatching lines). Note that d' may be represented by the vector $(-DY, DX)$.

Hence the base points q are all of the form

$$q \equiv b + \lambda d' \quad \text{for some } \lambda$$

This formulation naturally represents every point on the new line perpendicular to the hatching lines, but only its points of intersection with the hatching lines are required. Note that any non-zero scalar multiple of d' may also represent the direction of the new line, and choose $s \equiv (DIST/ |d'|) \times d'$. Here $|d'|$ represents the length of vector d', which means that vector s has length (or modulus) DIST. Now note that q can be considered:

$$q \equiv b + Ns \equiv b + N \times (DIST/|d'|) \times d' \quad \text{for some } N$$

If N is an integer, this vector combination gives all, but only, the points of intersection of the new line with a set of parallel lines of direction d in which neighbouring lines are a distance DIST apart. Since b is one of these intersections ($N = 0$), then this formulation contains the base vectors for the required set of hatching lines. However, lines still have to be restricted to those with 'c-values' that lie between CMIN and CMAX. This is achieved by insisting that the 'N-values' of the base points of the hatching lines lie between NMIN and NMAX, where

$$NMIN = \lceil (CMIN - CMID)/(DIST \times |d'|) \rceil$$

and

$$NMAX = \lfloor (CMAX - CMID)/(DIST \times |d'|) \rfloor$$

Here $\lceil r \rceil$ gives the smallest integer not less than r, and $\lfloor r \rfloor$ gives the largest integer not greater than r. Note that 0, the 'N-value' corresponding to b need not lie in this range.

Given any integer N, the corresponding vector q which then identifies one hatching line can be calculated. Intersect this line with the edges of the polygons defined by vectors $p_1, \ldots, p_n$. Suppose that there is an intersection between points p_i and p_{i+1}, then note that the intersection on this edge may be given in the form

$$p_i + \alpha(p_{i+1} - p_i) \quad \text{where} \quad 0 \leqslant \alpha \leqslant 1$$

as well as by $q + \mu d$ on the hatching line. If the α value does not lie between 0 and

1 then the hatching line does not cut the polygon at this edge. The μ value must be noted for each valid intersection.

Let i vary through all the edges of the polygon (when $i = n$ then p_{n+1} is identified with p_1) and calculate all the μ values of proper intersections and place them in increasing numerical order. Take care with rounding errors and coincident points! Repeat for each polygon. There will be an even number of these μ values. Find the points on the hatching line that correspond to the μ values and join the first to the second, the third to the fourth etc., and this gives the correct hatching on one line. Varying N between NMIN and NMAX gives the complete hatching for the polygons.

If the polygon is composed of a large number of vertices (n is large) there is no need to waste time calculating all the intersections, only to find that most of the α values do not lie between 0 and 1 and so are irrelevant. A trick to save time is to put the hatching line in functional form:

$$f(x) \equiv f(x, y) \equiv a_x y - b_x x - c$$

Now if consecutive vectors p_i and p_{i+1} are such that $f(p_i)$ and $f(p_{i+1})$ have the same sign, that is, both are positive or both are negative, then there cannot be a useful point of intersection between them.

Complete Programs

Experiment with different modes, palettes and colours. MERGE 'lib0' and 'lib1' into the programs.

  I. Listing 3.1 ('square outside squares'). Data required: HORIZ, try 4.
     Run in both modes 1 and 2.
 II. Listing 3.2 ('intersection of two lines'). Data required: four coordinate pairs.
     Try $(-1, 1), (3, 3); (2, 1), (0, 3)$.

Note. If you are not using release 2.0 of BASICA, from this point listing 3.3 ('clip' and a new version of 'lineto') will replace listing 2.5 in 'lib1'. 'angle' (listing 3.4) and 'polygon filler' (listing 3.5) are also added to the library.

III. The same as I above, but with the new 'lib1'. Change HORIZ to 1.
 IV. Listing 3.6 ('overlap' and main program). Data required: HORIZ, and the number of vertices of two convex polygons and their coordinates (taken in an anticlockwise orientation). Try HORIZ = 30, with 3, $(8, 8), (-8, 8), (0, 0)$ and 4, $(4, 4), (-4, 4), (-4, -4), (4, -4)$.

4 Matrix Representation of Transformations on Two-dimensional Space

Chapter 2 saw the need to translate pictures of objects about the screen. Rather than perpetually changing the screen coordinate system, it is conceptually much easier to define an object in the simplest terms possible (as vertices in the form of pixel or coordinate values, together with line and area information related to the vertices), and then transform the object to various parts of the screen, keeping the screen coordinate system fixed. Only linear transformations (see below) are considered in this book. It will often be necessary to transform a large number of vertices, and to do this efficiently the linear transformations are represented as *matrices*. Before looking at linear transformations and their matrix representations, it is first necessary to explain what is meant by a matrix, and also by a *column vector*. In fact only square matrices are required: so the explanation is restricted to 3 × 3 matrices (said 3 by 3) for the study of two-dimensional space, and later 4 × 4 matrices for considering three-dimensional space. Such a 3 × 3 matrix (A say) is simply a group of real numbers placed in a block of 3 rows by 3 columns: a column vector (D say) is a group of numbers placed in a column of 3 rows:

$$\begin{pmatrix} A_{11} & A_{12} & A_{13} \\ A_{21} & A_{22} & A_{23} \\ A_{31} & A_{32} & A_{33} \end{pmatrix} \quad \text{and} \quad \begin{pmatrix} D_1 \\ D_2 \\ D_3 \end{pmatrix}$$

A general entry in the matrix is usually written A_{ij}; the first subscript denotes the ith row, and the second subscript the jth column (for example, A_{23} represents the value in the second row, third column). The entry in the column vector, D_i, denotes the value in the ith row. All these named entries will be explicitly replaced by numerical values and it is important to realise that the *information* stored in a matrix or column vector is not just the individual values but it is also the position of these values within the matrix or vector. Naturally BASIC programs are written along a line (no subscripts or superscripts) and hence matrices and vectors are implemented as arrays and the subscript values appear inside round brackets, following the array identifier.

Matrices can be added. Matrix C = A + B, the sum of two matrices A and B, is defined by the general entry C_{ij} thus:

$$C_{ij} = A_{ij} + B_{ij} \quad 1 \leqslant i, j \leqslant 3$$

Matrix A can be multiplied by a scalar k to form a matrix B:

$$B_{ij} = k \times A_{ij} \quad 1 \leqslant i, j \leqslant 3$$

Matrix A can be multiplied by a column vector D to produce another column vector E thus:

$$E_i = A_{i1} \times D_1 + A_{i2} \times D_2 + A_{i3} \times D_3 = \sum_{k=1}^{3} A_{ik} \times D_k \quad \text{where } 1 \leqslant i \leqslant 3$$

The ith row element of the new column vector is the sum of the products of the corresponding elements of the ith row of the matrix with those in the column vector.

Furthermore, the product (matrix) $C = A \times B$ of two matrices A and B may be calculated:

$$C_{ij} = A_{i1} \times B_{1j} + A_{i2} \times B_{2j} + A_{i3} \times B_{3j} = \sum_{k=1}^{3} A_{ik} \times B_{kj} \quad \text{where } 1 \leqslant i, j \leqslant 3$$

The $(i, j)^{\text{th}}$ element of the product matrix is the sum of each element in the ith row of the first matrix multiplied by the corresponding element in the jth column of the second. It must be noted that the product of matrices is not necessarily *commutative* (that is, $A \times B$ need not be the same as $B \times A$). For example

$$\begin{pmatrix} 0 & 1 & 0 \\ 0 & 0 & 1 \\ 1 & 0 & 0 \end{pmatrix} \times \begin{pmatrix} 0 & 0 & 1 \\ 0 & 1 & 0 \\ 1 & 0 & 0 \end{pmatrix} = \begin{pmatrix} 0 & 1 & 0 \\ 1 & 0 & 0 \\ 0 & 0 & 1 \end{pmatrix}$$

$$\text{but} \quad \begin{pmatrix} 0 & 0 & 1 \\ 0 & 1 & 0 \\ 1 & 0 & 0 \end{pmatrix} \times \begin{pmatrix} 0 & 1 & 0 \\ 0 & 0 & 1 \\ 1 & 0 & 0 \end{pmatrix} = \begin{pmatrix} 1 & 0 & 0 \\ 0 & 0 & 1 \\ 0 & 1 & 0 \end{pmatrix}$$

Experiment with these ideas until you have enough confidence to use them in the theory that follows. For those who want more details about the theory of matrices, books by Finkbeiner (1978) and by Stroud (1982) are recommended.

There is a special matrix called the *identity matrix* I (sometimes called the unit matrix):

$$I = \begin{pmatrix} 1 & 0 & 0 \\ 0 & 1 & 0 \\ 0 & 0 & 1 \end{pmatrix}$$

Every square matrix A has a *determinant*: det(A).

$$\det(A) = A_{11} \times (A_{22} \times A_{33} - A_{23} \times A_{32}) + A_{12} \times (A_{23} \times A_{31} - A_{21} \times A_{33})$$
$$+ A_{13} \times (A_{21} \times A_{32} - A_{22} \times A_{31})$$

Any matrix whose determinant is non-zero is called *non-singular*, and those with zero determinant *singular*. All non-singular matrices A have an *inverse*, A^{-1}, which has the property that $A \times A^{-1} = I$ and $A^{-1} \times A = I$. For methods of calculating an inverse of a matrix see Finkbeiner (1978): a listing is given in chapter 7 (listing 7.4) which uses the Adjoint method.

Now consider the transformation of points in space. Suppose a point (x, y) – 'before' – is transformed to (x', y') – 'after'. The transformation is totally described if equations are given that relate points 'before' and 'after' the transformation. A linear transformation is one that defines the 'after' point in terms of linear combinations of the coordinates of the 'before' point (that is, the equations contain only multiples of x, y and additional real values): it includes neither non-unit powers or multiples of x and y, nor other variables. Such equations may be written

$$x' = A_{11} \times x + A_{12} \times y + A_{13}$$
$$y' = A_{21} \times x + A_{22} \times y + A_{23}$$

The A values are called the *coefficients* of the equation. The result of the transformation is a combination of multiples of x values, y values and unity. Another equation may be added:

$$1 = A_{31} \times x + A_{32} \times y + A_{33}$$

For this to be true for all values of x and y, it follows that $A_{31} = A_{32} = 0$ and $A_{33} = 1$. This may seem a rather contrived exercise, but it will prove very useful. For if each point vector (x, y) (also called a *row vector* for obvious reasons) is set in the form of a three-dimensional column vector

$$\begin{pmatrix} x \\ y \\ 1 \end{pmatrix}$$

then the above three equations can be written in the form of a matrix multiplying a column vector:

$$\begin{pmatrix} x' \\ y' \\ 1 \end{pmatrix} = \begin{pmatrix} A_{11} & A_{12} & A_{13} \\ A_{21} & A_{22} & A_{23} \\ A_{31} & A_{32} & A_{33} \end{pmatrix} \times \begin{pmatrix} x \\ y \\ 1 \end{pmatrix}$$

So if the transformation is stored as a matrix, then every point can be transformed by considering it a column vector and premultiplying it by the matrix.

Many writers of books on computer graphics do not like the use of column vectors. They prefer to extend the row vector, such as (x, y), to $(x, y, 1)$, and postmultiply the row vector by the matrix so that the above equations in matrix form become

$$(x', y', 1) = (x, y, 1) \times \begin{pmatrix} A_{11} & A_{21} & A_{31} \\ A_{12} & A_{22} & A_{32} \\ A_{13} & A_{23} & A_{33} \end{pmatrix}$$

Note that this matrix is the *transpose* of the matrix of coefficients in the equations.

This causes a great deal of confusion among those who are not confident in the use of matrices. It is for this reason that this book keeps to the column vector notation. As you get more practice in the use of matrices, it is a good idea to rewrite some (or all) of the following transformation routines in the other notation. It is not really important which method you finally use *as long as you are consistent*. (Note that the transpose B of a matrix A is given by $B_{ij} = A_{ji}$, where $1 \leqslant i, j \leqslant 3$.)

Combination of Transformations

A very useful property of this matrix representation of transformations is that the combination of two transformations (say transformation (= matrix) A followed by transformation B) is represented by their product $C = B \times A$: *note* the order of multiplication — the matrix representing the first transformation is *premultiplied* by the second. This is because the final matrix will be used to premultiply a column vector representing a point, and so the first transformation matrix must appear on the right of the product and the last on the left. (If the row vector method was used then the product would appear in the *natural order* from left to right — this is the price paid for identifying the transformation matrix with the coefficients of the equation.)

So a routine 'mult2' (listing 4.1) is introduced which forms the product of two matrices. The BASIC computer language does not allow the transmission of parameters, in particular arrays, into routines, so an efficient means of coping with this limitation must be found. It is assumed that all matrix multiplication within a program reduces to a matrix A multiplied by a matrix R giving the product matrix B. After the product is complete B is copied back into R. The reason for the choice of identifiers and the final copy will become evident later. A routine ('idR2') which sets R to the identity matrix is also needed. When the product of a sequence of matrices is required, first R is set to the identity matrix (I) and then, for each of the matrices from right to left, each matrix is named A and the routine 'mult2' is called in turn. At the end of the process R contains the matrix product of the sequence.

Listing 4.1

```
9100  'mult2
9101  '**in ** A(3,3),R(3,3)
9102  '**out** R(3,3)
9110  FOR I%=1 TO 3
9120  FOR J%=1 TO 3
9130  AR=0
9140  FOR K%=1 TO 3
9150  AR=AR+A(I%,K%)*R(K%,J%)
9160  NEXT K%
9170  B(I%,J%)=AR
9180  NEXT J%
9190  NEXT I%
9200  FOR I%=1 TO 3
9210  FOR J%=1 TO 3
```

```
9220  R(I%,J%)=B(I%,J%)
9230  NEXT J%
9240  NEXT I%
9250  RETURN

9300  'idR2
9302  '**out** R(3,3)
9310  FOR I%=1 TO 3
9320  FOR J%=1 TO 3
9330  R(I%,J%)=0
9340  NEXT J%
9350  R(I%,I%)=1
9360  NEXT I%
9370  RETURN
```

All natural transformations may be reduced to a combination of three basic forms of linear transformation: translation, scaling and rotation about the co-ordinate origin. It should also be noted that all valid applications of these transformations return non-singular matrices. The routines that follow generate a matrix called A for each of the three types of transformation, so that each transformation routine can be used in conjunction with 'mult2' to produce combinations of transformations.

Translation
A 'before' point (x, y) is moved by a vector (TX, TY) to (x', y') say. This produces the equations

$$x' = 1_{\times}x + 0_{\times}y + TX$$

$$y' = 0_{\times}x + 1_{\times}y + TY$$

so the matrix describing this transformation is

$$\begin{pmatrix} 1 & 0 & TX \\ 0 & 1 & TY \\ 0 & 0 & 1 \end{pmatrix}$$

And a routine, 'tran2', for generating such a matrix A, given the values TX and TY, is given in listing 4.2.

Listing 4.2

```
9000  'tran2
9001  '**in ** TX,TY
9002  '**out** A(3,3)
9010  FOR I%=1 TO 3
9020  FOR J%=1 TO 3
9030  A(I%,J%)=0
9040  NEXT J%
9050  A(I%,I%)=1
9060  NEXT I%
9070  A(1,3)=TX : A(2,3)=TY
9080  RETURN
```

Scaling

The x-coordinate of a point in space is scaled by a factor SX, and the y coordinate by SY, thus:

$$x' = SX_x x + 0_x y + 0$$

$$y' = 0_x x + SY_x y + 0$$

giving the matrix

$$\begin{pmatrix} SX & 0 & 0 \\ 0 & SY & 0 \\ 0 & 0 & 1 \end{pmatrix}$$

Usually SX and SY are both positive, but if one or both are negative this creates a reflection as well as a scaling. In particular, if $SX = -1$ and $SY = 1$, then the point is reflected about the y-axis. A program segment, 'scale2', to produce such a scaling matrix A, given SX and SY, is given in listing 4.3.

Listing 4.3

```
8900 'scale2
8901 '**in ** SX,SY
8902 '**out** A(3,3)
8910 FOR I%=1 TO 3
8920 FOR J%=1 TO 3
8930 A(I%,J%)=0
8940 NEXT J%
8950 NEXT I%
8960 A(1,1)=SX : A(2,2)=SY : A(3,3)=1
8970 RETURN
```

Rotation about the origin

The rotation of a point about the origin by an angle θ in an anticlockwise direction (the normal mathematical orientation) is given by the equations

$$x' = \cos\theta_x x - \sin\theta_x y + 0$$

$$y' = \sin\theta_x x + \cos\theta_x y + 0$$

and the matrix is

$$\begin{pmatrix} \cos\theta & -\sin\theta & 0 \\ \sin\theta & \cos\theta & 0 \\ 0 & 0 & 1 \end{pmatrix}$$

The routine, 'rot2', to produce a rotation matrix, A, for an angle θ (THETA) is given in listing 4.4

Listing 4.4

```
8600 ´rot2
8601 ´**in ** THETA
8602 ´**out** A(3,3)
8610 FOR I%=1 TO 3
8620 FOR J%=1 TO 3
8630 A(I%,J%)=0
8640 NEXT J%
8650 NEXT I%
8660 A(3,3)=1
8670 CT=COS(THETA) : ST=SIN(THETA)
8680 A(1,1)= CT : A(2,2)=CT
8690 A(1,2)=-ST : A(2,1)=ST
8700 RETURN
```

Inverse Transformations

For every transformation there is an inverse transformation which will restore the points in space to their original positions. If a transformation is represented by a matrix A, then the inverse transformation is represented by the inverse matrix A^{-1}. There is no need to calculate this inverse using listing 7.4, it can be found directly by using listings 4.2, 4.3 and 4.4, with parameters derived from the parameters of the original transformation:

(1) a translation by (TX, TY) is inverted by a translation by (−TX, −TY).
(2) a scaling by SX and SY is inverted by a scaling by 1/SX and 1/SY (naturally both SX and SY are non-zero, for otherwise the two-dimensional space would contract into a line or a point).
(3) a rotation by an angle θ is inverted by a rotation by an angle $-\theta$.
(4) if the transformation matrix is a product of a number of translation, scaling and rotation matrices A × B × C × . . . × L × M × N (say), then the inverse transformation matrix is

$$N^{-1} \times M^{-1} \times L^{-1} \times . . . \times C^{-1} \times B^{-1} \times A^{-1}$$

Note the order of multiplication!

The Placing of an Object

Objects are usually drawn at various points on the screen, and at arbitrary orientations. It would be very inefficient to calculate by hand the coordinates of vertices for each position of the object and input them to the program. Instead, an arbitrary but fixed coordinate system for two-dimensional space, which is called the ABSOLUTE system, will be defined. Next the coordinates of the vertices of the object are defined in some simple way, usually about the origin. This is called the SETUP position. Lines and areas within the object are defined in terms of the vertices. Matrices can be used to move the vertices of the object from the SETUP to the ACTUAL position in the ABSOLUTE system. The lines and areas maintain their relationship with the now transformed vertices. The matrix that relates the SETUP to ACTUAL position will be called P throughout this book (it sometimes has a letter subscript to identify it uniquely from other such matrices). Because of the restriction of not passing arrays as parameters into subprograms, P will not normally be explicitly generated, instead it will be implicitly used to update the array R.

Looking at the Object

Thus objects in a scene can be moved relative to the ABSOLUTE coordinate axes. When observing such a scene, the eye is assumed to be looking directly at point (DX, DY) of the ABSOLUTE system and the head to be tilted through an angle α (ALPHA). It would be convenient to assume that the eye is looking at the origin and there is no tilt of the head (called the OBSERVED position). Therefore another matrix is generated, which will transform space so that the eye is moved from its ACTUAL position to this OBSERVED position. The ACTUAL to OBSERVED matrix is named Q throughout this book, and is achieved by first translating all points in space by a vector $(-DX, -DY)$, matrix A, and then rotating them by an angle $-\alpha$, matrix B (note the minus signs!). Thus $Q = B \times A$, which is generated in routine 'look2', listing 4.5. Normally Q is not explicitly calculated since it is usually used to update R; however if it is necessary to use the values of the matrix repeatedly then obviously it is sensible to store Q.

Listing 4.5

```
8200  'look2/general
8202  '**out** R(3,3)
8210  INPUT"(DX,DY) ",DX,DY
8220  INPUT"ALPHA ",ALPHA
8229  'look at (DX,DY).
8230  LET TX=-DX : LET TY=-DY : GOSUB 9000 'tran2
8240  GOSUB 9100 'mult2
8249  'tilt head through ALPHA radians.
8250  THETA=-ALPHA : GOSUB 8600 'rot2
8260  GOSUB 9100 'mult2
8270  RETURN
```

Drawing an Object

The combination of the SETUP to ACTUAL matrix P with the ACTUAL to OBSERVED matrix Q creates the SETUP to OBSERVED matrix $R = Q \times P$ (R will always be used to denote this matrix: and remember R is always the result of the 'mult2' routine). Transforming all the SETUP vertices by R, with the corresponding movement of line and area information, means that the coordinates of the object are given relative to the observer who is looking at the origin of the ABSOLUTE coordinate system with head upright, and who is in fact really looking at a graphics screen. So the ABSOLUTE coordinate system is identified with the system of the screen to find the positions of the vertices on the screen, and then the vertices, lines and areas that compose the object are drawn. In practice this is achieved by a *construction routine* which uses matrix R. It will set up the vertex, line and area information, transform the vertices using R, and perhaps finally draw the object. See example 4.1 below. Later it will be seen that there are certain situations where it is more efficient to store the vertex, line and area information. For example, the vertex coordinates can be stored in arrays X and Y, line information in a two-dimensional array LIN% or area information in a two-dimensional array FACET%. Vertices may be stored in their SETUP, ACTUAL or OBSERVED position — it really depends on the context of the program. This SETUP to ACTUAL to OBSERVED method enables a dynamic series of scenes to be drawn. Objects can move relative to the ABSOLUTE axes, and to themselves, while simultaneously the observer can move independently around the scene. To start with, however, the simplest case of a fixed scene is considered.

Complicated Pictures — the 'Building Block' Method

Pictures containing a number of similar objects can be drawn with a minimum of extra effort. There is no need to produce a new routine for each occurrence of the object, each time simply calculate a new SETUP to OBSERVED matrix and enter this into the same routine. Naturally one routine is required for each new type of object in the picture. The final picture is achieved by the execution of a main program, named 'scene2'. This main program simply calls the 'start' routine, centres the coordinate system on the screen, and then declares necessary arrays and, if required, calls 'look2' to generate Q (if more than one object is to be drawn then Q is stored). Then 'scene2' calculates a matrix P and calls the required construction routine using R = Q × P for each individual object (or *block*). All the blocks finally build into the finished picture. To distinguish between different occurrences of these matrices in what follows, a subscript is sometimes added to the names P and R.

   This modular approach to solve the problem of defining and drawing a picture may not be the most efficient, but it does greatly clarify the situation for beginners, enabling them to ask the right questions about constructing a required scene. Also when dealing with multiple views (such as in animation), this approach will minimise problems in scenes where not only are the objects moving relative to one another, but also the observer himself is moving. Naturally if the head is upright then matrix Q can be replaced by a call to 'setorigin' which changes the screen coordinate system. Or if the eye is looking at the origin, head upright, then Q is the identity matrix I, hence it plays no part in transforming the picture and the 'look2' routine may be ignored. No such assumptions are made here, and only the most general situation is considered. It is a useful exercise running throughout this book for the reader to *cannibalise* the program listings in order to make them efficient for specific cases. This book aims to explain these concepts in the most general and straightforward terms, even if it is at the expense of efficiency and speed. The readers can return to these programs when they are ready and fully understand the ideas of transforming space. Later some hints are given on how to make these changes, but at the moment they would only confuse the issue.

However, the most important reason for this modular approach will be seen when it comes to drawing pictures of three-dimensional objects. These three-dimensional constructions will be described as an extension of the ideas above, and full understanding of two-dimensional transformations is essential before going on to higher dimensions.

Example 4.1

Consider a simple *flag* SETUP consisting of three coloured areas and two lines, defined by vertices (labelled 1 to 12) taken from the set $(5, 5), (-5, 5), (-5, -5)$, $(5, -5), (4, 5), (-4, 5), (-5, 4), (-5, -4), (-4, -5), (4, -5), (5, -4)$ and $(5, 4)$. The three areas (or *facets*) are given by vertices $1, 2, 3, 4$ (facet 1), $1, 5, 8, 3, 9, 12$ (facet 2) and $2, 7, 10, 4, 11, 6$ (facet 3). The two lines are given by vertices $1, 3$ (line 1) and $2, 4$ (line 2). This information is stored in a DATA statement and recalled when required. See figure 4.1 — a flag drawn on a screen with HORIZ = 24, where the SETUP to ACTUAL matrix is the identity and the ACTUAL to OBSERVED matrix is such that the observer is looking at the origin with head upright. Listing 4.6 gives the necessary 'scene2' main program which moves the object into position and takes a general view, and listing 4.7 is the required construction routine 'flag'. Note that 'flag', which uses matrix R to transform the vertices (and hence the object) into their OBSERVED positions, does not store the vertex values for this position in a permanent data-base. Instead the values are kept in arrays X

Figure 4.1

and Y for the duration of the routine and if the routine is re-entered to draw another
flag then these array locations are used again. Note the base area of the flag is in
colour 2, the two diagonal stripes are in colour 1, and the diagonal lines in colour 0.
The obvious PAPER% colour is therefore logical 3.

Listing 4.6

```
100 ´main program : scene2/look2 ; flag (not stored) ; single view
110 GOSUB 9700 ´start
120 DIM X(12),Y(12)
130 DIM A(3,3),B(3,3),R(3,3)
139 ´place the observer.
140 GOSUB 9300 ´idR2
150 GOSUB 8200 ´look2
160 GOSUB 60000 ´colour monitor
170 XMOVE=HORIZ/2 : YMOVE=VERT/2
180 GOSUB 9600 ´setorigin
189 ´define and draw the object.
190 GOSUB 6500 ´flag
200 GOSUB 60100 ´monochrome display
210 END
```

Listing 4.7

```
6500 ´flag / data not stored
6501 ´**in ** R(3,3)
6502 ´**out** NC%,XC(NC%),YC(NC%),COLFAC%,FOREGROUND%
6510 RESTORE 6520 : DIM XC(6),YC(6)
6520 DATA  5,5,   -5,5,  -5,-5,   5,-5,   4,5,   -4,5,
          -5,4, -5,-4, -4,-5,   4,-5,   5,-4,   5,4
6529 ´read vertex data and place in position with matrix R.
6530 FOR I%=1 TO 12
6540 READ XX,YY
6550 X(I%)=R(1,1)*XX+R(1,2)*YY+R(1,3)
6560 Y(I%)=R(2,1)*XX+R(2,2)*YY+R(2,3)
6570 NEXT I%
6579 ´draw base of flag in colour 2.
6580 NC%=4 : COLFAC%=2 : FOREGROUND%=2
6590 XC(1)=X(1) : YC(1)=Y(1)
6600 XC(2)=X(2) : YC(2)=Y(2)
6610 XC(3)=X(3) : YC(3)=Y(3)
6620 XC(4)=X(4) : YC(4)=Y(4)
6630 GOSUB 4000 ´filler
6639 ´draw two stripes of flag in colour 1.
6640 NC%=6 : COLFAC%=1 : FOREGROUND%=1
6650 XC(1)=X(1) : YC(1)=Y(1)
6660 XC(2)=X(5) : YC(2)=Y(5)
6670 XC(3)=X(8) : YC(3)=Y(8)
6680 XC(4)=X(3) : YC(4)=Y(3)
6690 XC(5)=X(9) : YC(5)=Y(9)
6700 XC(6)=X(12) : YC(6)=Y(12)
6710 GOSUB 4000 ´filler
6720 NC%=6 : COLFAC%=1 : FOREGROUND%=1
6730 XC(1)=X(2) : YC(1)=Y(2)
6740 XC(2)=X(7) : YC(2)=Y(7)
6750 XC(3)=X(10) : YC(3)=Y(10)
6760 XC(4)=X(4) : YC(4)=Y(4)
6770 XC(5)=X(11) : YC(5)=Y(11)
6780 XC(6)=X(6) : YC(6)=Y(6)
6790 GOSUB 4000 ´filler
6799 ´draw two diagonal lines in colour 0.
6800 LINE (X(1),Y(1))-(X(3),Y(3)),0
6810 LINE (X(2),Y(2))-(X(4),Y(4)),0
6820 ERASE XC,YC
6830 RETURN
```

Example 4.2

Draw figure 4.2. It includes four flags labelled (a), (b), (c) and (d) on a screen HORIZ = 300. For simplicity, in this picture Q is assumed to be the identity

Figure 4.2

matrix, so the head is upright and the eye looks at the SETUP origin. Flag (a) is placed identically at its SETUP position, that is, $R_a = I$, whereas flag (b) is moved from its SETUP to ACTUAL position by the following transformations:

(1) Scale the figure with SX = 4 and SY = 2, producing matrix A.
(2) Rotate the figure through $\pi/6$ radians, matrix B.
(3) Translate figure by TX = 30 and TY = 15, matrix C.

$$A = \begin{pmatrix} 4 & 0 & 0 \\ 0 & 2 & 0 \\ 0 & 0 & 1 \end{pmatrix} \quad B = \begin{pmatrix} \sqrt{3}/2 & -1/2 & 0 \\ 1/2 & \sqrt{3}/2 & 0 \\ 0 & 0 & 1 \end{pmatrix} \quad C = \begin{pmatrix} 1 & 0 & 30 \\ 0 & 1 & 15 \\ 0 & 0 & 1 \end{pmatrix}$$

The complete transformation is given by $R_b = Q \times P_b = I \times P_b = P_b = C \times B \times A$ (note the order of matrix multiplication, and that the subscript distinguishes the placing of flag (b) from the others).

If instead the order $A \times B \times C$ (giving matrix P_d) was used, then

$$P_b = \begin{pmatrix} 2\sqrt{3} & -1 & 30 \\ 2 & \sqrt{3} & 15 \\ 0 & 0 & 1 \end{pmatrix} \quad P_d = \begin{pmatrix} 2\sqrt{3} & -2 & 60\sqrt{3} - 30 \\ 1 & \sqrt{3} & 15\sqrt{3} + 30 \\ 0 & 0 & 1 \end{pmatrix}$$

which are obviously two different transformations. Matrix $R_d = Q \times P_d = I \times P_d$ produces flag (d). Note how this flag is not symmetrical about two mutually perpendicular axes as are the other 3 flags; be very careful with the use of the scaling transformation — remember scaling is defined about the origin and this will cause distortions in the shape of an object that is moved away from the origin!

To further illustrate this example, the ACTUAL positions of the four corners of flag (b) on the screen are calculated. The coordinates of the corners are put in the form of a column vector and premultiplied by matrix $R_b = I \times P_b$. For example

$$\begin{pmatrix} 2\sqrt{3} & -1 & 30 \\ 2 & \sqrt{3} & 15 \\ 0 & 0 & 1 \end{pmatrix} \times \begin{pmatrix} 5 \\ 5 \\ 1 \end{pmatrix} = \begin{pmatrix} 10\sqrt{3} + 25 \\ 5\sqrt{3} + 25 \\ 1 \end{pmatrix} \text{ etc.}$$

When returned to normal vector form the four vertices, $(5, 5), (-5, 5), (-5, -5)$ and $(5, -5)$, have been transformed to $(10\sqrt{3} + 25, 5\sqrt{3} + 25), (-10\sqrt{3} + 25, 5\sqrt{3} + 5)$, $(-10\sqrt{3} + 35, -5\sqrt{3} + 5)$ and $(10\sqrt{3} + 35, -5\sqrt{3} + 25)$ respectively.

Flag (c) is flag (b) reflected in the line $3y = -4x - 9$. This line cuts the y-axis at $(0, -3)$ and makes an angle $\alpha = \cos^{-1}(-3/5) = \sin^{-1}(4/5) = \tan^{-1}(-3/4)$ with the positive x-axis. If space is moved by a vector $(0, 3)$, matrix D say, this line will go through the origin. Furthermore, rotating space by $-\alpha$, matrix E say, means the line is now identical with the x-axis. Matrix F can reflect the flag in the x-axis, E^{-1} puts the line back at an angle α with the x-axis, and finally D^{-1} returns the line to its original position. Matrix $G = D^{-1} \times E^{-1} \times F \times E \times D$ will therefore reflect all the ACTUAL vertices of flag (b) about the line $3y = -4x - 9$, and $R_c = I \times P_c = G \times P_b$ can therefore be used to draw flag (c). That is, matrix P_b is used to move the flag to position (b) and then matrix G to place it in position (c).

$$D = \begin{pmatrix} 1 & 0 & 0 \\ 0 & 1 & 3 \\ 0 & 0 & 1 \end{pmatrix} \quad E = \begin{pmatrix} -3/5 & 4/5 & 0 \\ -4/5 & -3/5 & 0 \\ 0 & 0 & 1 \end{pmatrix} \quad F = \begin{pmatrix} 1 & 0 & 0 \\ 0 & -1 & 0 \\ 0 & 0 & 1 \end{pmatrix}$$

and

$$R_c = \frac{1}{25} \begin{pmatrix} -48 - 14\sqrt{3} & 7 - 24\sqrt{3} & -642 \\ 14 - 48\sqrt{3} & 24 + 7\sqrt{3} & -669 \\ 0 & 0 & 25 \end{pmatrix}$$

Figure 4.2 is drawn using the new 'scene2' main program of listing 4.8: note that this 'scene2' does not call 'look2', since it is assumed that the eye is looking at the origin with the head erect. The 'flag' routine, as well as all the graphics package routines, stay unchanged.

Listing 4.8

```
100 'main program : scene2/ 4 flags (not stored) ; fixed view
110 GOSUB 9700 'start
120 DIM X(12),Y(12)
130 DIM A(3,3),B(3,3),R(3,3)
140 GOSUB 60000 'colour monitor
150 XMOVE=HORIZ/2 : YMOVE=VERT/2
160 GOSUB 9600 'setorigin
169 'flag a)
```

```
170 GOSUB 9300 'idR2
179 'define and draw the object.
180 GOSUB 6500 'flag
189 'flag b) .
190 SX=4 : SY=2 : GOSUB 8900 'scale2
200 GOSUB 9100 'mult2
210 THETA=3.141493/6 : GOSUB 8600 'rot2
220 GOSUB 9100 'mult2
230 TX=30 : TY=15 : GOSUB 9000 'tran2
240 GOSUB 9100 'mult2
250 GOSUB 6500 'flag
259 'flag c)
260 TX=0 : TY=3 : GOSUB 9000 'tran2
270 GOSUB 9100 'mult2
280 AX=-3 : AY=4 : GOSUB 8800 'angle
290 THETA=-THETA : GOSUB 8600 'rot2
300 GOSUB 9100 'mult2
310 SX=1 : SY=-1 : GOSUB 8900 'scale2
320 GOSUB 9100 'mult2
330 THETA=-THETA : GOSUB 8600 'rot2
340 GOSUB 9100 'mult2
350 TX=0 : TY=-3 : GOSUB 9000 'tran2
360 GOSUB 9100 'mult2
370 GOSUB 6500 'flag
379 'flag d)
380 GOSUB 9300 'idR2
390 TX=30 : TY=15 : GOSUB 9000 'tran2
400 GOSUB 9100 'mult2
410 THETA=3.141493/6 : GOSUB 8600 'rot2
420 GOSUB 9100 'mult2
430 SX=4 : SY=2 : GOSUB 8900 'scale2
440 GOSUB 9100 'mult2
450 GOSUB 6500 'flag
460 GOSUB 60100 'monochrome display
470 END
```

Exercise 4.1

In order to convince yourself that this program may be used to deal with the general situation, you should run this program using non-zero values of DX, DY or α so that the ACTUAL to OBSERVED matrix Q is not the identity matrix. Your 'scene2' routine should call 'look2' to calculate Q, which must be stored. Then for each object in the scene, in turn, calculate the SETUP to ACTUAL matrix P (which 'mult2' places in R), premultiply it by Q (which has to be copied into matrix A for use with 'mult2') and finally enter the construction routine with the product matrix R = Q × P.

Exercise 4.2

Use the above routines to draw diagrams that are similar to figure 4.2, but where the number, positions and directions of the flags are read in from the keyboard. You can produce routines to draw more complicated objects; a very simple example was chosen here so that the algorithms would not be obscured by the complexity of objects. The above method can deal with as many vertices, lines and coloured areas as the IBM PC can handle within time and storage limitations.

Exercise 4.3

Loops in the program can be used to draw ordered sequences of the objects; for example, the objects may all have the same orientation but their points of reference (the origin in the SETUP position) are equally spaced along any line $p + \mu q$. A loop may be set up with index parameter μ and one flag drawn for each pass through the loop. For each value of μ the parameters of translation may be altered in a regular way within the loop (using μ, p and q). The new values of these parameters are used to calculate a different SETUP to ACTUAL matrix for each occurrence, and this moves the object into a new ACTUAL position. R = Q $\times$ P = I $\times$ P is used to observe and draw each object on the screen. With these ideas, construct a line of flags on the screen.

Efficient Use of Matrices

It is obvious that whatever combination of transformations is used, the third row of every matrix will always be (0 0 1). Working only with the top two rows of the matrix makes the routines much more efficient. The matrices are still DIMensioned as 3 $\times$ 3 arrays rather than 2 $\times$ 3 (all that is really needed), because other routines may have been written previously that assume the use of 3 $\times$ 3 matrices. ReDIMensioning the arrays could lead to array bound errors in the earlier routines — the cost of an extra three real numbers per matrix is a small price to pay to avoid such errors. ERASE can be used to set these arrays to zero and it is also more efficient to use explicit statements rather than loops. Listings 4.1, 4.2, 4.3 and 4.4 are rewritten to make use of these facts.

Listing 4.1a

```
9100 'mult2
9101 '**in ** A(3,3),R(3,3)
9102 '**out** R(3,3)
9110 FOR I%=1 TO 2
9120 FOR J%=1 TO 3
9130 B(I%,J%)=A(I%,1)*R(1,J%)+A(I%,2)*R(2,J%)
9140 NEXT J%
9150 B(I%,3)=B(I%,3)+A(I%,3)
9160 NEXT I%
9170 FOR J%=1 TO 3
9180 R(1,J%)=B(1,J%) : R(2,J%)=B(2,J%)
9190 NEXT J%
9200 RETURN

9300 'idR2
9302 '**out** R(3,3)
9310 ERASE R : DIM R(3,3)
9320 R(1,1)=1 : R(2,2)=1
9330 RETURN
```

Listing 4.2a

```
9000 ´tran2
9001 ´**in ** TX,TY
9002 ´**out** A(3,3)
9010 ERASE A : DIM A(3,3)
9020 A(1,1)= 1 : A(2,2)= 1
9030 A(1,3)=TX : A(2,3)=TY
9040 RETURN
```

Listing 4.3a

```
8900 ´scale2
8901 ´**in ** SX,SY
8902 ´**out** A(3,3)
8910 ERASE A : DIM A(3,3)
8920 A(1,1)=SX : A(2,2)=SY
8930 RETURN
```

Listing 4.4a

```
8600 ´rot2
8601 ´**in ** THETA
8602 ´**out** A(3,3)
8610 ERASE A : DIM A(3,3)
8620 CT=COS(THETA) : ST=SIN(THETA)
8630 A(1,1)= CT : A(2,2)=CT
8640 A(1,2)=-ST : A(2,1)=ST
8650 RETURN
```

The construction of figure 4.2 may seem rather contrived since the positions of the objects were chosen in an arbitrary way. However, in most diagrams the positioning of objects will be well defined, the values being implicit in the diagram required. See example 4.3 below.

Example 4.3
Write a program that draws an ellipse with major axis A, minor axis B and is centred at the point (CX, CY). The major axis makes an angle θ (THETA) with the positive x-direction. Note that the order of transformations is important: first rotate and then translate. Matrices need not be used to draw ellipses with major axis horizontal: simply use the routine set in exercise 2.3 and ideas similar to those in listing 2.9. Listing 4.9 gives a 'scene2' main program which reads in data about the ellipse, calculates the SETUP to OBSERVED matrix and then calls the construction routine 'ellipse' which draws the ellipse.

Listing 4.9

```
100 ´scene2/look2; ellipse (not stored)
110 GOSUB 9700 ´start
120 DIM A(3,3),B(3,3),R(3,3)
129 ´major axis A, minor axis B, centre (CX,CY), angle THETA.
130 INPUT"A,B,CX,CY,THETA ",A,B,CX,CY,THETA
140 GOSUB 9300 ´idR2
150 GOSUB 8600 ´rot2
```

```
160 GOSUB 9100 'mult2
170 TX=CX : TY=CY : GOSUB 9000 'tran2
180 GOSUB 9100 'mult2
190 GOSUB 60000 'colour monitor
200 XMOVE=HORIZ/2 : YMOVE=VERT/2
210 GOSUB 9600 'setorigin
220 GOSUB 6500 'ellipse
230 GOSUB 60100 'monochrome display
240 END

6500 'ellipse / not stored
6501 '**in ** R(3,3)
6509 'find points (XX,YY) on the ellipse with horizontal major
     axis and place them in position using matrix R.
6510 XPT=R(1,1)*A+R(1,3) : YPT=R(2,1)*A+R(2,3)
6520 GOSUB 9500 'moveto
6530 ALPHA=0 : ADIF=3.141593/50
6540 FOR I%=1 TO 100
6550 ALPHA=ALPHA+ADIF
6560 XX=A*COS(ALPHA) : YY=B*SIN(ALPHA)
6570 XPT=R(1,1)*XX+R(1,2)*YY+R(1,3)
6580 YPT=R(2,1)*XX+R(2,2)*YY+R(2,3)
6590 GOSUB 9400 'lineto
6600 NEXT I%
6610 RETURN
```

Exercise 4.4

Write a routine for drawing an individual matrix-transformable object (in this case
an *astroid*, as shown in figure 4.3a) and then use the matrix techniques to draw
combinations of these objects (as in figure 4.3b). An astroid is a closed curve with

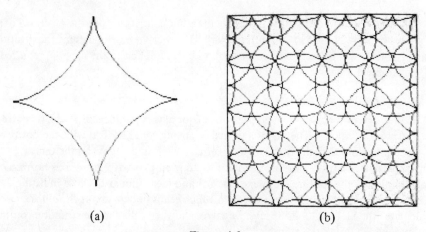

(a)   (b)

Figure 4.3

parametric form ($R_x\cos^3\theta$, $R_x\sin^3\theta$) with $0 \leqslant \theta \leqslant 2\pi$, where R is the radius (the
maximum distance from the centre of the object). The parameters needed by this
routine are the radius of the astroid and the transforming matrix. Figure 4.3b is
the combination of a large number of two different forms of the astroid. One has
radius 1 and is not rotated, the other has radius $\sqrt{2}$ and is rotated through $\pi/4$
radians.

Exercise 4.5

Experiment with these matrix techniques. Write a routine that generates the matrix necessary to rotate points in space by an angle θ about an arbitrary point (X, Y) in space (not necessarily the origin). Also produce another routine to generate the matrix that will reflect points about the general line $ay = bx + c$. (Use the ideas given in example 4.2 for the production of flag (c).)

Storing Information about Scenes

It was mentioned earlier that certain situations would arise when all the information about a particular scene would have to be stored in a large data-base if the information was not to be lost on leaving the construction routine. The data-base will consist of vertices, lines and facets, together with information on colour which can be explicitly or implicitly stored. Vertices are stored as arrays X and Y, of length greater than or equal to NOV%, the final number of vertices to be stored. (These vertices can be stored in SETUP, ACTUAL or OBSERVED position: it depends on the context of the problem.)

Line information is stored in a two-dimensional array LIN% whose first index is 1 or 2, and whose second index is a number between 1 and a value greater than or equal to NOL%, the final number of lines in the scene. The Ith line joins the two vertices with indices LIN% (1, I) to LIN% (2, I): and hence this information is independent of position, it simply says which two vertices are joined by the Ith line. The colours of lines are assumed to be implicitly defined in the program listings, usually logical colour 0.

Information about polygonal areas or facets ($\leqslant$ NOF% in number) may be stored in a two-dimensional array FACET% and two one-dimensional arrays SIZE% and COL%. SIZE% (J) holds the number of edges in facet J, COL% (J) explicitly defines its colour, and FACET% (J, K), where $1 \leqslant J \leqslant$ NOF% and $1 \leqslant K \leqslant$ SIZE% (J), holds the indices of the vertices that make up the facet. NOV%, NOL% and NOF% values are initialised in the 'scene 2' routine and incremented in the construction routines. Note that to colour the lines explicitly would require another array.

From now on the construction routines will no longer draw lines and facets, they will be used only to create the data-base of lines, vertices, facets etc. (transformed by the matrix R). After 'scene2' has constructed the final scene in memory it calls another routine 'drawit' which draws the final picture. The 'scene2' routine will be very similar to those mentioned earlier; for example, the routine for drawing figure 4.2 in this new way will be that given in listing 4.8 with the five minor changes listed below.

```
120 DIM X(48), Y(48), LIN%(2, 8), FACET%(6, 12), SIZE%(12), COL%(12)
150 XMOVE = HORIZ/2: YMOVE = VERT/2: NOV% = 0: NOL% = 0: NOF% = 0
460 GOSUB 7000 'drawit
```

470 GOSUB 60100 'monochrome monitor

480 END

This is used in conjunction with listing 4.10 which gives the 'flag' construction routine (which now only sets up the data) and 'drawit' routine.

Listing 4.10

```
6500 'flag / data stored
6501 '**in ** R(3,3)
6502 '**out** NOV%,X(NOV%),Y(NOV%),NOL%,LIN%(2,NOL%)
              NOF%,FACET%(6,NOF%),SIZE%(NOF%),COL%(NOF%)
6510 RESTORE 6520
6520 DATA 4,2,1,2,3,4, 6,1,1,5,8,3,9,12, 6,1,2,7,10,4,11,6
6530 DATA 1,3, 2,4
6540 DATA  5,5,  -5,5, -5,-5,  5,-5,  4,5,  -4,5,
           -5,4, -5,-4, -4,-5,  4,-5,  5,-4,  5,4
6549 'READ facet information.
6550 FOR I%=1 TO 3
6560 NOF%=NOF%+1 : READ SIZE%(NOF%),COL%(NOF%)
6570 FOR J%=1 TO SIZE%(NOF%)
6580 READ FVAL% : FACET%(J%,NOF%)=NOV%+FVAL%
6590 NEXT J% : NEXT I%
6599 'READ line information.
6600 FOR I%=1 TO 2
6610 NOL%=NOL%+1 : READ L1%,L2%
6620 LIN%(1,NOL%)=L1%+NOV% : LIN%(2,NOL%)=L2%+NOV%
6630 NEXT I%
6639 'READ vertex information.
6640 FOR I%=1 TO 12
6650 NOV%=NOV%+1 : READ XX,YY
6660 X(NOV%)=R(1,1)*XX+R(1,2)*YY+R(1,3)
6670 Y(NOV%)=R(2,1)*XX+R(2,2)*YY+R(2,3)
6680 NEXT I%
6690 RETURN

7000 'drawit
7001 '**in ** NOV%,X(NOV%),Y(NOV%),NOL%,LIN%(2,NOL),R(3,3),
              NOF%,FACET%(6,NOF%),SIZE%(NOF%),COL%(NOF%)
7010 DIM XC(6),YC(6)
7019 'draw the facets in explicit colour COLFAC%.
7020 FOR K%=1 TO NOF%
7030 FOREGROUND%=COL%(K%) : COLFAC%=COL%(K%) : NC%=SIZE%(K%)
7040 FOR J%=1 TO NC%
7050 M%=FACET%(J%,K%)
7060 XC(J%)=X(M%) : YC(J%)=Y(M%)
7070 NEXT J%
7080 GOSUB 4000 'polygon filler
7090 NEXT K%
7099 'draw the lines in implicit colour 0.
7100 FOREGROUND%=0
7110 FOR K%=1 TO NOL%
7120 M%=LIN%(1,K%) : XPT=X(M%) : YPT=Y(M%) : GOSUB 9500 'moveto
7130 M%=LIN%(2,K%) : XPT=X(M%) : YPT=Y(M%) : GOSUB 9400 'lineto
7140 NEXT K%
7150 ERASE XC,YC
7160 RETURN
```

It is often required to produce different views of the same scene (again figure 4.2 is used as an example); that is, the same SETUP to ACTUAL matrices P, but different ACTUAL to OBSERVED matrices Q. The obvious solution is to create a data-base for the scene with the vertices in ACTUAL position (use the 'flag' routine of listing 4.11). Now Q is calculated for each new OBSERVED position. It is entered into another 'drawit' routine (see listing 4.11 – different from listing 4.10) which transfers each vertex from its ACTUAL to OBSERVED position using Q, stores them in arrays XD and YD so as not to corrupt the X, Y data-base, and recalls them when they are required for drawing. When using this method to construct different views of figure 4.2, only the 'scene2' and 'drawit' routines differ from their earlier manifestations, and then only slightly. These are given in listing 4.11.

Listing 4.11

```
100 ´main program :  scene2/ 4 flags (stored) ; variable view
110 GOSUB 9700 ´start
120 DIM X(48),Y(48),XD(48),YD(48)
130 DIM LIN%(2,8),FACET%(6,12),SIZE%(12),COL%(12)
140 DIM A(3,3),B(3,3),R(3,3)
149 ´flag a)
150 NOV%=0 : NOL%=0 : NOF%=0
160 GOSUB 9300 ´idR2
170 GOSUB 6500 ´flag
179 ´flag b)
180 SX=4 : SY=2 : GOSUB 8900 ´scale2
190 GOSUB 9100 ´mult2
200 THETA=3.141493/6 : GOSUB 8600 ´rot2
210 GOSUB 9100 ´mult2
220 TX=30 : TY=15 : GOSUB 9000 ´tran2
230 GOSUB 9100 ´mult2
240 GOSUB 6500 ´flag
249 ´flag c)
250 TX=0 : TY=3 : GOSUB 9000 ´tran2
260 GOSUB 9100 ´mult2
270 AX=-3 : AY=4 : GOSUB 8800 ´angle
280 THETA=-THETA : GOSUB 8600 ´rot2
290 GOSUB 9100 ´mult2
300 SX=1 : SY=-1 : GOSUB 8900 ´scale2
310 GOSUB 9100 ´mult2
320 THETA=-THETA : GOSUB 8600 ´rot2
330 GOSUB 9100 ´mult2
340 TX=0 : TY=-3 : GOSUB 9000 ´tran2
350 GOSUB 9100 ´mult2
360 GOSUB 6500 ´flag
369 ´flag d)
370 GOSUB 9300 ´idR2
380 TX=30 : TY=15 : GOSUB 9000 ´tran2
390 GOSUB 9100 ´mult2
400 THETA=3.141493/6 : GOSUB 8600 ´rot2
410 GOSUB 9100 ´mult2
420 SX=4 : SY=2 : GOSUB 8900 ´scale2
430 GOSUB 9100 ´mult2
440 GOSUB 6500 ´flag
450 XMOVE=HORIZ/2 : YMOVE=VERT/2
460 GOSUB 9300 ´idR2
470 GOSUB 8200 ´look2
480 GOSUB 60000 ´colour monitor
490 GOSUB 9600 ´setorigin
500 GOSUB 7000 ´drawit
510 GOSUB 60100 ´monochrome display
520 XMOVE=0 : YMOVE=0
530 GOTO 460
540 END

7000 ´drawit
7001 ´**in ** NOV%,X(NOV%),Y(NOV%),NOL%,LIN%(2,NOL%),R(3,3),
               NOF%,FACET%(6,NOF%),SIZE%(NOF%),COL%(NOF%)
7010 DIM XC(6),YC(6)
```

```
7019 'move vertices to OBSERVED position.
7020 FOR K%=1 TO NOV%
7030 XD(K%)=R(1,1)*X(K%)+R(1,2)*Y(K%)+R(1,3)
7040 YD(K%)=R(2,1)*X(K%)+R(2,2)*Y(K%)+R(2,3)
7050 NEXT K%
7059 'draw the facets in explicit colour COLFAC%.
7060 FOR K%=1 TO NOF%
7070 FOREGROUND%=COL%(K%) : COLFAC%=COL%(K%).: NC%=SIZE%(K%)
7080 FOR J%=1 TO NC%
7090 M%=FACET%(J%,K%)
7100 XC(J%)=XD(M%) : YC(J%)=YD(M%)
7110 NEXT J%
7120 GOSUB 4000 'polygon filler
7130 NEXT K%
7139 'draw the lines in implicit colour 0.
7140 FOREGROUND%=0
7150 FOR K%=1 TO NOL%
7160 M%=LIN%(1,K%) : XPT=XD(M%) : YPT=YD(M%) : GOSUB 9500 'moveto
7170 M%=LIN%(2,K%) : XPT=XD(M%) : YPT=YD(M%) : GOSUB 9400 'lineto
7180 NEXT K%
7190 ERASE XC,YC
7200 RETURN
```

Exercise 4.6

Construct a dynamic scene. With each new view the flags will move relative to one another in some well-defined manner. The observer also should move in some simple way; for example, the eye can start looking at the origin, and twenty views later it is looking at the point (100, 100), and with each view the head is tilted a further 0.1 radians. You no longer need to INPUT the values of (DX, DY) and ALPHA into 'look2', instead they should be calculated by the program.

Exercise 4.7

Construct a scene that is a diagrammatic view of a room in your house — with schematic two-dimensional drawings of tables, chairs etc. placed in the room. Each different type of object has its own construction routine, and the 'scene2' routine should read in data to place these objects around the room. Once the scene is set produce a variety of views, looking from various points and orientations. Use the menu technique of chapters 5 and 6 to input information.

Or you can set up a line-drawing picture of a map, and again view it from various orientations. The number of possible choices of scene is enormous!

If a small value for HORIZ is chosen, then this has the effect of the observer zooming up close to parts of a scene, and all external lines and areas will be conveniently clipped off by the 'filler' routine.

Exercise 4.8

These programs take quite a time to execute, so this is a good time to think carefully about making programs more efficient. Replace calls to routines by explicit lines of code. Reorder the program lines to put the most commonly used routines at the front of the program. Use listing I.1 to take out all REMarks. If you understand the algorithms, you can reduce the length of the variable names. Those with a knowledge of assembly language can write an assembler program for 'filler'. If you are not too bothered about the *holes* left by PAINT then 'filler' can be replaced by a much faster program using this command. Finally you can always get a compiler!

Complete Programs

Listings 4.1a ('mult2' and 'idR2'), 4.2a ('tran2'), 4.3a ('scale2'), 4.4a ('rot2') and 4.5 ('look2') are grouped under the heading 'lib2'. All the programs in this chapter must have 'lib0', 'lib1' and 'lib2' MERGEd with them. Run the programs in MODE% = 1, with PALETTE% = 1, BACKGROUND% = FOREGROUND% = 0 and PAPER% = 3.

I. Listing 4.6 ('scene2'), and MERGE in listing 4.7 ('flag'). Data required: HORIZ, DX, DY and ALPHA. Try 24, 1, 1, 0.5. Keep any three of these values fixed and systematically make small changes in the other data value.

II. Listing 4.8 ('scene2'), and MERGE in listing 4.7 ('flag'). Data required: HORIZ. Try 240: 160: 80.

III. Listing 4.9 ('scene2' and 'ellipse'). Data required: HORIZ, A, B, CX, CY, THETA. Try 30, 6, 5, 1, 1, 0.5. Again fix all but one of the values and change the remaining value systematically.

IV. Listing 4.8 ('scene2' adjusted as described in text) and MERGE listing 4.10 ('flag' and 'drawit'). Data required: as II above.

V. Listing 4.10 ('flag' but not 'drawit'), and MERGE listing 4.11 ('scene2' and 'drawit'). Data required: HORIZ, DX, DY, ALPHA. Try 240, 5, 5, 1. Systematically change each of the data values in turn.

5 Character Graphics and Pixel Blocks

Chapter 1 introduced the idea of the ASCII code: integer numbers between 0 and 255 (hexadecimal &H00 to &HFF) referring to a character set for monochrome and colour monitors. PRINT (CHR$(I)) displays the Ith character of the set on the appropriate screen. The description of these 256 characters is fixed for the monochrome display. However, for a colour monitor in a graphics mode, the data is stored as two sets of information; one for codes from 0 to 127 (the fixed set) cannot be changed, the other for codes from 128 to 255 (the variable set) is user-definable. You should remember that the latter variable set must either be loaded by typing GRAFTABL before entering the BASICA interpreter or created in some other way (see later), in order to prevent garbage appearing on the screen in place of the required characters of the ASCII codes greater than 127. To display all the available characters, you should load and run listing 5.1 (merging in 'lib0' of course). Some characters are used as control codes and therefore are not PRINTed; they appear as solid red squares in this display.

Listing 5.1

```
100 MODE%=1
110 GOSUB 60000 'colour monitor
120 GOSUB 5000 'display
130 GOSUB 60100 'monochrome display
140 END

5000 'display routine
5009 'divide character set into fixed set ( 0<= ASCII code <128 )
                        and variable set ( 128<= ASCII code <256
5010 CLS : LOCATE 5,1
5020 PRINT"which character set do you want to see ?",
          "  type 1 for fixed or 2 for variable";
5030 KB$=INKEY$ : IF KB$="" THEN GOTO 5030
5040 IF KB$<>"1" AND KB$<>"2" THEN GOTO 5030
5050 BASE%=(VAL(KB$)-1)*128
5060 R%=0 : CLS : LOCATE 2,5
5070 IF BASE%=0 THEN PRINT SPC(6)"FIXED CHARACTER SET" :
                     PRINT SPC(9)"(CANNOT be redefined)"
                ELSE PRINT SPC(5)"VARIABLE CHARACTER SET" :
5079 'print out characters in specified set, 16 to a line.
5080 FOR I%=BASE% TO BASE%+112 STEP 16
5090 R%=R%+1 : LOCATE 2*R%+4,1
5100 PRINT I%;
5110 FOR J%=0 TO 15
5120 ACODE%=I%+J%
5130 LINE (46+J%*16,22+R%*16)-(57+J%*16,33+R%*16),2,BF
5140 IF ACODE%=7 OR (ACODE%>8 AND ACODE%<14 )
                 OR (ACODE%>27 AND ACODE%<32) THEN GOTO 5160
```

92

```
5150 LOCATE R%*2+4,5+J%*2+2 : PRINT CHR$(ACODE%);
5160 NEXT J%
5170 NEXT I%
5180 LOCATE 23,7 : PRINT"Do you wish to see the other set";
5190 LOCATE 24,16 : PRINT"Type Y or N";
5200 KB$=INKEY$ : IF KB$="" THEN GOTO 5200
5210 IF KB$="Y" OR KB$="y" THEN BASE%=128-BASE% : GOTO 5060
5220 RETURN
```

The variable character set is stored as a table of 8 × 128 bytes, that is, 8 bytes per character. In mode 2 (a screen of 640 by 200 pixels) each character is square, 8 rows of 8 pixels, drawn in white foreground on a black background. Each of the 8 bytes that describe one character represents one row of the character, the first byte for the top row, the eighth for the bottom. Each of the 8 bits in a byte represents one pixel in the row, bit 7 on the left and bit 0 on the right. A bit value of 0 will represent a black pixel on the row, and a bit value of 1 a white pixel. In mode 1 (screen 320 by 200 pixels) a bit value of 1 represents the foreground (normally logical colour 3, but which can be changed — see chapter 1), and a bit value of 0 the background (logical colour 0). In mode 2 the screen may be considered as 80 by 25 characters in size, and in mode 1 as 40 by 25.

Therefore, if the location in the Random Access Memory of the start of the variable character data table is known, offset ADDRESS% in segment PAGE% of the memory (say), then it is a simple task to create a new character equivalent to a given ASCII code (I say). The 8 memory locations, corresponding to the required character, are found using the code (these are the 8 locations starting at ADDRESS% + (I − 128) * 8 of segment PAGE%) and their contents changed to the 8 bytes of the new character — a very simple task given the values of ADDRESS% and PAGE%. These values are found directly from the interrupt vector &H1F hexadecimal, or in plain English from locations 124, 125, 126 and 127 (hexadecimal &H7C, &H7D, &H7E and &H7F) of segment zero. Typing

DEF SEG = 0

PAGE% = PEEK (127) * &H100 + PEEK (126)

ADDRESS% = PEEK (125) * &H100 + PEEK (124)

will evaluate the required values. For example, if these four locations held values 4, 1, 95 (hex &H5F) and 6 respectively, then PAGE% = &H65F and ADDRESS% = &H104, which would put the absolute location of the start of the table at PAGE% * &H10 + ADDRESS% (remember the value in a DEF SEG statement refers to an absolute location &H10 times that value), that is, &H66F4 in the example. Changing the contents of any of these four locations will force the PRINT statement to look at a different part of the memory for the character table. This means that many character sets may be stored simultaneously in the memory, each of which can be referred to with PRINT, by the simple expedient of putting the correct PAGE% and ADDRESS% values for that set into locations 124 to 127 of segment zero. For example, setting the contents of 125 to &HFC and the others to zero would start a variable character set at location &HFC00. Make sure that you do not dump character sets where they destroy essential information — like in the middle of a program. While still experimenting with character generation it is safer to use the locations reserved by GRAFTABL which, on loading, increases the resident size of DOS in the memory so that it can hold the character set, and also puts the values in locations 124 to 127 which point to this character set.

Exercise 5.1

It is essential, therefore, that you first enter GRAFTABL before running the programs from this chapter with the BASICA interpreter. Use listing 5.1 to study the variable character set created by GRAFTABL. PEEK at locations 124 to 127 of segment zero and calculate the start address of the table. POKE arbitrary 8-bit values into the table locations and view the effect with listing 5.1. Then POKE different values into the contents of locations 124 to 127 and observe that effect; for example, add 8 to the contents of address 124. Return these locations back to their original values before continuing.

Listing 5.2

```
100 MODE%=2
110 GOSUB 60000 ´colour monitor
119 ´PRINT CHR$(128) at top left corner of graphics screen.
120 PRINT CHR$(128)
130 GOSUB 60100 ´monochrome
139 ´set segment to graphics screen buffer.
140 DEF SEG=&HB800
150 ODDLINE%=0
159 ´get 8 bytes for character from screen memory.
160 DIM HOLD%(8)
170 FOR K%=1 TO 8
180 ADDRESS%=ODDLINE%*&H2000+INT((K%-1)/2)*80
190 HOLD%(K%)=PEEK(ADDRESS%)
200 ODDLINE%=1-ODDLINE%
210 PRINT HOLD%(K%);" ";
220 NEXT K%
230 PRINT´
238 ´look for character in computer memory.
239 ´divide memory into PAGEs of length &H1000.
240 FOR PAGE%=0 TO 20
250 DEF SEG=PAGE%*&H100
260 PRINT "checking page ";PAGE%
270 FOR I%=0 TO &HFFF
280 FOR J%=1 TO 8
290 IF PEEK(I%+J%-1) <> HOLD%(J%) GOTO 320
300 NEXT J%
310 PRINT "found CHR$(128) starting at ";HEX$(PAGE*&H1000+I%)
320 NEXT I%
330 NEXT PAGE%
340 END
```

If you want reassurance about the position of the character table, you can run listing 5.2 — it is also quite instructive regarding the structure of the computer memory. This program PRINTs CHR$ (128), the first character from the variable set, on a mode 2 screen. Then setting the segment to &HB800 (the screen buffer), it reads the 8 bytes corresponding to this character directly from the screen.

Remember that the even and odd lines of the screen are stored separately in memory. The program then searches systematically through the memory for consecutive sets of 8 bytes with the same values as the character and prints out the addresses holding the first byte, if and when it finds them.

Listing 5.3

```
100 DEF SEG=0
110 PAGE%=PEEK(127)*&H100+PEEK(126)
120 ADDRESS%=PEEK(125)*&H100+PEEK(124)
130 MODE%=1 : GOSUB 60000 'colour monitor
140 LOCATE 8,10 : PRINT"ROTATING CHARACTERS"
150 LOCATE 12,16 : PRINT"becomes"
160 LINE (142,70)-(153,81),2,BF
170 LINE (142,102)-(153,113),2,BF
179 'rotate fixed set characters (ASCII code between 32 and 126)
    and place them in variable set (codes between 160 and 254).
180 FOR ASCHAR%=32 TO 126
190 LOCATE 10,19 : PRINT CHR$(ASCHAR%)
200 GOSUB 6600 'rotate character
210 GOSUB 4500 'put character
220 NEXT ASCHAR%
230 GOSUB 5000 'display characters
240 GOSUB 2000 'example of vertical labelling
250 GOSUB 60100 'monochrome monitor
260 DEF SEG=PAGE%
270 BSAVE "B:ROTCHARS.DAT",ADDRESS%,&H400
280 END

1500 'vertical labelling / print routine
1501 '**in ** LABROW%,LABCOL%,LABEL$
1510 LENLABEL%=LEN(LABEL$)
1520 FOR LROW%=1 TO LENLABEL%
1530 LOCATE LABROW%+1-LROW%,LABCOL%
1540 ASCHAR%=ASC(MID$(LABEL$,LROW%,1))+128
1550 PRINT CHR$(ASCHAR%);
1560 NEXT LROW%
1570 RETURN

2000 'layout routine
2009 'sample of vertical labelling.
2010 CLS
2020 LABEL$="VERTICAL labelling"
2030 LABROW%=22 : LABCOL%=5
2040 GOSUB 1500 'vertical labelling
2050 LABEL$="0123456789!$%^&*()-+,:;"
2060 LABROW%=25 : LABCOL%=8
2070 GOSUB 1500 'vertical labelling
2080 RETURN

4500 'put routine
4501 ' **in ** PAGE%,ADDRESS%,ASCHAR%
4509 'take rotated character from screen and store in variable
     set at position equivalent to ASCII code ASCHAR%+128.
4510 DIM V%(8) : DEF SEG=PAGE%
4520 FOR J%=1 TO 8
4530 V%(J%)=0
4540 FOR I%=1 TO 8
4550 COL%=POINT(143+I%,104+J%)
4560 V%(J%)=V%(J%)*2+INT(COL%/3)
4570 NEXT I% : NEXT J%
4580 ADD%=ADDRESS%+ASCHAR%*8
4590 FOR J%=1 TO 8 : POKE ADD%,V%(J%) : ADD%=ADD%+1 : NEXT J%
4600 ERASE V%
4610 RETURN
```

```
5000 'display routine : see listing 5.1
5009 'divide character set into fixed set ( 0<= ASCII code <128 )
                      and variable set ( 128<= ASCII code <256 )
5220 RETURN

6600 'rotate character anticlockwise
6609 'use character with top left corner pixel (144,72),
     new character has bottom left corner pixel (144,111).
6610 FOR J%=0 TO 7
6620 FOR I%=0 TO 7
6630 COL%=POINT(144+I%,72+J%)
6640 PSET (144+J%,111-I%),COL%
6650 NEXT I% : NEXT J%
6670 RETURN
```

Many data graphs and diagrams need labelling (see chapter 6), and the standard horizontal alphanumeric characters are often not suitable. One obvious need is for a character set that will allow the PRINTing of character strings in a vertical direction instead of horizontally. Listing 5.3 creates such a character set, and also includes a routine, which given a character string LABEL$, PRINTs this string vertically upwards starting at text row LABROW% and column LABCOL%. The method of construction of the vertical character set is very simple. PRINT every character with ASCII code between 32 and 126 on the screen in turn. Then use POINT to find the colour of each pixel (I, J) in that character. By going through the 8 pixels of each column J of the character, the rows of the rotated character can be calculated. The resulting 8 bytes are then taken from the screen and stored in the table at a position corresponding to a character with ASCII code 128 greater than the original. Given a horizontal character string (all ASCII codes between 32 and 126 (127 is not used since ASCII code 255 = 127 + 128 is a control code)), the vertical PRINT routine isolates individual characters from within the string, finds each ASCII code, and PRINTs the equivalent vertical character by adding 128 to that code. The vertical set having been constructed, BSAVE is used to store the 8* 128 locations (= &H400 hexadecimal) of the table as the disk file "B:ROTCHARS.DAT" (or A: ... if you have a single disk drive), keeping it for future use in chapter 6.

Exercise 5.2

Construct your own character sets in which the horizontal set has either

(1) been rotated in the opposite direction to that above,
(2) been stored upside-down, or
(3) had the colours inverted — black to white and vice versa.

In each case write a suitable printout routine for these new characters.

A Character Generator

It is very tedious and error-prone to calculate the 8 bytes for each new individual character in a particular character set, and to POKE them separately into memory. It makes far more sense to construct a CHARACTER GENERATOR program.

Such a program, like the one given in listing 5.4, must be planned very carefully. You must break down the problem into a sequence of tasks, which themselves may be further broken down into further subtasks etc., until you have derived a structured plan of approach for writing the program. Then the subtasks (or modules) can be programmed and tested separately, before combining them all in the final structured program.

Listing 5.4

```
100                      CHARACTER GENERATOR
110 DEF SEG=0 : KEY OFF : OPTION BASE 1 : CLS
120 PRINT"Do you wish to change locations 124-127?: Y or N"
130 KB$=INKEY$ : IF KB$="" THEN GOTO 130
140 IF KB$<>"y" AND KB$<>"Y" THEN GOTO 190
150 FOR ADD%=124 TO 127
160 PRINT"Type contents of location ";ADD%;
170 INPUT CONTENTS% : POKE ADD%,CONTENTS%
180 NEXT ADD%
190 PAGE%=PEEK(127)*&H100+PEEK(126)
200 ADDRESS%=PEEK(125)*&H100+PEEK(124)
210 DEF SEG=PAGE%
220 PRINT"Do you wish to load a variable character set?: Y or N "
230 KB$=INKEY$ : IF KB$="" THEN GOTO 230
240 IF KB$="Y" OR KB$="y"
        THEN INPUT "Name of file ",F$ : BLOAD F$,ADDRESS%
249 'READ DATA for a 7x7 pixel block holding cursor symbol.
250 DIM CURSOR%(9)
260 DATA &HE,&H7,&HCC0,&H3030,&HC00C,&H3,&HC00C,&H3030,&HCC0
270 FOR I%=1 TO 9 : READ CURSOR%(I%) : NEXT I%
280 MODE%=1
290 GOSUB 60000  'colour monitor
300 GOSUB 2000   'layout
310 GOSUB 1000   'supervisor
320 GOSUB 60100  'monochrome monitor
330 PRINT"Do you wish to save this variable character set?: Y or N "
340 KB$=INKEY$ : IF KB$="" THEN GOTO 340
350 IF KB$="Y" OR KB$="y" THEN INPUT "Name of file ",F$ :
                          DEF SEG=PAGE% :
                          BSAVE F$,ADDRESS%,&H400
360 END

1000 'supervisor routine : loop through all legal keyboard input.
1009 'see ASCII codes in Appendix G of BASIC Manual.
1010 KB$=INKEY$ : IF KB$="" GOTO 1010
1020 LENKB%=LEN(KB$)
1030 IF LENKB%=1 THEN ASCKB%=ASC(KB$) : GOTO 1100
1039 'deal with keyboard input that creates two character string.
1040 ASCKB%=ASC(RIGHT$(KB$,1))
1050 IF ASCKB%=80 THEN MX%= 0 : MY%= 1 : GOSUB 3000 :
                       GOTO 1010 'cursor control
1060 IF ASCKB%=72 THEN MX%= 0 : MY%=-1 : GOSUB 3000 :
                       GOTO 1010 'cursor control
1070 IF ASCKB%=75 THEN MX%=-1 : MY%= 0 : GOSUB 3000 :
                       GOTO 1010 'cursor control
1080 IF ASCKB%=77 THEN MX%= 1 : MY%= 0 : GOSUB 3000 :
                       GOTO 1010 'cursor control
1090 GOTO 1010
1099 'deal with single character input, CAPITAL letters only.
1100 IF ASCKB%>90 THEN ASCKB%=ASCKB%-32
1110 IF ASCKB%=ASC("D") THEN GOSUB 5000 :
                          GOSUB 2000 'display codes
1120 IF ASCKB%=ASC("G") THEN GOSUB 4000 'get routine
1130 IF ASCKB%=ASC("P") THEN GOSUB 4500 'put routine
1140 IF ASCKB%=ASC("C") THEN GOSUB 3200 'change colour
```

```
1150 IF ASCKB%=ASC("X") THEN GOSUB 6200 'x-reflect routine
1160 IF ASCKB%=ASC("Y") THEN GOSUB 6400 'y-reflect routine
1170 IF ASCKB%=ASC("R") THEN GOSUB 6600 'rotate routine
1180 IF ASCKB%=ASC("I") THEN GOSUB 6000 'invert routine
1190 IF ASCKB%<>ASC("E") THEN GOTO 1010
1200 RETURN

2000 'layout the keyboard MENU.
2001 '**in ** CURSOR%
2002 '**out** CURX%,CURY%,GRIDX%,GRIDY%
2010 CLS
2020 LINE (8,8)-(138,138),2,BF
2030 LINE (10,10)-(136,136),0,BF
2040 FOR I%=25 TO 121 STEP 16
2050 LINE (I%,9)-(I%,137),2
2060 LINE (9,I%)-(137,I%),2
2070 NEXT I%
2080 LOCATE  1,22 : PRINT "E end generation";
2090 LOCATE  3,22 : PRINT "D display set";
2100 LOCATE  5,22 : PRINT "G get character";
2110 LOCATE  7,22 : PRINT "P put character";
2120 LOCATE  9,22 : PRINT "C change colour";
2130 LOCATE 11,22 : PRINT CHR$(24);" move cursor up";
2140 LOCATE 13,22 : PRINT CHR$(25);" move cursor down";
2150 LOCATE 15,22 : PRINT CHR$(26);" move cursor right";
2160 LOCATE 17,22 : PRINT CHR$(27);" move cursor left";
2170 LOCATE 19,22 : PRINT "X reflect in X axis";
2180 LOCATE 21,22 : PRINT "Y reflect in Y axis";
2190 LOCATE 23,22 : PRINT "R rotate";
2200 LOCATE 25,22 : PRINT "I invert colours";
2210 ASCHAR%=32
2220 GOSUB 2600 'character description
2230 CURX%=14 : CURY%=14 : GRIDX%=1 : GRIDY%=1
2240 PUT (CURX%,CURY%),CURSOR%
2250 RETURN

2400 'input ASCII code
2402 '**out** ASCHAR%
2410 LINE (0,152)-(160,199),0,BF
2419 ' input up to 3 numeric characters.
2420 LOCATE 21,2 : PRINT"Give ASCII code ";
2430 ASCHAR%=0
2440 FOR I%=1 TO 3
2450 KB$=INKEY$ : IF KB$="" THEN GOTO 2450
2460 IF ASC(KB$)=13 THEN GOTO 2510
2470 KBV%=INSTR("0123456789",KB$)
2480 IF KBV%<>0 THEN ASCHAR%=ASCHAR%*10+KBV%-1
2490 LOCATE 23,5 : PRINT ASCHAR%
2500 NEXT I%
2509 'illegal codes.
2510 IF ASCHAR%<1 OR ASCHAR%=7 OR (ASCHAR%>8 AND ASCHAR%<14 )
       OR (ASCHAR%>27 AND ASCHAR%<32) OR ASCHAR%>=255
     THEN GOTO 2410
2520 RETURN


2600 'description of present ASCII character
2601 '**in ** ASCHAR%
2610 LINE (0,152)-(160,199),0,BF
2620 LOCATE 20,1  : PRINT "Present character";
2630 LOCATE 21,4  : PRINT "actual size";
2640 LINE (70,174)-(81,185),2,BF
2650 LOCATE 23,10 : PRINT CHR$(ASCHAR%);
2660 LOCATE 25,1 : PRINT "ASCII code is ";ASCHAR%;
2670 RETURN

3000 'move the cursor by (MX%,MY%) : it must stay inside grid.
3001 '**in ** GRIDX%,GRIDY%,CURX%,CURY%,MX%,MY%,CURSOR%
3002 '**out** GRIDX%,GRIDY%,CURX%,CURY%
```

```
3010 NGX%=GRIDX%+MX%
3020 IF NGX%<1 OR NGX%>8 THEN RETURN
3030 NGY%=GRIDY%+MY%
3040 IF NGY%<1 OR NGY%>8 THEN RETURN
3050 GRIDX%=NGX% : GRIDY%=NGY%
3060 PUT (CURX%,CURY%),CURSOR%,XOR
3070 CURX%=CURX%+MX%*16 : CURY%=CURY%+MY%*16
3080 PUT (CURX%,CURY%),CURSOR%
3090 BEEP
3100 RETURN

3200 'change colour of specified pixel
3201 '**in ** GRIDX%,GRIDY%,CURX%,CURY%,CURSOR%
3209 'calculate pixel position (XP%,YP%) from grid value.
3210 XP%=71+GRIDX% : YP%=175+GRIDY%
3220 COL%=POINT(XP%,YP%)
3230 NEWCOL%=3-COL%
3240 LINE (CURX%-4,CURY%-4)-(CURX%+10,CURY%+10),NEWCOL%,BF
3250 PSET (XP%,YP%),NEWCOL%
3260 PUT (CURX%,CURY%),CURSOR%,XOR
3270 RETURN

3400 'create grid representation of ASCII character.
3410 FOR I%=0 TO 7
3420 FOR J%=0 TO 7
3430 COL%=POINT(I%+72,J%+176)
3440 X%=16*I%+10 : Y%=16*J%+10
3450 LINE (X%,Y%)-(X%+14,Y%+14),COL%,BF
3460 NEXT J% : NEXT I%
3470 GOTO 2230

4000 'get character from memory and place on grid and screen
4010 GOSUB 2400 'input ASCII code
4020 GOSUB 2600 'character description
4030 GOSUB 3400 'character to grid
4040 RETURN

4500 'put character from screen into memory
4501 '**in ** PAGE%,ADDRESS%
4509 'take new character from screen and store in variable
     set at position equivalent to ASCII code ASCHAR%.
4510 DIM V%(8) : DEF SEG=PAGE%
4520 FOR J%=1 TO 8
4530 V%(J%)=0
4540 FOR I%=1 TO 8
4550 COL%=POINT(71+I%,175+J%)
4560 V%(J%)=V%(J%)*2+INT(COL%/3)
4570 NEXT I% : NEXT J%
4579 'INPUT ASCHAR%
4580 GOSUB 2400 'input ASCII code
4589 'only change variable character set.
4590 IF ASCHAR%<128 THEN GOTO 4580
4600 ADD%=ADDRESS%+(ASCHAR%-128)*8
4610 FOR J%=1 TO 8 : POKE ADD%,V%(J%) : ADD%=ADD%+1 : NEXT J%
4620 GOSUB 2600 'character description
4630 ERASE V%
4640 RETURN

5000 'display routine : see listing 5.1
5009 'divide character set into fixed set ( 0<= ASCII code <128 )
                         and variable set ( 128<= ASCII code <256 )
5220 RETURN

6000 'invert colours of 8x8 block (72,176)-(79,183)
6010 FOR X=72 TO 79
6020 FOR Y=176 TO 183
6030 COL=POINT(X,Y) : NEWCOL=3-COL
6040 PSET (X,Y),NEWCOL
```

```
6050 NEXT Y : NEXT X
6060 GOSUB 3400 ´screen character to grid
6070 RETURN

6200 ´x-reflect 8x8 block (72,176)-(79,183)
6210 FOR X%=72 TO 79
6220 FOR Y%=176 TO 179
6230 COL1%=POINT(X%,Y%) : COL2%=POINT(X%,359-Y%)
6240 PSET (X%,Y%),COL2% : PSET (X%,359-Y%),COL1%
6250 NEXT Y% : NEXT X%
6260 GOSUB 3400 ´screen character to grid
6270 RETURN

6400 ´y-reflect 8x8 block (72,176)-(79,183)
6410 FOR X%=72 TO 75
6420 FOR Y%=176 TO 183
6430 COL1%=POINT(X%,Y%) : COL2%=POINT(151-X%,Y%)
6440 PSET (X%,Y%),COL2% : PSET (151-X%,Y%),COL1%
6450 NEXT Y% : NEXT X%
6460 GOSUB 3400 ´screen character to grid
6470 RETURN

6600 ´rotate 8x8 block (72,176)-(79,183)
6610 FOR J%=0 TO 7
6620 FOR I%=0 TO 7
6630 COL%=POINT(16*I%+10,16*J%+10)
6640 PSET (72+J%,183-I%),COL%
6650 NEXT I% : NEXT J%
6660 GOSUB 3400 ´screen character to grid
6670 RETURN
```

Listing 5.4 is intended as a guideline on how to approach a CHARACTER
GENERATOR and suchlike programs. Ambitious readers may attempt their own
generator program, but all readers should at least try to add a few extensions to the
listing. The modular form of its construction makes this task reasonably straightforward: more of this later.

Before generating any characters, it is sensible for the program to request changes
to the contents of locations 124 to 127 of segment zero in order to identify the
start of a variable character set. It must also allow a previously constructed character
set to be loaded into the table locations, to allow for further generation or alteration.

A character, being only 8 pixels square, appears rather small on the screen and it
is difficult to observe small changes. It is almost impossible to indicate individual
pixels within the character. So instead the program represents them on a mode 1
screen by an 8 by 8 grid of large squares (each of side 16 pixels, black with a red
surround), and each square corresponds to a pixel in the equivalent position in the
character. The top left-hand black pixel of the $(I, J)^{th}$ grid square is $(10 + 16 * I,$
$10 + 16 * J)$. The real-size character is also PRINTed beneath the grid: top left-hand
corner pixel (72, 176) and bottom right (79, 183). This makes any manipulation of
a character much easier to observe, while at the same time the real-size effect of any
change is also visible. Individual squares must be indicated in some way. The usual
method is to construct a special cursor symbol; for example, a cross, which can
move around the screen under external interactive control.

The display having thus been planned, the program must be constructed as a series
of operations (the modules) initiated from the keyboard. These affect the grid, and

hence change the equivalent character. The list of operations, together with the keyboard value that signifies each operation, is displayed in a menu alongside the grid. A 'supervisor' routine repeatedly checks the keyboard for input, and calls the subroutine module corresponding to the input. The program in listing 5.4 deals with some typical operations; however, since it was written in a structured fashion, the reader should have little difficulty adding other, more specialised, operations to the list below.

(1) "E" Ends the program, at which point the existing character set may be BSAVEd on disk.

(2) The keyboard cursor keys (↑, ↓, ←, →) are used to move a cross-cursor symbol up/down/left/right (MX% = 0, MY% = −1/MX% = 0, MY% = 1/MX% = −1, MY% = 0/MX% = 1, MY% = 0) on the grid to specify an individual pixel in the character. (CURX%, CURY%) is the pixel vector used to PUT (with XOR) a cross-cursor on the screen; PUTting (XOR) the cross in the same position deletes the cursor, so that a single cross-cursor may move about the grid − a animation technique first introduced in listing 1.17. The cross is drawn centred in a square. (GRIDX%, GRIDY%) is the number of squares, across and down respectively, of the current cursor position within the grid, that is, $1 \leqslant$ GRIDX%, GRIDY% $\leqslant 8$. The cross-cursor is READ as DATA into an integer array CURSOR% (9) which enables a 7 by 7 pixel block, holding the cross, to be PUT anywhere on the screen, in particular inside the grid squares at (CURX%, CURY%). If you wish to use pixel blocks READ in this way in your own programs and you are not sure what values to use, simply draw the object on the screen with graphics commands, GET it into an integer array and PRINT out the values.

(3) "D" Displays the present character sets. You must merge the 'display' routine from listing 5.1 if you wish to use this option.

(4) "G" Gets a character from the table (after an ASCII code is input), PRINTs it on the screen and draws the corresponding grid.

(5) "P" Puts the character, at present represented in the grid, into the character set at a position specified by the input of an ASCII code (> 128).

(6) "C" Changes (that is, inverts) the colour of the grid square at present pointed at by the cursor (CURX%, CURY%), and makes the same change to the corresponding pixel of the character (XP%, YP%).

(7) "X" takes the character at present on the screen, and reflects it about the X-direction through the centre of the character. The program finds each pixel (X%, Y%) in the character above the central X-direction line together with the corresponding pixel below the line (X%, 359 − Y%), and swaps their colours around. Then it copies the effect to the grid.

(8) "Y" takes the character at present on the screen, and reflects it about the Y-direction through the centre of the character. The program takes each pixel (X%, Y%) in the character left of the central Y-direction line, together with the corresponding pixel right of the line (151 − X%, Y%), and swaps their colours around. Then it copies the effect to the grid.

(9) "R" takes the current character and rotates it anticlockwise about its centre. The colour of each $(I\%, J\%)^{th}$, $0 < I\%, J\% < 9$, square in the grid is noted in turn, then the corresponding pixel position in the character is found and rotated about the character centre to find the new pixel position $(72 + J\%, 183 - I\%)$, and this pixel is then given the noted colour. When every pixel in the character has been rotated, the new character is copied to the grid.

(10) "I" inverts the colour of each $(X\%, Y\%)$ pixel in a character. Characters are defined as two colours, logical 3 foreground (which can be changed with a POKE) and logical 0 background. This operation changes each pixel of logical colour 3 to colour 0 and vice versa. Then the new character is copied to the grid.

Exercise 5.3

All 2^{64} possible 8 by 8 two-colour characters can be constructed with this routine, in particular those shown in figure 5.1, which are to be identified with codes 198 to 207. Create these characters with the generator program and store them as part of a file "B:PATTERN.DAT" which will be used by the next two programs.

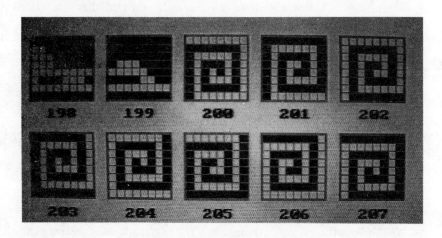

Figure 5.1

Listing 5.5

```
100 'simple tessellated pattern
110 DEF SEG=0
120 PAGE%=PEEK(127)*&H100+PEEK(126)
130 ADDRESS%=PEEK(125)*&H100+PEEK(124)
140 DEF SEG=PAGE%
150 BLOAD "B:PATTERN.DAT",ADDRESS%
160 MODE%=1
170 GOSUB 60000 'colour monitor
179 'print groups of 8 characters ( ASCII codes 200-207 )
     filling 40 columns of each of the first 23 rows.
```

```
180 NUM%=0
190 FOR ROW%=1 TO 23
200 FOR COL%=1 TO 40
210 ASCHAR%=200 + (NUM% MOD 8)
220 PRINT CHR$(ASCHAR%);
230 NUM%=NUM%+1
240 NEXT COL%
250 NUM%=NUM%+1
260 NEXT ROW%
270 GOSUB 60100 'monochrome monitor
280 END
```

Listing 5.5 draws an example of a tessellated pattern. The characters with codes 200 to 207 are symmetrically inter-related by rotations and inversions, and used to fill the first 23 rows of the screen (23 avoids scrolling!). Some unusual designs can result from such inter and intra-character symmetry.

Listing 5.6

```
100 'animation using PRINT.
110 DEF SEG=0
120 PAGE%=PEEK(127)*&H100+PEEK(126)
130 ADDRESS%=PEEK(125)*&H100+PEEK(124)
140 DEF SEG=PAGE%
150 BLOAD "B:PATTERN.DAT",ADDRESS%
160 MODE%=1 : BACKGROUND%=4 : FOREGROUND%=1
170 GOSUB 60000 'colour monitor
180 PLANE$=CHR$(32)+CHR$(198)+CHR$(199)
190 FOR I%=1 TO 38
200 LOCATE  8,I% : PRINT PLANE$;
210 LOCATE 12,I% : PRINT PLANE$;
220 LOCATE 16,I% : PRINT PLANE$;
230 LOCATE 20,I% : PRINT PLANE$;
240 NEXT I%
250 GOSUB 60100 'monochrome monitor
260 END
```

Listing 5.6 demonstrates simple animation by PRINTing. Codes 198 and 199 store the two halves of an airplane character. Printing a space (ASCII 32) with these two characters at steadily increasing column positions across the screen blots out the old plane and replaces it with a new one moved one character position to the right. Animation!

Exercise 5.4

Add extensions to this character generator. Allow reflection of characters along diagonals, or perhaps the merging together of two characters. There are numerous possibilities. Create complex animation scenes with your characters, for example, construct the front view of a plane using three characters, and move the plane about the screen under keyboard control.

A Pixel Block Generator

Characters are of limited use in many graphics applications because they are of only
two colours, they are of fixed size, and they obliterate everything in the 8 by 8
pixels placed under them. The IBM PC has a much more powerful and useful object
– the pixel block (called a sprite on some other machines). These are rectangular
areas of arbitrary size which can hold pixels in any mode-allowable colour. The
method of constructing these blocks with graphics commands, GETting them off
the screen, and PUTting them back using AND, OR, XOR etc. at any screen position
was described in chapter 1. Even the CHARACTER GENERATOR above had to
use a pixel block for the animated drawing of the cursor-cross. Obviously, a PIXEL
BLOCK GENERATOR constructed along similar lines to the CHARACTER
GENERATOR, that is, in a modular approach, is a very powerful tool. Listing 5.7
is such a program.

Listing 5.7

```
100 ´ PIXEL BLOCK GENERATOR
110 CLS : OPTION BASE 1
120 INPUT"Type size of pixel block : NX% by NY% ",NX%,NY%
130 IF NX%<1 OR NX%>24 OR NY%<1 OR NY%>24 THEN GOTO 120
139 ´prepare grid, a large scale copy of pixel block, each pixel
        will be represented by a square block N% by N% pixels, position
        of top left corner is (XT%,YT%) and bottom right (XB%,YB%).
140 N1%=INT(200/NX%) : N2%=INT(200/NY%)
150 IF N1%<N2% THEN N%=N1% ELSE N%=N2%
160 XT%=120+INT((200-N%*NX%)/2) : YT%=INT((200-N%*NY%)/2)
170 XB%=XT%+(NX%-1)*N% : YB%=YT%+(NY%-1)*N%
179 ´prepare actual size pixel block, stored in BLOCK%.
180 BSIZE%=2+INT(INT((NX%*2+7)/8)*NY%/2+.5)
190 DIM CURSOR%(7),BLOCK%(BSIZE%)
200 BLOCK%(1)=2*NX% : BLOCK%(2)=NY%
209 ´prepare cross-cursor - place at (CURX%,CURY%)
210 DATA &HA,&H5,&H4,&H4,&H4055,&H4,&H4
220 FOR I%=1 TO 7 : READ CURSOR%(I%) : NEXT I%
230 CURX%=XT%+N%/2-3 : CURY%=YT%+N%/2-3
239 ´prepare graphics screen
240 MODE%=1 : PALETTE%=0 : BORDER%=0
250 BACKGROUND%=0 : FOREGROUND%=1
259 ´store logical constants
260 TRUE%=-1 : FALSE%=0
270 GOSUB 60000 ´colour monitor
280 GOSUB 500 ´menu
290 GOSUB 1000 ´supervisor
300 GOSUB 60100 ´monochrome monitor
310 END

500 ´menu display
501 ´**in ** TRUE%
502 ´**out** MENUONSCREEN%
510 CLS
520 LOCATE  1,14 : PRINT "KEYBOARD MENU";
530 LOCATE  3,10 : PRINT "M : menu display";
540 LOCATE  5,10 : PRINT "E : end generation";
550 LOCATE  7,10 : PRINT "L : layout routine
560 LOCATE  9,10 : PRINT "G : get pixel block";
570 LOCATE 11,10 : PRINT "P : put pixel block";
580 LOCATE 13,4  : PRINT "0,1,2,3 : change colour";
590 LOCATE 15,8  :
        PRINT CHR$(24);",";CHR$(25);" : move cursor up or down";
```

```
600 LOCATE 17,8  :
    PRINT CHR$(26);",";CHR$(27);" : move cursor right or left";
610 LOCATE 19,10 : PRINT "X : reflect in X axis";
620 LOCATE 21,10 : PRINT "Y : reflect in Y axis";
630 LOCATE 23,10 : PRINT "R : rotate";
640 LOCATE 25,10 : PRINT "I : invert colours";
650 MENUONSCREEN%=TRUE%
660 RETURN


1000 'supervisor routine
1001 '**in ** CURX%,CURY%,CURSOR%,MENUONSCREEN%
1009 'input action character from keyboard.
1010 KB$=INKEY$ :IF KB$="" THEN GOTO 1010
1020 LENKB%=LEN(KB$)
1030 IF LENKB%=1 THEN ASCKB%=ASC(KB$) : GOTO 1100
1040 ASCKB%=ASC(RIGHT$(KB$,1))
1049 'cursor control section
1050 IF ASCKB%=80 THEN MX%= 0 : MY%= 1 : GOSUB 3000 :
                    GOTO 1010 'cursor control
1060 IF ASCKB%=72 THEN MX%= 0 : MY%=-1 : GOSUB 3000 :
                    GOTO 1010 'cursor control
1070 IF ASCKB%=75 THEN MX%=-1 : MY%= 0 : GOSUB 3000 :
                    GOTO 1010 'cursor control
1080 IF ASCKB%=77 THEN MX%= 1 : MY%= 0 : GOSUB 3000 :
                    GOTO 1010 'cursor control
1090 GOTO 1010
1099 'lower case action character changed to upper case.
1100 IF ASCKB%>90 THEN ASCKB%=ASCKB%-32
1109 'call subroutine equivalent to action character.
1110 IF ASCKB%=ASC("M") THEN GOSUB 500  'menu
1120 IF ASCKB%=ASC("L") THEN GOSUB 2000 'layout block
1130 IF ASCKB%=ASC("G") THEN GOSUB 4000 'get routine
1140 IF ASCKB%=ASC("P") THEN GOSUB 4500 'put routine
1150 IF ASCKB%>=ASC("0") AND ASCKB%<=ASC("3")
     THEN GOSUB 3200 'change colour
1160 IF ASCKB%=ASC("X") THEN GOSUB 6200 'x-reflect routine
1170 IF ASCKB%=ASC("Y") THEN GOSUB 6400 'y-reflect routine
1180 IF ASCKB%=ASC("R") THEN GOSUB 6600 'rotate routine
1190 IF ASCKB%=ASC("I") THEN GOSUB 6000 'invert routine
1200 IF MENUONSCREEN% THEN GOTO 1230
1210 PUT (CURX%,CURY%),CURSOR%,XOR
1220 PUT (CURX%,CURY%),CURSOR%,XOR
1229 'go back for next action.
1230 IF ASCKB%<>ASC("E") THEN GOTO 1010
1240 RETURN


2000 'layout pixel block and grid
2001 '**in ** CURX%,CURY%,CURSOR%,BLOCK%,FALSE%
2002 '**out** MENUONSCREEN%
2010 CLS
2020 LINE (120,0)-(319,199),1,BF
2030 LINE (0,0)-(NX%+1,NY%+1),1,B
2040 PUT (1,1),BLOCK%
2050 GOSUB 3400 'pixel block to grid
2059 'place cursor on grid
2060 PUT (CURX%,CURY%),CURSOR%,XOR
2070 MENUONSCREEN%=FALSE%
2080 RETURN


3000 'move the cursor by (MX%*N%,MY%*N%)
3001 '**in ** CURX%,CURY%,CURSOR%,MX%,MY%,N%,
              XT%,YT%,XB%,YB%,MENUONSCREEN%
3002 '**out** CURX%,CURY%
3010 IF MENUONSCREEN% THEN RETURN
3020 NEWX%=CURX%+MX%*N%
3030 IF NEWX%<XT% OR NEWX%>XB%+N% THEN RETURN
3040 NEWY%=CURY%+MY%*N%
3050 IF NEWY%<YT% OR NEWY%>YB%+N% THEN RETURN
```

```
3060 PUT (CURX%,CURY%),CURSOR%,XOR
3070 CURX%=NEWX% : CURY%=NEWY%
3080 PUT (CURX%,CURY%),CURSOR%,XOR
3090 BEEP
3100 RETURN

3200 'change colour of pixel
3201 '**in ** CURX%,CURY%,CURSOR%,BLOCK%,ASCKB%,N%,
                XT%,YT%,NX%,NY%,MENUONSCREEN%
3210 IF MENUONSCREEN% THEN RETURN
3219 'change ASCII code to 0,1,2 or 3.
3220 COL%=ASCKB%-48
3229 'find (XP%,YP%) in pixel block equivalent to
        (CURX%,CURY%) in grid.
3230 XG%=CURX%-N%/2+3 : XP%=1+(XG%-XT%)/N%
3240 YG%=CURY%-N%/2+3 : YP%=1+(YG%-YT%)/N%
3249 'change colour of grid square
3250 LINE (XG%,YG%)-(XG%+N%-1,YG%+N%-1),3-COL%,BF
3260 LINE (XG%+1,YG%+1)-(XG%+N%-2,YG%+N%-2),COL%,BF
3269 'change colour of pixel in block
3270 PSET (XP%,YP%),COL%
3279 'replace cursor
3280 PUT (CURX%,CURY%),CURSOR%,XOR
3289 'store pixel block
3290 GET (1,1)-(NX%,NY%),BLOCK%
3300 RETURN

3400 'pixel block to grid calculation
3401 '**in ** N%,XT%,YT%,NX%,NY%
3409 'look at each pixel (XP%,YP%) in pixel block.
3410 X%=XT%-N%
3420 FOR XP%=1 TO NX%
3430 Y%=YT%-N% : X%=X%+N%
3440 FOR YP%=1 TO NY%
3450 Y%=Y%+N% : COL%=POINT(XP%,YP%)
3459 'fill in equivalent grid square at (X%,Y%).
3460 LINE (X%,Y%)-(X%+N%-1,Y%+N%-1),3-COL%,BF
3470 LINE (X%+1,Y%+1)-(X%+N%-2,Y%+N%-2),COL%,BF
3480 NEXT YP% : NEXT XP%
3490 RETURN

3600 'grid to pixel block calculation
3601 '**in ** N%,XT%,YT%,XB%,YB%
3609 'look at each square (X%,Y%) in grid.
3610 XP%=0
3620 FOR X%=XT% TO XB% STEP N%
3630 YP%=0 : XP%=XP%+1
3640 FOR Y%=YT% TO YB% STEP N%
3650 YP%=YP%+1 : COL%=POINT(X%+1,Y%+1)
3659 'colour in equivalent pixel (XP%,YP%).
3660 PSET (XP%,YP%),COL%
3670 NEXT Y% : NEXT X%
3680 RETURN

4000 'get pixel block from disk
4001 '**in ** BSIZE%
4002 '**out** BLOCK%
4010 CLS
4020 LOCATE 10,1 : PRINT"Type name of file that holds pixel block";
4030 LOCATE 11,1 : PRINT"e.g.   B:BLOCK.DAT";
4040 LOCATE 14,1 : INPUT F$
4050 OPEN "I",#1,F$
4060 FOR I%=1 TO BSIZE%
4070 INPUT#1,BLOCK%(I%)
4080 NEXT I%
4090 CLOSE
4100 GOSUB 500 'menu
4110 RETURN
```

```
4500 ´put pixel block on disk
4501 ´**in ** BSIZE%,BLOCK%
4510 CLS
4520 LOCATE 10,1 :
     PRINT "Type name of file that will hold pixel block";
4530 LOCATE 11,1 : PRINT"e.g.  B:BLOCK.DAT";
4540 LOCATE 14,1 : INPUT F$
4550 OPEN F$ FOR APPEND AS #1
4560 FOR I%=1 TO BSIZE%
4570 PRINT#1,BLOCK%(I%)
4580 NEXT I%
4590 CLOSE
4600 GOSUB 500 ´menu
4610 RETURN


6000 ´invert routine
6001 ´**in ** N%,XT%,YT%,NX%,NY%,CURX%,CURY%,
               CURSOR%,BLOCK%,MENUONSCREEN%
6002 ´**out** BLOCK%
6010 IF MENUONSCREEN% THEN RETURN
6019 ´look at each pixel (XP%,YP%) from pixel block.
6020 X%=XT%-N%
6030 FOR XP%=1 TO NX%
6040 Y%=YT%-N% : X%=X%+N%
6050 FOR YP%=1 TO NY%
6060 Y%=Y%+N% : COL%=POINT(XP%,YP%)
6069 ´invert colour of equivalent grid square (X%,Y%).
6070 LINE (X%,Y%)-(X%+N%-1,Y%+N%-1),COL%,BF
6080 LINE (X%+1,Y%+1)-(X%+N%-2,Y%+N%-2),3-COL%,BF
6090 NEXT YP% : NEXT XP%
6099 ´copy grid back to pixel block.
6100 GOSUB 3600 ´grid to pixel block
6109 ´replace cursor.
6110 PUT (CURX%,CURY%),CURSOR%,XOR
6119 ´store pixel block.
6120 GET (1,1)-(NX%,NY%),BLOCK%
6130 RETURN


6200 ´x-reflect routine
6201 ´**in ** N%,XT%,YT%,NX%,NY%,CURX%,CURY%,
               CURSOR%,BLOCK%,MENUONSCREEN%
6202 ´**out** BLOCK%
6210 IF MENUONSCREEN% THEN RETURN
6219 ´look at each pixel (XP%,YP%) from pixel block.
6220 X%=XT%-N%
6230 FOR XP%=1 TO NX%
6240 Y%=YT%-N% : X%=X%+N%
6250 FOR YP%=1 TO NY%
6259 ´find colour of x-reflected pixel (XP%,1+NY%-YP%).
6260 Y%=Y%+N% : COL%=POINT(XP%,1+NY%-YP%)
6269 ´copy this colour into grid point (X%,Y%)
        equivalent to original (XP%,YP%).
6270 LINE (X%,Y%)-(X%+N%-1,Y%+N%-1),3-COL%,BF
6280 LINE (X%+1,Y%+1)-(X%+N%-2,Y%+N%-2),COL%,BF
6290 NEXT YP% : NEXT XP%
6299 ´copy grid back to pixel block.
6300 GOSUB 3600 ´grid to pixel block
6309 ´replace cursor.
6310 PUT (CURX%,CURY%),CURSOR%,XOR
6319 ´store pixel block.
6320 GET (1,1)-(NX%,NY%),BLOCK%
6330 RETURN


6400 ´y-reflect routine
6401 ´**in ** N%,XT%,YT%,NX%,NY%,CURX%,CURY%,
               CURSOR%,BLOCK%,MENUONSCREEN%
6402 ´**out** BLOCK%
6410 IF MENUONSCREEN% THEN RETURN
```

```
6419 'look at each pixel (XP%,YP%) from pixel block.
6420 X%=XT%-N%
6430 FOR XP%=1 TO NX%
6440 Y%=YT%-N% : X%=X%+N%
6450 FOR YP%=1 TO NY%
6459 'find colour of y-reflected pixel (1+NX%-XP%,YP%).
6460 Y%=Y%+N% : COL%=POINT(1+NX%-XP%,YP%)
6469 'copy this colour into grid point (X%,Y%)
        equivalent to original (XP%,YP%).
6470 LINE (X%,Y%)-(X%+N%-1,Y%+N%-1),3-COL%,BF
6480 LINE (X%+1,Y%+1)-(X%+N%-2,Y%+N%-2),COL%,BF
6490 NEXT YP% : NEXT XP%
6499 'copy grid back to pixel block.
6500 GOSUB 3600 'grid to pixel block
6509 'replace cursor.
6510 PUT (CURX%,CURY%),CURSOR%,XOR
6519 'store pixel block.
6520 GET (1,1)-(NX%,NY%),BLOCK%
6530 RETURN

6600 'rotate routine
6601 '**in ** N%,XT%,YT%,NX%,NY%,CURX%,CURY%,
              CURSOR%,BLOCK%,MENUONSCREEN%
6602 '**out** BLOCK%
6610 IF MENUONSCREEN% THEN RETURN
6619 'only rotate square pixel blocks.
6620 IF NX%<>NY% THEN RETURN ELSE X%=XT%-N%
6629 'look at each pixel (XP%,YP%) from pixel block.
6630 FOR XP%=1 TO NX%
6640 Y%=YT%-N% : X%=X%+N%
6650 FOR YP%=1 TO NY%                              ｜
6659 'find colour of rotated pixel (NX%-YP%+1,XP%)
6660 Y%=Y%+N% : COL%=POINT(NX%-YP%+1,XP%)
6669 'copy this colour into grid point (X%,Y%)
        equivalent to original (XP%,YP%).
6670 LINE (X%,Y%)-(X%+N%-1,Y%+N%-1),3-COL%,BF
6680 LINE (X%+1,Y%+1)-(X%+N%-2,Y%+N%-2),COL%,BF
6690 NEXT YP% : NEXT XP%
6699 'copy grid back to pixel block.
6700 GOSUB 3600 'grid to pixel block
6709 'replace cursor.
6710 PUT (CURX%,CURY%),CURSOR%,XOR
6719 'store pixel block.
6720 GET (1,1)-(NX%,NY%),BLOCK%
6730 RETURN
```

The program has a 'layout' routine which plots a real-scale pixel block in the top left-hand corner of the screen that is NX% pixels across by NY% pixels down (maximum 24), and stores it in an integer array BLOCK% of size BSIZE%, which naturally depends on NX% and NY%. A grid of squares is drawn to the right of the pixel block, and is a large-scale representation of that block. In order that the grid fits on the screen, the size of each square (N% pixels) depends on NX% and NY%. Each square in the grid is Block Filled with the LINE command relative to some reference point. The top left-hand corner square has reference point (XT%, YT%) and that of the bottom right has (XB%, YB%). A 5 by 5 pixel block cross-cursor is READ from DATA and stored in array CURSOR% (7), and this can be drawn as pixel vector (CURX%, CURY%) inside the grid, where it can be moved about under control of the cursor keys.

The grid and pixel block can be manipulated with a variety of operations, each denoted by a single keyboard character. The list of operations and corresponding keys is printed out by a 'menu' routine. Since menu and grid will not fit together on the screen, the program must draw them separately. A flag, MENUONSCREEN%, lets the program know whether the menu is on the screen (TRUE% = −1) or not (FALSE% = 0) at any given time. As with listing 5.4, there is a 'supervisor' routine which loops around, waiting on keyboard input that will initiate calls to grid/block or screen manipulation routines. The flag MENUONSCREEN% makes sure that blocks are not manipulated when the grid is not on the screen (since these modules GET the pixel block from the top left-hand corner of the screen).

Some typical calls are described below, although readers are expected to extend this list.

(1) "M" clears the screen and draws the Menu.

(2) "E" Ends the generation.

(3) "L" takes the pixel block from array BLOCK% (blank to start with), PUTs it on the screen and then draws the equivalent grid Layout.

(4) "G" Gets a single pixel block from a file on disk and stores it in the array BLOCK%, PUTs it on the screen and then constructs the equivalent grid.

(5) "P" Puts the pixel block onto disk by APPENDing to the back of a specified file. In this way a complete set of pixel blocks can be stored in a file for future use, for example, see listing 5.8.

(6) "0", "1", "2" or "3" changes both the grid square pointed to by the cursor (top left-hand corner (XG%, YG%)) and the equivalent pixel in the block (pixel (XP%, YP%)) to the specified numeric logical colour.

(7) The cursor keys are used to move the cross-cursor over the grid, in a manner similar to that in the CHARACTER GENERATOR; however, now the increment size depends on the size of the grid.

(8) "X" takes the colour of each (XP%, YP%) pixel from the block, finds the grid square (X%, Y%) that is equivalent to the pixel reflected about a line in the X-direction through the block centre, and gives the square that colour. Finally the grid is copied back to the block.

(9) "Y" takes the colour of each (XP%, YP%) pixel from the block, finds the grid square (X%, Y%) that is equivalent to the pixel reflected about a line in the Y-direction through the block centre, and gives the square that colour. Finally the grid is copied back to the block.

(10) "R" Rotates square pixel blocks. It takes the colour of each (XP%, YP%) pixel from the block, finds the grid square (X%, Y%) that is equivalent to that pixel rotated anticlockwise about the centre, and gives it that colour. Finally the grid is copied back to the block.

(11) "I" Inverts all the colours in a pixel block. It takes the colour of each (XP%, YP%) pixel from the block, finds the grid square (X%, Y%) that is equivalent to the pixel, and gives it the inverted colour: logical colour I ($0 \leqslant I \leqslant 3$) is inverted to colour $3 - I$. Finally the grid is copied back to the block.

Exercise 5.5
Extend the PIXEL BLOCK GENERATOR. Allow merging of blocks, or have a
variety of colour changes (not just inversion). You could have a symmetric fill
option; that is, given one-quarter of the pixel block, the computer fills in the other
three by reflection or rotation.

Exercise 5.6
The PIXEL BLOCK GENERATOR creates pixel blocks for mode 1 displays. Alter
the program so that the blocks created may be used with mode 2.

The use of pixel blocks is a very powerful facility of the IBM PC and the PIXEL
BLOCK GENERATOR, together with any extensions you may add, should prove
extremely useful. Two examples of its use are given. The first is a recursive solution
of the Eight Queens Problem, that of placing eight queens on an 8 by 8 chessboard
so that no queen captures any other. Note that a queen may capture along horizontal, vertical, and the major and minor diagonal directions. Since there can only be
one queen in any given column, we store a solution to the problem in an array
ROWINCOL%. That is, the queen in column I lies in row ROWINCOL% (I). Also
since there can only be one queen in any one row, the 8 values of ROWINCOL%
must be a permutation of the first 8 positive integers. Therefore, a solution to the
problem is found by just running through all the permutations of the list of numbers
1 to 8, checking to see if any of the corresponding queens are captured diagonally
from the left.

Recursion is used to solve the general problem of permuting a list of N elements.
The first element of the list is fixed and the remaining N − 1 permuted. Then the
original list is rotated one place to the left, a new first element is fixed and the
remaining N − 1 elements are permuted. Repeating this process N times completes
the permutation. That is, permutation is defined in terms of permutation − and so
a routine that solves this problem calls itself! At any time during execution, the
number of calls to the recursive routine that can be traced directly back to the first
call is called the level of recursion at that time. This process will not go on
indefinitely (that is, it will not have infinite level) since recursion stops when
eventually an empty list is reached.

This method is used for the Eight Queens Problem. The numbers 1 to 8 are
placed in the array ROWINCOL% and these 8 elements are permuted. At level 1
the list is rotated into 8 separate positions, and the first position is fixed for each
and the routine called at level 2 to permute the last 7 elements in the array. Each
of these calls consists of 7 separate rotations in which the second element is fixed
and the last 6 elements in the array are permuted at level 3, and so on to level 9.
If at any time a level is reached (COL% say) where the equivalent queen in column
COL%, row ROWINCOL% (COL%) is captured from the left by a queen fixed at an
earlier level, then there is no need to continue with the sequence of recursion: just
give up and go back to level COL% − 1. The permutation routine has to keep track
of the rotations occurring at all levels. In some computer languages it is possible to

have local variables which take on new values whenever a recursive routine is entered, and recoup their old values on exit. This is not available in BASICA so instead the program uses an array INDEX% (8) to store the one variable needing the local property; INDEX% (COL%) stores a value denoting how many rotations have been completed at the present incarnation of level COL%.

The chessboard is constructed as an 8 by 8 grid of squares, each square being 24 pixels square. Best results are achieved by RUNning the program in MODE% = 1 and PALETTE% = 0. The squares are made from two types of pixel blocks: BLANK1% holds a black (logical 0) square with red (logical 2) edge, and BLANK2% is a brown (logical 3) square with a red edge. The program alternates the PUTting of the blocks on the grid to give the checkerboard pattern. Two more pixel blocks, QUEEN1% and QUEEN2%, are used to hold a red queen on black and brown squares (with red edges) respectively. All four pixel blocks are stored on a file "B:PIECES.DAT" constructed by the PIXEL BLOCK GENERATOR. Figure 5.2 gives a description of QUEEN1%.

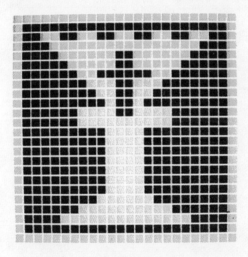

Figure 5.2

The program draws a queen at the correct position whenever it fixes an array value for a given column in the recursive routine, and blanks it out when it finishes with that value. The position of the grid is used to define whether a black or a brown square is used.

Exercise 5.7
Use the PIXEL BLOCK GENERATOR to create a complete chess set. Use the knight to program the Knight's Tour Problem. Really ambitious programmers can program their IBM PC to play chess (see Liffick, 1979).

Listing 5.8

```
100 ´ THE EIGHT QUEENS PROBLEM
109 ´prepare screen.
110 OPTION BASE 1
120 MODE%=1 : PALETTE%=0 : FALSE%=0
130 GOSUB 60000 ´colour monitor
139 ´ROWINCOL%(I) is the row position of the queen in column I%.
        INDEX% is used for recursion.
140 DIM ROWINCOL%(8),INDEX%(8)
149 ´setup so each row and each column contains only one queen.
150 FOR I%=1 TO 8 : ROWINCOL%(I%)=I% : NEXT I%
160 GOSUB 3000 ´draw the board
169 ´permute so property (149) is maintained, however,
        we must also check no diagonal contains >1 queen.
        Start in first column.
170 COL%=1 : GOSUB 1000 ´place queens from column COL to right.
180 GOSUB 60100 ´monochrome display
190 END


1000 ´place queens from column COL% to right.
1001 ´**in ** COL%,INDEX%,ROWINCOL%,FALSE%,
                BLANK1%,BLANK2%,QUEEN1%,QUEEN2%
1002 ´**out** COL%,INDEX%,ROWINCOL%
1009 ´no column 9, queens have been successfully placed.
1010 IF COL%=9 THEN GOSUB 2000 : RETURN ´we have a solution
1018 ´no local variables, so FOR loop replaced by WHILE loop,
        with loop index of present COL% stored in INDEX%(COL%).
        All the possible ROW% positions for present COL% that
1019 ´prevent horizontal capture by a queen to the left are
        in ROWINCOL%(COL% -> 8). Rotate through these ROWs.
1020 INDEX%(COL%)=COL%
1030 WHILE INDEX%(COL%)<9
1039 ´queen in column COL% is now in row ROW%.
1040 ROW%=ROWINCOL%(COL%)
1049 ´check background of square and draw queen.
1050 IF (ROW%+COL%) MOD 2 = 0
        THEN PUT(-20+24*COL%,-20+24*ROW%),QUEEN1%,PSET
        ELSE PUT(-20+24*COL%,-20+24*ROW%),QUEEN2%,PSET
1059 ´check if this queen is taken diagonally by queens to its left.
1060 TAKEN%=FALSE%
1070 IF COL%=1 THEN GOTO 1120
1080 FOR I%=1 TO COL%-1
1090 TAKEN%=TAKEN% OR ((COL%-I%)=ABS(ROWINCOL%(COL%)-ROWINCOL%(I%)))
1100 NEXT I%
1110 IF TAKEN% THEN GOTO 1150
1119 ´recursively place queens from column COL%+1 to right.
1120 COL%=COL%+1
1130 GOSUB 1000 ´place queens to right
1139 ´try next position of queen in present column COL%.
1140 COL%=COL%-1
1149 ´next ROW% position cannot be in ROWINCOL%(1 -> COL%-1),
        so rotate section of the array ROWINCOL%(COL% ->8).
1150 IF COL%=8 THEN GOTO 1210
1160 ROW%=ROWINCOL%(COL%)
1170 FOR I%=COL%+1 TO 8
1180 ROWINCOL%(I%-1)=ROWINCOL%(I%)
1190 NEXT I%
1200 ROWINCOL%(8)=ROW%
1209 ´blank out queen in column COL%, and find next queen.
1210 IF (ROW%+COL%) MOD 2 = 0
        THEN PUT(-20+24*COL%,-20+24*ROW%),BLANK1%,PSET
        ELSE PUT(-20+24*COL%,-20+24*ROW%),BLANK2%,PSET
1220 INDEX%(COL%)=INDEX%(COL%)+1
1230 WEND
1240 RETURN
```

```
2000 ´solution message
2010 LOCATE 3,29 : PRINT"You have a"
2020 LOCATE 5,30 : PRINT"solution"
2030 LOCATE 7,33 : PRINT"to"
2040 LOCATE 19,28 : PRINT"type any key"
2050 LOCATE 21,28 : PRINT"to CONTINUE"
2059 ´play a tune!
2060 PLAY"MF MS T140 O2 L16 EFG O3 C+10 O2 G+ O3 C+4"
2069 ´before continuing blank out solution message.
2070 A$=INKEY$ : IF A$="" THEN GOTO 2070
2080 LINE (200,0)-(319,56),0,BF
2090 LINE (200,144)-(319,199),0,BF
2100 RETURN

3000 ´ draw the board
3002 ´**out** BLANK1%,BLANK2%,QUEEN1%,QUEEN2%
3009 ´pieces can be on a black or a yellow square.
     INPUT data on two blanks and two queens,
     each is a 24 by 24 pixel block.
3010 DIM BLANK1%(74),BLANK2%(74),QUEEN1%(74),QUEEN2%(74)
3020 OPEN "I",#1,"B:PIECES.DAT"
3030 FOR I%=1 TO 74 : INPUT #1,BLANK1%(I%) : NEXT I%
3040 FOR I%=1 TO 74 : INPUT #1,BLANK2%(I%) : NEXT I%
3050 FOR I%=1 TO 74 : INPUT #1,QUEEN1%(I%) : NEXT I%
3060 FOR I%=1 TO 74 : INPUT #1,QUEEN2%(I%) : NEXT I%
3070 CLOSE
3079 ´draw background.
3080 LINE (0,0)-(199,199),1,BF
3090 LINE (3,3)-(196,196),2,BF
3099 ´alternate between black and yellow squares.
3100 FLAG%=0
3110 FOR COL%=4 TO 172 STEP 24
3120 FOR ROW%=4 TO 172 STEP 24
3130 IF FLAG%=0 THEN PUT(COL%,ROW%),BLANK1%,PSET
              ELSE PUT(COL%,ROW%),BLANK2%,PSET
3140 FLAG%=1-FLAG%
3150 NEXT ROW% : FLAG%=1-FLAG% : NEXT COL%
3159 ´print title.
3160 LOCATE 9,33 : PRINT "The"
3170 LOCATE 11,32 : PRINT "Eight"
3180 LOCATE 13,32 : PRINT "QUEENS"
3190 LOCATE 15,31 : PRINT "Problem"
3200 RETURN
```

Exercise 5.8

The previous program used two different blanks and two queens. By clever use of
PUT (with AND, OR etc.) it is possible to use fewer pixel blocks (but more PUTs?).
Change the program to do this, using the PIXEL BLOCK GENERATOR to create
any blocks that you need. You could also use multicoloured rather than two-
coloured pixel blocks for the queen, in which case limiting the number of versions
of each symbol could be more difficult.

The second application of pixel blocks will be very useful for drawing data
diagrams in chapter 6. Diagrams in mode 2 have 80 horizontal columns in which to
put character labels. Mode 1, however, only allows 40 columns, which is unsuitable,
especially when several numerical labels are needed on a horizontal axis. One
solution is to construct 'narrow' numerals as pixel blocks and store them as a file
"B:NARROW.DAT". Figure 5.3 shows a set of 13, 4 by 8 pixel blocks, representing the decimal digits, plus, minus and decimal point. Listing 5.9 includes a routine

Figure 5.3

that uses these blocks to take a numeric character string and turn it into an equivalent string of narrow pixel blocks on the screen.

Listing 5.9

```
100 OPTION BASE 1
110 MODE%=1
120 GOSUB 5000 ´setup narrow characters
130 GOSUB 60000 ´colour monitor
139 ´prepare narrow string NUM$ and position it at (X%,Y%).
140 NUM$="1234567890+-."
150 X%=20 : Y%=20
160 GOSUB 5500 ´narrow print
170 GOSUB 60100 ´monochrome display
180 END

5000 ´setup narrow characters from disk
5002 ´**out** NARROW%,BUFFER%
5010 DIM NARROW%(78),BUFFER%(6)
5020 OPEN "I",#1,"B:NARROW.DAT"
5030 FOR I%=1 TO 78
5040 INPUT#1,NARROW%(I%)
5050 NEXT I%
5060 CLOSE
5070 RETURN

5500 ´narrow print routine
5501 ´**in ** X%,Y%,NUM$,NARROW%,BUFFER%
5510 XP%=X%
5519 ´look at each character in string.
5520 FOR I%=1 TO LEN(NUM$)
5530 CHAR$=MID$(NUM$,I%,1)
5540 IF CHAR$>="0" AND CHAR$<="9" THEN CHAR%=(ASC(CHAR$)-48)*6
     ELSE IF CHAR$="+" THEN CHAR%=60
           ELSE IF CHAR$="-" THEN CHAR%=66 ELSE CHAR%=72
5549 ´copy narrow version of character into buffer.
5550 FOR J%=1 TO 6
```

```
5560 BUFFER%(J%)=NARROW%(CHAR%+J%)
5570 NEXT J%
5579 'PUT narrow symbol on screen.
5580 PUT (XP%,Y%),BUFFER%
5590 XP%=XP%+4
5600 NEXT I%
5610 RETURN
```

Exercise 5.9

Extend the narrow set by adding %, =, * etc., and change the printout routine accordingly. Then produce another narrow set that can be used to print vertical narrow labels.

Exercise 5.10

Extend the PIXEL BLOCK GENERATOR to enable you to construct a set of large-scale alphabetic symbols, pixel blocks 16 pixels square (double the size of a normal character in both dimensions), and use them in a labelling routine. The routine should print a normal-size character in the bottom left-hand corner of the screen and copy it onto the 16 by 16 grid, so that each pixel in the character is drawn as a 2 by 2 pixel block in the grid. The double-size character thus created will look rather ragged, so you should use the original GENERATOR program to tidy it up.

As it stands, this pixel block will be of logical 3 foreground colour on a logical 0 background. You do not need to redefine a new pixel block for each symbol if you want to display it with different choices of BACKGROUND% and FORE-GROUND% colour. Use LINE with Block Fill in colour FOREGROUND% XOR BACKGROUND% to create a 16 by 16 pixel block in the screen area that will hold the final symbol, and PUT (AND) the double-size symbol on top. Then GET this new symbol into a buffer that is capable of holding a block of this size. Use a Block Filled LINE to refill the area in colour BACKGROUND% and PUT (XOR) the buffer on top to get the required effect. A simplified version of this method is used in chapter 6 to PRINT coloured characters. Can you think of any other way of solving this problem?

Having mentioned data diagrams on a number of occasions in this chapter, it is time to lead on to the construction of these figures in the next chapter.

Complete Programs

'lib0' must be MERGED with all the listings given below.

  I. Listing 5.1 ('display of character sets'). Initially type "1" for the fixed set and "2" for the variable set. Subsequently type "Y" to see the alternative set; any other key terminates the program.
 II. Listing 5.2 ('search through memory'). No data required.

III. Listing 5.3 ('rotate characters'). Add the 'display' routine of listing 5.1. No
data required. Program creates file "B:ROTCHARS.DAT".
IV. Listing 5.4 ('CHARACTER GENERATOR'). Add the 'display' routine of
listing 5.1. Extensive number of operations available: see the text for full
details.
V. Listing 5.5 ('tessellated pattern'). Use listing 5.4 to create file
"B:PATTERN.DAT" on disk — see figure 5.1 of the text. This is the only
data required.
VI. Listing 5.6 ('airplane animation'). Use listing 5.4 to create file
"B:PATTERN.DAT" on disk — see figure 5.1 of the text. This is the only
data required.
VII. Listing 5.7 ('PIXEL BLOCK GENERATOR'). Extensive number of operations
available: see the text for full details.
VIII. Listing 5.8 ('Eight Queens Problem'). Program requires pixel blocks from disk
file "B:PIECES.DAT", created with listing 5.7 using figure 5.2.
IX. Listing 5.9 ('narrow symbols'). Program creates disk file "B:NARROW.DAT".
Data required is indicated by figure 5.3 of text.

All three files 'ROTCHARS.DAT", "PIECES.DAT" and "NARROW.DAT"
are to be found on the diskette accompanying this book.

6 Data Diagrams

The use of computer-generated diagrams to represent massive amounts of information in a simple, easy to understand pictorial form is probably the most widely used
application of microcomputer graphics. Data collection of every kind has exploded
with the advent of low-cost personal computers. Even the smallest companies now
rely on computers like the IBM PC to keep records, to send bills and, just as
important, to keep statistics on the state of the business. Reams of tabular numerical output are certainly not suitable for interpreting such masses of information.
Data diagrams are the answer. Scientists have always used such pictures, but business-
men have considered them to be of secondary importance, mainly because of the
time and expense needed for their construction. Computer graphics has ended all
that. Now it is relatively straightforward to use microcomputers to construct
instantaneously bar-charts, histograms, pie-charts, continuous and discrete graphs,
as well as many other types of figure. This chapter will describe some techniques
needed to produce an interactive programming package that will draw the above-
mentioned diagrams. It is hoped that the reader will take the package and extend it,
and then use the ideas presented here to create a program that will draw other types
of diagram. Before running any of the programs given below, in fact before entering
the BASICA interpreter, the user should type GRAPHICS so that the Print Screen
key can dump out any diagram on the printer, and GRAFTABL so that space in the
memory for a character set is organised and the pointers to this set are initialised.

It is essential that a well-organised modular approach is used to construct the
package. The brief outline view presented in this chapter is a typical approach for
solving the problem of drawing data diagrams on a microcomputer. The package is
divided into five major sections:

(a) preparation and supervision: listing 6.1.
(b) labelling diagrams: listing 6.2.
(c) constructing bar-charts or histograms: listings 6.3 and 6.4.
(d) constructing pie-charts: listing 6.5.
(e) constructing scientific graphs: listing 6.6.

These major tasks are broken down into inter-related subtasks, each subtask
being programmed as a separate subroutine. All five sections must now be considered at length, so that the reader may understand the underlying organisation
given here before going on to bigger and better programs. It is hoped that the reader
will extend these sections as indicated in the text, and eventually add new extra
sections.

Preparation and Supervision

All programming packages need a section in which elements fundamental to the package as a whole must be created. This section, programmed in listing 6.1, initialises information, declares arrays, reads in data from external files and lays out utility subroutines needed by the other four sections. All data diagrams given in this package are drawn in graphical mode 1 in order to take advantage of colour on the IBM PC, a fact declared at this stage. It is here that the palette, colour of paper and background and the aspect ratio are defined. Certain areas will be filled by tile-PAINTing in the later four sections, so arrays with information about sixteen different tiles and associated boundary colours are initialised (the first four tiles relate to the four logical colours). If they wish, users may increase the number of tiles or change any of the sixteen values; however, care must be taken to avoid Illegal Function Calls in a PAINT call (see chapter 1).

Control of this section of the program is given to the 'diagram supervisor' routine (the same idea was used in the GENERATOR programs of chapter 5), which loops waiting for keyboard input. The input of certain characters initiates calls to the various routines.

(1) "M" calls a Menu routine which clears the screen and displays all the options with the corresponding characters. This means that any diagram on the screen must be cleared before the menu is displayed. It is essential that a copy of that diagram is made, so that it may be restored to the screen for future additions. The contents of the screen buffer are therefore regularly stored in the integer array SKREEN% (8002): two integer locations hold the x and y information on the pixel block, and the remaining 8000 hold the 16000 bytes of the screen buffer.

(2) "E" Ends the diagram construction, terminates the program and returns control to the monochrome display.

(3) "N" clears the screen in a requested PAPER colour, ready for a New diagram. Initially the PAPER% colour is set to logical 3.

(4) "S" clears the screen and requests the name of a disk file, PUTs SKREEN% back on the screen and then Stores the screen buffer, locations &H0 to &H3FFF of segment &HB800, on disk as the named file.

(5) "R" clears the screen and requests the name of the disk file holding a previously stored screen buffer. The routine Reloads this information back onto the screen. GET is then used to store the redrawn diagram in SKREEN%.

(6) "B" Brings the diagram stored in SKREEN% to the screen, destroying any previous display. This is used mainly for over-drawing the menu display.

The remaining five entries are for the separate diagram construction sections ((b), (c), (d) and two forms of (e)) mentioned above.

(7) "L" calls the routine for interactively Labelling a diagram.

(8) "H" initiates the Histogram or bar-chart routine.

(9) "P" initiates the Pie-chart routine.

(10) "C" calls a routine for drawing Continuous graphs.

(11) "D" calls a routine for drawing Discrete graphs.

Listing 6.1

```
100 ´    DATA DIAGRAM PROGRAM
110 CLS : OPTION BASE 1
119 ´prepare cursor-cross.
120 DIM CURSOR%(7),SKREEN%(8002),BLANK%(18)
130 RESTORE 140
140 DATA &HA,&H5,&H4,&H4,&H4055,&H4,&H4
150 FOR I%=1 TO 7 : READ CURSOR%(I%) : NEXT I%
160 CURX%=160 : CURY%=100 : INC%=8
170 GOSUB 5000 ´setup narrow characters
179 ´load character set : remember to load GRAFTABL first
180 DEF SEG=0
190 PAGE%=PEEK(127)*&H100+PEEK(126)
200 ADDRESS%=PEEK(125)*&H100+PEEK(124)
210 DEF SEG=PAGE% : BLOAD"B:ROTCHARS.DAT",ADDRESS%
219 ´prepare screen.
220 MODE%=1 : ASPECT=1
230 INPUT"palette and background ? ",PALETTE%,BACKGROUND%
239 ´setup logical values.
240 TRUE%=-1 : FALSE%=0
250 DIM TILE$(16),BOUND%(16)
260 BOUND%(1)=2
270 BOUND%(2)=1
280 BOUND%(3)=0
290 BOUND%(4)=3
300 TILE$(5)=CHR$(&H11)+CHR$(&H44)  : BOUND%(5)=2
310 TILE$(6)=CHR$(&H22)+CHR$(&H88)  : BOUND%(6)=1
320 TILE$(7)=CHR$(&H33)+CHR$(&HCC)  : BOUND%(7)=0
330 TILE$(8)=CHR$(&H66)+CHR$(&H99)  : BOUND%(8)=0
340 TILE$(9)=CHR$(&H77)+CHR$(&HDD)  : BOUND%(9)=2
350 TILE$(10)=CHR$(&HBB)+CHR$(&HEE) : BOUND%(10)=1
360 TILE$(11)=CHR$(&H0)+CHR$(&HA)  : BOUND%(11)=0
370 TILE$(12)=CHR$(&H0)+CHR$(&H2A)+CHR$(&H2A)+CHR$(&F2A) :
    BOUND%(12)=0
380 TILE$(13)=CHR$(&H1B)+CHR$(&H6A)+CHR$(&HB1)+CHR$(&HA6) :
    BOUND%(13)=0
390 TILE$(14)=CHR$(&H55)+CHR$(&H11) : BOUND%(14)=0
400 TILE$(15)=CHR$(&H55)+CHR$(&H66) : BOUND%(15)=1
410 TILE$(16)=CHR$(&HFF)+CHR$(&HEE) : BOUND%(16)=2
420 GOSUB 60000 ´colour monitor
430 PAPER%=3 : GOSUB 2540 ´new screen
440 GOSUB 1500   ´diagram menu
450 GOSUB 1000   ´diagram supervisor
460 GOSUB 60100 ´monochrome monitor
470 END

1000 ´ diagram supervisor routine
1010 GOSUB 2000 ´keyboard input
1020 IF LENKB%=2 THEN GOTO 1010
1030 IF ASCKB%>90 THEN ASCKB%=ASCKB%-32
1040 IF ASCKB%=ASC("M") THEN GOSUB 1500 ´diagram menu
1050 IF ASCKB%=ASC("N") THEN GOSUB 2500 : GOSUB 1500 ´new diagram
1060 IF ASCKB%=ASC("R") THEN GOSUB 4000 ´reload diagram routine
1070 IF ASCKB%=ASC("S") THEN GOSUB 4500 ´store diagram routine
1080 IF ASCKB%=ASC("B") THEN PUT (0,0),SKREEN%,PSET
1090 IF ASCKB%=ASC("L") THEN GOSUB 10000 ´label routine
1100 IF ASCKB%=ASC("H") THEN GOSUB 20000 ´histogram routine
1110 IF ASCKB%=ASC("P") THEN GOSUB 30000 ´pie-chart routine
1120 IF ASCKB%=ASC("C") THEN GOSUB 40000 ´continuous graph
1130 IF ASCKB%=ASC("D") THEN GOSUB 50000 ´discrete graph
1140 IF ASCKB%<>ASC("E") THEN GOTO 1010
1150 RETURN
```

```
1500 ´diagram menu routine
1510 CLS
1520 LOCATE  2,14 : PRINT "DIAGRAM MENU";
1530 LOCATE  4,10 : PRINT "M : menu routine";
1540 LOCATE  6,10 : PRINT "E : end generation";
1550 LOCATE  8,10 : PRINT "N : new diagram";
1560 LOCATE 10,10 : PRINT "R : reload diagram";
1570 LOCATE 12,10 : PRINT "S : store diagram";
1580 LOCATE 14,10 : PRINT "B : bring diagram to screen";
1590 LOCATE 16,10 : PRINT "L : label diagram";
1600 LOCATE 18,10 : PRINT "H : histogram or bar-chart";
1610 LOCATE 20,10 : PRINT "P : pie-chart";
1620 LOCATE 22,10 : PRINT "C : continuous graph";
1630 LOCATE 24,10 : PRINT "D : discrete graph";
1640 RETURN

2000 ´ keyboard input routine
2002 ´**out** ASCKB%,LENKB%
2009 ´find ASCII code ASCKB% of key pressed.
2010 KB$=INKEY$ : LENKB%=LEN(KB$)
2020 IF LENKB%=2 THEN KB$=RIGHT$(KB$,1)
2030 IF KB$="" THEN GOTO 2010
2040 ASCKB%=ASC(KB$)
2050 RETURN

2500 ´ new diagram / clear the screen
2502 ´**out** PAPER%,SKREEN%
2509 ´fill SKREEN% with colour PAPER%.
2510 CLS : INPUT"ARE YOU SURE?(Y/N) ";F$
2520 IF F$<>"Y" AND F$<>"y" THEN RETURN
2530 INPUT"colour of paper ";PAPER%
2540 LINE (0,0)-(319,199),PAPER%,BF
2550 GET (0,0)-(319,199),SKREEN%
2560 RETURN

3000 ´ cursor control
3001 ´**in ** CURX%,CURY%,CURSOR%,MENUONSCREEN%
3002 ´**out** CURX%,CURY%
3010 IF MENUONSCREEN% THEN RETURN
3019 ´cursor centre is (CURX%,CURY%) so PUT the 5 by 5
     pixel block at (CURX%-2,CURY%-2).
3020 PUT (CURX%-2,CURY%-2),CURSOR%,XOR
3029 ´cursor movement controlled by keyboard input.
3030 GOSUB 2000 ´keyboard input
3039 ´Home key swaps cursor increment step between 1 and 8.
3040 IF ASCKB%=71 THEN INC%= 9-INC% : GOTO 3030
3049 ´cursor keys move cursor cross down,up,left,right.
3050 IF ASCKB%=80 THEN MX%= 0 : MY%= INC% : GOSUB 3500 : GOTO 3030
3060 IF ASCKB%=72 THEN MX%= 0 : MY%=-INC% : GOSUB 3500 : GOTO 3030
3070 IF ASCKB%=75 THEN MX%=-INC% : MY%= 0 : GOSUB 3500 : GOTO 3030
3080 IF ASCKB%=77 THEN MX%= INC% : MY%= 0 : GOSUB 3500 : GOTO 3030
3089 ´keys 0,1,2 or 3 puts dot of that colour at cursor centre.
3090 IF ASCKB%>47 AND ASCKB%<52
     THEN PSET (CURX%,CURY%),(ASCKB%-48) XOR 1 : GOTO 3030
3099 ´End key terminates cursor control.
3100 IF ASCKB%=79 THEN PUT (CURX%-2,CURY%-2),CURSOR%,XOR : RETURN
3110 GOTO 3030

3500 ´move the cursor cross at (CURX%,CURY%) by (MX%,MY%)
3501 ´**in ** CURX%,CURY%,CURSOR%,MX%,MY%
3502 ´**out** CURX%,CURY%
3509 ´find new position of cursor cross (NEWX%,NEWY%) and
     check that the cross lies totally on the screen.
3510 NEWX%=CURX%+MX%
3520 IF NEWX%<2 OR NEWX%>317 THEN RETURN
3530 NEWY%=CURY%+MY%
3540 IF NEWY%<2 OR NEWY%>197 THEN RETURN
3549 ´remove old cursor cross.
3550 PUT (CURX%-2,CURY%-2),CURSOR%,XOR
```

```
3560 CURX%=NEWX%  :  CURY%=NEWY%
3569 ´draw new cursor cross.
3570 PUT (CURX%-2,CURY%-2),CURSOR%,XOR
3580 BEEP
3590 RETURN

4000 ´reload diagram from disk : GET it in SKREEN%
4002 ´**out** SKREEN%
4010 CLS
4020 LOCATE 10,1 : PRINT"Type name of file that holds picture";
4030 LOCATE 11,1 : PRINT"e.g.  B:PICCY.PIC";
4040 LOCATE 14,1 : INPUT F$
4050 DEF SEG=&HB800 : BLOAD F$,0
4060 GET (0,0)-(319,199),SKREEN%
4070 RETURN

4500 ´store diagram on disk from SKREEN%
4501 ´**in ** SKREEN%
4510 CLS
4520 LOCATE 10,1 : PRINT"Type name of file that will hold picture";
4530 LOCATE 11,1 : PRINT"e.g.  B:DIAGRAM.PIC";
4540 LOCATE 14,1 : INPUT F$
4550 CLS : PUT (0,0),SKREEN%,PSET
4560 DEF SEG=&HB800 : BSAVE F$,0,&H3FFF
4570 GOSUB 1500 ´diagram menu
4580 RETURN

5000 ´setup narrow characters from disk
5002 ´**out** NARROW%,BUFFER%
5010 DIM NARROW%(78),BUFFER%(6)
5020 OPEN "I",#1,"B:NARROW.DAT"
5030 FOR I%=1 TO 78
5040 INPUT#1,NARROW%(I%)
5050 NEXT I%
5060 CLOSE
5070 RETURN

5500 ´narrow print routine
5501 ´**in ** X%,Y%,NUM$,NARROW%,BUFFER%
5510 XP%=X%
5519 ´look at each character in string.
5520 FOR I%=1 TO LEN(NUM$)
5530 CHAR$=MID$(NUM$,I%,1)
5540 IF CHAR$>="0" AND CHAR$<="9" THEN CHAR%=(ASC(CHAR$)-48)*6
     ELSE IF CHAR$="+" THEN CHAR%=60
         ELSE IF CHAR$="-" THEN CHAR%=66 ELSE CHAR%=72
5549 ´copy narrow version of character into buffer.
5550 FOR J%=1 TO 6
5560 BUFFER%(J%)=NARROW%(CHAR%+J%)
5570 NEXT J%
5579 ´PUT narrow symbol on screen.
5580 PUT (XP%,Y%),BUFFER%
5590 XP%=XP%+4
5600 NEXT I%
5610 RETURN
```

Listing 6.1 also contains utility routines needed by the diagram construction routines. One routine returns the ASCII code (ASCKB%) of any key that is pressed on the keyboard. The 'narrow' pixel block symbols of chapter 5 must be loaded from file "B:NARROW.DAT" together with its printout procedure of listing 5.9. The character set "B:ROTCHARS.DAT" created by listing 5.3 is loaded into locations pointed to by the contents of addresses 124 to 127 of segment 0. This set may be extended, using the CHARACTER GENERATOR, to include other symbols needed for specific labelling tasks.

Like all interactive graphics programs, a cursor-cross (or similar symbol) capable of control from the keyboard (or another input device) must be defined. The method of cursor-cross animation is exactly that used in the previous chapter. A cursor-control routine loops through a sequence of keyboard inputs; each input initiates a call to another routine which executes a single step movement of the cursor-cross using PUT (with XOR) both to delete the old cursor-cross and to redraw it in a new position on the screen. The cross is stored as a small 5 by 5 pixel block centred at pixel (CURX%, CURY%) in the integer array CURSOR% and defined like that in the GENERATOR programs of chapter 5. The cursor is capable of vertical or horizontal jumps of INC% pixels, where INC% flips between 1 and 8 by pressing the Home key. The control routine is executed only when there is a diagram on the screen. The use of a flag MENUONSCREEN% avoids any possibility of moving the cursor over a menu. In later exercises (such as 6.1) it will be necessary to move a different cursor-cross over the menu! Exit from the cursor-control routine is not automatic: the operator must press the End key to return the present centre position (CURX%, CURY%) of the cursor-cross to the calling routine.

Typing a numeric key 0, 1, 2 or 3 while still in the cursor routine causes a dot of that logical colour to be drawn at the centre of the cursor-cross. This will be used in a labelling routine that follows.

Labelling

Whatever diagram is being constructed, at some point it will be necessary to add extra text labelling, points, lines, rectangles etc. to the picture. There are two possible approaches. The first method, used in batch systems on mainframes, is to call individual routines, each of which achieves one particular aim, explicitly in the program code. Position, text labels, ends of lines etc. are specified with large numbers of parameters to each routine. A far better approach when using microcomputers is to have interactive routines that change the screen under control of the keyboard, or some other input device (joystick, lightpen, mouse etc.). It is this method that is used in listing 6.2.

Listing 6.2

```
10000 ´ label supervisor routine
10001 ´**in ** SKREEN%
10002 ´**out** SKREEN%,MENUONSCREEN%,FOREGROUND%,BACKGROUND%
10010 FOREGROUND%=0 : BACKGROUND%=3
10020 GOSUB 13060 ´change colours
10030 GOSUB 2000 ´keyboard input
10040 IF LENKB%<>1 THEN GOTO 10030
10050 IF ASCKB%>90 THEN ASCKB%=ASCKB%-32
10060 IF ASCKB%=ASC("M") THEN GOSUB 10500 ´label menu
10070 IF ASCKB%=ASC("B") THEN PUT (0,0),SKREEN%,PSET :
                              MENUONSCREEN%=FALSE%
10080 IF ASCKB%=ASC("G") THEN GET (0,0)-(319,199),SKREEN%
10090 IF ASCKB%=ASC("C") THEN GOSUB 13000 ´change colours
10100 IF ASCKB%=ASC("V") THEN GOSUB 11000 ´vertical label routine
10110 IF ASCKB%=ASC("H") THEN GOSUB 12000 ´horizontal label
```

```
10120 IF ASCKB%=ASC("N") THEN GOSUB 17000 'narrow label
10130 IF ASCKB%=ASC("P") THEN GOSUB 3000 'cursor start
10140 IF ASCKB%=ASC("L") THEN GOSUB 16000 'draw a line
10150 IF ASCKB%=ASC("D") THEN GOSUB 14000 'drag a block
10160 IF ASCKB%=ASC("F") THEN GOSUB 15000 'fill a block
10170 IF ASCKB%=ASC("T") THEN GOSUB 18000 'tile-paint
10180 IF ASCKB%<>ASC("X") THEN GOTO 10030
10190 GOSUB 1500 'diagram menu
10200 RETURN

10500 'label menu routine
10502 '**out** MENUONSCREEN%
10510 CLS
10520 LOCATE  1,13 : PRINT "LABELLING MENU";
10530 LOCATE  3,10 : PRINT "M : menu routine";
10540 LOCATE  5,10 : PRINT "X : exit labelling";
10550 LOCATE  7,10 : PRINT "B : bring picture to screen";
10560 LOCATE  9,10 : PRINT "G : store picture in array";
10570 LOCATE 11,10 : PRINT "C : change colours";
10580 LOCATE 13,10 : PRINT "V : vertical labels";
10590 LOCATE 15,10 : PRINT "H : horizontal labels";
10600 LOCATE 17,10 : PRINT "N : narrow labels";
10610 LOCATE 19,10 : PRINT "P : draw a point";
10620 LOCATE 21,10 : PRINT "L : draw a line";
10630 LOCATE 23,10 : PRINT "D : drag a block";
10640 LOCATE 25, 5 : PRINT "T or F : tile-paint or fill a block";
10650 MENUONSCREEN%=TRUE%
10660 RETURN


11000 'vertical label routine
11001 '**in ** MENUONSCREEN%,CURX%,CURY%,BLANK%,SKREEN%
11002 '**out** CURX%,CURY%
11010 IF MENUONSCREEN% THEN RETURN
11019 'cursor places start of string at (LABCOL%,LABROW%).
11020 GOSUB 3000 'cursor control
11030 LABCOL%=INT(CURX%/8)+1
11040 LABROW%=INT(CURY%/8)+1
11049 'request LABEL$ in top two lines of screen.
11050 LINE (0,0)-(319,15),0,BF
11060 LOCATE 1,1 : PRINT "label ?"
11070 LOCATE 2,1 : INPUT LABEL$
11079 'replace top two lines of screen.
11080 PUT (0,0),SKREEN%,PSET
11090 LENLAB%=LEN(LABEL$)
11100 FOR LROW%=1 TO LENLAB%
11110 LOCATE LABROW%+1-LROW%,LABCOL%
11120 ASCHAR%=ASC(MID$(LABEL$,LROW%,1))+128
11130 PRINT CHR$(ASCHAR%);
11140 NEXT LROW%
11149 'colour background of vertical string.
11150 CURX%=LABCOL%*8-8 : CURY%=LABROW%*8-8
11160 FOR LROW%=1 TO LENLAB%
11170 PUT (CURX%,CURY%),BLANK%
11180 CURY%=CURY%-8
11190 NEXT LROW%
11200 RETURN

12000 'horizontal label routine
12001 '**in ** MENUONSCREEN%,CURX%,CURY%,SKREEN%,BLANK%
12002 '**out** CURX%,CURY%
12010 IF MENUONSCREEN% THEN RETURN
12019 'cursor places start of string at (LABCOL%,LABROW%).
12020 GOSUB 3000 'cursor control
12030 LABCOL%=INT(CURX%/8)+1
12040 LABROW%=INT(CURY%/8)+1
12049 'request LABEL$ in top two lines of screen.
12050 LINE (0,0)-(319,15),0,BF
12060 LOCATE 1,1 : PRINT "label ?"
12070 LOCATE 2,1 : INPUT LABEL$
```

```
12079 ´replace top two lines of screen.
12080 PUT (0,0),SKREEN%,PSET
12090 LOCATE LABROW%,LABCOL% : PRINT LABEL$;
12100 CURX%=LABCOL%*8-8 : CURY%=LABROW%*8-8
12110 LENLAB%=LEN(LABEL$)
12120 FOR LROW%=1 TO LENLAB%
12130 PUT (CURX%,CURY%),BLANK%
12140 CURX%=CURX%+8
12150 NEXT LROW%
12159 ´integer truncation of LABCOL% and LABROW% may place
        cross cursor off screen, so adjust (CURX%,CURY%).
12160 IF CURX%>312 THEN CURX=312
12170 IF CURY%<8 THEN CURY%=8
12180 RETURN


13000 ´change foreground and background text colours
13002 ´**out** FOREGROUND%,BACKGROUND%,BLANK%
13010 CLS : INPUT "foreground colour ";FOREGROUND%
13020 IF FOREGROUND%<0 OR FOREGROUND%>3 THEN GOTO 13010
13030 INPUT "background colour ";BACKGROUND%
13040 IF BACKGROUND%<0 OR BACKGROUND%>3 THEN GOTO 13030
13049 ´prepare BLANK% to PUT over text in order to
        create correct background and foreground colours.
13050 LINE (0,0)-(7,7),BACKGROUND%,BF
13060 GET (0,0)-(7,7),BLANK%
13069 ´change foreground so that when BLANK% is PUT over
        the text with XOR, the correct foreground appears.
13070 IF BACKGROUND%<>FOREGROUND%
        THEN DEF SEG : POKE &H4E,FOREGROUND% XOR BACKGROUND%
13080 GOSUB 10500 ´label menu
13090 RETURN


14000 ´drag a block
14001 ´**in ** MENUONSCREEN%,CURX%,CURY%,CURSOR%,PAPER%
14002 ´**out** CURX%,CURY%
14010 IF MENUONSCREEN% THEN RETURN
14019 ´define the block with two ends of a line :-
        (CURX1%,CURY1%) and (CURX2%,CURY2%).
14020 GOSUB 16500 ´define a line
14030 PUT (CURX1%-2,CURY1%-2),CURSOR%
14040 PUT (CURX2%-2,CURY2%-2),CURSOR%
14049 ´store area under block.
14050 SIZ%=2+INT(2*(ABS(CURX2%-CURX1%)+8)/8)*
                (ABS(CURY2%-CURY1%)+1)
14060 DIM HOLD%(SIZ%)
14070 GET (CURX1%,CURY1%)-(CURX2%,CURY2%),HOLD%
14079 ´draw outline of block.
14080 LINE (CURX1%,CURY1%)-(CURX2%,CURY2%),3-PAPER%,B
14089 ´find new position for block.
14090 GOSUB 3000 ´cursor start
14099 ´erase old block.
14100 LINE (CURX1%,CURY1%)-(CURX2%,CURY2%),PAPER%,BF
14109 ´put block in new position.
14110 PUT (CURX%,CURY%),HOLD%,PSET
14120 ERASE HOLD%
14130 RETURN


15000 ´ fill a block
15001 ´**in ** MENUONSCREEN%,CURSOR%,FOREGROUND%,BACKGROUND%
15010 IF MENUONSCREEN% THEN RETURN
15019 ´define the block with two ends of a line :-
        (CURX1%,CURY1%) and (CURX2%,CURY2%).
15020 GOSUB 16500 ´define a line
15030 PUT (CURX1%-2,CURY1%-2),CURSOR%
15040 PUT (CURX2%-2,CURY2%-2),CURSOR%
15049 ´fill block with BACKGROUND%, and edge FOREGROUND%.
15050 LINE (CURX1%,CURY1%)-(CURX2%,CURY2%),BACKGROUND%,BF
15060 LINE (CURX1%,CURY1%)-(CURX2%,CURY2%),FOREGROUND%,B
15070 RETURN
```

```
16000 'draw a line
16001 '**in ** MENUONSCREEN%,CURSOR%,FOREGROUND%
16002 '**out** CURX%,CURY%
16010 IF MENUONSCREEN% THEN RETURN
16019 'find the two ends of a line using the cursor:-
         (CURX1%,CURY1%) and (CURX2%,CURY2%).
16020 GOSUB 16500 'define a line
16029 'delete cursor crosses.
16030 PUT (CURX1%-2,CURY1%-2),CURSOR%
16040 PUT (CURX2%-2,CURY2%-2),CURSOR%
16049 'draw the line.
16050 LINE (CURX1%,CURY1%)-(CURX2%,CURY2%),FOREGROUND%
16060 RETURN

16500 'define a line
16501 '**in ** CURSOR%
16502 '**out** CURX%,CURY%,CURX1%,CURY1%,CURX2%,CURY2%
16510 GOSUB 3000 'start cursor
16519 'find the two ends of a line using the cursor:-
         (CURX1%,CURY1%) and (CURX2%,CURY2%).
16520 CURX1%=CURX% : CURY1%=CURY%
16530 PUT (CURX%-2,CURY%-2),CURSOR%
16539 'move cursor 1 character block out of the way.
16540 IF CURX%>309 THEN CURX%=CURX%-8 ELSE CURX%=CURX%+8
16550 IF CURY%>189 THEN CURY%=CURY%-8 ELSE CURY%=CURY%+8
16560 GOSUB 3000 'start cursor
16570 CURX2%=CURX% : CURY2%=CURY%
16580 PUT (CURX%-2,CURY%-2),CURSOR%
16590 RETURN

17000 'narrow horizontal label
17001 '**in ** MENUONSCREEN%,SKREEN%
17002 '**out** CURX%,CURY%
17010 IF MENUONSCREEN% THEN RETURN
17019 'find position of start of label.
17020 GOSUB 3000 'cursor start
17029 'input the narrow label.
17030 LINE (0,0)-(319,15),0,BF
17040 LOCATE 1,1 : PRINT "label ?"
17050 LOCATE 2,1 : INPUT NUM$
17059 'reset the screen.
17060 PUT (0,0),SKREEN%,PSET
17069 'call routine to print narrow labels.
17070 X%=CURX% : Y%=CURY%
17080 GOSUB 5500 'narrow labels
17090 RETURN

18000 'tile-paint an area
18001 '**in ** MENUONSCREEN%,SKREEN%,TILE$,BOUND%
18002 '**out** CURX%,CURY%
18010 IF MENUONSCREEN% THEN RETURN
18019 'input the tile number.
18020 LINE (0,0)-(319,15),0,BF
18030 LOCATE 1,1 : PRINT "tile number ?"
18040 LOCATE 2,1 : INPUT TILE%
18049 'reset the screen.
18050 PUT (0,0),SKREEN%,PSET
18059 'define the block with two ends of a line :-
         (CURX1%,CURY1%) and (CURX2%,CURY2%).
18060 GOSUB 16500 'define a line
18070 PUT (CURX1%-2,CURY1%-2),CURSOR%
18080 PUT (CURX2%-2,CURY2%-2),CURSOR%
18089 'fill block with 3-BOUND%(TILE%) and edge BOUND%(TILE%).
18090 LINE (CURX1%,CURY1%)-(CURX2%,CURY2%),3-BOUND%(TILE%),BF
18100 LINE (CURX1%,CURY1%)-(CURX2%,CURY2%),BOUND%(TILE%),B
18109 'tile-paint block.
18110 IF TILE%>4 THEN PAINT ((CURX1%+CURX2%)/2,(CURY1%+CURY2%)/2),
                            TILE$(TILE%),BOUND%(TILE%)
18120 RETURN
```

By pressing the key "L" in the 'diagram supervisor' routine, control is passed to an inner 'label supervisor' routine. The control loops inside this routine waiting for character input from the keyboard to initiate specific labelling tasks — a technique used earlier in a number of routines including the 'diagram supervisor'. These tasks and the character indicators are listed below.

(1) "M" clears the screen and draws a label Menu of all the tasks and equivalent characters. Characters used in the two menus (diagram and label) should be readily identifiable with the task they represent (for example, "M" for Menu). Ideally each character should be identified with a unique task in both menus. Realistically, this is not always possible as the number of tasks increases. For example, "L" is used in the diagram menu to indicate the Labelling routine, however in the label menu it indicates drawing a Line (see later). It is difficult to avoid this duplication with keyboard input. One way out of this problem is to use arbitrary indicators (which is totally unsatisfactory); another, and better solution, is to use lower case characters or combinations of characters. This problem does not arise at all if other forms of input are used.

   For example, a 'mouse' can be used to indicate a particular entry in the menu. No character indicators are needed, only an explicit description of a different task on each screen line. A (new) cursor symbol can be moved over the line containing the required menu entry, and a button on the mouse pressed to indicate the choice.

(2) "X" eXits from the 'label supervisor' routine and returns control to the 'diagram supervisor'. If "E" had been used in this routine as well as in the 'diagram supervisor', holding down the "E" key too long would cause an exit from both supervisors, and the program would end prematurely.

(3) "B" Brings the present SKREEN% diagram to the screen, and sets the flag MENUONSCREEN% to FALSE%. The following routines will not execute unless a diagram is visible, that is, there is no menu on the screen.

(4) "G" GETs the present picture from the screen and loads it into array SKREEN%. Mistakes are quite common when labelling interactively. If a picture is not explicitly stored with GET on completion of particular tasks, then mistakes are automatically erased by Bringing the old SKREEN% back to the screen or by going on to other types of label construction.

(5) "C" Changes the FOREGROUND% and BACKGROUND% (logical) colours of text (it does not change the actual colour of logical colour 0). It also creates an array BLANK% holding an 8 by 8 pixel block of BACKGROUND% colour, used to change the normal PRINT text background from logical 0 to BACKGROUND%, and foreground from logical 3 to FOREGROUND%. This change is achieved by XORing the BLANK% over a new text foreground which is set to logical colour FOREGROUND% XOR BACKGROUND% by POKEing this value into location &H4E of the BASIC segment. The routine is called on entry to the label supervisor to initialise BACKGROUND% and FOREGROUND% to logical 3 and 0 respectively.

(6) "V" indicates Vertical text labels using the "B:ROTCHARS.DAT" characters created by listing 5.3. The start position of the text is pointed at by the cursor (press the End key when it is in the correct position). The top two lines of the screen are cleared and the text label is requested. After input the screen is reset with SKREEN%, and the label drawn vertically upwards starting at the character block containing the cursor.

(7) "H" is used for Horizontal labels and is of a similar construction to the vertical label routine, but uses the standard character set.

(8) "N" calls the Narrow label routines of listing 5.9 which are incorporated in listing 6.1.

(9) "P" calls the cursor routine, so enabling the user to draw a Point of logical colour 0, 1, 2 or 3 by pressing the corresponding key. Once inside the cursor control program, as many points as needed can be drawn by moving the cursor-cross into the required position and pressing keys 0 to 3. The Home key alternates the cursor increment between 1 and 8 pixels, and the End key returns control to the 'label supervisor'. After End, remember to GET any changes into SKREEN% before continuing, or otherwise changes to the picture may be lost.

(10) "L" draws a Line. The line is defined with two calls to the cursor control program. After the first call a fixed cursor-cross is left on the screen, and the movable cross moved away in order that the XOR operation does not obliterate the fixed cross. When both ends of the line have been indicated, the crosses are deleted and a line drawn between the points in FOREGROUND% colour.

(11) "D" Drags a rectangular pixel block portion of the screen to another part of the screen. Two corners of the block are defined by two calls to the cursor control (as in the Line routine) and a box is drawn around the area. The pixel block area is stored in an array HOLD%, the old area blanked out in BACKGROUND% colour and the HOLD% block PUT back on the screen at a position indicated by another call to the cursor routine (remember the Hold and End keys).

(12) "T" Tile-PAINTs a pixel block area defined by two cursor calls. The top two lines of the screen hold the TILE-number request. These lines are again reset by SKREEN%.

(13) "F" LINE Fills a rectangular pixel block defined by two cursor calls, in BACKGROUND% colour with an edge of FOREGROUND%.

Exercise 6.1

These are just some of the numerous labelling options that are possible. Many of the diagrams from this book were constructed using this routine (for example, the figures from chapter 5). Readers should extend the program, adding other options.

So many may be added that more than one menu may be needed to hold all the options! Some such extras could be:

(a) Define a pixel block by outlining it with the cursor, and make a Copy of it on another part of the screen.
(b) Invert all the colours inside a pixel block specified by two cursor positions.
(c) Tile-PAINT a polygonal area whose vertices are indicated by calls to the cursor routines.
(d) Move the whole screen up/down/left/right by a specified number of pixels.
(e) Change the input method as indicated in the text. Instead of keyboard input, use another cursor-cross (under control of a lightpen, mouse or joystick if you have them, or keyboard if you do not) as an indicator that moves up and down the menus, using the End key (or other terminator) to indicate your choice of option.

There are many, many more possible extensions. This program was written to enable you to make these additions with very little difficulty. The modular approach means that you can cannibalise the programs with ease, keeping routines that are useful and deleting and replacing those that are no longer required.

Now having the ability to add labels and adjust diagrams, the obvious next step is to construct the data diagrams themselves, starting with bar-charts.

Bar-charts and Histograms

This part of the package is entered by typing "H" (for histogram) in the 'diagram supervisor' routine. Strictly speaking, the following two listings 6.3 and 6.4 construct bar-charts (a histogram is a bar-chart with no gaps between bars: it also has a continuous numerical horizontal scale). The letter "B" (for Bar-chart) has already been used by the 'diagram supervisor' for another task (see listing 6.1), so we use "H" instead.

Listing 6.3 enables you to read in the data on a number of bars (NBAR%). This data on each bar consists of the height of the bar, and the tile number (defined in listing 6.1) needed to fill it. The upper and lower bounds for this vertical data are also requested in order to label and scale the vertical coordinate axis. The axes are drawn, and five small equi-spaced hatch marks are placed on the vertical axis as well as narrow numerical labels at these marks. Four equal subdivisions of the vertical axis is a reasonable number; choosing too many, with the limited resolution available, could obscure the 'narrow' labels and the data presentation. The program then assumes that the width of each bar is twice the GAP between bars, so enabling the GAP value (in pixels) to be calculated. Then all the bars can be drawn individually. The pixel row corresponding to the top of each bar can be calculated using the scaling factor found earlier, and the pixel column position of the left-hand side of the bar found, it being a simple multiple of the GAP value offset from the vertical axis. Thus a bar is drawn from the horizontal base line of the diagram up to this pixel row at the top, with width GAP, and positioned properly on the base line. The final step is to tile-PAINT each bar to create the final bar-chart. Returning command to the 'diagram supervisor' now allows the user to add extra labels and/or adjust the diagram. Figure 6.1, showing the annual rainfall in the London area, is an example of a diagram constructed in this way. Having divided the problem of diagram construction into major tasks, a complete description of the implementation of the solutions to these problems would be tedious at this stage. The reader should study the fully REMarked programs, such as listing 6.3, in order to understand how the program is segmented, and to see how each individual module is programmed in BASIC for running on the IBM PC.

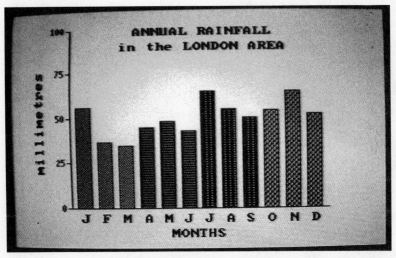

Figure 6.1

Listing 6.3

```
20000 ´ BAR-CHART ROUTINE (type 1)
20001 ´**in ** TILE$,BOUND%,PAPER%
20002 ´**out** SKREEN%
20010 CLS
20019 ´input data for bar-chart.
20020 INPUT"lower bound of vertical range ";YLO
20030 INPUT"upper bound of vertical range ";YHI
20040 IF YLO >= YHI THEN GOTO 20010
20050 YSCALE=150/(YHI-YLO)
20060 INPUT "number of bars ",NBAR%
20070 DIM BARVAL(NBAR%),TILENUM%(NBAR%)
20080 FOR I%=1 TO NBAR%
20090 PRINT "value and tile number for bar ";STR$(I%)
20100 INPUT BARVAL(I%),TILENUM%(I%)
20110 NEXT I%
20119 ´draw axes.
20120 PUT (0,0),SKREEN%,PSET
20130 LINE (50,25)-(50,175),3-PAPER%
20140 LINE (50,175)-(270,175),3-PAPER%
20149 ´place 5 labels on vertical axis.
20150 YV=YLO : YDIF=(YHI-YLO)/4
```

```
20160 FOR K%=1 TO 5
20169 'place small mark on axis.
20170 Y%=175-INT((YV-YLO)*YSCALE+.5)
20180 LINE (50,Y%)-(47,Y%),3-PAPER%
20189 'place narrow label at mark.
20190 NUM$=STR$(INT(YV))
20200 IF YV>=0 THEN NUM$=RIGHT$(NUM$,LEN(NUM$)-1)
20210 IF LEN(NUM$)>3 THEN NUM$="..."
20220 X%=46-4*LEN(NUM$) : Y%=Y%-4
20230 GOSUB 5500 'narrow characters
20240 YV=YV+YDIF
20250 NEXT K%
20259 'place NBAR% bars in diagram, each bar has width 2*GAP
       and there is a distance GAP between neighbouring bars.
20260 GAP=220/(3*NBAR%+1)
20270 FOR I%=1 TO NBAR%
20279 'x-pixels of I%'th bar are from X% to X%+2*GAP.
20280 X%=50+INT(GAP*(3*I%-2))
20290 TILE%=TILENUM%(I%)
20299 'y-pixels go from 175 up to YPIXEL.
20300 YPIXEL=175-YSCALE*(BARVAL(I%)-YLO)
20309 'draw bar in colour 3-BOUND%(TILE%)
       with edge colour BOUND%(TILE%).
20310 LINE (X%,175)-(X%+2*GAP,YPIXEL),3-BOUND%(TILE%),BF
20320 LINE (X%,175)-(X%+2*GAP,YPIXEL),BOUND%(TILE%),B
20329 'if bar is non-empty then PAINT with a tile.
20330 IF YPIXEL>173 THEN GOTO 20350
20340 IF TILE%>4 THEN PAINT(X%+1,174),TILE$(TILE%),BOUND%(TILE%)
20350 NEXT I%
20359 'store final diagram in SKREEN%.
20360 GET (0,0)-(319,199),SKREEN%
20370 ERASE BARVAL,TILENUM%
20380 RETURN
```

Exercise 6.2

Adjust the above program so that there is no gap between the bars. Also assume a
continuous numerical scale on the horizontal *x*-axis. That is, draw a proper histogram with the bars centred on equi-spaced points on the horizontal axis.

Another listing (6.4) may be substituted for listing 6.3 in the program, so that
another kind of bar-chart can be created from the very same program structure.
This program draws what appear to be three-dimensional bars. The six-sided outline of each bar is constructed with LINEs, the interior PAINTed, and then internal
LINEs added to give the three-dimensional effect. Each bar has front and back faces
of width 2 * GAP pixels, and side faces, slanting away from the front to the right,
of width GAP pixels. There is a distance GAP + 4 pixels between bars. Knowing the
number of bars and the width of the diagram allows the program to calculate GAP,
and hence position the bars on the screen.

The diagram consists of two rows of bars, the front drawn in logical colour 2 and
the back in colour 1. The pixel positions of the top of each bar and the external
and internal lines may be calculated given the data value for the bar, whether it is
in the front or back row, and its position within that row. The two rows are drawn
in two separate stages. Firstly, the front row is constructed and stored in the array
SKREEN%. Then the second row is drawn and the first row is PUT (AND) over it.
Where the two different colours (1 and 2) overlap, logical colour 0 is produced, and

this gives the observer the impression of transparent bars, and by implication a clearer understanding of the relationship between the two sets of data.

An example of its use, showing the maximum and minimum temperatures in the London area, is given in figure 6.2. Again a full understanding of the techniques involved can be achieved by using the REMarks to analyse the listing.

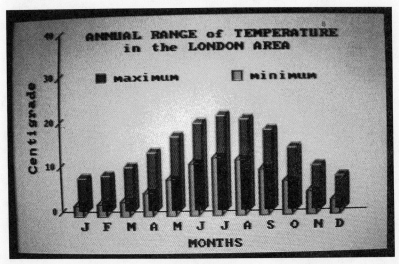

Figure 6.2

Listing 6.4

```
20000 ´ BAR-CHART ROUTINE (type 2)
20002 ´**out** SKREEN%
20010 CLS
20019 ´input data for 3-D bar-chart.
20020 INPUT"lower bound of vertical range ";YLO
20030 INPUT"upper bound of vertical range ";YHI
20040 IF YLO >= YHI THEN GOTO 20010
20050 YSCALE=150/(YHI-YLO)
20060 INPUT "number of bars in each row ",NBAR%
20070 DIM BARVAL(2,NBAR%)
20080 FOR I%=1 TO NBAR%
20090 PRINT "front and back values for bar ";STR$(I%)
20100 INPUT BARVAL(1,I%),BARVAL(2,I%)
20110 NEXT I%
20119 ´draw axes.
20120 LINE (0,0)-(319,199),3,BF
20130 LINE (40,25)-(40,175),0
20140 LINE (40,175)-(300,175),0
20149 ´place 5 labels on vertical axis.
20150 YV=YLO : YDIF=(YHI-YLO)/4
20160 FOR K%=1 TO 5
20169 ´place small diagonal mark on axis.
20170 Y%=175-INT((YV-YLO)*YSCALE+.5)
20180 LINE (43,Y%-3)-(37,Y%+3),0
20189 ´place narrow label at mark.
20190 NUM$=STR$(INT(YV))
20200 IF YV>=0 THEN NUM$=RIGHT$(NUM$,LEN(NUM$)-1)
```

```
20210 IF LEN(NUM$)>3 THEN NUM$="..."
20220 X%=36-4*LEN(NUM$) : Y%=Y%-4
20230 GOSUB 5500 ´narrow characters
20240 YV=YV+YDIF
20250 NEXT K%
20259 ´place two ROW%s of bars in diagram.
       Maximum width of each 3-D bar is 3*GAP and there
       is a distance GAP+4 between neighbouring bars.
20260 GAP=INT(260/NBAR%/4-1) : EXTRA=GAP+(260-4*NBAR%*(GAP+1))/2
20269 ´calculate (XS,YS), start position for bars in each ROW%.
       Variable EXTRA is used to centre diagram.
20270 FOR ROW%=1 TO 2
20280 XS=40+EXTRA-GAP*(2-ROW%) : YS=175+GAP*(2-ROW%)
20289 ´draw I%´th bar in ROW%.
20290 FOR I%=1 TO NBAR%
20299 ´x-pixels of I´th bar are from X to X+3*GAP.
20300 X=XS+4*(GAP+1)*(I%-1)
20309 ´y-pixels may range from YS up to YPIXEL-GAP.
20310 YPIXEL=YS-YSCALE*(BARVAL(ROW%,I%)-YLO)
20319 ´draw outer edges of 3-D bar in colour ROW%.
20320 LINE (X,YS)-(X+2*GAP,YS),ROW%
20330 LINE -(X+3*GAP,YS-GAP),ROW%
20340 LINE -(X+3*GAP,YPIXEL-GAP),ROW%
20350 LINE -(X+GAP,YPIXEL-GAP),ROW%
20360 LINE -(X,YPIXEL),ROW%
20370 LINE -(X,YS),ROW%
20379 ´PAINT inside of bar in colour 3-ROW%.
20380 IF YPIXEL<200 THEN PAINT(X+2*GAP,YPIXEL),3-ROW%,ROW%
                    ELSE PAINT(X+2*GAP,199),3-ROW%,ROW%
20389 ´draw inner edges of 3-D bar in colour ROW%.
20390 LINE (X+2*GAP,YS)-(X+2*GAP,YPIXEL),ROW%
20400 LINE (X,YPIXEL)-(X+2*GAP,YPIXEL),ROW%
20410 LINE -(X+3*GAP,YPIXEL-GAP),ROW%
20420 NEXT I%
20429 ´store the front ROW% and axes, clear the screen,
       draw the back ROW%, and PUT(AND) front ROW% on top.
20430 IF ROW%=1 THEN GET (0,0)-(319,199),SKREEN% :
                    LINE (0,0)-(319,199),3,BF
                 ELSE PUT (0,0),SKREEN%,AND
20440 NEXT ROW%
20449 ´store final diagram in SKREEN%.
20450 GET (0,0)-(319,199),SKREEN%
20460 ERASE BARVAL
20470 RETURN
```

Exercise 6.3

Write a variation on listing 6.4, in which each pair of data values is combined to form a single bar in the bar-chart; each bar has two sections corresponding to the two data items, one directly above the other.

Pie-Charts

Pie-charts are very popular data diagrams with economists. Any pie-chart program must be capable of taking a set of positive numerical values, calculating their total, and representing each individual value as a slice of a circle (a pie). The angle at the centre of a pie slice should be the same proportion of the full circle as the corresponding data item is of the sum total of the data. It is also necessary that a pie can be positioned anywhere on the screen and be given any radius. Also, it must be possible to pull individual slices away from the centre of the pie. It should also be possible to superimpose different pies in a single diagram. Listing 6.5 is a routine that achieves all these requirements; it is entered by typing "P" in the 'diagram supervisor'. Figure 6.3, showing the breakdown of radiation doses for a typical human, was generated by this listing and the 'label' routine.

Listing 6.5

```
30000  ' pie-chart routine
30001  '**in ** CURX%,CURY%,CURSOR%,SKREEN%,TILE$,BOUND%
30002  '**out** CURX%,CURY%,SKREEN%
30009  'input data for pie-chart.
30010  CLS : INPUT "number of segments ",NSEG%
30020  DIM SEGVAL(NSEG%),TILENUM%(NSEG%)
30030  TOTAL=0
30040  FOR I%=1 TO NSEG%
30050  PRINT "value and tile number for segment ";STR$(I%)
30060  INPUT SEGVAL(I%),TILENUM%(I%)
30069  'don't draw PAPER% coloured lines on PAPER% background.
30070  IF BOUND%(TILENUM%(I%))=PAPER% THEN GOTO 30050
30080  TOTAL=TOTAL+SEGVAL(I%)
30090  NEXT I%
30099  'place centre of pie with cursor.
30100  PUT (0,0),SKREEN%,PSET
30110  LINE (0,0)-(319,7),0,BF
30120  LOCATE 1,1 : PRINT"centre pie ?",
30130  GOSUB 3000 'cursor start
30140  XC%=CURX% : YC%=CURY%
30150  PUT (XC%-2,YC%-2),CURSOR%
30159  'calculate radius from cursor position.
30160  LOCATE 1,1 : PRINT"radius ?",
30170  CURY%=CURY%+8
30180  GOSUB 3000 'cursor start
30190  PUT (XC%-2,YC%-2),CURSOR%
30200  RAD=INT(SQR((CURX%-XC%)^2+(CURY%-YC%)^2)+.5)
30210  ASTART=6.283186 : ASCALE=ASTART/TOTAL
30219  'draw the I%'th slice of the pie-chart.
30220  FOR I%=1 TO NSEG%
30229  'recoup data on I%'th slice.
30230  TILE%=TILENUM%(I%)
30240  T$=TILE$(TILE%) : BCOL%=BOUND%(TILE%)
30249  'place apex of slice with the cursor.
30250  LOCATE 1,1 : PRINT"centre segment ?",
30260  CURX%=XC% : CURY%=YC%
30270  GOSUB 3000 'cursor start
30280  PUT (0,0),SKREEN%,PSET
30290  ADIF=ASCALE*SEGVAL(I%)
30300  AMID=ADIF*.5-ASTART
30310  IF CURX%=XC% AND CURY%=YC% THEN GOTO 30350
30320  DIST=SQR((CURX%-XC%)^2+(CURY%-YC%)^2)
30330  CURX%=XC%+INT(DIST*COS(AMID)+.5)
30340  CURY%=YC%+INT(DIST*SIN(AMID)+.5)
30349  'draw the outline of slice.
30350  AEND=ASTART-ADIF
30360  IF AEND<=0 THEN AEND=.000001
30370  CIRCLE (CURX%,CURY%),RAD,BCOL%,-AEND,-ASTART,ASPECT
30379  'tile-paint the slice.
30380  PX%=CURX%+INT((RAD-5)*COS(AMID)+.5)
30390  PY%=CURY%+INT((RAD-5)*SIN(AMID)+.5)
30400  PAINT (PX%,PY%),3-BCOL%,BCOL%
30410  IF TILE%>4 THEN PAINT (PX%,PY%),T$,BCOL%
30419  'store picture and go back for next slice.
30420  GET (0,0)-(319,199),SKREEN%
30430  ASTART=AEND
30440  NEXT I%
30450  ERASE SEGVAL,TILENUM%
30460  RETURN
```

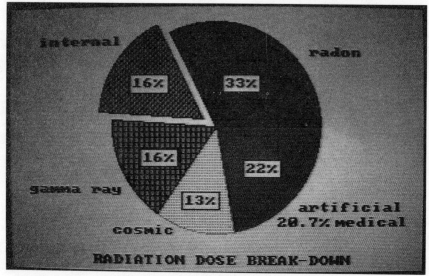

Figure 6.3

The program requests the number of slices, and the value and tile number for each slice. It calculates the total of the data values so it can be used to calculate the angular value of each slice. The program first requests the centre of the pie, indicated by the cursor-cross. Then the radius of the pie-chart is found by the cursor, indicating any point on the pie circumference: the radius is the distance of the circumference from the centre. Each pie slice is now drawn in turn. The angle and orientation of the slice is calculated: it is bounded by two lines which make angles ASTART and AEND with the positive x-direction. The apex of the pie need not be the centre of the pie. The cursor-cross is used to indicate the distance of the slice apex from the centre. This distance (and not the cursor position) is used to place the slice at pixel (PX%, PY%). CIRCLE (with the correct ASPECT) is used to outline the shape, before it is tile-PAINTed. The labelling routine can then be used to finish off the picture.

Scientific Graphs: Continuous and Discrete

The type of diagram most used by scientists is the 'graph', which is composed of a sequence of line segments that approximate to a curve. There are many variations on this basic idea, two of which are given below. The first is where the curve is defined by a single-valued mathematical formula, in which case every x-value on the curve has a unique corresponding y-value: this is the continuous graph called by an entry "C" in the 'diagram supervisor'. The second type of curve is one where no formula is given; here y-values are known for a set of x-values: this is the discrete graph called by "D" in the 'diagram supervisor'.

Both types of graph require the construction of x and y axes. Listing 6.6 gives the routines for constructing both types of graph, as well as another routine for constructing and scaling the axes; axes and graphs are drawn in black (logical 0 identified with actual 0) on white background (logical 1 in palette 1). This latter routine requests the lower and upper bounds of both x and y axes. It then calculates the different x and y scales to map and draw these axes onto the pixels of the IBM PC screen. The lower bound of x is mapped onto pixel column 50, and the upper bound onto pixel column 270; the lower bound of y is mapped onto pixel row 175 and the upper bound onto row 25. The intersection of the axes on the screen (the origin) is carefully chosen to be pixel (XORG, YORG): the value of XORG is explained below, YORG follows by a similar explanation. If a zero x-value lies between the lower and upper bounds of x, that is, using the x-scaling factor it maps onto a pixel column between 50 and 270, then XORG is set to that pixel column. If zero is less than the lower bound then XORG is set to the pixel column 50, otherwise it is set to the upper bound pixel (270). Each axis has five hatch marks which divide it into four equal lengths, and if requested the axis may be labelled with narrow characters. Four equal subdivisions of each axis were chosen for the reasons mentioned above.

Listing 6.6

```
40000  ´continuous graph
40002  ´**out** SKREEN%
40010  GOSUB 45000 ´prepare screen and axes
40019  ´vary x from XLO to XHI, that is
          through all pixels PX from 50 to 270.
40020  X=XLO : GOSUB 40500 ´find y-value from X
40029  ´calculate Y value for each X, and then find
        ´ the corresponding pixel value PY.
40030  PY%=INT(175-(Y-YLO)*YSCALE)
40040  PSET (50,PY%),0
40050  FOR PX%=51 TO 270
40060  X=(PX%-50)/XSCALE+XLO : GOSUB 40500 ´find y-value
40070  PY%=INT(175-(Y-YLO)*YSCALE)
40079  ´draw lines between neighbouring (PX%,PY%).
40080  LINE -(PX%,PY%),0
40090  NEXT PX%
40100  GET (0,0)-(319,199),SKREEN%
40110  RETURN

40500  ´find Y-value from X
40501  ´**in ** X
40502  ´**out** Y
40510  Y=SIN(X)+COS(X)
40520  RETURN

45000  ´ prepare screen and axes for both types of graph
45001  ´**in ** SKREEN%
45002  ´**out** XLO,YLO,XSCALE,YSCALE
45009  ´input data for axes.
45010  CLS
45020  INPUT"Lower and Upper Bounds for X ? ",XLO,XHI
45030  IF XHI<XLO THEN GOTO 45020
45040  INPUT"Lower and Upper Bounds for Y ? ",YLO,YHI
45050  IF YHI<YLO THEN GOTO 45040
45059  ´calculate X- and Y-scaling factors.
45060  XSCALE=220/(XHI-XLO) : YSCALE=150/(YHI-YLO)
```

```
45069 'place axes through pixel (XORG%,YORG%).
45070 IF XHI<=0 THEN XORG%=270
      ELSE IF XLO>=0 THEN XORG%=50
           ELSE XORG%=INT(50-XLO*XSCALE)
45080 IF YHI<=0 THEN YORG%=25
      ELSE IF YLO>=0 THEN YORG%=175
           ELSE YORG%=INT(175+YLO*YSCALE)
45089 'input data for labelling.
45090 INPUT"Do you want X-axis labelled Y/N ? ",F$
45100 XLAB%=(F$="y") OR (F$="Y")
45110 INPUT"Do you want Y-axis labelled Y/N ? ",F$
45120 YLAB%=(F$="y") OR (F$="Y")
45129 'draw lines for axes.
45130 PUT(0,0),SKREEN%,PSET
45140 LINE (XORG%,25)-(XORG%,175),0
45150 LINE (50,YORG%)-(270,YORG%),0
45159 'place 5 marks on X-axis
45160 XMARK=0 : MDIF=(XHI-XLO)/4
45170 FOR MARK%=1 TO 5
45180 PX%=50+INT(XMARK*XSCALE+.5)
45190 LINE(PX%,YORG%)-(PX%,YORG%+3),0
45199 'label axes if requested.
45200 IF NOT XLAB% THEN GOTO 45260
45210 NUM$=STR$(XMARK+XLO)
45220 IF XMARK+XLO>=0 THEN NUM$=RIGHT$(NUM$,LEN(NUM$)-1)
45230 IF LEN(NUM$)>3 THEN NUM$="..."
45240 X%=PX%-4*LEN(NUM$)+6 : Y%=YORG%+4
45250 GOSUB 5500 'narrow characters
45260 XMARK=XMARK+MDIF
45270 NEXT MARK%
45279 'place 5 marks on Y-axis
45280 YMARK=0 : MDIF=(YHI-YLO)/4
45290 FOR MARK%=1 TO 5
45300 PY%=175-INT(YMARK*YSCALE+.5)
45310 LINE(XORG%,PY%)-(XORG%-3,PY%),0
45319 'label axes if requested.
45320 IF NOT YLAB% THEN GOTO 45380
45330 NUM$=STR$(YMARK+YLO)
45340 IF YMARK+YLO>=0 THEN NUM$=RIGHT$(NUM$,LEN(NUM$)-1)
45350 IF LEN(NUM$)>3 THEN NUM$="..."
45360 X%=XORG%-4*LEN(NUM$)-1 : Y%=PY%-8
45370 GOSUB 5500 'narrow characters
45380 YMARK=YMARK+MDIF
45390 NEXT MARK%
45400 RETURN


50000 ' discrete graph
50009 'input discrete data.
50010 CLS : INPUT"Number of points ? ",NOP%
50020 DIM X(NOP%),Y(NOP%)
50030 FOR I%=1 TO NOP%
50040 PRINT"Type X(";I%;") and Y(";I%;")";
50050 INPUT X(I%),Y(I%)
50060 NEXT I%
50069 'put data in increasing order of X.
50070 FOR I%=1 TO NOP%-1
50080 FOR J%=I%+1 TO NOP%
50090 IF X(I%)>X(J%) THEN TEMP=X(I%) : X(I%)=X(J%) : X(J%)=TEMP :
                          TEMP=Y(I%) : Y(I%)=Y(J%) : Y(J%)=TEMP
50100 NEXT J%
50110 NEXT I%
50120 GOSUB 45000 'prepare screen and axes
50129 'draw symbol at first data point (PX%,PY%).
50130 PX%=INT(50+(X(1)-XLO)*XSCALE)
50140 PY%=INT(175-(Y(1)-YLO)*YSCALE)
50150 PSET (PX%,PY%),0
50160 GOSUB 55000 'draw symbol
50169 'find remaining data points (PX%,PY%) and draw
      line between neighbouring points.
```

```
50170 FOR I%=2 TO NOP%
50180 PX%=INT(50+(X(I%)-XLO)*XSCALE)
50190 PY%=INT(175-(Y(I%)-YLO)*YSCALE)
50200 LINE -(PX%,PY%),0
50210 GOSUB 55000 'draw symbol
50220 NEXT I%
50229 'store picture.
50230 GET (0,0)-(319,199),SKREEN%
50240 RETURN

55000 'draw symbol at (PX%,PY%)
55001 '**in ** PX%,PY%
55010 PSET (PX%+2,PY%+2),0
55020 LINE -(PX%-2,PY%+2),0
55030 LINE -(PX%-2,PY%-2),0
55040 LINE -(PX%+2,PY%-2),0
55050 LINE -(PX%+2,PY%+2),0
55060 PSET (PX%,PY%),0
55070 RETURN
```

To draw the continuous graph on such axes it is first necessary to write a routine for the mathematical formula starting at program line 40500: given an x-value it must return a unique y-value.

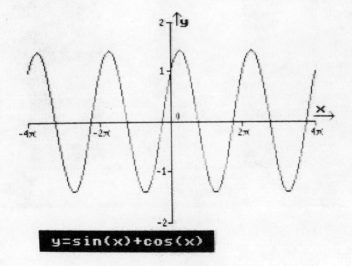

Figure 6.4

Listing 6.6 gives a simple routine for the function:

$$y = \sin(x) + \cos(x)$$

which is drawn in figure 6.4. Starting at pixel column 50 and moving right in single pixel steps to column 270, the x-value X corresponding to each column PX% is calculated. This is passed into the formula routine and the y-value Y returned. This y-value is then mapped into a pixel row PY%. Consecutive values of (PX%, PY%) are joined with LINEs to give the required approximation to the curve. Then the figure is labelled to complete the diagram.

Exercise 6.4

Change the code so that a number of different curves can be drawn on the same axes. Give each curve a different colour, and perhaps use different types of LINE style.

The discrete curve is drawn on the axes in a similar manner. The number of points (NOP%) is requested and each point (X(I), Y(I)), $1 \leqslant I \leqslant$ NOP% read in. These are reorganised into increasing order of X. A corresponding pixel (PX%, PY%) is calculated for each *x*, *y* value and a simple symbol is drawn at that point on the screen. LINEs join these points starting from left to right. Figure 6.5 is an example of the use of this program, and shows the pH levels in river water at various times of the day.

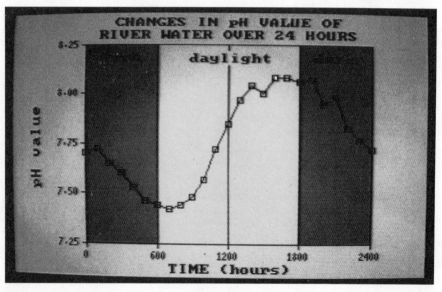

Figure 6.5

Exercise 6.5

Use different LINE styles to draw dashed lines between the points. Change the listing so that a number of different discrete curves, each with its own unique symbol, can be drawn on the screen at the same time. Also place a 'key' of the symbols on the screen with the label routine.

Exercise 6.6

Change the program so that no symbols are drawn. Instead the sequence of lines that define the curve must start at the lower bound and end on the upper bound, and the area under the curve must be PAINTed a different colour from that over the curve. Perhaps use a number of different curves in the same diagram, and use a different tile-colour under each.

Having constructed these mode 1 diagrams it is often necessary to create utility programs to adjust them in some way. For example, quite often a picture that has a good colour balance on the screen, when dumped to a printer has a totally unsatisfactory grey-scale effect. Listing 6.7 loads in a mode 1 picture from disk, changes the colour of each pixel in some predefined way, and finally stores the adjusted picture back on disk. Each byte in the screen buffer (an 8-bit number) is broken down from left to right into four 2-bit numbers C4%, C3%, C2% and C1%. Each 2-bit number corresponds to one of the four logical colours. Each colour is to be changed: colour I changes to colour COL%(I). The four colours above can be altered in this way, recombined into an 8-bit number and stored back in the original position in the screen buffer.

Listing 6.7

```
100 ´colour transfer program
109 ´pixels of logical colour I% are changed
    to logical colour MAP%(I%) : 0<=I%<=3.
110 OPTION BASE 0 : DIM MAP%(3)
120 FOR I%=0 TO 3
130 PRINT "Type in new value of logical colour ";I%;
140 INPUT MAP%(I%)
150 NEXT I%
160 MODE%=1 : PALETTE%=0 : BACKGROUND%=0
170 INPUT "What picture file do you require? ",F$
179 ´load picture into screen buffer.
180 GOSUB 60000 ´colour monitor
190 DEF SEG=&HB800
200 BLOAD F$,0
209 ´look at even (I%=0) and odd (I%=1) lines of the screen.
    Data for lines stored in addresses START% to START%+7999.
    Even lines START% at offset 0, odd lines at offset &H2000.
210 START%=0
220 FOR I%=0 TO 1
230 FOR ADDRESS%=START% TO START%+7999
239 ´take each byte in turn (OLDBYTE% say).
240 OLDBYTE%=PEEK(ADDRESS%)
249 ´break it down into constituent pixel colours C4%,C3%,C2%,C1%.
250 C1%=(OLDBYTE% AND 3)
260 C2%=(OLDBYTE% AND 12)/4
270 C3%=(OLDBYTE% AND 48)/16
280 C4%=(OLDBYTE% AND 192)/64
289 ´reconstitute byte (NEWBYTE%) using MAP%.
290 NEWBYTE%=MAP%(C4%)*64+MAP%(C3%)*16+MAP%(C2%)*4+MAP%(C1%)
299 ´make the colour change, and go to next byte.
300 POKE ADDRESS%,NEWBYTE%
310 NEXT ADDRESS%
319 ´look at odd lines.
320 START%=&H2000
330 NEXT I%
340 GOSUB 60100 ´monochrome monitor
350 INPUT"Do you wish to save this picture?: Y or N ",Q$
360 IF Q$="Y" OR Q$="y" THEN INPUT "Name of file ",F$ :
                        DEF SEG=&HB800 : BSAVE F$,0,&H3FFF
370 END
```

Exercise 6.7

This utility program takes a long time to execute. Write an assembler program using the same algorithm.

Exercise 6.8

BLOAD a previously saved picture into the memory at a location near to the screen buffer, such as &HB8004 or &HB7FF8. You will notice that the original picture has been translated. Incorporate this idea in a program that translates a diagram around the screen. It may be necessary to add Block-Filled LINEs to fill in blank areas.

Exercise 6.9

This DATA DIAGRAM package was designed for use with mode 1, in order to make use of the colour capabilities of that mode. As an exercise, rewrite this package so that it can be used in mode 2. You lose colour but you gain higher resolution.

There are many more types of data diagram. This chapter should have given you ideas on how to approach their construction. Remember always to use the structured approach — you will then find that a number of previously written (tried and tested) routines will be usable in later programs, and this will save a great deal of time at the construction and debugging stages.

Complete Programs

There are two variations of the data diagram programs available. Both programs need two disk files. "B:ROTCHARS.DAT" created with listing 5.3, and "B:NARROW.DAT" created with listing 5.9. These files are on the diskette accompanying this book.

I. Listings 6.1 ('supervisor'), 6.2 ('label'), 6.3 ('bar-chart type 1'), 6.5 ('pie-chart'), 6.6 ('graphs') and 'lib0' must be MERGEd together.
II. Listings 6.1 ('supervisor'), 6.2 ('label'), 6.4 ('bar-chart type 2'), 6.5 ('pie-chart'), 6.6 ('graphs') and 'lib0' must be MERGEd together.

There are numerous ways of using these programs. See the text for all possible inputs.

III. Listing 6.7 ('colour change utility') MERGEd with 'lib0'. Data required: four integers between zero and three. Try 1, 3, 0 and 1. Program BLOADs any mode 1 picture, such as one stored by the above programs, and changes every occurrence of the logical colours. In the above example, logical 0 changes to 1, 1 to 3 etc.

7 Three-Dimensional Coordinate Geometry

Before we lead on to a study of the graphical display of objects in three-dimensional space, we first have to come to terms with the three-dimensional Cartesian coordinate geometry. As in two-dimensional space, we arbitrarily fix a point in the space, named the *coordinate origin* (or *origin* for short). We then imagine three mutually perpendicular lines through this point, each line going off to infinity in both directions. These are the *x-axis*, the *y-axis* and the *z-axis*. Each axis is thought to have a positive and a negative half, both starting at the origin; that is, distances measured from the origin along the axis are positive on one side and negative on the other. We may think of the x-axis and y-axis in the same way as we did for two-dimensional space, both lying on the page of this book say, the positive x-axis 'horizontal' and to the right of the origin, and the positive y-axis 'vertical' and above the origin. This just leaves the position of the z-axis: it has to be perpendicular to the page (since it is perpendicular to both the x-axis and the y-axis). The positive z-axis can be into the page (the so-called *left-handed triad* of axes) or out of the page (the *right-handed triad*). *In this book we always use the left-handed triad notation.* What we say in the remainder of the book, using left-handed axes, has its equivalent in the right-handed system — it does not matter which notation you finally decide to use *as long as you are consistent.*

We specify a general point p in space by a coordinate triple or vector (X, Y, Z), where the individual coordinate values are the perpendicular projections of the point on to the respective x-axis, y-axis and z-axis. By projection we mean the unique point on the specified axis such that a line from that point to p is perpendicular to that axis.

Initially there are two operations we need to consider for three-dimensional vectors. Suppose we have two vectors $p_1 \equiv (x_1, y_1, z_1)$ and $p_2 \equiv (x_2, y_2, z_2)$ then

scalar multiple: we multiply the three individual coordinate values by a scalar number k

$$kp_1 = (k \times x_1, k \times y_1, k \times z_1)$$

vector addition: we add the x-coordinates together, then the y-coordinates and finally the z-coordinates to form a new vector

$$p_1 + p_2 \equiv (x_1 + x_2, y_1 + y_2, z_1 + z_2)$$

Definition of a Straight Line

A *straight line* in three-dimensional space that passes through two points such as $p_1 \equiv (x_1, y_1, z_1)$ and $p_2 \equiv (x_2, y_2, z_2)$ is the next object to be defined. We may do this by describing the coordinates of a general point $p \equiv (x, y, z)$ on the line by three equations

$$(x - x_1) \times (y_2 - y_1) = (y - y_1) \times (x_2 - x_1)$$

$$(y - y_1) \times (z_2 - z_1) = (z - z_1) \times (y_2 - y_1)$$

$$(z - z_1) \times (x_2 - x_1) = (x - x_1) \times (z_2 - z_1)$$

Although these are three equations in three unknowns, we shall see that they are inter-related (or so-called *linearly dependent*) and so there is no unique solution (this is natural since we are generating a general point on the line, not just one point). These equations enable us to calculate two of the coordinates in terms of a third (see example 7.1).

As with two dimensions, this is not the only way of representing a line, in fact the second way we introduce is possibly more useful. The general point on the line is represented as a vector that is dependent on only one real number μ, and is given as the vector sum of two scalar multiples of vectors:

$$p(\mu) \equiv (1 - \mu)p_1 + \mu p_2 \quad \text{where} \quad -\infty < \mu < \infty$$

That is

$$p(\mu) \equiv ((1 - \mu) \times x_1 + \mu \times x_2, (1 - \mu) \times y_1 + \mu \times y_2, (1 - \mu) \times z_1 + \mu \times z_2)$$

This form is exactly equivalent to the two-dimensional parametric form of a line that we saw in chapter 3. Here we place μ in brackets after p to demonstrate the dependence of p on μ; however, when this concept has been fully investigated, then (μ) will be ignored. Note that when $\mu = 0$ the equation returns point p_1 and when $\mu = 1$ it gives point p_2.

We may rewrite this vector expression as

$$p(\mu) \equiv p_1 + \mu(p_2 - p_1)$$

Like its counterpart in two dimensions, p_1 is called a *base vector* and $(p_2 - p_1)$ a *directional vector*. Again we see the dual interpretation of a vector. A vector may be used to specify a point uniquely in three-dimensional space, or it may be considered as a general direction, namely any line parallel to the line that joins the origin to the vector (considered as a point). We can move along a line in one of two directions, so we say that the direction from the origin to the point has *positive sense*, and the direction from the point to the origin has *negative sense*. Hence vectors $d \equiv (x, y, z)$ and $-d \equiv (-x, -y, -z)$ represent the same line in space but their directions are of opposite senses. We define the length of a vector $d \equiv (x, y, z)$ (sometimes called its modulus, or absolute value) as $|d|$, and the distance of the point vector from the origin is

$$|d| = \sqrt{(x^2 + y^2 + z^2)}$$

So any point on the line $p + \mu d$ is found by moving to the point p and then travelling along a line that is parallel to the direction d, a distance of $\mu \,|d\,|$ in the positive sense of d if μ is positive, and in the negative sense otherwise. Note that any point on the line can act as a base vector, and the directional vector may be replaced by any non-zero scalar multiple of itself.

If the directional vector $d \equiv (x, y, z)$ makes angles of θ_x, θ_y and θ_z with the respective positive x-direction, y-direction and z-direction, then

$$x : y : z = \cos \theta_x : \cos \theta_y : \cos \theta_z$$

which means that

$$d \equiv (\lambda \times \cos \theta_x, \lambda \times \cos \theta_y, \lambda \times \cos \theta_z) \text{ for some } \lambda$$

We know from the properties of three-dimensional geometry that

$$\cos^2 \theta_x + \cos^2 \theta_y + \cos^2 \theta_z = 1$$

Hence $\lambda = |d\,|$, and if the directional vector has unit modulus (that is, modulus = $\lambda = 1$), then the coordinates of this vector must be $(\cos \theta_x, \cos \theta_y, \cos \theta_z)$. The coordinates of a directional vector given in this way are called the *direction cosines* of the set of lines that is generated by the vector. In general, if the direction vector is $d \equiv (x, y, z)$ then the direction cosines are

$$\left(\frac{x}{|d\,|}, \frac{y}{|d\,|}, \frac{z}{|d\,|} \right)$$

Example 7.1
Describe the line joining $(1, 2, 3)$ to $(-1, 0, 2)$, by using the three methods shown so far.

The general point (x, y, z) on the line satisfies the equations

$$(x - 1) \times (0 - 2) \quad = (y - 2) \times (-1 - 1)$$
$$(y - 2) \times (2 - 3) \quad = (z - 3) \times (0 - 2)$$
$$(z - 3) \times (-1 - 1) \quad = (x - 1) \times (2 - 3)$$

That is

$$-2x + 2y = 2 \tag{7.1}$$
$$-y + 2z = 4 \tag{7.2}$$
$$-2z + x = -5 \tag{7.3}$$

Note that equation (7.1) is -2 times the sum of equations (7.2) and (7.3). Thus we need consider only these latter two equations, to get

$$x = 2z - 5$$
$$y = 2z - 4$$

Hence the general point on the line depends only on one variable, in this case z, and it is given by $(2z - 5, 2z - 4, z)$. This result can easily be checked by noting that when $z = 3$ we get $(1, 2, 3)$ and when $z = 2$ we get $(-1, 0, 2)$, the two original points that define the line.

In vector form the general point on the line (depending on μ) is

$$p(\mu) \equiv (1 - \mu)(1, 2, 3) + \mu(-1, 0, 2) \equiv (1 - 2\mu, 2 - 2\mu, 3 - \mu)$$

Again the coordinates depend on just one variable (μ), and to check the validity of this representation of a line we note that $p(0) \equiv (1, 2, 3)$ and $p(1) \equiv (-1, 0, 2)$.

If we put the line into base/directional vector form we see that

$$p(\mu) \equiv (1, 2, 3) + \mu(-2, -2, -1)$$

with $(1, 2, 3)$ as the base vector and $(-2, -2, -1)$ as the direction (which incidently has modulus $\sqrt{(4 + 4 + 1)} = \sqrt{9} = 3$). We also noted that any point on the line can act as a base vector, and so we can give another form for the general point on this line, p':

$$p'(\mu) \equiv (-1, 0, 2) + \mu(-2, -2, -1)$$

We can change the directional vector into its direction cosine form $(-2/3, -2/3, -1/3)$ and represent the line in another version of the base/direction form:

$$p''(\mu) \equiv (1, 2, 3) + \mu(-2/3, -2/3, -1/3)$$

Naturally the same μ value will give different points for different representations of the line; for example, $p(3) \equiv (-5, -4, 0), p'(3) \equiv (-7, -6, -1)$ and $p''(3) \equiv (-1, 0, 2)$. The direction of this line makes angles of 131.81 degrees (= $\cos^{-1}(-2/3)$), 131.81 degrees and 109.47 degrees (= $\cos^{-1}(-1/3)$) with the positive x-direction, y-direction and z-direction respectively.

The Angle between Two Directional Vectors

In order to calculate such an angle we first introduce the operator $\cdot$, the *dot product* or *scalar product*. This operates on two vectors and returns a scalar (real) result thus:

$$p \cdot q = (x_1, y_1, z_1) \cdot (x_2, y_2, z_2) = x_1 \times x_2 + y_1 \times y_2 + z_1 \times z_2$$

If p and q are both unit vectors (that is, they are in direction cosine form), and θ is the angle between the lines, then $\cos \theta = p \cdot q$ (see chapter 3 for the equivalent two-dimensional relationship). In general, therefore, the angle between two directional vectors p and q (we can assume they meet at the origin) is

$$\cos^{-1}\left(\frac{p}{|p|} \cdot \frac{q}{|q|}\right)$$

Obviously p and q are mutually perpendicular directions if and only if $p \cdot q = 0$.

Definition of a Plane

The plane is the next object we must consider in three-dimensional space. The general point $x \equiv (x, y, z)$ on the plane is given by the vector equation:

$$n \cdot x = k$$

where k is a scalar, and n is the directional vector of the set of lines that are perpendicular to (or *normal* to) the plane (see example 7.2). If a is any point on the plane then naturally $n \cdot a = k$, and so by replacing k in the above equation, we may rewrite it as

$$n \cdot x = n \cdot a \quad \text{or} \quad n \cdot (x - a) = 0$$

This latter equation is self-evident from the property of the dot product — two mutually perpendicular lines have zero dot product. For any point $x \equiv (x, y, z)$ in the plane that is not equal to a, we know that $(x - a)$ can be considered as the direction of a line in the plane. Since n is normal to the plane, and incidently perpendicular to every line in the plane, then $n \cdot (x - a) = \cos(\pi/2) = 0$.

By expanding the original equation of the plane with normal $n \equiv (n_1, n_2, n_3)$, we get the usual coordinate representation of a plane:

$$(n_1, n_2, n_3) \cdot (x, y, z) = n_1 \times x + n_2 \times y + n_3 \times z = k$$

Note that two planes with normals n and m (say) are parallel if and only if one normal is a scalar multiple of the other, that is if $n = \lambda m$ for some $\lambda \neq 0$.

The Point of Intersection of a Line and a Plane

Suppose the line is given by $b + \mu d$ and the plane by $n \cdot x = k$. Since the point of intersection lies on both the line and the plane we have to find the unique value of μ (if one exists) for which

$$n \cdot (b + \mu d) = k$$

that is

$$\mu = (k - n \cdot b)/(n \cdot d) \text{ provided } n \cdot d \neq 0$$

$n \cdot d = 0$ if the line and plane are parallel and so either there is no point of intersection or the line is in the plane.

The Distance of a Point from a Plane

The distance of a point p_1 from a plane $n \cdot x = k$ is the distance of p_1 from the nearest point p_2 on the plane. Hence the normal from the plane at p_2 must pass through p_1. This line can be written $p_1 + \mu n$, and the μ value that defines p_2 is such that

$$\mu = (k - n \cdot p_1)/(n \cdot n)$$

from the equation above, and the distance of the point $p_2 \equiv p_1 + \mu n$ from p_1 is

$$\mu \times |n| = |k - n \cdot p_1|/|n|$$

In particular, if p_1 is the origin O then the distance of the plane from the origin is $|k|/|n|$. Furthermore, if n is a direction cosine vector we see that the distance of the origin from the plane is $|k|$, the absolute value of the real number k.

Example 7.2

Find the point of intersection of the line joining $(1, 2, 3)$ to $(-1, 0, 2)$ with the plane $(0, -2, 1) \cdot x = 5$, and also find the distance of the plane from the origin.

$$n \equiv (0, -2, 1)$$
$$b \equiv (1, 2, 3)$$
$$d \equiv (-1, 0, 2) - (1, 2, 3) \equiv (-2, -2, -1)$$
$$n \cdot b = (0 \times 1 + -2 \times 2 + 1 \times 3) = -1$$
$$n \cdot d = (0 \times -2 + -2 \times -2 + 1 \times -1) = 3$$

hence the μ value of the point of intersection is $(5 - (-1))/3 = 2$, and the point vector is

$$(1, 2, 3) + 2(-2, -2, -1) \equiv (-3, -2, 1)$$

and the distance from the origin is $5/|n| = 5/\sqrt{5} = \sqrt{5}$.

The program given in listing 7.1 enables us to calculate the point of intersection (array P) of a line and a plane. The line has base vector B and direction D, and the plane has normal N and plane constant K. Note that, since we are working with decimal numbers, and thus are subject to rounding errors, we cannot check if a dot product is zero. We can find only if it is sufficiently small to be considered zero, and what is meant by sufficiently small is left to the programmer (on the IBM PC about six places after the decimal point is reasonable).

The Point of Intersection of Two Lines

Suppose we have two lines $b_1 + \mu d_1$ and $b_2 + \lambda d_2$. Their point of intersection, if it exists (if the lines are not coplanar or are parallel then they will not intersect), is identified by finding unique values for μ and λ that satisfy the vector equation (three separate coordinate equations):

$$b_1 + \mu d_1 = b_2 + \lambda d_2$$

Listing 7.1

```
100 'Intersection of a line and a plane in 3-D space.
110 DIM B(3),D(3),N(3),P(3)
120 CLS
130 LOCATE 3,5
140 PRINT "INTERSECTION of LINE  and PLANE"
149 'INPUT data on line and plane.
150 LOCATE 5,1
160 INPUT " Base vector of line ",B(1),B(2),B(3)
170 INPUT " Direction vector of ",D(1),D(2),D(3)
180 INPUT " Normal to plane ",N(1),N(2),N(3)
190 INPUT " Plane constant ",K
200 DOT=N(1)*D(1)+N(2)*D(2)+N(3)*D(3)
210 CLS
219 'output data on the lines.
220 LOCATE 3,5
230 PRINT "INTERSECTION of LINE  and PLANE"
240 LOCATE 5,5  : PRINT "base vector of line "
250 LOCATE 6,5  : PRINT "(";B(1);",";B(2);",";B(3);")"
260 LOCATE 8,5  : PRINT "direction vector of line "
270 LOCATE 9,5  : PRINT "(";D(1);",";D(2);",";D(3);")"
280 LOCATE 11,5 : PRINT "normal to plane "
290 LOCATE 12,5 : PRINT "(";N(1);",";N(2);",";N(3);")"
300 LOCATE 14,5 : PRINT "plane constant "
310 LOCATE 15,5 : PRINT K
320 LOCATE 18,5 : PRINT "Point of Intersection"
329 'find point of intersection ( if any ).
330 IF ABS(DOT)<.000001 THEN LOCATE 18,26 :
                         PRINT " does not exist" : GOTO 390
340 MU=(K-N(1)*B(1)-N(2)*B(2)-N(3)*B(3))/DOT
350 FOR I%=1 TO 3
360 P(I%)=B(I%)+MU*D(I%)
370 NEXT I%
380 LOCATE 19,5 : PRINT "(";P(1);",";P(2);",";P(3);")"
390 LOCATE 22,1
400 END
```

Three equations in two unknowns means that for the equations to be meaningful there must be at least one pair of the equations that are independent, and the remaining equation must be a combination of these two. Two lines are parallel if one directional vector is a scalar multiple of the other. So we take two independent equations, find the values of μ and λ (we have two equations in two unknowns), and put them in the third equation to see if they are consistent. Example 7.3 will demonstrate this method, and listing 7.2 is a way of implementing it on a computer. The first line has base and direction stored in arrays B and D, and the second line in C and E: the calculated point of intersection goes into array P.

Note that if the two independent equations are

$$a_{11} \times \mu + a_{12} \times \lambda = b_1$$

$$a_{21} \times \mu + a_{22} \times \lambda = b_2$$

then the *determinant* of this pair of equations, $\Delta = a_{11} \times a_{22} - a_{12} \times a_{21}$, will be non-zero (because the equations are not related), and we have the solutions:

$$\mu = (a_{22} \times b_1 - a_{12} \times b_2)/\Delta \quad \text{and} \quad \lambda = (a_{11} \times b_2 - a_{21} \times b_1)/\Delta$$

Listing 7.2

```
100 'Intersection of two lines in 3-D space.
110 DIM B(3),D(3),C(3),E(3),N(3),P(3)
120 CLS
130 LOCATE 3,5
140 PRINT "INTERSECTION of TWO LINES"
149 'INPUT data on two lines.
150 LOCATE 5,1
160 INPUT " base vector for first line ",B(1),B(2),B(3)
170 INPUT " direction vector for first line ",D(1),D(2),D(3)
180 INPUT " base vector for second line ",C(1),C(2),C(3)
190 INPUT " direction vector for second line ",E(1),E(2),E(3)
200 CLS
209 'output data on the lines.
210 LOCATE 3,5
220 PRINT "INTERSECTION of TWO LINES"
230 LOCATE 5,5   : PRINT "base vector for first line "
240 LOCATE 6,5   : PRINT "(";B(1);",";B(2);",";B(3);")"
250 LOCATE 8,5   : PRINT "direction vector for first line "
260 LOCATE 9,5   : PRINT "(";D(1);",";D(2);",";D(3);")"
270 LOCATE 11,5  : PRINT "base vector for second line "
280 LOCATE 12,5  : PRINT "(";C(1);",";C(2);",";C(3);")"
290 LOCATE 14,5  : PRINT "direction vector for second line "
300 LOCATE 15,5  : PRINT "(";E(1);",";E(2);",";E(3);")"
310 LOCATE 18,5  : PRINT "Point of Intersection"
319 'find independent equations.
320 FOR I%=1 TO 3
330 J%=(I% MOD 3)+1
340 DELTA=E(I%)*D(J%)-E(J%)*D(I%)
350 IF ABS(DELTA)>.000001 THEN GOTO 390
360 NEXT I%
369 'find point of intersection.
370 LOCATE 18,26 : PRINT " does not exist"
380 GOTO 470
390 MU=(E(I%)*(C(J%)-B(J%))-E(J%)*(C(I%)-B(I%)))/DELTA
400 LAMBDA=(D(I%)*(C(J%)-B(J%))-D(J%)*(C(I%)-B(I%)))/DELTA
410 K%=(J% MOD 3)+1
420 IF ABS(B(K%)+MU*D(K%)-C(K%)-LAMBDA*E(K%))>.000001 THEN GOTO 370
430 FOR I%=1 TO 3
440 P(I%)=B(I%)+MU*D(I%)
450 NEXT I%
460 LOCATE 19,5  : PRINT "(";P(1);",";P(2);",";P(3);")"
470 LOCATE 22,1
480 END
```

Example 7.3

Find the point of intersection (if any) of
(a) $(1, 1, 1) + \mu(2, 1, 3)$ with $(0, 0, 1) + \lambda(-1, 1, 1)$;
(b) $(2, 3, 4) + \mu(1, 1, 1)$ with $(-2, -3, -4) + \lambda(1, 2, 3)$.
   In (a) the three equations are

$$1 + 2\mu = 0 - \lambda \tag{7.4}$$

$$1 + \mu = 0 + \lambda \tag{7.5}$$

$$1 + 3\mu = 1 + \lambda \tag{7.6}$$

From equations (7.4) and (7.5) we get $\mu = -2/3$ and $\lambda = 1/3$, which when substituted in equation (7.6) gives $1 + 3 \times (-2/3) = -1$ on the left-hand side and $1 + 1 \times (1/3) = 4/3$ on the right-hand side, which are obviously unequal so the lines do not intersect.
   From (b) we get the equations

$$2 + \mu = -2 + \lambda \tag{7.7}$$

$$3 + \mu = -3 + 2\lambda \tag{7.8}$$

$$4 + \mu = -4 + 3\lambda \tag{7.9}$$

and from equations (7.7) and (7.8) we get $\mu = -2$ and $\lambda = 2$, and these values also satisfy equation (7.9) (left-hand side = right-hand side = 2). So the point of intersection is

$$(2, 3, 4) - 2(1, 1, 1) = (-2, -3, -4) + 2(1, 2, 3) = (0, 1, 2)$$

The Plane through Three Non-collinear Points

In order to solve this problem we must introduce a new vector operator, $\times$ the *vector product*, which operates on two vectors p and q (say) giving the vector result

$$p \times q = (p_1, p_2, p_3) \times (q_1, q_2, q_3)$$

$$= (p_2 \times q_3 - p_3 \times q_2, p_3 \times q_1 - p_1 \times q_3, p_1 \times q_2 - p_2 \times q_1)$$

If p and q are non-parallel directional vectors then $p \times q$ is the directional vector that is perpendicular to both p and q. It should also be noted that this operation is *non-commutative*. That is, in general for given values of p and q we note that $p \times q \neq q \times p$; these two vector products will represent directions on the same line but with opposite sense. For example $(1, 0, 0) \times (0, 1, 0) = (0, 0, 1)$ but $(0, 1, 0) \times (1, 0, 0) = (0, 0, -1); (0, 0, 1)$ and $(0, 0, -1)$ are both parallel to the z-axis (and so perpendicular to the directions $(1, 0, 0)$ and $(0, 1, 0)$), but they are of opposite sense. Listing 7.3 gives a main program that calls the routines 'vecprod' (for the vector product of two vectors L and M returning vector N) and 'dotprod' (which calculates the dot product DOT of the vectors L and M).

Suppose we are given three non-collinear points p_1, p_2 and p_3. Then the two vectors $p_2 - p_1$ and $p_3 - p_1$ represent the directions of two lines that are coincident at p_1, both of which lie in the plane that contains the three points. We know that the normal to the plane is perpendicular to every line in the plane, in particular to the two lines mentioned above. Also, because the points are not collinear, $p_2 - p_1 \neq p_3 - p_1$, the normal to the plane is $(p_2 - p_1) \times (p_3 - p_1)$, and since p_1 lies in the plane the equation is

$$((p_2 - p_1) \times (p_3 - p_1)) \cdot (x - p_1) = 0$$

Example 7.4
Give the coordinate equation of the plane through the points $(0, 1, 1), (1, 2, 3)$ and $(-2, 3, -1)$.

Listing 7.3

```
100 ' Example of Dot and Vector Product.
110 DIM L(3),M(3),N(3)
120 CLS
130 LOCATE 5,5  : PRINT "Example of Dot and Vector Product"
140 LOCATE 20,1 : INPUT "Type in vector L ",L(1),L(2),L(3)
150 LOCATE 20,1 : PRINT SPC(79)
160 LOCATE 7,5
170 PRINT "Vector L  :  (";L(1);",";L(2);",";L(3);")"
180 LOCATE 20,1 : INPUT "Type in vector m ",M(1),M(2),M(3)
190 LOCATE 20,1 : PRINT SPC(79)
200 LOCATE 9,5
210 PRINT "Vector M  :  (";M(1);",";M(2);",";M(3);")"
220 GOSUB 500 'dotprod
230 GOSUB 600 'vecprod
240 LOCATE 12,5
250 PRINT "Dot Product   = ";DOT
260 LOCATE 14,5
270 PRINT "Vector Product = (";N(1);",";N(2);",";N(3);")"
280 LOCATE 20,1
290 END

500 ' dotprod
501 ' **in ** L(3),M(3)
502 ' **out** DOT
510 DOT=L(1)*M(1)+L(2)*M(2)+L(3)*M(3)
520 RETURN

600 ' vecprod
601 ' **in ** L(3),M(3)
602 ' **out** N(3)
610 FOR I%=1 TO 3
620 J%=(I% MOD 3)+1 : K%=(J% MOD 3)+1
630 N(I%)=L(J%)*M(K%)-L(K%)*M(J%)
640 NEXT I%
650 RETURN
```

This is given by the general point $x \equiv (x, y, z)$ where

$$(((1, 2, 3) - (0, 1, 1)) \times ((-2, 3, -1) - (0, 1, 1))) \cdot ((x, y, z)$$
$$- (0, 1, 1)) = 0$$

that is

$$((1, 1, 2) \times (-2, 2, -2)) \cdot (x, y - 1, z - 1) = 0$$

or

$$(-6, -2, 4) \cdot (x, y - 1, z - 1) = 0$$

which in coordinate form is $-6x - 2y + 4z - 2 = 0$ or in the equivalent form $3x + y - 2z = -1$.

The Point of Intersection of Three Planes

We assume that the three planes are defined by equations (7.10) to (7.12) below. The point of intersection of these three planes, $b \equiv (x, y, z)$, must lie in all three planes and satisfy

$$n_1 \cdot x = k_1 \qquad (7.10)$$

$$n_2 \cdot x = k_2 \qquad (7.11)$$

$$n_3 \cdot x = k_3 \qquad (7.12)$$

where $n_1 \equiv (n_{11}, n_{12}, n_{13})$, $n_2 \equiv (n_{21}, n_{22}, n_{23})$ and $n_3 \equiv (n_{31}, n_{32}, n_{33})$. We can rewrite these three equations as one matrix equation

$$\begin{pmatrix} n_{11} & n_{12} & n_{13} \\ n_{21} & n_{22} & n_{23} \\ n_{31} & n_{32} & n_{33} \end{pmatrix} \times \begin{pmatrix} x \\ y \\ z \end{pmatrix} = \begin{pmatrix} k_1 \\ k_2 \\ k_3 \end{pmatrix}$$

and so the solution for b is given by the *column vector*

$$\begin{pmatrix} x \\ y \\ z \end{pmatrix} = \begin{pmatrix} n_{11} & n_{12} & n_{13} \\ n_{21} & n_{22} & n_{23} \\ n_{31} & n_{32} & n_{33} \end{pmatrix}^{-1} \times \begin{pmatrix} k_1 \\ k_2 \\ k_3 \end{pmatrix}$$

So any calculation that requires the intersection of three planes necessarily involves the inversion of a 3 × 3 matrix. Listing 7.4 gives the Adjoint method of finding NINV, the inverse of matrix N. It also returns variable SNG% which equals 0 if N is non-singular and 1 otherwise.

Listing 7.4

```
1000 'inverse of 3 by 3 matrix
1001 ' **in ** N(3,3)
1002 ' **out** SNG,NINV(3,3)
1009 'find NINV, the inverse of 3x3 matrix N : Adjoint method.
1010 DET=0 : NI%=2 : NNI%=3
1019 'find DET, the determinant of matrix N.
1020 FOR I%=1 TO 3
1030 DET=DET+N(1,I%)*(N(2,NI%)*N(3,NNI%)-N(3,NI%)*N(2,NNI%))
1040 NI%=NNI% : NNI%=(NNI% MOD 3)+1
1050 NEXT I%
1059 'if DET=0 then the matrix N is singular.
1060 IF ABS(DET)<.000001 THEN SNG%=1 : RETURN
1070 SNG%=0 : NI%=2 : NNI%=3
1080 FOR I%=1 TO 3
1090 NJ%=2 : NNJ%=3
1100 FOR J%=1 TO 3
1110 NINV(J%,I%)=
        (N(NI%,NJ%)*N(NNI%,NNJ%)-N(NI%,NNJ%)*N(NNI%,NJ%))/DET
1120 NJ%=NNJ% : NNJ%=(NNJ% MOD 3)+1
1130 NEXT J%
1140 NI%=NNI% : NNI%=(NNI% MOD 3)+1
1150 NEXT I%
1160 RETURN
```

Again in the program to solve this problem (listing 7.5), vectors are represented as one-dimensional arrays, thus array B will contain the solution of the equations (*b*); array K will contain the plane constants. We are given the normals n_1, n_2 and n_3 in the form of a 3 × 3 array N, so the values in B are found by the following code. Obviously if any two of the planes are parallel or the three meet in a line, then SNG% equals 1 and there is no unique point of intersection.

Listing 7.5

```
100 'Intersection of three planes in 3-D space.
110 DIM N(3,3),NINV(3,3),K(3),B(3)
120 CLS
130 LOCATE 3,5
140 PRINT "INTERSECTION of THREE PLANES"
149 'INPUT data on planes.
150 LOCATE 5,1
160 INPUT " Normal to first plane ",N(1,1),N(1,2),N(1,3)
170 INPUT " Constant of first plane ",K(1)
180 INPUT " Normal to second plane ",N(2,1),N(2,2),N(2,3)
190 INPUT " Constant of second plane ",K(2)
200 INPUT " Normal to third plane ",N(3,1),N(3,2),N(3,3)
210 INPUT " Constant of third plane ",K(3)
220 CLS
229 'output data on the planes.
230 LOCATE 3,5
240 PRINT "INTERSECTION of THREE PLANES"
250 LOCATE 5,5  : PRINT "Normal and constant of first plane "
260 LOCATE 6,5  : PRINT "(";N(1,1);",";N(1,2);",";N(1,3);")    ";K(1)
270 LOCATE 8,5  : PRINT "Normal and constant of second plane "
280 LOCATE 9,5  : PRINT "(";N(2,1);",";N(2,2);",";N(2,3);")    ";K(2)
290 LOCATE 11,5 : PRINT "Normal and constant of third plane "
300 LOCATE 12,5 : PRINT "(";N(3,1);",";N(3,2);",";N(3,3);")    ";K(3)
310 LOCATE 18,5 : PRINT "Point of Intersection "
319 'find B, the point of intersection ( if any ).
    Find NINV, the inverse of 3x3 matrix N.
320 GOSUB 1000 'inverse
330 IF SNG%=1 THEN LOCATE 18,26 : PRINT "does not exist" : GOTO 410
340 FOR I%=1 TO 3
350 B(I%)=0
360 FOR J%=1 TO 3
370 B(I%)=B(I%)+NINV(I%,J%)*K(J%)
380 NEXT J%
390 NEXT I%
400 LOCATE 19,5 : PRINT "(";B(1);",";B(2);",";B(3);")"
410 LOCATE 22,1
420 END
```

Example 7.5

Find the point of intersection of the three planes $(0, 1, 1) \cdot x = 2, (1, 2, 3) \cdot x = 4$ and $(1, 1, 1) \cdot x = 0$.

In the matrix form we have

$$\begin{pmatrix} 0 & 1 & 1 \\ 1 & 2 & 3 \\ 1 & 1 & 1 \end{pmatrix} \times \begin{pmatrix} x \\ y \\ z \end{pmatrix} = \begin{pmatrix} 2 \\ 4 \\ 0 \end{pmatrix}$$

The inverse of $\begin{pmatrix} 0 & 1 & 1 \\ 1 & 2 & 3 \\ 1 & 1 & 1 \end{pmatrix}$ is $\begin{pmatrix} -1 & 0 & 1 \\ 2 & -1 & 1 \\ -1 & 1 & -1 \end{pmatrix}$

and so

$$\begin{pmatrix} x \\ y \\ z \end{pmatrix} = \begin{pmatrix} -1 & 0 & 1 \\ 2 & -1 & 1 \\ -1 & 1 & -1 \end{pmatrix} \times \begin{pmatrix} 2 \\ 4 \\ 0 \end{pmatrix} = \begin{pmatrix} -2 \\ 0 \\ 2 \end{pmatrix}$$

This solution is easily checked: $(0, 1, 1) \cdot (-2, 0, 2) = 2$, $(1, 2, 3) \cdot (-2, 0, 2) = 4$ and $(1, 1, 1) \cdot (-2, 0, 2) = 0$, which means the point $(-2, 0, 2)$ lies on all three planes and so is their point of intersection.

The Line of Intersection of Two Planes

Let the two planes be

$$p \cdot x = (p_1, p_2, p_3) \cdot x = k_1$$

and

$$q \cdot x = (q_1, q_2, q_3) \cdot x = k_2$$

We assume that the planes are not parallel, and so $p \neq \lambda q$ for all λ. The line common to the two planes naturally lies in each plane, and so it must be perpendicular to the normals of both planes (p and q). Thus the direction of this line must be $d \equiv p \times q$ and the line can be written in the form $b + \mu d$, where b can be any point on the line. In order completely to classify the line we have to find one such b. We find a point that is the intersection of the two planes together with a third that is neither parallel to them nor cuts them in a common line. By choosing a plane with normal $p \times q$ we shall satisfy these conditions (and remember we have already calculated this vector product). We still need a value for k_3, but any value will do, so we take $k_3 = 0$ in order that this third plane goes through the origin. Thus b is given by the column vector

$$b = \begin{pmatrix} p_1 & p_2 & p_3 \\ q_1 & q_2 & q_3 \\ p_2 \times q_3 - p_3 \times q_2 & p_3 \times q_1 - p_1 \times q_3 & p_1 \times q_2 - p_2 \times q_1 \end{pmatrix}^{-1} \times \begin{pmatrix} k_1 \\ k_2 \\ 0 \end{pmatrix}$$

Example 7.6

Find the line that is common to the planes $(0, 1, 1) \cdot x = 2$ and $(1, 2, 3) \cdot x = 2$.

$p = (0, 1, 1)$ and $q = (1, 2, 3)$, and so $p \times q = (1 \times 3 - 1 \times 2, 1 \times 1 - 0 \times 3, 0 \times 2 - 1 \times 1) = (1, 1, -1)$. We require the inverse of

$$\begin{pmatrix} 0 & 1 & 1 \\ 1 & 2 & 3 \\ 1 & 1 & -1 \end{pmatrix} = \frac{1}{3} \begin{pmatrix} -5 & 2 & 1 \\ 4 & -1 & 1 \\ -1 & 1 & -1 \end{pmatrix}$$

and hence the point of intersection of the three planes is

$$\frac{1}{3} \begin{pmatrix} -5 & 2 & 1 \\ 4 & -1 & 1 \\ -1 & 1 & -1 \end{pmatrix} \times \begin{pmatrix} 2 \\ 2 \\ 0 \end{pmatrix} = \frac{1}{3} \begin{pmatrix} -6 \\ 6 \\ 0 \end{pmatrix} = \begin{pmatrix} -2 \\ 2 \\ 0 \end{pmatrix}$$

and the line is $(-2, 2, 0) + \mu(1, 1, -1)$.

It is easy to check this result, because all the points on the line should lie in both planes:

$(0, 1, 1) \cdot ((-2, 2, 0) + \mu(1, 1, -1))$

$= (0, 1, 1) \cdot (-2, 2, 0) + \mu(0, 1, 1) \cdot (1, 1, -1) = 2$ for all μ

and

$(1, 2, 3) \cdot ((-2, 2, 0) + \mu(1, 1, -1))$

$= (0, 1, 1) \cdot (-2, 2, 0) + \mu(1, 2, 3) \cdot (1, 1, -1) = 2$ for all μ

The program to solve this problem is given as listing 7.6; note that it is very similar to the previous program. Also note that arrays are not explicitly used for p and q – these values are stored in the first two rows of array N. Array B holds the base vector of the line of intersection, but we do not place d in an array because the values are already in the third row of N.

Functional Representation of a Surface

In our study of two-dimensional space in chapter 3 we noted that curves can be represented in a functional notation. This idea can be extended into three dimensions when we study surfaces. The simplest form of surface is an infinite plane with normal $n \equiv (n_1, n_2, n_3)$, which we have seen can be given as a coordinate equation:

$$n \cdot x - k = n_1 \times x + n_2 \times y + n_3 \times z - k = 0$$

This can be rewritten in functional form for a general point $x \equiv (x, y, z)$ on the surface:

$$f(x) \equiv f(x, y, z) \equiv n_1 \times x + n_2 \times y + n_3 \times z - k \equiv n \cdot x - k$$

which is a simple expression in variables x, y and z (x). This enables us to divide all the points in space into three sets, those with $f(x) = 0$ (the zero set), those with $f(x) < 0$ (the negative set) and those with $f(x) > 0$ (the positive set). A point x lies on the surface if and only if it belongs to the zero set. If the surface divides space into two halves (each half being *connected*, that is any two points in a given half can be joined by a curve that does not cross the surface) then these two halves may be identified with the positive and negative sets. Again

Listing 7.6

```
100 'Intersection of two planes in 3-D space.
110 DIM N(3,3),NINV(3,3),K(3),B(3)
120 CLS
130 LOCATE 3,5
140 PRINT "INTERSECTION of TWO PLANES"
149 'INPUT data on planes.
150 LOCATE 5,1
160 INPUT " Normal to first plane ",N(1,1),N(1,2),N(1,3)
170 INPUT " Constant of first plane ",K(1)
180 INPUT " Normal to second plane ",N(2,1),N(2,2),N(2,3)
190 INPUT " Constant of second plane ",K(2)
199 'find third rows of N and K.
200 N(3,1)=N(1,2)*N(2,3)-N(1,3)*N(2,2)
210 N(3,2)=N(1,3)*N(2,1)-N(1,1)*N(2,3)
220 N(3,3)=N(1,1)*N(2,2)-N(1,2)*N(2,1)
230 K(3)=0
240 CLS
249 'output data on the planes.
250 LOCATE 3,5
260 PRINT "INTERSECTION of TWO PLANES"
270 LOCATE 5,5 : PRINT "Normal and constant of first plane "
280 LOCATE 6,5 : PRINT "(";N(1,1);",";N(1,2);",";N(1,3);")"    ";K(1)
290 LOCATE 8,5 : PRINT "Normal and constant of second plane "
300 LOCATE 9,5 : PRINT "(";N(2,1);",";N(2,2);",";N(2,3);")"    ";K(2)
309 'compare with previous listing.
310 LOCATE 12,5 : PRINT "Line of Intersection"
320 GOSUB 1000 'inverse
330 IF SNG%=1 THEN LOCATE 12,25 : PRINT " does not exist" : GOTO 440
340 FOR I%=1 TO 3
350 B(I%)=0
360 FOR J%=1 TO 3
370 B(I%)=B(I%)+NINV(I%,J%)*K(J%)
380 NEXT J%
390 NEXT I%
399 'output line of intersection.
400 LOCATE 14,5 : PRINT "Base vector "
410 LOCATE 15,5 : PRINT "(";B(1);",";B(2);",";B(3);")"
420 LOCATE 17,5 : PRINT "Directional vector"
430 LOCATE 18,5 : PRINT "(";N(3,1);",";N(3,2);",";N(3,3);")"
440 LOCATE 22,1
450 END
```

beware, there are many surfaces that divide space into more than two connected volumes and then it is impossible to relate functional representation with connected sets; for example $f(x, y, z) \equiv \cos(y) - \sin(x^2 + z^2)$. There are, however, many useful well-behaved surfaces with this property, the sphere of radius r for example:

$$f(x) \equiv r^2 - |x|^2$$

that is

$$f(x, y, z) \equiv r^2 - x^2 - y^2 - z^2$$

If $f(x) = 0$ then x lies on the sphere, if $f(x) < 0$ then x lies outside the sphere, and if $f(x) > 0$ then x lies inside the sphere.

The functional representation of a surface is a very useful concept. It can be used to define sets of equations that are necessary in calculating the intersections of various objects. The major use, however, is to determine whether or not two points p and q (say) lie on the same side of a surface that divides space into two parts. All we need do is to compare the signs of $f(p)$ and $f(q)$. If they are of opposite signs then a line joining p and q must cut the surface. Some examples are now given.

Is a point on the same side of a plane as the origin?
Suppose the plane is defined (as earlier) by three non-collinear points p_1, p_2 and p_3. Then the equation of the plane is

$$((p_2 - p_1) \times (p_3 - p_1)) \cdot (x - p_1) = 0$$

We may rewrite this in functional form

$$f(x) \equiv ((p_2 - p_1) \times (p_3 - p_1)) \cdot (x - p_1)$$

So all we need do for a point e (say) is to compare $f(e)$ with $f(O)$, where O is the origin. We assume here that neither O nor e lies in the plane.

We shall see that this idea will be of great use in the study of hidden surface algorithms.

Example 7.7

Are the origin and point $(1, 1, 3)$ on the same side of the plane defined by points $(0, 1, 1), (1, 2, 3)$ and $(-2, 3, -1)$?

From example 7.4 we see that the functional representation of the plane is

$$f(x) \equiv (-6, -2, 4) \cdot (x - (0, 1, 1))$$

Thus

$$f(0, 0, 0) = -(-6, -2, 4) \cdot (0, 1, 1) = -2$$

and

$$f(1, 1, 3) = (-6, -2, 4) \cdot ((1, 1, 3) - (0, 1, 1)) = 2$$

Hence $(1, 1, 3)$ lies on the opposite side of the plane to the origin and so a line segment that joins the two points will cut the plane at a point $(1 - \mu)(0, 0, 0) + \mu(1, 1, 3)$ where $0 < \mu < 1$.

Is an oriented convex polygon of vertices in two-dimensional space clockwise or anticlockwise?
We start by assuming that the polygon is a triangle that is defined by the three vertices $p_1 \equiv (x_1, y_1), p_2 \equiv (x_2, y_2)$ and $p_3 \equiv (x_3, y_3)$. Although these points are in two-dimensional space we can assume they lie in the x/y plane through the origin of three-dimensional space by giving them all a z-coordinate value of zero. We systematically define the directions of the edges of the polygon to be

$(p_2 - p_1), (p_3 - p_2)$ and $(p_1 - p_3)$. Since these lines all lie in the x/y plane through the origin we know that for all $i = 1, 2$ or 3 and for some real numbers r_i that depend on i

$$(p_{i+1} - p_i) \times (p_{i+2} - p_{i+1}) = (0, 0, r_i)$$

This is because this vector product is perpendicular to the x/y plane and so only z-coordinate values may be non-zero. The addition of subscripts is modulo 3. Because the vertices were taken systematically, note that the signs of these r_i values are always the same; but what is more important, if the p_i values are clockwise then the r_i values are all negative, and if the p_i values are anticlockwise the r_i values are all positive.

Given an oriented convex polygon we need only consider the first three vertices to find if it is clockwise or anticlockwise. This technique will prove to be invaluable when we deal with hidden line/surface algorithms later in this book. Listing 7.7 allows us to find whether or not three ordered two-dimensional vertices form an anticlockwise triangle.

Listing 7.7

```
100 'Orientation of a 2-D triangle.
110 DIM X(3),Y(3)
120 CLS : LOCATE 5,5
130 PRINT "Triangle defined by vertices :-"
140 ROW%=8
149 'INPUT/OUTPUT vertices of triangle.
150 FOR I%=1 TO 3
160 LOCATE 20,1
170 PRINT "Type coordinates of vertex ";I%
180 INPUT X(I%),Y(I%)
190 LOCATE 20,1 : PRINT SPC(40)
200 LOCATE 21,1 : PRINT SPC(40)
210 LOCATE ROW%,5
220 PRINT "Vertex ";I%;"   :   (";X(I%);",";Y(I%);")"
230 ROW%=ROW%+2
240 NEXT I%
249 'form two directional vectors (DX1,DY1,0) and (DX2,DY2,0).
250 DX1=X(2)-X(1) : DY1=Y(2)-Y(1)
260 DX2=X(3)-X(2) : DY2=Y(3)-Y(2)
270 LOCATE 15,5
280 PRINT "is oriented ";
289 'check signs of z-coordinate of their vector product.
290 IF DX1*DY2-DX2*DY1 > 0 THEN PRINT"ANTI-";
300 PRINT"CLOCKWISE"
310 LOCATE 22,1
320 END
```

Example 7.8

Why is the polygon given in example 3.4 anticlockwise?

The vertices (considered in three dimensions) are $(1, 0, 0), (5, 2, 0), (4, 4, 0)$ and $(-2, 1, 0)$. The directions of the edges are $(4, 2, 0), (-1, 2, 0), (-6, -3, 0)$ and $(3, -1, 0)$.

$$(4, 2, 0) \times (-1, 2, 0) = (0, 0, 10)$$

$$(-1, 2, 0) \times (-6, -3, 0) = (0, 0, 15)$$

$$(-6, -3, 0) \times (3, -1, 0) = (0, 0, 15)$$

$$(3, -1, 0) \times (4, 2, 0) = (0, 0, 10)$$

Since these are all positive, the orientation of the polygon is anticlockwise. But be careful, if you lose this consistent order for calculating the vector product you can get the wrong answer. For example

$$(-6, -3, 0) \times (4, 2, 0) = (0, 0, 0) - \text{the lines are parallel!}$$

or

$$(-1, 2, 0) \times (3, -1, 0) = (0, 0, -5) - \text{the edges have been taken out}$$
of sequence.

Complete Programs

The programs in this chapter do not require any library routines.

  I. Listing 7.1 (intersection of line and plane). Data required: a base vector (B(1), B(2), B(3)) and direction vector (D(1), D(2), D(3)) for the line, a normal (N(1), N(2), N(3)) and constant K for the plane. Try $(1, 2, 3), (0, 2, -1), (1, 0, 1)$ and 2 respectively.

 II. Listing 7.2 (intersection of two lines). Data required: a base and direction vectors for the two lines (B(1), B(2), B(3)) and (D(1), D(2), D(3)), and (C(1), C(2), C(3)) and (E(1), E(2), E(3)). Try $(1, 2, 3), (1, 1, -1)$, and $(-1, 1, 3)$, $(1, 0, 1)$.

III. Listing 7.3 (main program, 'vecprod' and 'dotprod'). Data required: two vectors (L(1), L(2), L(3)) and (M(1), M(2), M(3)). Try $(1, 2, 3), (1, 1, -1)$.

 IV. Listing 7.5 (intersection of three planes). MERGE in listing 7.4 ('inv'). Data required: normal (N(I, 1), N(I, 2), N(I, 3)) and constant K(I) for the three planes, $1 \leqslant I \leqslant 3$. Try $(1, 2, 3), 0, (1, 1, -1), 1, (1, 0, 1), 2$.

  V. Listing 7.6 (intersection of two planes). MERGE in listing 7.4 ('inv'). Data required: normal (N(I, 1), N(I, 2), N(I, 3)) and constant K(I) for the two planes, $1 \leqslant I \leqslant 2$. Try $(1, 2, 3), 0, (1, 1, -1), 1$.

 IV. Listing 7.7 (orientation of 2-D triangle). Data required: the vertices (X(I), Y(I)), $1 \leqslant I \leqslant 3$. Try $(1, 2), (2, 3)$ and $(-1, 1)$.

8 *Matrix Representation of Transformations on Three-Dimensional Space*

In chapter 4 we saw the need for transforming objects in two-dimensional space. When we draw three-dimensional pictures there will be many times when we need to make the equivalent linear transformations on three-dimensional space. As in the lower dimension, there are three basic types of transformation: translation, scaling and rotation. We will represent transformations as square matrices (now they will be 4 × 4). A general point in space relative to a fixed coordinate triad, the row vector (x, y, z), must be considered as a four-rowed column vector:

$$\begin{pmatrix} x \\ y \\ z \\ 1 \end{pmatrix}$$

All the operations on matrices (addition, scalar multiple, transpose, premultiplication of a column vector and matrix product) that we saw in chapter 4 are easily extended to cope with 4 × 4 matrices and column vectors by simply changing the upper bound of the index ranges from 3 to 4. In this way we can generate a routine 'mult3' (see listing 8.1) for multiplying two 4 × 4 matrices together. It is exactly equivalent to routine 'mult2' in the two-dimensional case, and for the very same reasons. The routine multiplies matrix A by matrix R to give matrix B, which is then copied into R. We also need the routine 'idR3' (see listing 8.1) which sets R to the identity matrix.

Consider the case of a general linear transformation on points in three-dimensional space. A point (x, y, z) – 'before' – is transformed into (x', y', z') – 'after' – according to three *linear equations*:

$$x' = A_{11} \times x + A_{12} \times y + A_{13} \times z + A_{14}$$

$$y' = A_{21} \times x + A_{22} \times y + A_{23} \times z + A_{24}$$

$$z' = A_{31} \times x + A_{32} \times y + A_{33} \times z + A_{34}$$

and as usual we add the extra equation:

$$1 = A_{41} \times x + A_{42} \times y + A_{43} \times z + A_{44}$$

which if it is to be true for all x, y and z means that $A_{41} = A_{42} = A_{43} = 0$ and that $A_{44} = 1$.

Then the equations may be written as a matrix equation where a column vector representing the 'after' point is the product of a matrix and the 'before' column vector:

$$\begin{pmatrix} x' \\ y' \\ z' \\ 1 \end{pmatrix} = \begin{pmatrix} A_{11} & A_{12} & A_{13} & A_{14} \\ A_{21} & A_{22} & A_{23} & A_{24} \\ A_{31} & A_{32} & A_{33} & A_{34} \\ A_{41} & A_{42} & A_{43} & A_{44} \end{pmatrix} \times \begin{pmatrix} x \\ y \\ z \\ 1 \end{pmatrix}$$

So if we store the transformation as a matrix, we can transform every required point by considering it as a column vector and *premultiplying* it by a transformation matrix. As before, transformations may be combined simply by obeying the sequence of transformations in order. If their equivalent matrices are A, B, C, . . . , L, M, N, then the matrix equivalent to the combination is N × M × L × . . . × C × B × A. Remember the order. Since we are premultiplying a column vector, then the first transformation appears on the right of the matrix product and the last on the left.

As with the two-dimensional case, we note that the 'bottom row' of all transformation matrices is always $(0, 0, 0, 1)$, and it is of no real use in calculations. It is added only to form square matrices which are necessary for the formal definition of matrix multiplication. We may adjust this definition, and that of the multiplication of a matrix and a column vector, so that instead we use only the top three rows of the 4×4 matrices (in chapter 4 we used the top two rows of 3×3 matrices in listings 4.2a, 4.3a, 4.4a and 4.5a).

Listing 8.1

```
9100  'mult3
9101  '**in ** A(4,4),R(4,4)
9102  '**out** R(4,4)
9110  FOR I%=1 TO 3
9120  FOR J%=1 TO 4
9130  B(I%,J%)=A(I%,1)*R(1,J%)+A(I%,2)*R(2,J%)+A(I%,3)*R(3,J%)
9140  NEXT J%
9150  B(I%,4)=B(I%,4)+A(I%,4)
9160  NEXT I%
9170  FOR J%=1 TO 4
9180  R(1,J%)=B(1,J%) : R(2,J%)=B(2,J%) : R(3,J%)=B(3,J%)
9190  NEXT J%
9200  RETURN

9300  'idR3
9302  '**out** R(4,4)
9310  ERASE R : DIM R(4,4)
9320  R(1,1)=1 : R(2,2)=1 : R(3,3)=1
9330  RETURN
```

Translation

Every point to be transformed is moved by a vector (TX, TY, TZ) say. This produces the following equations which relate the 'before' and 'after' coordinates:

$$x' = 1 \times x + 0 \times y + 0 \times z + TX$$

$$y' = 0 \times x + 1 \times y + 0 \times z + TY$$

$$z' = 0 \times x + 0 \times y + 1 \times z + TZ$$

so that the matrix describing the translation is

$$\begin{pmatrix} 1 & 0 & 0 & TX \\ 0 & 1 & 0 & TY \\ 0 & 0 & 1 & TZ \\ 0 & 0 & 0 & 1 \end{pmatrix}$$

The routine 'tran3' for producing such a matrix A, given the parameters TX, TY and TZ, is given in listing 8.2.

Listing 8.2

```
9000 'tran3
9001 '**in ** TX,TY,TZ
9002 '**out** A(4,4)
9010 ERASE A : DIM A(4,4)
9020 A(1,1)= 1 : A(2,2)= 1 : A(3,3)= 1
9030 A(1,4)=TX : A(2,4)=TY : A(3,4)=TZ
9040 RETURN
```

Scaling

The x-coordinate of every point to be transformed is scaled by a factor SX, the y-coordinate by SY and the z-coordinate by SZ, thus

$$x' = SX \times x + 0 \times y + 0 \times z + 0$$

$$y' = 0 \times x + SY \times y + 0 \times z + 0$$

$$z' = 0 \times x + 0 \times y + SZ \times z + 0$$

giving the matrix

$$\begin{pmatrix} SX & 0 & 0 & 0 \\ 0 & SY & 0 & 0 \\ 0 & 0 & SZ & 0 \\ 0 & 0 & 0 & 1 \end{pmatrix}$$

Usually the scaling values are positive, but if any of the values are negative then this leads to a reflection as well as (possibly) scaling. For example, if SX = −1 and SY = SZ = 1 then points are reflected in the y/z plane through the origin. A routine 'scale3' to produce such a scaling matrix A given SX, SY and SZ is shown in listing 8.3.

Listing 8.3

```
8900 'scale3
8901 '**in ** SX,SY,SZ
8902 '**out** A(4,4)
8910 ERASE A : DIM A(4,4)
8920 A(1,1)=SX : A(2,2)=SY : A(3,3)=SZ
8930 RETURN
```

Rotation about a Coordinate Axis

In order to consider the rotation about a general axis $p + \mu q$ by a given angle it is first necessary to simplify the problem by considering rotation about one of the coordinate axes.

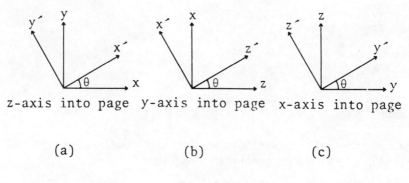

z-axis into page   y-axis into page   x-axis into page

(a)   (b)   (c)

Figure 8.1

(a) Rotation by an angle θ about the x-axis
Referring to figure 8.1c, the axis of rotation is perpendicular to the page (the positive x-axis being into the page), and since we are using left-handed axes the figure shows the point (x', y', z') that results from the transformation of an arbitrary point (x, y, z). We see that the rotation actually reduces to a two-dimensional rotation in the y/z plane that passes through the point; that is, after the rotation the x-coordinate remains unchanged. By using the ideas explained in chapter 4 we get the equations

$$x' = x$$

$$y' = \cos \theta \times y - \sin \theta \times z$$

$$z' = \sin \theta \times y + \cos \theta \times z$$

and thus the matrix is

$$\begin{pmatrix} 1 & 0 & 0 & 0 \\ 0 & \cos \theta & -\sin \theta & 0 \\ 0 & \sin \theta & \cos \theta & 0 \\ 0 & 0 & 0 & 1 \end{pmatrix}$$

(b) Rotation by an angle θ about the y-axis
Referring to figure 8.1b, we now have the positive *y*-axis into the page, and because of the left-handedness of the axes the positive *z*-axis is horizontal and to the right of the origin and the positive *x*-axis is above the origin. This leads us to the equations

$$x' = \sin \theta \times z + \cos \theta \times x$$

$$y' = y$$

$$z' = \cos \theta \times z - \sin \theta \times x$$

which gives the matrix

$$\begin{pmatrix} \cos \theta & 0 & \sin \theta & 0 \\ 0 & 1 & 0 & 0 \\ -\sin \theta & 0 & \cos \theta & 0 \\ 0 & 0 & 0 & 1 \end{pmatrix}$$

(c) Rotation by an angle θ about the z-axis
Referring to figure 8.1a we get the equations

$$x' = \cos \theta \times x - \sin \theta \times y$$

$$y' = \sin \theta \times x + \cos \theta \times y$$

$$z' = z$$

and the matrix

$$\begin{pmatrix} \cos \theta & -\sin \theta & 0 & 0 \\ \sin \theta & \cos \theta & 0 & 0 \\ 0 & 0 & 1 & 0 \\ 0 & 0 & 0 & 1 \end{pmatrix}$$

A subprogram 'rot3' to produce such a matrix A, given the angle THETA and the axis number AXIS% (AXIS% = 1 for the x-axis, AXIS% = 2 for the y-axis and AXIS% = 3 for the z-axis) is given in listing 8.4.

Listing 8.4

```
8600 ´rot3
8601 ´**in ** THETA,AXIS%
8602 ´**out** A(4,4)
8610 ERASE A : DIM A(4,4)
8620 AX1%=(AXIS% MOD 3)+1 : AX2%=(AX1% MOD 3)+1
8630 CT=COS(THETA) : ST=SIN(THETA)
8640 A(AXIS%,AXIS%)=1
8650 A(AX1%,AX1%)=CT : A(AX1%,AX2%)=-ST
8660 A(AX2%,AX1%)=ST : A(AX2%,AX2%)=CT
8670 RETURN
```

Inverse Transformations

Before we can consider the general rotation transformation, it is necessary to look at inverse transformations. An inverse transformation returns the points transformed by a given transformation back to their original position. If a transformation is represented by a matrix A, then the inverse transformation is given by matrix A^{-1}, the inverse of A. There is no need to explicitly calculate the inverse of a matrix by using such techniques as the Adjoint method (listing 7.4): we can use listings 8.2, 8.3 and 8.4 with parameters that are derived from the parameters of the original transformation:

(1) A translation by (TX, TY, TZ) is inverted with a translation by ($-$TX, $-$TY, $-$TZ).
(2) A scaling by SX, SY and SZ is inverted with a scaling by 1/SX, 1/SY and 1/SZ.
(3) A rotation by an angle θ about a given axis is inverted with a rotation by an angle $-\theta$ about the same axis.
(4) If the transformation matrix is the product of a number of translation, scaling and rotation matrices A $\times$ B $\times$ C $\times$ . . . $\times$ L $\times$ M $\times$ N, then the inverse transformation is

$$N^{-1} \times M^{-1} \times L^{-1} \times \ldots \times C^{-1} \times B^{-1} \times A^{-1}$$

Rotation of Points by an Angle γ about a General Axis $p + \mu q$

Assume $p \equiv$ (PX, PY, PZ) and $q \equiv$ (QX, QY, QZ). We break down the task into a number of subtasks:

(a) We translate all of space so that the axis of rotation goes through the origin. This is achieved by adding a vector $-p$ to every point in space with a matrix F say, which is generated by a call to 'tran3' with parameters $-PX$, $-PY$ and $-PZ$. The inverse matrix F^{-1} will be needed later and is found by a call to 'tran3' with parameters PX, PY and PZ. After this transformation the axis of rotation is the line $O + \mu q$ that passes through the origin.

$$F = \begin{pmatrix} 1 & 0 & 0 & -PX \\ 0 & 1 & 0 & -PY \\ 0 & 0 & 1 & -PZ \\ 0 & 0 & 0 & 1 \end{pmatrix} \qquad F^{-1} = \begin{pmatrix} 1 & 0 & 0 & PX \\ 0 & 1 & 0 & PY \\ 0 & 0 & 1 & PZ \\ 0 & 0 & 0 & 1 \end{pmatrix}$$

(b) We then rotate space about the z-axis by an angle $-\alpha$, where (ALPHA =) $\alpha = \tan^{-1}(QY/QX)$, given by the matrix G. The matrix may be generated by a call to 'rot3', with parameters angle $-ALPHA$ and axis 3, and the inverse matrix G^{-1} by a call to 'rot3' with ALPHA and 3. At this stage the axis of rotation is a line lying in the x/z plane that passes through the point $(v, 0, QZ)$.

$$G = \frac{1}{v} \begin{pmatrix} QX & QY & 0 & 0 \\ -QY & QX & 0 & 0 \\ 0 & 0 & v & 0 \\ 0 & 0 & 0 & v \end{pmatrix} \qquad G^{-1} = \frac{1}{v} \begin{pmatrix} QX & -QY & 0 & 0 \\ QY & QX & 0 & 0 \\ 0 & 0 & v & 0 \\ 0 & 0 & 0 & v \end{pmatrix}$$

where v is the positive number given by $v^2 = QX^2 + QY^2$.

(c) We now rotate space about the y-axis by an angle $-\beta$, where (BETA =) $\beta = \tan^{-1}(v/QZ)$, given by the matrix H which is obtained by the call 'rot3' with parameters angle $-$ BETA and axis 2, and the inverse matrix H^{-1} by a 'rot3' call with parameters BETA and 2.

$$H = \frac{1}{w} \begin{pmatrix} QZ & 0 & -v & 0 \\ 0 & w & 0 & 0 \\ v & 0 & QZ & 0 \\ 0 & 0 & 0 & w \end{pmatrix} \qquad H^{-1} = \frac{1}{w} \begin{pmatrix} QZ & 0 & v & 0 \\ 0 & w & 0 & 0 \\ -v & 0 & QZ & 0 \\ 0 & 0 & 0 & w \end{pmatrix}$$

where w is the positive number given by $w^2 = v^2 + QZ^2 = QX^2 + QY^2 + QZ^2$. So the point $(v, 0, QZ)$ is transformed to $(0, 0, w)$, hence the axis of rotation is along the z-axis.

(d) We can now rotate space by an angle γ (GAMMA) about the axis of rotation by using matrix W which is generated by 'rot3' (with angle GAMMA and axis 3):

$$W = \begin{pmatrix} \cos\gamma & -\sin\gamma & 0 & 0 \\ \sin\gamma & \cos\gamma & 0 & 0 \\ 0 & 0 & 1 & 0 \\ 0 & 0 & 0 & 1 \end{pmatrix}$$

(e) We need to return the axis of rotation to its original position so we multiply by H^{-1}, G^{-1} and finally F^{-1}.

Thus the final matrix P that rotates space by the angle γ about the axis $\boldsymbol{p} + \mu\boldsymbol{q}$ is $P = F^{-1} \times G^{-1} \times H^{-1} \times W \times H \times G \times F$. Naturally some of these matrices may reduce to the identity matrix in some special cases and can be ignored. For example if the axis of rotation goes through the origin then F and F^{-1} are identical to the identity matrix I and can be ignored.

So it is possible to write a special routine 'genrot' (listing 8.5) which achieves this rotation and returns the required matrix P given GAMMA, (PX, PY, PZ) and (QX, QY, QZ).

Listing 8.5

```
5000 'genrot / rotation of a point about a general axis
5001 '**in ** PX,PY,PZ,QX,QY,QZ,GAMMA
5002 '**out** R(4,4)
5009 'place origin on axis of rotation.
5010 TX=-PX : TY=-PY : TZ=-PZ : GOSUB 9000 'tran3
5020 GOSUB 9100 'mult3
5029 'rotate axis of rotation into x/z plane through origin.
5030 AX=QX : AY=QY
5040 GOSUB 8800 'angle
5050 ALPHA=THETA : THETA=-ALPHA : AXIS%=3 : GOSUB 8600 'rot3
5060 GOSUB 9100 'mult3
5069 'rotate axis of rotation onto z-axis.
5070 AX=QZ : AY=SQR(QX*QX+QY*QY)
5080 GOSUB 8800 'angle
5090 BETA=THETA : THETA=-BETA : AXIS%=2 : GOSUB 8600 'rot3
5100 GOSUB 9100 'mult3
5109 'rotate space by angle GAMMA about axis of rotation.
5110 THETA=GAMMA : AXIS%=3 : GOSUB 8600 'rot3
5120 GOSUB 9100 'mult3
5129 'put axis of rotation back in its original position.
5130 THETA=BETA  : AXIS%=2 : GOSUB 8600 'rot3
5140 GOSUB 9100 'mult3
5150 THETA=ALPHA : AXIS%=3 : GOSUB 8600 'rot3
5160 GOSUB 9100 'mult3
5170 TX=PX : TY=PY : TZ=PZ : GOSUB 9000 'tran3
5180 GOSUB 9100 'mult3
5190 RETURN
```

Example 8.1

What happens to the points $(0, 0, 0), (1, 0, 0), (0, 1, 0), (0, 0, 1)$ and $(1, 1, 1)$ if space is rotated by $\pi/4$ radians about an axis $(1, 0, 1) + \mu(3, 4, 5)$.

Using the above theory we note that

$$F = \begin{pmatrix} 1 & 0 & 0 & -1 \\ 0 & 1 & 0 & 0 \\ 0 & 0 & 1 & -1 \\ 0 & 0 & 0 & 1 \end{pmatrix} \qquad F^{-1} = \begin{pmatrix} 1 & 0 & 0 & 1 \\ 0 & 1 & 0 & 0 \\ 0 & 0 & 1 & 1 \\ 0 & 0 & 0 & 1 \end{pmatrix}$$

$$G = \frac{1}{5} \begin{pmatrix} 3 & 4 & 0 & 0 \\ -4 & 3 & 0 & 0 \\ 0 & 0 & 5 & 0 \\ 0 & 0 & 0 & 5 \end{pmatrix} \qquad G^{-1} = \frac{1}{5} \begin{pmatrix} 3 & -4 & 0 & 0 \\ 4 & 3 & 0 & 0 \\ 0 & 0 & 5 & 0 \\ 0 & 0 & 0 & 5 \end{pmatrix}$$

$$H = \frac{1}{\sqrt{2}} \begin{pmatrix} 1 & 0 & -1 & 0 \\ 0 & \sqrt{2} & 0 & 0 \\ 1 & 0 & 1 & 0 \\ 0 & 0 & 0 & \sqrt{2} \end{pmatrix} \qquad H^{-1} = \frac{1}{\sqrt{2}} \begin{pmatrix} 1 & 0 & 1 & 0 \\ 0 & \sqrt{2} & 0 & 0 \\ -1 & 0 & 0 & 0 \\ 0 & 0 & 0 & \sqrt{2} \end{pmatrix}$$

$$W = \frac{1}{\sqrt{2}} \begin{pmatrix} 1 & -1 & 0 & 0 \\ 1 & 1 & 0 & 0 \\ 0 & 0 & \sqrt{2} & 0 \\ 0 & 0 & 0 & \sqrt{2} \end{pmatrix} \quad \text{and}$$

$$P = \frac{1}{50\sqrt{2}} \begin{pmatrix} 41 + 9\sqrt{2} & -12 - 13\sqrt{2} & -15 + 35\sqrt{2} & -26 + 6\sqrt{2} \\ -12 + 37\sqrt{2} & 34 + 16\sqrt{2} & -20 + 5\sqrt{2} & 32 - 42\sqrt{2} \\ -15 - 5\sqrt{2} & -20 + 35\sqrt{2} & 25 + 25\sqrt{2} & -10 + 30\sqrt{2} \\ 0 & 0 & 0 & 50\sqrt{2} \end{pmatrix}$$

where $P = F^{-1} \times G^{-1} \times H^{-1} \times W \times H \times G \times F$ is the matrix representation of the required transformation. Premultiplying the column vectors equivalent to $(0, 0, 0), (1, 0, 0), (0, 1, 0), (0, 0, 1)$ and $(1, 1, 1)$ by P and changing the resulting column vectors back into row form and taking out a factor $1/50\sqrt{2}$ gives the coordinates $(-26 + 6\sqrt{2}, 32 - 42\sqrt{2}, -10 + 30\sqrt{2}), (15 + 15\sqrt{2}, 20 - 5\sqrt{2}, -25 + 25\sqrt{2}), (-38 - 7\sqrt{2}, 66 - 26\sqrt{2}, -30 + 65\sqrt{2}), (-41 + 41\sqrt{2}, 12 - 37\sqrt{2}, 15 + 55\sqrt{2})$ and $(-12 + 37\sqrt{2}, 34 + 16\sqrt{2}, -20 + 85\sqrt{2})$ respectively. Naturally, translating and rotating space should leave relative positions unchanged; in particular the angles between direction vectors should be unchanged (the same cannot be said about the scaling transformation which in general does alter relative positions). In the original system the three lines from $(0, 0, 0)$ to $(1, 0, 0)$, $(0, 1, 0)$ and $(0, 0, 1)$, respectively, are mutually perpendicular (that is, the dot product of pairs of these directions should be zero). The dot product of the directions in the transformed system should also be zero: the three directional vectors (with $1/50\sqrt{2}$ factored out) are $(41 + 9\sqrt{2}, -12 + 37\sqrt{2}, -15 - 5\sqrt{2})$, $(-12 - 13\sqrt{2}, 34 + 16\sqrt{2}, -20 + 35\sqrt{2})$ and $(-15 + 35\sqrt{2}, -20 + 5\sqrt{2}, 25 + 25\sqrt{2})$, and the dot product of any pair is zero.

Similarly the dot product of the direction vector from the origin to $(1, 1, 1)$ in the original system, taken with any of the original directions above, gives the same value $(= 1)$. This is also true in the transformed system: the fourth direction is $(14 + 31\sqrt{2}, 2 + 58\sqrt{2}, -10 + 55\sqrt{2})$, and when we take the dot product with each of the three direction vectors above we get the value 5000, which when we take into account the factor $(1/50\sqrt{2})^2$ gives the value 1.

A program that reads in the axis of rotation $(PX, PY, PZ) + \mu(QX, QY, QZ)$ and the angle GAMMA, and rotates any point (XX, YY, ZZ) about this axis by an angle GAMMA is given in listing 8.6.

Listing 8.6

```
100 'Rotation about a given axis.
110 DIM A(4,4),B(4,4),R(4,4)
120 CLS
130 LOCATE 3,5
140 PRINT "ROTATION ABOUT A GIVEN AXIS"
149 'INPUT data on axis of rotation.
150 LOCATE 5,1
160 INPUT " base vector of axis ",PX,PY,PZ
170 INPUT " direction vector of axis ",QX,QY,QZ
180 INPUT " angle of rotation ",GAMMA
190 CLS
199 'output data on the axis.
200 LOCATE 2,5
210 PRINT "ROTATION ABOUT A GIVEN AXIS"
220 LOCATE 4,5   : PRINT "base vector of axis "
230 LOCATE 5,5   : PRINT "(";PX;",";PY;",";PZ;")"
240 LOCATE 7,5   : PRINT "direction vector of axis "
250 LOCATE 8,5   : PRINT "(";QX;",";QY;",";QZ;")"
260 LOCATE 10,5  : PRINT "angle of rotation "
270 LOCATE 11,5  : PRINT GAMMA;" radian(s)"
279 'calculate the rotation matrix R.
280 GOSUB 9300 'idR3
290 GOSUB 5000 'genrot
300 LOCATE 20,1 : PRINT " Type coordinates of point"
310 INPUT XX,YY,ZZ
320 LOCATE 20,1 : PRINT SPC(79),SPC(79)
330 LOCATE 13,5 : PRINT " Point   (";XX;",";YY;",";ZZ;")"
340 RX=R(1,1)*XX+R(1,2)*YY+R(1,3)*ZZ+R(1,4)
350 RY=R(2,1)*XX+R(2,2)*YY+R(2,3)*ZZ+R(2,4)
360 RZ=R(3,1)*XX+R(3,2)*YY+R(3,3)*ZZ+R(3,4)
370 LOCATE 14,5 : PRINT " is transformed to"
380 LOCATE 15,5 : PRINT "         (";RX;",";RY;",";RZ;")"
390 LOCATE 20,1 : PRINT " Press any key to continue"
400 A$=INKEY$ : IF INKEY$="" THEN GOTO 400
410 LOCATE 13,1
420 FOR I%=13 TO 16
430 PRINT SPC(79)
440 NEXT I%
450 GOTO 300
460 END
```

Exercise 8.1
Experiment with these ideas. You can always make a check on your final transformation matrix by considering simple values as above, and you can use the previous listings to check your answer. It is essential that you are confident in the use of matrices, and the best way to get this confidence is to experiment. You will make lots of arithmetic errors initially, but you will soon come to think of transformations in terms of their matrix representation, and this will greatly ease the study of drawing three-dimensional objects.

Exercise 8.2
You will have noticed that the routine 'rot3' is usually called with THETA generated by 'angle' which uses values AX and AY as input parameters. 'rot3' calculates the cosine and sine of angle THETA — but we know these are $AX/\sqrt{(AX^2 + AY^2)}$ and $AY/\sqrt{(AX^2 + AY^2)}$ respectively. Write another rotation routine 'rotxy' that calculates the rotation matrix direction from AX and AY without resorting to 'angle'.

Exercise 8.3
In chapter 4 we noted that some writers use row rather than column vectors, and postmultiply rather than premultiply. I decided against this interpretation so that the matrix of a transformation would correspond directly with the coefficients of the transformation equations. In this other interpretation it is the transpose of the matrix that is identical to the coefficients. It is useful to be aware of this other method, so use it to rewrite all the programs given in this chapter (and the remainder of this book). Remember though, it is not important which method you finally decide to use *as long as you are consistent*. I have used the column vector notation because I have found it causes less confusion in the early stages of learning the subject!

Complete Programs

I. All the listings in this chapter, 8.1 ('mult3' and 'idR3'), 8.2 ('tran3'), 8.3 ('scale3'), 8.4 ('rot3'), 8.5 ('genrot') and 8.6 (main program) together with listing 3.4 ('angle' from 'lib1'), form one program. Required data: base vector (PX, PY, PZ) and direction vector (QX, QY, QZ) of the axis of rotation and the angle GAMMA. Then any number of three-dimensional coordinates (XX, YY, ZZ). Try $(0, 0, 0), (1, 1, 1)$ and $\pi/4$, and points $(1, 0, 1), (1, 1, 1), (1, 2, 3)$.

9 Orthographic Projections

We may now address the problem of drawing views of three-dimensional objects on our (necessarily) two-dimensional graphics screen. The simple method we describe here is a direct generalisation of the method introduced in chapter 4 for two-dimensional objects. Again it involves the use of (up to) three *positions*. To illustrate these ideas we first give a brief outline, and then expand on this by using pictorial and numerical examples. We start by defining an arbitrary but fixed triad of axes in space which we call the ABSOLUTE system. Then, as in the two-dimensional case, we consider the three positions: (1) the SETUP position, (2) the ACTUAL position and (3) the OBSERVED position.

(1) The SETUP Position

Most scenes will be composed of simple objects (such as cube(s) — see example 9.1) which are set at a particular position and orientation in space. It is very inefficient to calculate by hand the complicated coordinates of every vertex of these objects and input them into the program. Instead we look at each object in turn and initially define it in an elementary way relative to the ABSOLUTE triad, usually setting it about the origin. The information required will be that of vertices (x-coordinate, y-coordinate and z-coordinate), and perhaps lines (which join pairs of vertices) or (later when we consider hidden surface algorithms) facets, which are polygonal planar areas bounded by the above-mentioned lines. This elementary definition of the object is called its SETUP position. We could also have other information such as the colour of the object.

(2) The ACTUAL Position

We may then use the matrix techniques of the last chapter to generate a matrix that will move the object from its SETUP position to its required ACTUAL position relative to the ABSOLUTE axes. We shall call this the SETUP to ACTUAL matrix P.

(3) The OBSERVED Position

Viewing an object in three-dimensional space naturally involves an observer (the eye — and note only one eye!) placed at a position (EX, EY, EZ) relative to the ABSOLUTE axes looking in a fixed direction: this direction of view can be uniquely determined by any other point on the line of sight (DX, DY, DZ), say. The head can also be tilted, but more of this later. What the eye sees when it looks at a three-dimensional object is a projection of the vertices, lines and facets of the object on to a (two-dimensional) *view plane* which is normal to the line of sight. In order to calculate such projections we must standardise our approach. We use matrix methods to transform all the points in space so that the eye is placed at the origin, and the line of sight is along the positive z-axis. This is the OBSERVED position, and the matrix that transforms the ACTUAL to OBSERVED position is called Q throughout this book. The method for calculating Q will be dealt with in detail later, but for the time being we shall assume that the eye is already at the origin and is looking along the z-axis: so in this simple case Q is the identity matrix.

When all the points in space have been moved into this OBSERVED position we note that the view plane is now parallel to the x/y plane through the origin. Having moved the eye into the correct position, we are now ready to project the object on to the view plane. But note, as yet we have neither defined the position of the view plane (we have only its normal), nor have we described the type of projection of three-dimensional space on to the plane. These two requirements are closely related. In this book we shall consider three possible projections — in a later chapter we shall deal with the *perspective and stereoscopic projections*, but first we introduce the simplest projection — the *orthographic*.

The Orthographic Projection

Nothing could be simpler. In the orthographic projection we can set the view plane to be *any* plane with normal vector along the line of sight. When transformed into the OBSERVED position, the view plane will be any plane that is parallel to the x/y plane given by the equation $z = 0$. For simplicity we take the x/y plane through the origin. The vertices of the object are projected on to the view plane by the simple expedient of setting their z-coordinates to zero. Thus any two different points in the OBSERVED position, (x, y, z) and (x, y, z') say (where $z \neq z'$), are projected on to the same point $(x, y, 0)$ on the view plane. Then we identify the x/y values on the plane with points in the graphics screen coordinate system (usually centred on the screen) by using the methods of chapter 2. Once the vertices have been projected on to the view plane and then on to the screen, we can construct the projection of lines and facets. These are related to the projected vertices in exactly the same way as the original lines and facets are related to the original vertices.

Before considering in detail the general case where the eye and direction of view are arbitrarily positioned, we shall consider an elementary example to demonstrate the orthographic projection.

Example 9.1

Use the above ideas to draw an orthographic projection of a cube. Figures such as those in figure 9.1 are called *wire diagrams* or *skeletons* (for obvious reasons).

In the SETUP position the cube may be thought to consist of eight vertices $(1, 1, 1), (1, 1, -1), (1, -1, -1), (1, -1, 1), (-1, 1, 1), (-1, 1, -1), (-1, -1, -1)$ and $(-1, -1, 1)$: vertices are labelled numerically 1 to 8. The twelve lines that form the wire cube join vertices 1 to 2, 2 to 3, 3 to 4, 4 to 1; 5 to 6, 6 to 7, 7 to 8, 8 to 1; 1 to 5, 2 to 6, 3 to 7 and 4 to 8.

Figure 9.1a shows the simplest possible example of an orthographic projection of the cube, where even the SETUP to ACTUAL matrix is the identity matrix, that is the cube stays in its SETUP position. We get a square: pairs of parallel lines from the front and back of the cube project into the same line on the screen. We put a '+' in these diagrams to show the position of the z-axis in the OBSERVED position (into the screen).

Figure 9.1b shows the same cube drawn after the following three transformations place it in its ACTUAL position:

(a) Rotate the cube by an angle $\alpha = -0.927295218$ radian about the z-axis — matrix A. This example is contrived so that $\cos \alpha = 3/5$ and $\sin \alpha = -4/5$, so ensuring that the rotation matrices consist of uncomplicated elements.
(b) Translate it by the vector $(-1, 0, 0)$ — matrix B.
(c) Rotate it by an angle $-\alpha$ about the y-axis — matrix C.

The SETUP to ACTUAL matrix is thus $P = C \times B \times A$, where

$$A = \begin{pmatrix} 3/5 & 4/5 & 0 & 0 \\ -4/5 & 3/5 & 0 & 0 \\ 0 & 0 & 1 & 0 \\ 0 & 0 & 0 & 1 \end{pmatrix} \quad B = \begin{pmatrix} 1 & 0 & 0 & -1 \\ 0 & 1 & 0 & 0 \\ 0 & 0 & 1 & 0 \\ 0 & 0 & 0 & 1 \end{pmatrix} \quad C = \begin{pmatrix} 3/5 & 0 & 4/5 & 0 \\ 0 & 1 & 0 & 0 \\ -4/5 & 0 & 3/5 & 0 \\ 0 & 0 & 0 & 1 \end{pmatrix}$$

and P is given by the matrix

$$P = \frac{1}{25} \begin{pmatrix} 9 & 12 & 20 & -15 \\ -20 & 15 & 0 & 0 \\ -12 & -16 & 15 & 20 \\ 0 & 0 & 0 & 25 \end{pmatrix}$$

So the above eight vertex coordinate triples in the SETUP position are transformed into the following eight ACTUAL coordinate triples: $(26/25, -5/25,$

7/25), (−14/25, −5/25, −23/25), (−38/25, −35/25, 9/25), (2/25, −35/25, 39/25), (8/25, 35/25, 31/25), (−32/25, 35/25, 1/25), (−56/25, 5/25, 33/25), (−16/25, 5/25, 63/25).

For example (1, 1, 1) is transformed into (26/25, −5/25, 7/25) because

$$\frac{1}{25} \begin{pmatrix} 9 & 12 & 20 & -15 \\ -20 & 15 & 0 & 0 \\ -12 & -16 & 15 & 20 \\ 0 & 0 & 0 & 25 \end{pmatrix} \times \begin{pmatrix} 1 \\ 1 \\ 1 \\ 1 \end{pmatrix} = \frac{1}{25} \begin{pmatrix} 26 \\ -5 \\ 7 \\ 25 \end{pmatrix}$$

Since the ACTUAL to OBSERVED matrix Q is the identity matrix, the projected coordinates on the view plane are thus (26/25, −5/25), (−14/25, −5/25), (−38/25, −35/25), (2/25, −35/25), (8/25, 35/25), (−32/25, 35/25), (−56/25, 5/25), (−16/25, 5/25). We can place these points on the screen and join them with lines in the same order as they were defined in the SETUP cube.

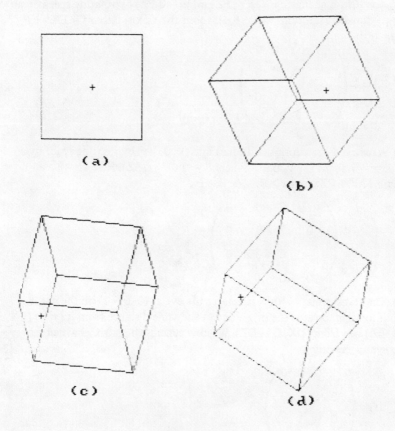

(a)

(b)

(c)

(d)

Figure 9.1

Construction of the ACTUAL to OBSERVED Matrix Q

We assume that the eye is at (EX, EY, EZ) relative to the ABSOLUTE axes, looking towards the point (DX, DY, DZ). The OBSERVED position is achieved in the following sequence of steps.

(1) A matrix D translates all the points in space by a vector $(-DX, -DY, -DZ)$ so that now the eye is at $(EX - DX, EY - DY, EZ - DZ) = (FX, FY, FZ)$ say, looking towards the origin:

$$D = \begin{pmatrix} 1 & 0 & 0 & -DX \\ 0 & 1 & 0 & -DY \\ 0 & 0 & 1 & -DZ \\ 0 & 0 & 0 & 1 \end{pmatrix}$$

(2) A matrix E changes (FX, FY, FZ) into $(r, 0 \ FZ)$ by rotating space by an angle $-\alpha$, where $\alpha = \tan^{-1}$ (FY/FX), about the z-axis. Here $r^2 = FX^2 + FY^2$ and $r > 0$:

$$E = \frac{1}{r} \begin{pmatrix} FX & FY & 0 & 0 \\ -FY & FX & 0 & 0 \\ 0 & 0 & r & 0 \\ 0 & 0 & 0 & r \end{pmatrix}$$

(3) A matrix F transforms $(r, 0, FZ)$ into $(0, 0, -s)$ by rotating space by an angle $\pi - \theta$ about the y-axis — where $\theta = \tan^{-1}$ (r/FZ). Here $s^2 = r^2 + FZ^2 = FX^2 + FY^2 + FZ^2$ and $s > 0$:

$$F = \frac{1}{s} \begin{pmatrix} -FZ & 0 & r & 0 \\ 0 & s & 0 & 0 \\ -r & 0 & -FZ & 0 \\ 0 & 0 & 0 & s \end{pmatrix}$$

(4) The transformation thus far places the eye at $(0, 0, -s)$ on the negative z-axis looking towards the origin and at the same distance from it (s) as (EX, EY, EZ) was from (DX, DY, DZ). We now generate a matrix G which moves the eye to the origin:

$$G = \begin{pmatrix} 1 & 0 & 0 & 0 \\ 0 & 1 & 0 & 0 \\ 0 & 0 & 1 & s \\ 0 & 0 & 0 & 1 \end{pmatrix}$$

(5) If in example 9.1 we now premultiply $P = C \times B \times A$ by our first approximation to the ACTUAL to OBSERVED matrix $Q (= G \times F \times E \times D)$ to find the SETUP to OBSERVED matrix $R = Q \times P = G \times F \times E \times D \times C \times B \times A$, we draw figure 9.1c by orthographic projection. This is a view of the scene observed from $(1, 1, 1)$ towards the origin. This view is not really satisfactory because the matrix Q places the cube at an arbitrary orientation within the view plane. It is much better to standardise our view, and one of the most popular ways is to *maintain the vertical*, that is a line that was vertical (that is, parallel to the y-axis) in its ACTUAL position remains vertical after transformation by Q into its OBSERVED position. Take the vertical line from (DX, DY, DZ) to $(DX, DY + 1, DZ)$. Because of this peculiar construction, we note that intermediate matrix K $(F \times E \times D)$ transforms this line into one that joins $(0, 0, 0)$ to $(K(1, 2), K(2, 2), K(3, 2)) = (p, q, r)$, say. So if we further rotate about the z-axis by an angle $\beta = \tan^{-1} (K(1, 2)/K(2, 2)) = \tan^{-1} (p/q) = \tan^{-1} (-FY \times FZ/(s \times FX))$ using a matrix H, before multiplying by G, then the vertical is maintained:

$$H = \frac{1}{t} \begin{pmatrix} q & -p & 0 & 0 \\ p & q & 0 & 0 \\ 0 & 0 & t & 0 \\ 0 & 0 & 0 & t \end{pmatrix}$$

where $t^2 = p^2 + q^2$ and thus

$$H \times \begin{pmatrix} p \\ q \\ r \\ 1 \end{pmatrix} = \frac{1}{t} \begin{pmatrix} q & -p & 0 & 0 \\ p & q & 0 & 0 \\ 0 & 0 & t & 0 \\ 0 & 0 & 0 & t \end{pmatrix} \times \begin{pmatrix} p \\ q \\ r \\ 1 \end{pmatrix} \begin{pmatrix} 0 \\ t \\ r \\ 1 \end{pmatrix}$$

Thus the complete transformation (figure 9.1d) is achieved by the matrix $R = Q \times P = G \times H \times F \times E \times D \times C \times B \times A$, and the projection of the line joining points (DX, DY, DZ) to $(DX, DY + 1, DZ)$ is the line joining $(0, 0)$ to $(0, t)$ on the screen; that is, the vertical — matrix G does not affect the x/y values. Note that this technique works in all cases except where (EX, EY, EZ) is vertically above (DX, DY, DZ) to start with, and naturally in this case maintaining the vertical makes no sense. The routine 'look3' (listing 9.1), given (EX, EY, EZ) and (DX, DY, DZ), generates the ACTUAL to OBSERVED matrix in the steps shown above, and at each step premultiplies the matrix R: so at the end of the process R will hold its original matrix value premultiplied by Q. If we wish to store Q explicitly then we need first to set R to the identity matrix (using 'idR3'), then call 'look3', and finally copy array R into array Q. Routine 'look3' can be radically reduced if we assume that the eye always looks at the origin (that is, $DX = DY = DZ = 0$). Furthermore with the orthographic projection the OBSERVED position of the eye need not be at the origin, it merely needs to be on the z-axis: again the routine can be cut down. We give the general case, which will be essential for later perspective projections.

Listing 9.1

```
8200  ´look3/maintain vertical
8202  ´**out** R(4,4)
8210  INPUT "(EX,EY,EZ) ",EX,EY,EZ
8220  INPUT "(DX,DY,DZ) ",DX,DY,DZ
8229  ´move origin to (DX,DY,DZ).
8230  LET TX=-DX : LET TY=-DY : TZ=-DZ
8240  GOSUB 9000 ´tran3
8250  GOSUB 9100 ´mult3
8259  ´move eye onto negative z-axis, looking at origin.
8260  FX=EX-DX : FY=EY-DY : FZ=EZ-DZ
8270  AX=FX : AY=FY : GOSUB 8800 ´angle
8280  THETA=-THETA : AXIS%=3 : GOSUB 8600 ´rot3
8290  GOSUB 9100 ´mult3
8300  DIST=SQR(FX*FX+FY*FY)
8310  AX=FZ : AY=DIST : GOSUB 8800 ´angle
8320  THETA=3.141593-THETA : AXIS%=2 : GOSUB 8600 ´rot3
8330  GOSUB 9100 ´mult3
8339  ´maintain the vertical.
8340  TZ=SQR(DIST*DIST+FZ*FZ)
8350  AX=TZ*FX : AY=-FY*FZ : GOSUB 8800 ´angle
8360  AXIS%=3 : GOSUB 8600 ´rot3
8370  GOSUB 9100 ´mult3
8379  ´move the eye to the origin : space now in OBSERVED position.
8380  LET TX=0 : LET TY=0
8390  GOSUB 9000 ´tran3
8400  GOSUB 9100 ´mult3
8410  RETURN
```

If required, we can extend this program to deal with the situation where the head is tilted through an angle γ from the vertical. This is achieved by further rotating space by $-\gamma$ about the z-axis. Thus matrix H should then rotate about the z-axis by an angle $\beta - \gamma$.

The construction of the ACTUAL to OBSERVED matrix is obviously independent of everything other than the position of the eye, line of sight and the tilt of the head. So if we wish to view a series of objects from the same position, we can store Q and use it repeatedly for placing each object.

How to Define an Object

It is now time to deal with the problem of representing objects to the computer. There is no definite solution, it really depends on what is being drawn and how it is projected. In this section we describe various ways of setting up a data-base to hold the information that is necessary for drawing any given scene, but make no comment on their usefulness. This is considered in the remainder of the book where we give examples to illustrate the value of particular methods in different situations. We shall be using arrays to hold large sets of data, and so naturally the amount of space given to arrays will depend on the amount of information that is required for a scene: be sure that when you declare these arrays there is enough space for all the information — if in doubt, overestimate your store requirements.

Vertices
We will always need to define vertices and other special reference points in a
scene, and these we store as x-coordinates, y-coordinates and z-coordinates in
arrays X, Y and Z respectively, assuming that if the total number is not known
explicitly then this value is calculated as NOV%. So there must be space for not
less than NOV% values in each of the three arrays. These vertices may be in the
SETUP, the ACTUAL or the OBSERVED position, it depends on the context
of the problem. There will also be situations (perspective in particular) when we
need to store the x/y coordinates of the projections of these NOV% vertices — in
arrays XD and YD. Naturally this is unnecessary in the case of an orthographic
projection of points in the OBSERVED position since we can use the values
already stored in the X and Y arrays. The choice of data-base really depends
on the scene and type of projection.

Lines
We can store information on NOL% (say) line segments in the two-dimensional
integer array LIN%. The Ith line is defined by the integer indices (between 1 and
NOV%) of the two points at each end of the line — we store the indices in
LIN%(1, I) and LIN%(2, I). The true coordinate values of the two points at each
end of the line segment can be found from the X, Y and Z arrays. We normally
assume that these lines are coloured implicitly by the program, usually black
(actual colour 0 = logical colour 0). For the time being it will be assumed that the
screen background (the paper colour) will be logical colour 3 (brown in palette 0.
or white in palette 1).

Facets
A facet is a convex polygonal area on the surface of a three-dimensional object,
and can be defined in a number of ways. Most facets will be triangular or quadrilateral, rarely greater than six-sided, so we usually assume than no facet has
more than six sides in order to minimise waste of store. The NOF% facets can
be defined in terms of the indices of the vertices at their corners in array FACET%:
FACET%(I, J) is the index of the Ith vertex on the Jth facet. Naturally if the facet
is not hexagonal then some of the values are *garbage* so we need to store array
SIZE%, the number of vertices/edges on each facet. We can implicitly colour
each facet or store it as an integer array COL%, and we may implicitly colour
the lines that form the edges of the facet. Another method is to store the facet in
terms of the indices of the lines in the object in array FACET%, which would thus
refer to array LIN%: FACET%(I, J) would now be the index of the Ith line on the
edge of the Jth facet. There are many other methods for representing these, and
other elements of a three-dimensional object: you choose the one most suitable
to your particular situation.

Construction Subroutines and the 'Building Block' Method

For any required object we define a *construction routine* that needs as parameters a matrix R to move vertices into position and any other information about the size of the object (if the object is to be stored in the SETUP position then naturally no matrix is needed). The routine can then define the vertices, lines, facets or any other elements of the object, and use the matrix R to move the vertices of the object into the required position. Depending on the context of the program the routine can then either draw the object, or extend a data-base that contains this information. We shall give examples of both methods.

We can construct a scene that contains a number of similar objects (so the data will be in either the ACTUAL or the OBSERVED position). There is no need to produce a new construction routine for each occurrence of the object, all we do each time is calculate a new SETUP to ACTUAL matrix P, and enter it (for the ACTUAL position) or Q × P (for the OBSERVED position) into the same routine. Naturally we shall require one new routine for each different type of object.

Three-dimensional scenes are manipulated in a manner similar to the two-dimensional case. A main program ('scene3') calls the 'start' routine to prepare the screen and then organises the construction and observation of the overall scene.

'scene3' declares all the arrays that are required for storing information about a scene, together with matrices A, B, R and (perhaps) Q for moving objects into position. If required the values of NOV% and NOL% (or NOF%) are initialised, and these will be updated in later construction routines. For each individual object (a 'block'), 'scene3' must calculate a matrix P that moves this block into the ACTUAL position, and then call the construction routine by using the correct matrix R (perhaps SETUP to ACTUAL or SETUP to OBSERVED). All the blocks finally construct the finished scene. Sometimes the drawing of the projection is done inside the construction routine, or it can be elsewhere in other routines that are specifically designed for special forms of drawing (as in hidden line and hidden surface pictures): it depends on what is being drawn and what is required of the view. As usual, because of the restriction of not passing parameters (in particular array parameters) into routines, we do not normally explicitly generate P and Q: we usually rely on updating matrix R. If we require the ACTUAL to OBSERVED matrix then this routine calls 'look3'. Should we need to store Q then we must first call 'idR3' which sets matrix R to the identity – remember all matrix operations are done via matrices A and R, using matrix B to hold intermediate values.

Our first example of this method is listing 9.2, which is the 'scene3' main program that is needed to construct a picture of a single cube as shown in figure 9.1d. The scene can be viewed from any position with the vertical maintained. We also have a construction routine 'cube' (listing 9.3) which generates the data for a cube with sides of length 2. It places the vertices, eight sets of coordinate triples, in arrays X, Y and Z. There is no need to store the lines of the cube explicitly, we get the information from a DATA statement and draw the lines straight away. The data for figure 9.1d are HORIZ = 8, (EX, EY, EZ) = (1, 1, 1) and (DX, DY, DZ) = (0, 0, 0).

Listing 9.2

```
100 ´main program : scene3 - draw a wire cube
110 GOSUB 9700 ´start
120 DIM X(8),Y(8),Z(8)
130 DIM A(4,4),B(4,4),R(4,4)
139 ´calculate SETUP to ACTUAL matrix R.
140 GOSUB 9300 ´idR3
150 THETA=-.927295 : AXIS%=3 : GOSUB 8600 ´rot3
160 GOSUB 9100 ´mult3
170 TX=-1 : TY=0 : TZ=0 : GOSUB 9000 ´tran3
180 GOSUB 9100 ´mult3
190 THETA=.927295 : AXIS%=2 : GOSUB 8600 ´rot3
200 GOSUB 9100 ´mult3
209 ´change R : premultiply it by the ACTUAL to OBSERVED matrix.
210 GOSUB 8200 ´look3
220 GOSUB 60000 ´colour monitor
230 XMOVE=HORIZ/2 : YMOVE=VERT/2
240 GOSUB 9600 ´setorigin
249 ´call the construction routine.
250 GOSUB 6500 ´cube
260 GOSUB 60100 ´monochrome monitor
270 END
```

Listing 9.3

```
6500 ´cube / data not stored, lines drawn
6501 ´**in ** R(4,4)
6510 DATA 1,1,1, 1,1,-1, 1,-1,-1, 1,-1,1,
     -1,1,1, -1,1,-1, -1,-1,-1, -1,-1,1
6520 DATA 1,2, 2,3, 3,4, 4,1, 5,6, 6,7, 7,8, 8,5, 1,5, 2,6, 3,7, 4,8
6529 ´INPUT the SETUP vertices and move them into OBSERVED position.
6530 RESTORE 6510
6540 FOR I%=1 TO 8
6550 READ XX,YY,ZZ
6560 X(I%)=R(1,1)*XX+R(1,2)*YY+R(1,3)*ZZ+R(1,4)
6570 Y(I%)=R(2,1)*XX+R(2,2)*YY+R(2,3)*ZZ+R(2,4)
6580 Z(I%)=R(3,1)*XX+R(3,2)*YY+R(3,3)*ZZ+R(3,4)
6590 NEXT I%
6599 ´INPUT line information : draw lines by joining pairs of vertices.
6600 FOR I%=1 TO 12
6610 READ L1%,L2%
6620 XPT=X(L1%) : YPT=Y(L1%) : GOSUB 9500 ´moveto
6630 XPT=X(L2%) : YPT=Y(L2%) : GOSUB 9400 ´lineto
6640 NEXT I%
6650 RETURN
```

We could have more than one cube in the scene. For example, should he rewrite 'scene3' as in listing 9.4, keeping all the other routines the same, we would get figure 9.2. Note that the X, Y and Z values of the previous cube are over-written in the second call to 'cube'. Also, because we have the same ACTUAL to **OBSERVED** matrix for both cubes (they have different SETUP to ACTUAL matrices) we need to store Q so that it can also be used for the second cube. Remember Q must premultiply the array P that moves the second cube into the

ACTUAL position. The data for figure 9.2 are HORIZ = 8, (EX, EY, EZ) = (3, 2, 1) and (DX, DY, DZ) = (0, 0, 0).

Listing 9.4

```
100 ´scene3 / two cubes ( not stored)
110 GOSUB 9700 ´start
120 DIM X(8),Y(8),Z(8)
130 DIM A(4,4),B(4,4),R(4,4),Q(4,4)
140 GOSUB 9300 ´idR3
150 GOSUB 8200 ´look3
159 ´store ACTUAL to OBSERVED matrix in Q.
160 FOR I%=1 TO 4 : FOR J%=1 TO 4
170 Q(I%,J%)=R(I%,J%)
180 NEXT J% : NEXT I%
190 GOSUB 60000 ´colour monitor
200 XMOVE=HORIZ/2 : YMOVE=VERT/2
209 ´store ACTUAL to OBSERVED matrix in Q.
210 GOSUB 9600 ´setorigin
219 ´create and draw first cube.
220 GOSUB 6500 ´cube
229 ´create and draw second cube.
230 GOSUB 9300 ´idR3
240 GOSUB 9300 ´idR3
250 TX=3 : TY=1.5 : TZ=2 : GOSUB 9000 ´tran3
260 GOSUB 9100 ´mult3
270 FOR I%=1 TO 4 : FOR J%=1 TO 4
280 A(I%,J%)=Q(I%,J%)
290 NEXT J% : NEXT I%
300 GOSUB 9100 ´mult3
310 GOSUB 6500 ´cube
320 GOSUB 60100 ´monochrome monitor
330 END
```

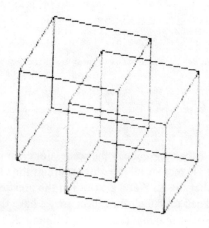

Figure 9.2

Exercise 9.1

Extend routine 'cube' so that information about the size of a rectangular block is input, so enabling the routine to construct a block of length LH, breadth BH and height HT: multiply the *x*-values of the SETUP cube by LH/2, the *y*-values by HT/2 and the *z*-values by BH/2.

Again it should be noted that the modular approach we have adopted may not be the most efficient method of drawing three-dimensional pictures. We chose this descriptive method in order to break down the complex situation into manageable pieces. Once the reader has mastered these concepts he should *cannibalise* our programs for the sake of efficiency. However, to show the value of this modular approach we give another example, which illustrates just how quickly programs can be altered to draw new scenes and situations. As the scenes get more complicated, there will be problems with storage and time. Insistence on proper formatting, labelling and modular construction of programs exacerbates the problem. For efficiency, you should delete unnecessary library routines from programs (for example, 'scale'), and 'derem' of listing I.1 can delete REMarks. Perhaps reduce the size of variable names, take out spaces or rearrange the order of routines. Calls to routines can be replaced with explicit calls to BASIC statements (such as 'lineto' and 'moveto' replaced with calls to LINE). Even with all these changes there will still be problems. The only certain way to enhance these programs is to get a compiler, or perhaps hand-compile commonly used routines.

Example 9.2

We wish to view a fixed scene (for example, the one shown in figure 9.2) from a variety of observation points.

In this case it is better to store the vertex coordinates of the scene in the ACTUAL position, rather than the OBSERVED position, and store the line information in array LIN%. The 'scene3' routine (listing 9.5) must first set NOV% and NOL% to zero and then place the objects in their ACTUAL position by using matrix R = P. The construction routine 'cube' (listing 9.6) must therefore be altered to update the data-base (but note that the same routine could be used to store vertices in their OBSERVED position: it needs only a different R = Q × P). Then for each different view point and direction the 'scene3' routine must clear the screen, set R to the identity matrix and call 'look3', and then call a special new 'drawit' routine (listing 9.7) which uses the matrix R (which holds the values of Q, the ACTUAL to OBSERVED matrix) to put the points in the OBSERVED position and orthographically project them into arrays XD and YD (we cannot use X and Y because this would corrupt our ACTUAL data-base). Routine 'drawit' which was called in 'scene3' can then use the information in array LIN% to draw the picture on the screen.

If the observer is travelling in a straight line and always looking in the same direction we need not even calculate Q each time, but simply initially manipulate space so that the observer is looking along the *z*-axis; then we can use the 'setorigin' routine to move the observer instead! After you have gained expertise in drawing three-dimensional projections, you should choose your construction and viewing method with care. You will rarely need to go through the complete method given in this chapter, there will always be short-cuts.

Listing 9.5

```
100 'scene3 : two cubes stored
110 GOSUB 9700 'start
120 DIM X(16),Y(16),Z(16),XD(16),YD(16)
130 DIM A(4,4),B(4,4),R(4,4),LIN%(2,24)
140 NOV%=0 : NOL%=0
149 'store first cube in ACTUAL position.
150 GOSUB 9300 'idR3
160 GOSUB 6500 'cube
169 'store second cube in ACTUAL position.
170 TX=3 : TY=1.5 : TZ=2 : GOSUB 9000 'tran3
180 GOSUB 9100 'mult3
190 GOSUB 6500 'cube
200 XMOVE=HORIZ/2 : YMOVE=VERT/2
209 'loop through variety of views.
210 GOSUB 9300 'idR3
220 GOSUB 8200 'look3
230 GOSUB 60000 'colour monitor
240 GOSUB 9600 'setorigin
250 GOSUB 7000 'drawit
260 GOSUB 60100 'monochrome monitor
270 XMOVE=0 : YMOVE=0
280 GOTO 210
290 END
```

Listing 9.6

```
6500 'cube / add to data base
6501 '**in ** NOV%,NOL%,LIN%(2,NOL%),X(NOV%),Y(NOV%),Z(NOV%),R(4,4)
6502 '**out** NOV%,NOL%,LIN%(2,NOL%),X(NOV%),Y(NOV%),Z(NOV%)
6510 DATA 1,2, 2,3, 3,4, 4,1, 5,6, 6,7, 7,8, 8,5, 1,5, 2,6, 3,7, 4,8
6520 DATA 1,1,1, 1,1,-1, 1,-1,-1, 1,-1,1,
         -1,1,1, -1,1,-1, -1,-1,-1, -1,-1,1
6529 'store line information.
6530 RESTORE 6510
6540 FOR I%=1 TO 12
6550 READ L1%,L2% : NOL%=NOL%+1
6560 LIN%(1,NOL%)=L1%+NOV% : LIN%(2,NOL%)=L2%+NOV%
6570 NEXT I%
6579 'store vertex information : positioned using R.
6580 FOR I%=1 TO 8
6590 READ XX,YY,ZZ : NOV%=NOV%+1
6600 X(NOV%)=R(1,1)*XX+R(1,2)*YY+R(1,3)*ZZ+R(1,4)
6610 Y(NOV%)=R(2,1)*XX+R(2,2)*YY+R(2,3)*ZZ+R(2,4)
6620 Z(NOV%)=R(3,1)*XX+R(3,2)*YY+R(3,3)*ZZ+R(3,4)
6630 NEXT I%
6640 RETURN
```

Listing 9.7

```
7000 ´drawit
7001 ´**in ** NOV%,NOL%,LIN%(2,NOL%),X(NOV%),Y(NOV%),Z(NOV%),R(4,4)
7009 ´store vertices in OBSERVED position.
7010 FOR I%=1 TO NOV%
7020 XD(I%)=R(1,1)*X(I%)+R(1,2)*Y(I%)+R(1,3)*Z(I%)+R(1,4)
7030 YD(I%)=R(2,1)*X(I%)+R(2,2)*Y(I%)+R(2,3)*Z(I%)+R(2,4)
7040 NEXT I%
7049 ´draw the lines.
7050 FOR I%=1 TO NOL%
7060 L1%=LIN%(1,I%) : L2%=LIN%(2,I%)
7070 XPT=XD(L1%) : YPT=YD(L1%) : GOSUB 9500 ´moveto
7080 XPT=XD(L2%) : YPT=YD(L2%) : GOSUB 9400 ´lineto
7090 NEXT I%
7100 RETURN
```

Exercise 9.2
Produce construction routines for a tetrahedron, pyramid etc. For example

(a) Tetrahedron: vertices $(1, 1, 1), (1, -1, -1), (-1, 1, -1)$ and $(-1, -1, 1)$; lines 1 to 2, 1 to 3, 1 to 4, 2 to 3, 2 to 4 and 3 to 4.
(b) Pyramid with square of side 1 and height HT: vertices $(0, HT, 0), (1, 0, 1)$, $(1, 0, -1), (-1, 0 -1)$ and $(-1, 0, 1)$; lines 1 to 2, 1 to 3, 1 to 4, 1 to 5, 2 to 3, 3 to 4, 4 to 5 and 5 to 2.

Exercise 9.3
Set up a line drawing of any planar object in the x/y plane (for example, the outline of an alphabetic character or string of characters) and view it in various orientations in three-dimensional space. You can place such planar objects on the side of a cube. All you need do is extend the 'cube' routine above to include extra vertices and lines to define the symbols.

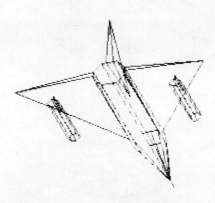

Figure 9.3

Thus far we have restricted our pictures to those of the simple cube. This is so that the methods we give are not obscured by the complexity of defining objects. Our programs will work for any object provided that it fits within the limitations of store (and time) that are available on the IBM PC. For complex objects we merely extend the size of our arrays, although some objects will have properties that enable us to minimise store requirements. Consider the *jet* shown in figure 9.3 — it possesses two-fold symmetry, which can be used to our advantage. We assume that the plane of symmetry is the y/z plane, and so for every point (x, y, z) on the jet there is also a corresponding point $(-x, y, z)$. To draw figure 9.3 we use all the graphics and 4×4 matrix routines, listings 9.1 and 9.2, together with listing 9.8, 'scene3' and construction routine 'jet' which generates all the vertices of the aeroplane that have positive x-coordinates, and thus stores information only about one-half of the jet. To construct the complete aeroplane we also need a 'drawit' routine (also in listing 9.8) which draws one side of the jet and then, by reversing the signs of all the x-values, draws the other.

It is simple to construct these figures, just plan your object in various sections on a piece of graph paper, number the important vertices and note which pairs of vertices are joined by lines. The coordinate values can be read directly from the grid on the paper. The data for figure 9.3 are HORIZ = 160, (EX, EY, EZ) = (1, 2, 3) and (DX, DY, DZ) = (0, 0, 0).

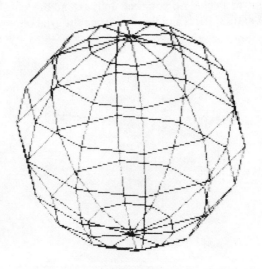

Figure 9.4

Listing 9.8

```
100 'scene3 / jet
110 GOSUB 9700 'start
120 DIM X(37),Y(37),Z(37),XD(37),YD(37),LIN%(2,46)
130 DIM A(4,4),B(4,4),R(4,4)
140 GOSUB 9300 'idR3
150 GOSUB 8200 'look3
160 GOSUB 6500 'jet
170 GOSUB 60000 'colour monitor
180 XMOVE=HORIZ/2 : YMOVE=VERT/2
190 GOSUB 9600 'setorigin
200 GOSUB 7000 'drawit
210 GOSUB 60100 'monochrome monitor
220 END

6500 'jet
6502 ' **out** NOV%,NOL%,X(NOV%),Y(NOV%),Z(NOV%),LIN%(2,NOL%)
6510 DATA 0,0,80, 0,0,64, 0,8,32, 4,8,32, 8,4,32, 8,0,32,
          4,-4,32, 0,8,-32, 4,8,-32, 8,4,-32, 8,0,-32, 4,-4,-32,
          0,-4,-32, 8,0,24, 48,0,-32, 8,2,-32, 0,8,0, 2,8,-32
6520 DATA 0,32,-32, 28,-4,-24, 30,-2,-24, 32,-2,-24, 34,-4,-24,
          32,-6,-24, 30,-6,-24, 28,-4,8, 30,-2,8, 32,-2,8,
6530 DATA 34,-4,8, 32,-6,8, 30,-6,8, 31,0,-24, 31,-2,-24,
          31,-2,-12, 31,0,-12, 0,6,40, 3,6,40
6540 DATA 1,2, 2,3, 2,4, 2,5, 2,6, 2,7, 3,4, 4,9, 5,10, 6,11, 7,12,
          8,9, 9,10, 10,11, 11,12, 12,13, 14,15, 15,10, 15,16, 14,16,
          17,18, 17,19, 18,19
6550 DATA 20,21, 21,22, 22,23, 23,24, 24,25, 25,20, 26,27, 27,28,
          28,29, 29,30, 30,31, 31,26, 20,26, 21,27, 22,28, 23,29,
          24,30, 25,31, 32,33, 33,34, 34,35, 35,32, 36,37
6559 'SETUP vertex and line information for half of the jet.
6560 RESTORE 6510
6570 NOV%=37 : NOL%=46
6580 FOR I%=1 TO NOV%
6590 READ X(I%),Y(I%),Z(I%)
6600 NEXT I%
6610 FOR I%=1 TO NOL%
6620 READ LIN%(1,I%),LIN%(2,I%)
6630 NEXT I%
6640 RETURN

7000 'drawit / two halves of the jet
7001 '**in ** NOV%,NOL%,X(NOV%),Y(NOV%),Z(NOV%),LIN%(2,NOL%),R(4,4)
7010 SIDE%=1
7019 'loop through two halves of jet.
7020 FOR J%=1 TO 2
7029 'put vertices in OBSERVED position.
7030 FOR I%=1 TO NOV%
7040 XX=SIDE%*X(I%) : YY=Y(I%) : ZZ=Z(I%)
7050 XD(I%)=R(1,1)*XX+R(1,2)*YY+R(1,3)*ZZ+R(1,4)
7060 YD(I%)=R(2,1)*XX+R(2,2)*YY+R(2,3)*ZZ+R(2,4)
7070 NEXT I%
7079 'draw the lines.
7080 FOR I%=1 TO NOL%
7090 L1%=LIN%(1,I%) : L2%=LIN%(2,I%)
7100 XPT=XD(L1%) : YPT=YD(L1%) : GOSUB 9500 'moveto
7110 XPT=XD(L2%) : YPT=YD(L2%) : GOSUB 9400 'lineto
7120 NEXT I%
7130 SIDE%=-1
7140 NEXT J%
7150 RETURN
```

Bodies of Revolution

This far in our construction of objects we have relied on DATA to input all the information about lines and vertices. We now consider a type of object where only a small amount of information is required for a quite complex object — this is a body of revolution, an example of which is shown in figure 9.4.

The method is simply to create a defining sequence of NUMV% lines in the x/y plane through the origin; this is called the *definition set*. We then revolve this set about the vertical (y-axis) NUMH% − 1 further times to create new vertical sets. The NUMV% lines in the definition set are formed by joining the NUMV% + 1 vertices (XD(I), YD(I), 0) (where $1 \leqslant I \leqslant$ NUMV% + 1) in order. From this we generate NUMH% different vertical sets: the Jth vertical set is the definition set rotated through an angle PHI + 2π (J − 1)/NUMH% about the vertical y-axis, for some input value PHI(ϕ). As well as the set of NUMH% × NUMV% vertical lines we also introduce horizontal lines. We consider a single point (XD(I), YD(I), 0) at the end of a line segment in the definition set: as we rotate about the vertical axis it moves into NUMH% positions (provided that the point is not on the axis of rotation):

$$(XD(I) \times \cos(\theta + \phi),\ YD(I),\ XD(I) \times \sin(\theta + \phi)) \quad \text{where}$$
$$\theta = 2\pi\,(J - 1)/\text{NUMH\%} \text{ with } 1 \leqslant J \leqslant \text{NUMH\%}$$

These NUMH% points are joined in order, and the NUMH%th position is joined back to the first, to give the Ith horizontal set. So there are (NUMH% − n) × NUMV% horizontal lines, where n is the number of vertices on the axis of rotation. Listing 9.9 is a construction routine 'revbod', which draws the body of revolution when given NUMV%, NUMH%, PHI, the original set of vertices in XD and YD and the positional matrix R. Listing 9.10 is the 'scene3' routine which creates the scene of a spheroid in figure 9.4 by placing eight points from a semicircle into the definition set: HORIZ = 3.6, PHI = $\pi/25$, NUMH% = 10, NUMV% = 8, viewed from (1, 2, 3) looking at (0, 0, 0). This technique was also used to create figure I.1 of the Introduction.

Listing 9.9

```
6500 ´revbod
6501 ´**in ** PHI,NUMH%,NUMV%,N1%,XD(N1%),YD(N1%),R(4,4)
6510 THETA=PHI : TD=3.141593*2/NUMH%
6519 ´create first vertical set.
6520 C=COS(PHI) : S=SIN(PHI)
6530 FOR I%=1 TO N1%
6540 XX=XD(I%)*C : YY=YD(I%) : ZZ=XD(I%)*S
6550 X(I%)=R(1,1)*XX+R(1,2)*YY+R(1,3)*ZZ+R(1,4)
6560 Y(I%)=R(2,1)*XX+R(2,2)*YY+R(2,3)*ZZ+R(2,4)
6570 NEXT I%
6579 ´loop through second vertical set.
6580 FOR J%=1 TO NUMH%
6590 THETA=THETA+TD : C=COS(THETA) : S=SIN(THETA)
6600 FOR I%=1 TO N1%
```

```
6610 XX=XD(I%)*C : YY=YD(I%) : ZZ=XD(I%)*S
6620 X(I%+N1%)=R(1,1)*XX+R(1,2)*YY+R(1,3)*ZZ+R(1,4)
6630 Y(I%+N1%)=R(2,1)*XX+R(2,2)*YY+R(2,3)*ZZ+R(2,4)
6640 NEXT I%
6649 'draw lines in first vertical set.
6650 XPT=X(1) : YPT=Y(1) : GOSUB 9500 'moveto
6660 FOR I%=2 TO N1%
6670 XPT=X(I%) : YPT=Y(I%) : GOSUB 9400 'lineto
6680 NEXT I%
6689 'join corresponding horizontal vertices on 2 vertical sets.
6690 FOR I%=1 TO N1%
6700 XPT=X(I%) : YPT=Y(I%) : GOSUB 9500 'moveto
6710 XPT=X(I%+N1%) : YPT=Y(I%+N1%) : GOSUB 9400 'lineto
6719 'copy second vertical set into first and repeat process.
6720 X(I%)=X(I%+N1%) : Y(I%)=Y(I%+N1%)
6730 NEXT I% : NEXT J%
6740 RETURN
```

Listing 9.10

```
100 'scene3 / spheroid
110 GOSUB 9700 'start
120 INPUT "Number of horizontal lines ",NUMH%
130 INPUT "Number of vertical lines ",NUMV%
140 INPUT "Initial rotation ",PHI
150 N1%=NUMV%+1 : THETA=3.141593/2 : TD=3.141593/NUMV%
160 DIM X(2*N1%),Y(2*N1%),Z(2*N1%),XD(N1%),YD(N1%)
170 DIM A(4,4),B(4,4),R(4,4)
179 'generate definition set.
180 FOR I%=1 TO N1%
190 XD(I%)=COS(THETA) : YD(I%)=SIN(THETA)
200 THETA=THETA+TD
210 NEXT I%
220 GOSUB 9300 'idR3
230 GOSUB 8200 'look3
240 GOSUB 60000 'colour monitor
250 XMOVE=HORIZ/2 : YMOVE=VERT/2
260 GOSUB 9600 'setorigin
270 GOSUB 6500 'revbod
280 GOSUB 60100 'monochrome monitor
290 END
```

Exercise 9.4

Experiment with this technique — any line sequence will do. Try an ellipsoid: this is essentially the same as the spheroid except that the definition set is produced from a semi-ellipse rather than a semicircle. There is no need to produce only convex bodies: lines can cut one another or cross to and fro over the *y*-axis, and *x*-values can move up and down. You have already seen an example of this method with the goblet shown in figure I.1 of the Introduction.

This idea can be extended into a *body of rotation*. Now as the set of lines moves around the central axis, the *y*-values of the points do not stay fixed. They can move in a regular manner, that is they can drop by the same amount with each rotation through 2π/NUMH%. Now, of course, the lines may make more than one complete rotation about the axis — see figure 9.5. Write a program to implement a body of rotation.

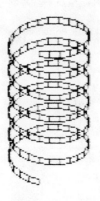

Figure 9.5

Complete Programs

From now on listings 8.1 ('mult3' and 'idR3'), 8.2 ('tran3'), 8.3 ('scale3'), 8.4 ('rot3') and 9.1 ('look3') will be referred to as the 'lib3' library. All the programs below need 'lib0', 'lib1' and 'lib3' MERGEd with them. Run the programs in MODE% = 1 with PALETTE% = 1, BACKGROUND% = FOREGROUND% = 0 and PAPER% = 3.

  I. Listing 9.2 ('scene3') and MERGE in listing 9.3 ('cube'). Data required: HORIZ, (EX, EY, EZ) and (DX, DY, DZ). Try 6, (1, 2, 3), (−1, 0, 1). Use modes 1 and 2.

  II. Listing 9.4 ('scene3') and MERGE 9.3 ('cube'). Data required: HORIZ, (EX, EY, EZ) and (DX, DY, DZ). Try 8, (1, 2, 3), (−1, 0, 1). Make systematic changes to one of these input values and keep all the other parameters fixed.

  III. Listings 9.5 ('scene3') and MERGE both listings 9.6 ('cube') and 9.7 ('drawit'). Data required: HORIZ, and then repeated input of (EX, EY, EZ) and (DX, DY, DZ). Try 8, then (1, 2, 3), (−1, 0, 1): (3, 2, 1), (0, 0, 1). Again make systematic changes to one of the input parameters.

  IV. Listing 9.8 ('scene3', 'jet' and 'drawit'). Data required: HORIZ and then repeated input of (EX, EY, EZ) and (DX, DY, DZ). Try 200, then (1, 2, 31), (−1, 0, 30): (3, 2, 20), (0, 0, 21). Again make systematic changes to one of the input parameters.

  V. Listings 9.10 ('scene3') and MERGE listing 9.9 ('revbod'). Data required: HORIZ, NUMH, NUMV, PHI, (EX, EY, EZ) and (DX, DY, DZ). Try 4, 10, 10, 1, (1, 2, 3), (0, 0, 0): (3, 2, 1), (0, 0, 0).

10 Simple Hidden Line and Hidden Surface Algorithms

Having drawn a cube and other wire objects, the lack of solidity in the figures soon causes irritation. It is preferable to consider solid objects, in which case the facets at the front of the object will obviously restrict the view of the facets (and boundary lines) at the back. Such pictures require the introduction of a hidden surface algorithm; or a hidden line algorithm if all, but only, the visible lines on the object are to be drawn. There are many, many such algorithms — some elementary for specially restricted situations, others very sophisticated for viewing general complicated scenes. The time and storage limitations of microcomputers bar the implementation of the very complex algorithms. Nevertheless, by limiting the types and number of objects in the scenes it is possible to get most acceptable pictures. A relatively complex algorithm is discussed in chapter 12, but here two special types of scene are considered — the properties implicit in these special configurations are used to minimise the work needed to discover which surfaces and lines are hidden. Later in this chapter, a simple method for drawing mathematically defined three-dimensional surfaces is described, but to start with an algorithm for drawing a single solid convex body in three-dimensional space is described.

In this work on hidden line and surface algorithms, the NOV% vertices of a scene (in the OBSERVED position) are stored in arrays X, Y and Z as usual. Now, however, facet rather than line information is used. This data may be implicit in the program or the NOF% facets are explicitly stored in an array FACET%. The integer code for the colour of the facet may be implicit, but if necessary it can be stored in an array COL%. Should the facet data be stored, then an array (SIZE%) is needed for the number of edges on each polygonal facet: and to save space insist that no polygonal facet has more than six edges. Should more edges be needed then the facet must be broken down into a set of smaller polygons. In order to make the hidden surface algorithm easier, a restriction is made on the order of vertices within the array FACET%. The vertices must be stored (or are understood to be) in the order in which they occur around the edge of the facet, and when viewed from the outside of an object they must be in an anticlockwise orientation. Naturally from the inside the vertices taken in this same order would appear clockwise. It will also be assumed that all lines are the junction of two facets. Individual lines not related to facets must be added as degenerate two-sided facets.

The Orientation of a Three-dimensional Triangle

Once the object is planned in terms of vertices and facets, there is still the problem
of deciding whether the facets are actually stored anticlockwise? Simply write a
program! The orientation of any convex polygon can be calculated from any three
of its vertices taken in order, so any ordered triangle of vertices from the facet will
give this information. A method for calculating the orientation of a two-dimensional
triangle was described in chapter 7. The problem is solved if the three-dimensional
situation can be reduced down into two dimensions.

For simplicity it is assumed that all objects are SETUP about and containing the
origin. It is also essential that an infinite plane containing any facet on the surface
of an object does not pass through the origin. Rotate space so that one of the
vertices of the triangle in question lies on the negative z-axis (compare with routine
'look3', listing 9.1). Since the origin is assumed to be inside the object and the eye
is outside, all that is needed is to project the transformed triangle back onto the
x/y plane (that is, ignore the z-coordinates) and treat it like a two-dimensional
triangle (in fact one of the three vertices will be $(0, 0)$). Listing 10.1 is one solution
of the problem.

Listing 10.1

```
100  ´ Orientation of a 3-D triangle.
110 DIM X(3),Y(3),Z(3)
120 DIM A(4,4),B(4,4),R(4,4)
130 CLS : LOCATE 5,5
140 PRINT "Triangle defined by vertices :-"
150 ROW%=8
160 FOR I%=1 TO 3
169 ´INPUT/OUTPUT vertices of triangle.
170 LOCATE 20,1
180 PRINT "Type coordinates of vertex ";I%
190 INPUT X(I%),Y(I%),Z(I%)
200 LOCATE 20,1 : PRINT SPC(40)
210 LOCATE 21,1 : PRINT SPC(40)
219 ´output data about the triangle.
220 LOCATE ROW%,5
230 PRINT "Vertex ";I%;"  :  (";X(I%);",";Y(I%);",";Z(I%);")"
240 ROW%=ROW%+2
250 NEXT I%
259 ´matrix R places first vertex on negative z-axis.
260 GOSUB 9300 ´idR3
270 AX=X(1) : AY=Y(1) : GOSUB 8800 ´angle
280 THETA=-THETA : AXIS%=3 : GOSUB 8600 ´rot3
290 GOSUB 9100 ´mult3
300 AX=Z(1) : AY=SQR(X(1)*X(1)+Y(1)*Y(1)) : GOSUB 8800 ´angle
310 THETA=3.141593-THETA : AXIS%=2 : GOSUB 8600 ´rot3
320 GOSUB 9100 ´mult3
329 ´position 3 vertices with R.
330 FOR I%=1 TO 3
340 XX=X(I%) : YY=Y(I%) : ZZ=Z(I%)
350 X(I%)=R(1,1)*XX+R(1,2)*YY+R(1,3)*ZZ+R(1,4)
360 Y(I%)=R(2,1)*XX+R(2,2)*YY+R(2,3)*ZZ+R(2,4)
370 NEXT I%
379 ´form two directional vectors (DX1,DY1,0) and (DX2,DY2,0).
380 DX1=X(2)-X(1) : DY1=Y(2)-Y(1)
390 DX2=X(3)-X(2) : DY2=Y(3)-Y(2)
400 LOCATE 15,5
410 PRINT "is oriented ";
```

```
419 'check signs of z-coordinate of their vector product.
420 IF DX1*DY2-DX2*DY1 > 0 THEN PRINT"ANTI-";
430 PRINT"CLOCKWISE"
440 LOCATE 16,5
450 PRINT "if eye and origin are on opposite sides of the facet."
460 LOCATE 22,1
470 END
```

Exercise 10.1

Rewrite the wire-figure routines of the previous chapter using the assumption that the data is given as vertices and anticlockwise polygonal facets, and not as lines. Check your facet data with the above program. The line information is still there of course, implicit in the facet data — as the edges of the facet considered as pairs of vertices. Within this information each line occurs twice, once on each of two neighbouring facets. It is a waste of time drawing lines twice! Because of the anti-clockwise manner of constructing the figures, it is noted that if a line joins vertex I to vertex J on one facet then the equivalent line on the neighbouring facet joins vertex J to I. So for wire figures stored as facets, lines will be drawn from vertex I to vertex J if and only if I < J.

A Hidden Surface Algorithm for a Single Closed Convex Body

A finite *convex body* is one in which any line segment joining two points inside the body lies totally within the body: a direct extension of the definition in two-dimensional space. It is automatically closed, and thus it is impossible to get inside the body without crossing through its surface. Project all the vertices of the object orthographically onto the view plane, noting that a projection of a convex polygon with n sides in three-dimensional space is an n-sided convex polygon (or degenerates to a line) in the view plane. Taking the projected vertices of any facet in the same order as the original, either the new two-dimensional polygon is in anticlockwise orientation, in which case the outside of the facet is being observed, or the new vertices are clockwise and the observer is looking at the underside. Since the object is closed, only the outside facets may be seen, the view of their underside being blocked by the bulk of the object. Therefore only the anticlockwise polygonal facets need be drawn — a very simple algorithm, which can be implemented in either construction or 'drawit' routines.

For example, an adjusted construction routine 'cube' for eliminating the hidden surfaces from an orthographic picture of a cube is given as listing 10.2. Here the facets are not stored, but instead the information is READ from DATA, and the visible facets drawn immediately. The facet data, including colour, is implied in the program listing. This program was used to produce figure 10.1, a hidden surface version of figure 9.1d. This figure is drawn with the very same routines that drew figure 9.1d, except of course for the construction routine which sets up the data as vertices and facets, and draws the object (listing 10.2 replaces listing 9.3 in the program for drawing figure 9.1d). Naturally the data needed was the same as that used for figure 9.1d. Note that if the facets are coloured with the same logical colour as the background, then a hidden line as well as a hidden surface algorithm is achieved.

Listing 10.2

```
6500 'cube / data not stored, hidden surfaces removed
6501 '**in ** R(4,4)
6510 DATA 1,1,1, 1,1,-1, 1,-1,-1, 1,-1,1,
        -1,1,1, -1,1,-1, -1,-1,-1, -1,-1,1
6520 DATA 1,2,3,4, 5,8,7,6, 1,5,6,2, 2,6,7,3, 3,7,8,4, 4,8,5,1
6529 'INPUT the SETUP vertices and move into OBSERVED position.
6530 RESTORE 6510 : DIM XC(4),YC(4)
6539 'position the vertices.
6540 FOR J%=1 TO 8
6550 READ XX,YY,ZZ
6560 X(J%)=R(1,1)*XX+R(1,2)*YY+R(1,3)*ZZ+R(1,4)
6570 Y(J%)=R(2,1)*XX+R(2,2)*YY+R(2,3)*ZZ+R(2,4)
6580 Z(J%)=R(3,1)*XX+R(3,2)*YY+R(3,3)*ZZ+R(3,4)
6590 NEXT J%
6599 'INPUT line information : draw lines by joining 2 vertices.
6600 FOR J%=1 TO 6
6609 'read facet data and check orientation.
6610 READ F1%,F2%,F3%,F4%
6620 DX1=X(F2%)-X(F1%) : DY1=Y(F2%)-Y(F1%)
6630 DX2=X(F3%)-X(F2%) : DY2=Y(F3%)-Y(F2%)
6639 'if anticlockwise then draw the facet.
6640 IF DX1*DY2-DX2*DY1 < 0 THEN GOTO 6710
6650 NC%=4 : COLFAC%=1 : FOREGROUND%=2
6660 XC(1)=X(F1%) : YC(1)=Y(F1%)
6670 XC(2)=X(F2%) : YC(2)=Y(F2%)
6680 XC(3)=X(F3%) : YC(3)=Y(F3%)
6690 XC(4)=X(F4%) : YC(4)=Y(F4%)
6700 GOSUB 4000 'filler
6710 NEXT J%
6720 ERASE XC,YC
6730 RETURN
```

If the colours of the facets were stored in the array COL% then naturally the 'filler' routine can be called with colour parameter COL%(I) (and perhaps black FOREGROUND%?) to fill the Ith facet.

A hidden surface construction routine for an icosahedron is now given (listing 10.3). Change line 120 of listing 9.2 'scene3' to allow for twelve, rather than eight, vertices.

Listing 10.3

```
6500 'icosahedron / data not stored, hidden surfaces removed
6501 '**in ** R(4,4)
6510 DATA 0,1,2, 2,0,1, 1,2,0, 0,-1,2, 2,0,-1, -1,2,0, 0,1,-2,
        -2,0,1, 1,-2,0, 0,-1,-2, -2,0,-1, -1,-2,0
6520 DATA 1,3,2, 1,2,4, 1,4,8, 1,8,6, 1,6,3, 2,3,5, 2,9,4, 4,12,8,
        8,11,6, 3,6,7, 2,5,9, 4,9,12, 8,12,11, 6,11,7, 3,7,5,
        5,10,9, 9,10,12, 12,10,11, 11,10,7, 7,10,5
6530 RESTORE 6510 : DIM XC(3),YC(3)
6540 D=(1+SQR(5))/2
6549 'INPUT the SETUP vertices and move them into OBSERVED position.
6550 FOR J%=1 TO 12
6560 READ XX,YY,ZZ
6570 IF ABS(XX)=2 THEN XX=SGN(XX)*D
```

```
6580 IF ABS(YY)=2 THEN YY=SGN(YY)*D
6590 IF ABS(ZZ)=2 THEN ZZ=SGN(ZZ)*D
6599 'position the vertices.
6600 X(J%)=R(1,1)*XX+R(1,2)*YY+R(1,3)*ZZ+R(1,4)
6610 Y(J%)=R(2,1)*XX+R(2,2)*YY+R(2,3)*ZZ+R(2,4)
6620 Z(J%)=R(3,1)*XX+R(3,2)*YY+R(3,3)*ZZ+R(3,4)
6630 NEXT J%
6639 'read facet data and check orientation.
6640 FOR J%=1 TO 20
6650 READ F1%,F2%,F3%
6660 DX1=X(F2%)-X(F1%) : DY1=Y(F2%)-Y(F1%)
6670 DX2=X(F3%)-X(F2%) : DY2=Y(F3%)-Y(F2%)
6679 'if anticlockwise then draw the facet.
6680 IF DX1*DY2-DX2*DY1 < 0 THEN GOTO 6740
6690 NC%=3 : COLFAC%=1 : FOREGROUND%=2
6700 XC(1)=X(F1%) : YC(1)=Y(F1%)
6710 XC(2)=X(F2%) : YC(2)=Y(F2%)
6720 XC(3)=X(F3%) : YC(3)=Y(F3%)
6730 GOSUB 4000 'filler
6740 NEXT J%
6750 ERASE XC,YC
6760 RETURN
```

Exercise 10.2

Change listing 10.2 so that it can draw a rectangular block of length LH, breadth BH and height HT, where LH, BH and HT are input parameters to the routine. Then draw a hidden line picture of it. Draw hidden line pictures of tetrahedra, pyramids, octahedra etc. Add extra parameters to distort these figures so that they are no longer regular, but are still convex.

Exercise 10.3

Rather than have a one-colour cube with black edges drawn in on a white background, give it three colours (red, green and black: PALETTE% = 0) where opposite faces have the same colour and the edges are not drawn. The information on the colour of a facet should be stored in DATA alongside the vertices, so the program would contain

READ F1%, F2%, F3%, F4%, COLOUR%

When it comes to colouring in a facet you must call the 'filler' routine with colour parameter COLFAC% set to COLOUR% and edges set to the present FOREGROUND% colour.

Also draw an icosahedron in two colours (cyan and magenta: that is, PALETTE% = 1) with edges in black.

Instead of creating a hidden surface picture of a cube with facets drawn in one colour, it is possible to put patterns on the visible sides. The routines in listing 10.4 can be used in conjunction with 'lib0', 'lib1' and 'lib3' to draw a flag, similar to that of the two-dimensional example 4.1, on the side of a cube (see figure 10.2).

Figure 10.1

Listing 10.4

```
100 'scene3 / cube with flag faces ( hidden lines removed )
110 GOSUB 9700 'start
120 DIM X(8),Y(8),Z(8)
130 DIM A(4,4),B(4,4),R(4,4)
140 GOSUB 9300 'idR3
150 GOSUB 8200 'look3
160 GOSUB 60000 'colour monitor
170 XMOVE=HORIZ/2 : YMOVE=VERT/2
180 GOSUB 9600 'setorigin
190 GOSUB 6500 'cube
200 GOSUB 60100 'monochrome monitor
210 END

6500 'cube / data not stored
6510 DATA 1,1,1, 1,1,-1, 1,-1,-1, 1,-1,1,
        -1,1,1, -1,1,-1, -1,-1,-1, -1,-1,1
6520 DATA 1,2,3,4, 5,8,7,6, 1,5,6,2, 2,6,7,3, 3,7,8,4, 4,8,5,1
6530 RESTORE 6510
6539 'position the vertices.
6540 FOR J%=1 TO 8
6550 READ XX,YY,ZZ
6560 X(J%)=R(1,1)*XX+R(1,2)*YY+R(1,3)*ZZ+R(1,4)
6570 Y(J%)=R(2,1)*XX+R(2,2)*YY+R(2,3)*ZZ+R(2,4)
6580 Z(J%)=R(3,1)*XX+R(3,2)*YY+R(3,3)*ZZ+R(3,4)
6590 NEXT J%
6599 'read facet data and check orientation.
6600 FOR J%=1 TO 6
6610 READ F1%,F2%,F3%,F4%
6620 DX1=X(F2%)-X(F1%) : DY1=Y(F2%)-Y(F1%)
6630 DX2=X(F3%)-X(F2%) : DY2=Y(F3%)-Y(F2%)
6639 'if anticlockwise then draw the facet.
6640 IF DX1*DY2-DX2*DY1 < 0 THEN GOTO 6720
6649 'draw flags on visible faces.
6650 GOSUB 7000 'flagface
6659 'draw lines in colour 0 around flag.
6660 FOREGROUND%=0
```

```
6670 XPT=X(F4%) : YPT=Y(F4%) : GOSUB 9500 'moveto
6680 XPT=X(F1%) : YPT=Y(F1%) : GOSUB 9400 'lineto
6690 XPT=X(F2%) : YPT=Y(F2%) : GOSUB 9400 'lineto
6700 XPT=X(F3%) : YPT=Y(F3%) : GOSUB 9400 'lineto
6710 XPT=X(F4%) : YPT=Y(F4%) : GOSUB 9400 'lineto
6720 NEXT J%
6730 RETURN


7000 'flagface
7001 '**in ** F1%,F2%,F3%,F4%
7010 DIM FACE%(4),XD(12),YD(12),XC(6),YC(6)
7020 FACE%(1)=F1% : FACE%(2)=F2% :
     FACE%(3)=F3% : FACE%(4)=F4% : K%=4
7029 'calculate 12 reference points on the flag face.
7030 FOR M%=1 TO 4
7040 XD(M%)=X(FACE%(M%)) : YD(M%)=Y(FACE%(M%))
7050 NEXT M%
7060 FOR M%=1 TO 4
7070 N%=(M% MOD 4)+1 : K%=K%+1
7080 XD(K%)=.9*X(FACE%(M%))+.1*X(FACE%(N%))
7090 YD(K%)=.9*Y(FACE%(M%))+.1*Y(FACE%(N%))
7100 K%=K%+1
7110 XD(K%)=.1*X(FACE%(M%))+.9*X(FACE%(N%))
7120 YD(K%)=.1*Y(FACE%(M%))+.9*Y(FACE%(N%))
7130 NEXT M%
7139 'draw base of flag in colour 1.
7140 NC%=4 : COLFAC%=1 : FOREGROUND%=1
7150 XC(1)=XD(1) : YC(1)=YD(1)
7160 XC(2)=XD(2) : YC(2)=YD(2)
7170 XC(3)=XD(3) : YC(3)=YD(3)
7180 XC(4)=XD(4) : YC(4)=YD(4)
7190 GOSUB 4000 'filler
7199 'draw diagonals of flag in colour 2.
7200 NC%=6 : COLFAC%=2 : FOREGROUND%=2
7210 XC(1)=XD(1)  : YC(1)=YD(1)
7220 XC(2)=XD(5)  : YC(2)=YD(5)
7230 XC(3)=XD(8)  : YC(3)=YD(8)
7240 XC(4)=XD(3)  : YC(4)=YD(3)
7250 XC(5)=XD(9)  : YC(5)=YD(9)
7260 XC(6)=XD(12) : YC(6)=YD(12)
7270 GOSUB 4000 'filler
7280 NC%=6 : COLFAC%=2 : FOREGROUND%=2
7290 XC(1)=XD(2)  : YC(1)=YD(2)
7300 XC(2)=XD(7)  : YC(2)=YD(7)
7310 XC(3)=XD(10) : YC(3)=YD(10)
7320 XC(4)=XD(4)  : YC(4)=YD(4)
7330 XC(5)=XD(11) : YC(5)=YD(11)
7340 XC(6)=XD(6)  : YC(6)=YD(6)
7350 GOSUB 4000 'filler
7360 ERASE FACE%,XD,YD,XC,YC
7370 RETURN
```

Exercise 10.4

Draw a hidden surface picture of a red die with black spots (PALETTE% = 0), and with edges also drawn in black. Remember that the values on opposite faces of a die sum to seven.

Bodies of Revolution

This anticlockwise *versus* clockwise method can be used to produce hidden surface pictures of bodies of revolution that were defined in chapter 9. Going through the

NUMH% revolutions as defined in the wire-body of revolution, NUMV% facets are created with each move. Provided that these quadrilateral (or perhaps degenerate triangular) facets are carefully constructed in an anticlockwise orientation then the same algorithm may be used. Listing 10.5 is such a 'revbod' routine which produces figure 10.3, a hidden surface version of figure 9.4 (and it uses the same input data).

Figure 10.2

Again, because of the modular design of the programs, all the routines needed to draw figure 10.3, except 'revbod', are the same as those given in chapter 9. Now, however, only convex bodies of revolution may be considered.

Listing 10.5

```
6500 'revbod / hidden lines removed
6501 ' **in ** PHI,NUMV%,NUMH%,N1%,XD(N1%),YD(N1%),R(4,4)
6510 DIM XC(4),YC(4) : THETA=PHI : TD=3.141593*2/NUMH%
6519 'create first vertical set.
6520 C=COS(PHI) : S=SIN(PHI)
6530 FOR I%=1 TO N1%
6540 XX=XD(I%)*C : YY=YD(I%) : ZZ=XD(I%)*S
6550 X(I%)=R(1,1)*XX+R(1,2)*YY+R(1,3)*ZZ+R(1,4)
6560 Y(I%)=R(2,1)*XX+R(2,2)*YY+R(2,3)*ZZ+R(2,4)
6570 Z(I%)=R(3,1)*XX+R(3,2)*YY+R(3,3)*ZZ+R(3,4)
6580 NEXT I%
6589 'loop through second vertical set.
6590 FOR J%=1 TO NUMH%
6600 THETA=THETA+TD : C=COS(THETA) : S=SIN(THETA)
6610 FOR I%=1 TO N1%
6620 XX=XD(I%)*C : YY=YD(I%) : ZZ=XD(I%)*S
6630 X(I%+N1%)=R(1,1)*XX+R(1,2)*YY+R(1,3)*ZZ+R(1,4)
6640 Y(I%+N1%)=R(2,1)*XX+R(2,2)*YY+R(2,3)*ZZ+R(2,4)
6650 Z(I%+N1%)=R(3,1)*XX+R(3,2)*YY+R(3,3)*ZZ+R(3,4)
6660 NEXT I%
6669 'facet formed by F1%,F2%,F3% (and F4%) is SETUP anticlockwise.
6670 FOR I%=1 TO NUMV%
```

```
6680 Fl%=I% : F2%=I%+1
6690 IF I%=NUMV% THEN F3%=F2%+NUMV% ELSE F3%=F2%+N1%
6700 DX1=X(F2%)-X(Fl%) : DY1=Y(F2%)-Y(Fl%) : DZ1=Z(F2%)-Z(Fl%)
6710 DX2=X(F3%)-X(F2%) : DY2=Y(F3%)-Y(F2%) : DZ2=Z(F3%)-Z(F2%)
6720 F3%=F2%+N1% : F4%=F3%-1
6729 'if OBSERVED anticlockwise then facet is visible.
     Vector (NX,NY,NZ) needed by later shading program.
6730 NZ=DX1*DY2-DX2*DY1
6740 IF NZ < 0 THEN GOTO 6840
6750 NY=DZ1*DX2-DZ2*DX1
6760 NX=DY1*DZ2-DY2*DZ1
6769 'join corresponding horizontal vertices on the 2 vertical sets.
6770 F3%=F2%+N1% : F4%=F3%-1
6779 'colour-in visible facet.
6780 NC%=4 : COLFAC%=1 : FOREGROUND%=2
6790 XC(1)=X(Fl%) : YC(1)=Y(Fl%)
6800 XC(2)=X(F2%) : YC(2)=Y(F2%)
6810 XC(3)=X(F3%) : YC(3)=Y(F3%)
6820 XC(4)=X(F4%) : YC(4)=Y(F4%)
6830 GOSUB 4000 'filler
6840 NEXT I%
6849 'copy second vertical set into first vertical set.
6850 FOR I%=1 TO N1%
6860 X(I%)=X(I%+N1%) : Y(I%)=Y(I%+N1%) : Z(I%)=Z(I%+N1%)
6870 NEXT I% : NEXT J%
6880 ERASE XC,YC
6890 RETURN
```

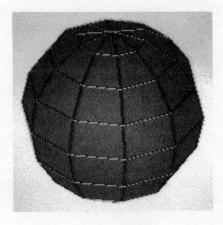

Figure 10.3

As the routine rotates the definition set of lines about the vertical axis, it stores the vertices of two consecutive vertical sets of lines. These form the vertical edges of one *slice* of facets. The vertices on these facets are immediately transformed by R (the SETUP to OBSERVED matrix) and stored in arrays X and Y. In such a configuration of pairs of vertical lines the first set of vertices has indices from 1 to NUMV% + 1 (= N1%), and the second from N1% + 1 to 2 * N1%. The Ith facet is bounded by four lines, two vertical joining vertex I to I + 1, and I + N1% to I + N1% + 1, and two horizontal joining I to I + N1%, and I + 1 to I + N1% + 1.

Adjustments must be made if one of the original vertices is on the axis of rotation, in which case the quadrilateral degenerates to a triangle. The order of vertices in each facet is carefully chosen so that they are in anticlockwise orientation when viewed from outside the object. Checking the orientation of each projected facet gives a simple algorithm for drawing the object with the hidden surfaces suppressed.

Exercise 10.5

Experiment with this technique. Any initial set of lines will do provided that it starts and ends on the vertical axis and the polygon thus formed in the x/y plane is convex.

Variations on the Sphere Program (listing 10.5 etc.)

The sphere program of the previous section is extended in two ways: (1) to demonstrate animation, and (2) to display a form of shading. These two new programs will show the immediate benefit of a structured approach to programming.

(1) Animation – a rotating sphere

A method of animation using GET and PUT was given in chapter 1. A rotating sphere is achieved in the same way. Listing 10.6 creates five separate pictures of a sphere, each rotated $\pi/25$ from the previous one. Therefore by setting PHI = 0 and NUMH% = 10, the five 'frames' appear to be intermediate stages of rotation. Since the angular difference between consecutive vertical edges is $2\pi/10$ (2π/NUMH%), the choice of PHI = $\pi/25$ gives the impression of five intermediate stages in a rotation of the sphere by $2\pi/10$. Rotation by I $*$ $2\pi/10$ will naturally create the same pictures for all integral values I. Therefore repeatedly drawing the five frames in order, over and over again, creates the impression of the sphere rotating.

Because PUT tends to be slow for drawing large areas of the screen (implying a jittery animation), the size of the block to be stored is restricted to 100 pixels square at the centre of the screen. To get a sphere completely inside this restricted area the value of HORIZ must be set to at least 8. Try the program with HORIZ = 8, NUMH% = NUMV% = 10, PHI = 0, (EX, EY, EZ) = (1, 2, 3) and (DX, DY, DZ) = (0, 0, 0).

Listing 10.6

```
100 'scene3 / spheroid movie
110 GOSUB 9700 'start
120 DIM STO1%(1252),STO2%(1252),STO3%(1252),STO4%(1252),STO5%(1252)
130 NUMH%=10 : NUMV%=10
140 N1%=NUMV%+1 : THETA=3.141593/2 : TD=.3141593
150 DIM X(2*N1%),Y(2*N1%),Z(2*N1%),XD(N1%),YD(N1%)
160 DIM A(4,4),B(4,4),R(4,4)
170 FOR I%=1 TO N1%
180 XD(I%)=COS(THETA) : YD(I%)=SIN(THETA)
190 THETA=THETA+TD
200 NEXT I%
```

```
210 PHI=0 : ROTBIT=3.141593/25
220 GOSUB 9300 'idR3
230 GOSUB 8200 'look3
240 GOSUB 60000 'colour monitor
250 XMOVE=HORIZ/2 : YMOVE=VERT/2
260 GOSUB 9600 'setorigin
269 'draw 5 frames, each 100 pixels square at centre of screen.
270 XL=PMAP(110,2) : YL=PMAP(50,3)
280 XR=PMAP(209,2) : YR=PMAP(149,3)
290 FOR FRAME%=1 TO 5
299 'in each frame the sphere rotates by a further pi/25.
300 PHI=PHI+ROTBIT
310 LINE (XL,YL)-(XR,YR),PAPER%,BF
320 GOSUB 6500 'revbod
329 'store each frame.
330 IF FRAME%=1 THEN GET (XL,YL)-(XR,YR),STO1%
    ELSE IF FRAME%=2 THEN GET (XL,YL)-(XR,YR),STO2%
        ELSE IF FRAME%=3 THEN GET (XL,YL)-(XR,YR),STO3%
340 IF FRAME%=4 THEN GET (XL,YL)-(XR,YR),STO4%
    ELSE GET(XL,YL)-(XR,YR),STO5%
350 NEXT FRAME%
359 'animation loop
360 PUT (XL,YL),STO1%,PSET
370 PUT (XL,YL),STO2%,PSET
380 PUT (XL,YL),STO3%,PSET
390 PUT (XL,YL),STO4%,PSET
400 PUT (XL,YL),STO5%,PSET
410 GOTO 360
420 END
```

(2) Shading

There are only a limited number of colours available, so it is impossible to have subtle variations of shade and colour on the screen. It is nevertheless possible to approximate to shading by filling each polygonal facet with a combination of colours, rather than a single colour. Also it is no longer necessary to draw the outline of each polygon. The shading is achieved by varying the proportions of colours within each facet (see figure 10.4 listing 10.7, and the cover).

Figure 10.4

Listing 10.7

```
100 'scene3 / spheroid shaded
110 GOSUB 9700 'start
120 INPUT "Number of horizontal lines ",NUMH%
130 INPUT "Number of vertical lines ",NUMV%
140 INPUT "Initial rotation ",PHI
150 N1%=NUMV%+1 : THETA=3.141593/2 : TD=3.141593/NUMV%
160 DIM X(2*N1%),Y(2*N1%),Z(2*N1%),XD(N1%),YD(N1%)
170 DIM A(4,4),B(4,4),R(4,4)
179 'generate definition set.
180 FOR I%=1 TO N1%
190 XD(I%)=COS(THETA) : YD(I%)=SIN(THETA)
200 THETA=THETA+TD
210 NEXT I%
220 INPUT "OBSERVED direction of Illumination ",DIX,DIY,DIZ
230 DXYZ=SQR(DIX*DIX+DIY*DIY+DIZ*DIZ)
240 GOSUB 9300 'idR3
250 GOSUB 8200 'look3
260 GOSUB 60000 'colour monitor
270 XMOVE=HORIZ/2 : YMOVE=VERT/2
280 GOSUB 9600 'setorigin
290 GOSUB 6500 'revbod
300 GOSUB 60100 'monochrome monitor
310 END


4000 'shaded polygon filler
4001 '**in ** NC%,XC(NC%),YC(NC%),MODE%,NX,NY,NZ,DIX,DIY,DIZ,DXYZ
4009 'find the Y-extremes of the polygon.
4010 YMAX=-1 : YMIN=200
4020 DIM PX(NC%),PY(NC%)
4030 FOR V%=1 TO NC%
4039 'pixel vector (PX(V%),PY(V%)) equivalent to (XC(V%),YC(V%))
4040 PX(V%)=PMAP(XC(V%),0) : PY(V%)=PMAP(YC(V%),1)
4050 IF PY(V%)<YMIN THEN YMIN=PY(V%)
4060 IF PY(V%)>YMAX THEN YMAX=PY(V%)
4070 NEXT V%
4080 IF YMIN<0 THEN YMIN=0
4090 IF YMAX>199 THEN YMAX=199
4100 IF YMAX<YMIN THEN RETURN
4109 'find cosine of angle between plane normal and direction of li
       and incorporate in value of SHADE.
4110 NXYZ=SQR(NX^2+NY^2+NZ^2)
4120 SHADE=50-50*(DIX*NX+DIY*NY+DIZ*NZ)/(NXYZ*DXYZ)
4129 'look at each pixel Y-line in turn.
4130 FOR Y=YMIN TO YMAX
4139 'find the X-extremes of the polygon on this Y-line.
4140 XMAX=-1 : XMIN=320*MODE%
4149 'for each edge of the polygon, a line segment joining
       (PX(V%),PY(V%)) to (PX(NV%),PY(NV%)), find its point of
       intersection (X,Y) (if any) with the Y-line.
4150 FOR V%=1 TO NC%
4160 NV%=(V% MOD NC%)+1
4170 IF (PY(V%)-PY(NV%))=0 THEN GOTO 4230
4180 MU=(Y-PY(V%))/(PY(NV%)-PY(V%))
4190 IF MU<0 OR MU>1 THEN GOTO 4230
4200 X=PX(V%)+INT(MU*(PX(NV%)-PX(V%))+.5)
4210 IF X<XMIN THEN XMIN=X
4220 IF X>XMAX THEN XMAX=X
4230 NEXT V%
4240 IF XMIN <0 THEN XMIN=0
4250 IF XMAX>=320*MODE% THEN XMAX=320*MODE%-1
4260 IF XMAX<XMIN THEN GOTO 4310
4269 'calculate the COLOR% of each pixel and shade it in.
4270 FOR X=XMIN TO XMAX
4280 GOSUB 4500 'shade it
4290 PSET (PMAP(X,2),PMAP(Y,3)),COLOR%
4300 NEXT X
```

```
4310 NEXT Y
4320 ERASE PX,PY
4330 RETURN

4500 'shade it
4501 '**in ** SHADE
4502 '**out** COLOR%
4510 IF SHADE<35 THEN COLOR%=2 : RETURN
4520 IF SHADE>95 THEN COLOR%=3 : RETURN
4530 IF SHADE > 85 THEN GOTO 4560
4540 IF 35+RND*50 < SHADE THEN COLOR%=1 ELSE COLOR%=2
4550 RETURN
4560 IF 85+RND*10 < SHADE THEN COLOR%=3 ELSE COLOR%=1
4570 RETURN
```

It is assumed that there is an external light source, called an illumination vector (given in OBSERVED coordinates). The light emitted is parallel to the direction from this vector to the origin (DX, DY, DZ). The cosine of the angle of incidence of this light on any facet is calculated by the dot product of the normal to the plane containing the facet with the illumination vector. This value is adjusted to range between 0 and 100. Running in MODE% = 1, the facet is coloured with a combination of either logical 1 and 3, or logical 1 and 2, depending on the cosine value. The routine to calculate the proportional choice of colours is given in the 'shade' routine, and the colouring of a facet is given in a new 'filler' routine of listing 10.7: compare it with the 'filler' in 'lib1'.

Loading the program for drawing figure 10.3, and MERGEing in listing 10.7 enables you to create pictures like figure 10.4. Try the program with HORIZ = 8, illumination vector $(1, 2, -3)$, (EX, EY, EZ) = $(1, 2, 3)$ and (DX, DY, DZ) = $(0, 0, 0)$. The sphere itself should have NUMH% = NUMV% = 40 and PHI = 0. If you use small values of NUMH% and NUMV% (for example, 10) then the facets will stand out through the shading.

The BACK to FRONT method

The call for pictures of convex solids is limited, so another simple algorithm which can be used with non-convex figures is now described. You will have noticed that, when colouring a new area, all the colours previously placed in that section of the screen are obliterated. This creates a very simple hidden surface algorithm: namely draw the areas in an order furthest from the eye first to the nearest last. Exactly what is meant by furthest/nearest is not that straightforward, however there are certain situations (such as that described in the next section, and the stack of cubes of figure 11.5) where this phrase has a very simple meaning and the algorithm is easy to implement. See chapter 12 for a general solution.

Drawing a Special Three-dimensional Surface

The construction of a restricted type of three-dimensional surface is considered, in which the y-coordinate of each point on the surface is given by a single-valued function 'f' of the x and z coordinates of that point. 'f' will be included as a

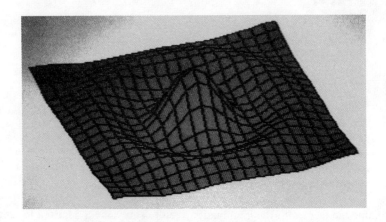

Figure 10.5

routine in the program – one such example is given in listing 10.8, the function $y = 4 \times SIN(XZ)/XZ$ where $XZ = \sqrt{(x^2 + z^2)}$, which is shown in figure 10.5. The data required was HORIZ = 30, NX% = NZ% = 20, MINX = MINZ = −10, MAXX = MAXZ = 10, (EX, EY, EZ) = (3, 2, 1), (DX, DY, DZ) = (0, 0, 0).

Listing 10.8

```
100 ´scene3 / mathematical surface
110 GOSUB 9700 ´start
120 DIM A(4,4),B(4,4),R(4,4)
129 ´INPUT grid data.
130 INPUT "NX%,MINX,MAXX ",NX%,MINX,MAXX
140 INPUT "NZ%,MINZ,MAXZ ",NZ%,MINZ,MAXZ
150 XD=(MAXX-MINX)/NX% : ZD=(MAXZ-MINZ)/NZ%
160 NX1%=NX%+1 : COLFAC%=1 : FOREGROUND%=2
169 ´view from (EX,EY,EX) looking at (0,0,0) : EX>0 and EZ>0.
170 GOSUB 9300 ´idR3
180 GOSUB 8200 ´look3
190 GOSUB 60000 ´colour monitor
200 XMOVE=HORIZ/2 : YMOVE=VERT/2
210 GOSUB 9600 ´setorigin
219 ´draw the surface.
220 GOSUB 6500 ´surface
230 GOSUB 60100 ´monochrome monitor
240 END

6500 ´surface
6501 ´**in ** NZ%,NX1%,XD,ZD,MINZ
6510 DIM X(2,NX1%),Y(2,NX1%),XC(4),YC(4)
6520 ZV=MINZ : INDEX%=1 : GOSUB 6700 ´setpoint
6529 ´loop through consecutive pairs of fixed-z lines.
6530 FOR LZ%=1 TO NZ%
6540 LXM1%=1 : ZV=ZV+ZD : INDEX%=2 : GOSUB 6700 ´setpoint
6549 ´move along polygons formed between these two lines.
6550 FOR LX%=2 TO NX1%
6560 GOSUB 7000 ´polygon
6570 LXM1%=LX%
```

```
6580 NEXT LX%
6589 'reset first line.
6590 FOR LX%=1 TO NX1%
6600 X(1,LX%)=X(2,LX%) : Y(1,LX%)=Y(2,LX%)
6610 NEXT LX%
6620 NEXT LZ%
6630 ERASE XC,YC
6640 RETURN


6700 'setpoint
6701 '**in ** R(4,4),ZV,NX1%,INDEX%,MINX
6702 '**out** X(2,NX1%),Y(2,NX1%)
6709 'points on fixed-z = ZV line are put into OBSERVED position.
6710 XV=MINX
6720 FOR LX%=1 TO NX1%
6730 GOSUB 6900 'f(unction evaluation)
6740 X(INDEX%,LX%)=R(1,1)*XV+R(1,2)*YV+R(1,3)*ZV+R(1,4)
6750 Y(INDEX%,LX%)=R(2,1)*XV+R(2,2)*YV+R(2,3)*ZV+R(2,4)
6760 XV=XV+XD
6770 NEXT LX%
6780 RETURN


6900 'f(unction evaluation)
6901 '**in ** XV,ZV
6902 '**out** YV
6910 RAD=SQR(XV*XV+ZV*ZV)
6920 IF RAD<.000001 THEN YV=4 ELSE YV=4*SIN(RAD)/RAD
6930 RETURN


7000 'polygon
7001 '**in ** X(2,NX1%),Y(2,NX1%),LX%,LXM1%
7010 DX1=X(1,LX%)-X(1,LXM1%) : DY1=Y(1,LX%)-Y(1,LXM1%)
7020 DX2=X(2,LX%)-X(1,LX%)  : DY2=Y(2,LX%)-Y(1,LX%)
7030 ZPROD1=DX1*DY2-DX2*DY1
7040 DX1=X(2,LXM1%)-X(2,LX%)   : DY1=Y(2,LXM1%)-Y(2,LX%)
7050 DX2=X(1,LXM1%)-X(2,LXM1%) : DY2=Y(1,LXM1%)-Y(2,LXM1%)
7060 ZPROD2=DX1*DY2-DX2*DY1
7069 'grid rectangle transforms into a quadrilateral or 2 triangles.
7070 IF SGN(ZPROD1)<>SGN(ZPROD2) GOTO 7150
7079 'draw the quadrilateral.
7080 NC%=4
7090 XC(1)=X(1,LXM1%) : YC(1)=Y(1,LXM1%)
7100 XC(2)=X(1,LX%)   : YC(2)=Y(1,LX%)
7110 XC(3)=X(2,LX%)   : YC(3)=Y(2,LX%)
7120 XC(4)=X(2,LXM1%) : YC(4)=Y(2,LXM1%)
7130 GOSUB 4000 'filler
7140 RETURN
7149 'find the intersection (A5,B5) of lines from (A1,B1) to (A2,B2)
         and from (A3,B3) to (A4,B4).
7150 A1=X(1,LXM1%) : B1=Y(1,LXM1%)
7160 A2=X(1,LX%)   : B2=Y(1,LX%)
7170 A3=X(2,LX%)   : B3=Y(2,LX%)
7180 A4=X(2,LXM1%) : B4=Y(2,LXM1%)
7190 FOR L%=1 TO 2
7200 C11=A2-A1 : C12=A3-A4 : C21=B2-B1 : C22=B3-B4
7210 D1=A3-A1 : D2=B3-B1 : DET=C11*C22-C21*C12
7220 IF ABS(DET) < .000001 THEN GOTO 7360
7230 MU=(D1*C22-D2*C12)/DET
7240 IF MU<0 OR MU>1 THEN GOTO 7360
7250 A5=A1+MU*C11 : B5=B1+MU*C21
7259 'draw the two triangles : (A1,B1) to (A4,B4) to (A5,B5)
                        and   (A2,B2) to (A3,B3) to (A5,B5) .
7260 NC=3
7270 XC(1)=A1 : YC(1)=B1
7280 XC(2)=A4 : YC(2)=B4
7290 XC(3)=A5 : YC(3)=B5
7300 GOSUB 4000 'filler
7310 XC(1)=A2 : YC(1)=B2
7320 XC(2)=A3 : YC(2)=B3
```

```
7330 XC(3)=A5 : YC(3)=B5
7340 GOSUB 4000 'filler
7350 RETURN
7359 'no intersection so swap (A2,B2) with (A4,B4).
7360 AA=A2 : A2=A4 : A4=AA
7370 AA=B2 : B2=B4 : B4=AA
7380 NEXT L%
7390 RETURN
```

Since it is impossible to draw every point on the surface, a subset of these surface points is considered as an approximation. The only points chosen are those which, when viewed orthographically directly from above (thus ignoring the y-values), form a rectangular grid. This grid is composed of NX% by NZ% rectangles in the x/z plane. The x-coordinates of the vertices are equi-spaced and vary between MINX and MAXX (MINX < MAXX) and the equi-spaced z-values vary between MINZ and MAXZ (MINZ < MAXZ). There are thus (NX% + 1)×(NZ% + 1) vertices (X, Z) in the grid which can be identified by the pair of integers (i, j):

$$X = MINX + i_\times XV \text{ where } 0 \leqslant i \leqslant NX\% \text{ and } XV = (MAXX - MINX)/NX\%$$

$$Z = MINZ + j_\times ZV \text{ where } 0 \leqslant j \leqslant NZ\% \text{ and } ZV = (MAXZ - MINZ)/NZ\%$$

The equivalent point on the surface is (X, Y, Z) where $Y = f(X, Z)$. Every one of the (NX% + 1)×(NZ% + 1) points generated in this way is joined to its four immediate neighbours along the grid (that is, those with equal x or equal z values), unless it lies on the edge in which case it is joined to three, or in the case of corners to two, neighbours.

The approximation to the surface that is formed in this way may undulate, so not all the facets need be visible from a given view point − in fact some may even be partially visible. A very simple method for eliminating the hidden surfaces is to work from the back of the surface to the front. To simplify the algorithm the eye is always assumed to be in the positive quadrant (that is, EX > 0 and EZ > 0) and always looking at the origin (DX = DY = DZ = 0). If the function is non-symmetrical and a view from another quadrant is needed, then simply change the sign of x and/or z in the function. The surface is then transformed into the OBSERVED position.

Loop through the set of NX% facets generated from the consecutive fixed-x grid lines $x = MINX + i_\times XV$ and $x = MINX + (i + 1)_\times XV$ from the back (i = 0) to the front (i = NX% − 1) (naturally the term back to front is used in the sense of the final OBSERVED position). Within each set, loop through the individual facets generated by the intersection of the fixed-x lines with the fixed-z grid lines starting at $z = MINZ$ and $z = MINZ + ZV$, working through to $z = MAXZ - ZV$ and $z = MAXZ$. The four grid points created in this way may be labelled (1, K) and (1, K + 1) − on the fixed-x line with smaller x-value − and (2, K) and (2, K + 1) − on the fixed-x line with larger value. (K + 1 is called J in the program, and in the explanation below.) 'f' is used to form four points on the surface from these grid points, which when transformed onto the view plane either form a quadrilateral or two triangles. Distinguish between the two possibilities by finding the orientation of the two triangles formed by grid points (1, K), (1, J) and (2, J), and (2, J), (2, K) and (1, K). If they have the same orientation (both clockwise or both anti-clockwise) then they form a quadrilateral, otherwise two triangles. The extra vertex of the two triangles is found from either the intersection of the lines joining (1, K) to (1, J) and (2, J) to (2, K), or from (1, K) to (2, K) and (1, J) to (2, J): other combinations are topologically impossible. Having found the quadrilateral or two triangles, they are coloured in and their edges also drawn, and the back to front construction (because EX and EZ are positive) ensures a correct hidden surface picture.

Exercise 10.6
Change the functions 'f' used by this program. For example, use f = 4SIN(t) where $t = \sqrt{(x^2 + z^2)}$.

Exercise 10.7
Extend the above program so that it draws the top side of the surface in a different colour from the underside.

___

Complete Programs

All the programs below (except I which needs only 'angle' from 'lib1') need 'lib0', 'lib1' and 'lib3' MERGEd with them. Run the programs in MODE% = 1 with PALETTE% = 1, BACKGROUND% = FOREGROUND% = 0 and PAPER% = 3.

   I. Listing 10.1. Data required: the vertex coordinates of a triangle (X(I), Y(I), Z(I)), where $1 \leqslant I \leqslant 3$. Try (1, 0, 1), (1, 1, 0) and (0, 1, 1): also the same vertices in a different order, say (1, 1, 0), (1, 0, 1) and (0, 1, 1).

  II. Listing 9.2 ('scene3') and MERGE listing 10.2 ('cube'). Data required: HORIZ, (EX, EY, EZ), (DX, DY, DZ). Try 8, (1, 2, 3), (0, 0, −1).

 III. Listing 9.2 ('scene3' and change 'cube' to 'icosa' and increase the number of vertices in line 120 from 8 to 12) and MERGE listing 10.3 ('icosa'). Data required: HORIZ, (EX, EY, EZ) and (DX, DY, DZ). Try same data as that used in II.

  IV. Listing 10.4 ('cube', 'flag' etc.). Data required: HORIZ, (EX, EY, EZ) and (DX, DY, DZ). Try same data as that used in II.

   V. Listing 9.9 ('scene3') and MERGE listing 10.5 ('revbod'). Data required: HORIZ, NUMH%, NUMV%, PHI, (EX, EY, EZ), (DX, DY, DZ). Try 4, 10, 10, 1, (1, 2, 3), (0, 0, −1).

  VI. Listing 10.6 ('scene3') and MERGE listing 10.5 ('revbod'). Data required: HORIZ, NUMH%, NUMV%, PHI, (EX, EY, EZ), (DX, DY, DZ). Try 12, 10, 10, 1, (1, 2, 3), (0, 0, 0).

 VII. Listing 10.7 ('scene3', 'shade' etc.) and MERGE listing 10.5 ('revbod'). Data required: HORIZ, NUMH%, NUMV%, PHI, vector direction of illumination,

(EX, EY, EZ), (DX, DY, DZ). Try 4, 40, 40, 0, (1, 2, −3), (1, 2, 3), (0, 0, 0).
VIII. Listing 10.8 ('scene3', 'surface', 'setpt', 'f' etc.). Data required: HORIZ, NX%, MINX, MAXX, NZ%, MINZ, MAXZ, (EX, EY, EZ) where EX and EZ are non-negative, (DX, DY, DZ) the origin. Try 28, 16, −8, 8, 16, −8, 8, (1, 2, 3) and (0, 0, 0).

11 Perspective and Stereoscopic Projections

Perspective

We have seen that the orthographic projection has the property that parallel
lines in three-dimensional space are projected into parallel lines on the view
plane. Although very useful, such views do look odd! Our brains are used to the
perspective phenomenon of three-dimensional space, and so they attempt to
interpret orthographic figures as if they were perspective views. For example,
the cubes of figures 9.1 and 10.1 look distorted.

So it is essential to produce a projection that displays perspective phenomena,
that is, parallel lines should meet on the horizon – an object should appear
smaller as it moves away from the observer. The *drawing-board* methods devised
by artists over the centuries are of no value to us. Three-dimensional coordinate
geometry and the concept of ACTUAL to OBSERVED positions, however,
furnish us with a relatively straightforward technique.

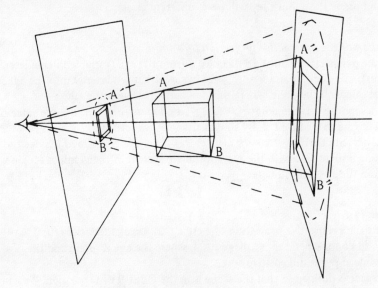

Figure 11.1

What is perspective vision?

To produce a perspective view we introduce a very simple definition of what we mean by vision. We imagine that every visible point in space is sending out a ray which enters the eye. Naturally the eye cannot see all of space, it is limited to the cone of rays that fall on the retina, the so-called *cone of vision*, which is outlined by the dashed lines of figure 11.1. The axis of this cone is called the *straight-ahead ray*. We imagine that space has been transformed into the OBSERVED position with the eye at the origin and the straight-ahead ray identified with the positive z-axis.

We place the view plane (which we call the *perspective plane* in this special case) perpendicular to the axis of the cone of vision at a distance d from the eye. In order to form the perspective projection we mark the points of intersection of each ray with this plane. Since there is an infinity of such rays this appears to be an impossible task. Actually the problem is not that great because we need consider only the rays that emanate from the important points in the scene, that is the vertices at the ends of line segments or the corners of polygonal facets. The final view is formed by relating the projected points on the perspective plane with lines and facets in exactly the same way as they are related in three-dimensional space, and then by identifying the view plane with the graphics screen.

Figure 11.1 shows a cube that is observed by an eye and projected on to two planes: the whole scene is also drawn in perspective! Two example rays are shown: the first from the eye to A, one of the near corners of the cube (relative to the eye), and the second to B, one of the far corners of the cube. The perspective projections of these points on to the near plane are A′ and B′, and on to the far plane A″ and B″. Note that the projections will have the same shape and orientation, but they will be of different sizes.

Calculation of the perspective projection of a point

We let the perspective plane be a distance d from the eye (variable PPD in later programs). Consider a point $P = (x, y, z)$ in space that sends a ray into the eye. We must calculate the point where this line cuts the view plane (the $z = d$ plane) — suppose it is the point $P' \equiv (x', y', d)$. Let us first consider the value of y' by referring to figure 11.2. By similar triangles we see that $y'/d = y/z$, that is $y' = y \times d/z$. Similarly $x' = x \times d/z$. Hence $P' \equiv (x \times d/z, y \times d/z, d)$. Since the view plane is identified with the x/y coordinate system of the graphics screen we can ignore the $z = d$ coordinate.

Example 11.1

Calculate the perspective projection of a cube that has eight vertices $(0, 0, 4) + (\pm 1, \pm 1, \pm 1)$ on the perspective plane $z = 4$, where the eye is origin and the straight-ahead ray is the positive z-axis.

The space is defined so that the scene is in the OBSERVED position. We can calculate the projections of the eight vertices by using the above method. For

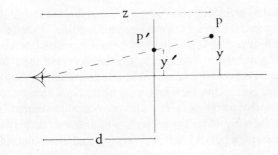

Figure 11.2

example $(1, 1, 3)$ is projected to $(1 \times 4/3, 1 \times 4/3, 4) = (4/3, 4/3, 4) \rightarrow (4/3, 4/3)$ on the screen. So we get the eight projections:

$(1, 1, 3) \rightarrow (4/3, 4/3)$ $\qquad$ $(1, -1, 3) \rightarrow (4/3, -4/3)$

$(-1, 1, 3) \rightarrow (-4/3, 4/3)$ $\qquad$ $(-1, -1, 3) \rightarrow (-4/3, -4/3)$

$(1, 1, 5) \rightarrow (4/5, 4/5)$ $\qquad$ $(1, -1, 5) \rightarrow (4/5, -4/5)$

$(-1, 1, 5) \rightarrow (-4/5, 4/5)$ $\qquad$ $(-1, -1, 5) \rightarrow (-4/5, -4/5)$

and the resulting diagram is shown in figure 11.3a.

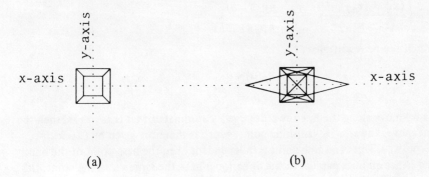

(a) $\qquad\qquad\qquad\qquad\qquad\qquad$ (b)

Figure 11.3

Properties of the perspective transformation
(1) The perspective transformation of a straight line (Γ_3 say) is a straight line (Γ_2 say). This is obvious because the origin (the eye) and the line Γ_3 form a plane (Ω say) in three-dimensional space and all the rays emanating from points on Γ_3 lie in this plane. (If the line enters the eye, Ω degenerates into a line.) Naturally Ω cuts the perspective plane in a line Γ_2 (or degenerates to a point) and so the perspective projection of a point on the original line Γ_3 now lies on the new line Γ_2. It is important to realise that a straight line does not become curved on perspective projection.

(2) The perspective transformation of a polygonal facet (a closed sequence of coplanar line segments) is a facet in the perspective plane. If the facet is an area bounded by n coplanar line segments then the transform of this facet is naturally an area in the $z = d$ plane that is bounded by the transforms of the n line segments. Again note that no curves are introduced in this projection: if they were, then the task of producing perspective pictures would be far more complicated.

(3) The projection of a convex facet is also convex. Suppose that facet F_3 is projected on to facet F_2. Since the projection of a closed facet is also closed and lines go into lines, then points inside F_3 are projected into points inside F_2. Suppose F_2 is not convex. Then there exist two points p_1 and p_2 inside F_2 such that the line joining them goes outside this facet. Hence there is at least one point p on the line outside F_2. If p_1 and p_2 are projections of points q_1 and q_2 from F_3, then p is the projection of some point q on the line joining q_1 and q_2. Since F_3 is convex then q must be inside F_3 and thus p must be inside F_2 — a contradiction and our proposition is thus proved.

(4) All infinitely long parallel lines appear to meet at one point, their so-called *vanishing point*. If we take a general line (with base vector p) from a set of parallel lines with direction vector h

$$p + \mu h \equiv (x_p, y_p, z_p) + \mu(x_h, y_h, z_h)$$

where $z_h > 0$, then the perspective transform of a general point on this line is

$$\left(\frac{(x_p + \mu x_h) \times d}{(z_p + \mu z_h)}, \frac{(y_p + \mu y_h) \times d}{(z_p + \mu z_h)} \right)$$

which can be rewritten as

$$\left(\frac{(x_h + x_p/\mu) \times d}{(z_h + z_p/\mu)}, \frac{(y_h + y_p/\mu) \times d}{(z_h + z_p/\mu)} \right)$$

As we move along the line towards large z-coordinates, that is as $\mu \to \infty$, then the line moves towards its vanishing point, which is therefore given by $(d \times x_h/z_h, d \times y_h/z_h)$. This vanishing point is independent of p, the base point of the line, and hence all lines parallel to the direction h have the same vanishing point. Of course the case $z_h < 0$ is ignored because the line would disappear outside the cone of vision as $\mu \to \infty$.

(5) The vanishing points of all lines in parallel planes are collinear. Suppose that the set of parallel planes has a common normal direction $n \equiv (x_n, y_n, z_n)$. If a general line in one of these planes has direction $h \equiv (x_h, y_h, z_h)$, then h is perpendicular to n (all lines in these planes are perpendicular to the normal to the plane n). Thus $n \cdot h = 0$, which in coordinate form is

$$x_n \times x_h + y_n \times y_h + z_n \times z_h = 0$$

Dividing by z_h gives

$$x_n \times x_h/z_h + y_n \times y_h/z_h + z_n = 0$$

and so the vanishing point $(d \times x_h/z_h, d \times y_h/z_h)$ lies on the straight line

$$x_n \times x + y_n \times y + d \times z_n = 0$$

and the statement is proved.

Example 11.2
Find the vanishing points of the edges of the cube in example 11.1, and of the diagonals of its top and bottom planes.

We divide the twelve edges of the cube into three sets of four edges; each set is parallel to the x-axis, y-axis and z-axis respectively and so has directional vectors $(1, 0, 0), (0, 1, 0)$ and $(0, 0, 1)$. The first two sets have zero z-values, and so their extended edges disappear outside the cone of vision and are ignored, whereas the third direction has the vanishing point $(4 \times 0/1, 4 \times 0/1) \equiv (0, 0)$ on the view plane. On the top and bottom faces the diagonals have directions $(1, 0, 1)$, the major diagonal, and $(-1, 0, 1)$, the minor diagonal. The major diagonal on the top plane is $(-1, 1, 3) + \mu(1, 0, 1)$, and so the vanishing point is $(4 \times 1/1, 4 \times 0/1) \equiv (4, 0)$. The minor diagonal on the top plane is $(1, 1, 3) + \mu(-1, 0, 1)$ and has the vanishing point $(4 \times -1/1, 4 \times 0/1) \equiv (-4, 0)$. By similar calculations we find that the vanishing points of the major and minor diagonals on the lower face are also $(4, 0)$ and $(-4, 0)$ respectively. The relevant edges are extended to their vanishing points in figure 11.3b. Note that all the lines mentioned lie in the two parallel planes (the top and bottom faces of the cube) and so the vanishing points should be collinear: they are because $(4, 0), (0, 0)$ and $(-4, 0)$ all lie on the x-axis. By a similar calculation we would find that the vanishing points of the diagonals of the side faces lie on a vertical line through the origin.

Exercise 11.1
Draw a perspective view of a tetrahedron with vertices $(1, 1, 5), (1, -1, 3)$, $(-1, 1, 3)$ and $(-1, -1, 5)$. Find the vanishing points (inside the cone of vision) of lines that join pairs of mid-points of the edges of the tetrahedron.

Programming the perspective transformation
The main program for drawing a perspective view of any scene is the same as that for the orthographic view, namely that created by routine 'scene3', which is similar to those discussed in chapter 9. We shall often need to calculate explicitly the ACTUAL to OBSERVED matrix, so that the eye is in the OBSERVED position at the origin and looking along the positive z-axis. This is achieved by routine 'look3' given in chapter 9 (listing 9.1). Calls are made to construction routines, each having a matrix R as parameter. Finally the figure must be drawn, inside the construction routines or in a 'drawit' routine.

Note that the only difference between the program that draws a perspective view and that of the orthographic view of chapter 9 is in the calculation of the coordinates of the projected image on the view plane. Unlike the orthographic, in the perspective projection the coordinates on the view plane cannot be identified with the x-value and the y-value of the point in the OBSERVED position. We need to store the perspective transformation of the vertices in the arrays XD and YD: the Ith vertex $(X(I), Y(I), Z(I))$ in the OBSERVED position is projected to $(XD(I), YD(I))$. The values in arrays XD and YD are given by

$$XD(I) = X(I)*PPD/Z(I) \quad \text{and} \quad YD(I) = Y(I)*PPD/Z(I) \quad \text{for } I = 1, 2, \ldots, NOV\%$$

The value of PPD is set to 3 * VERT in 'scene 3' — the reason for this is given in the next section. The calculation of XD and YD can be made in the construction routine, or in the 'scene3' or 'drawit' routines: it simply depends on the scene that is being considered.

Example 11.3
We draw a fixed scene (the two cubes that are described in example 9.2) in perspective from a variety of observation points, setting HORIZ = 1. Rerun the program with HORIZ = 10 (is there any difference?). The necessary 'scene3' main program will be almost the same as listing 9.5 except that it calculates PPD. It has the one addition:

$$140 \text{ NOV}\% = 0: \text{NOL}\% = 0: \text{PPD} = 3 * \text{VERT}$$

It places the group of cubes in their ACTUAL position by using the 'cube' routine of listing 9.6, and then loops through a number of different OBSERVED positions. For each time through the loop we call 'look3' which requires (EX, EY, EZ) and (DX, DY, DZ) to calculate the ACTUAL to OBSERVED matrix. Then the perspective 'drawit' routine (listing 11.1) is called. This uses the matrix to transform the vertices from their (stored) ACTUAL position to the OBSERVED position, and places the projected vertex coordinates in arrays XD and YD, according to the above equations. The routine can then finally draw the edges of the cubes in perspective.

Figure 11.4 was drawn by using $(EX, EY, EZ) \equiv (15, 10, 5)$ and $(DX, DY, DZ) \equiv (0, 0, 0)$. Compare this with the orthographic view of the same scene given in figure 9.2.

Exercise 11.2
Draw various perspective views of a wire tetrahedron and a pyramid.

The choice of perspective plane
The only value required for the perspective transformation that we have not yet discussed is that of PPD, the distance of the perspective plane from the eye. We can see from figure 11.1 that different values of PPD produce pictures of different sizes. Which one do we choose? Is there a correct value?

  If we consider the practical situation, we note that the observer is sitting

Listing 11.1

```
7000 'drawit : perspective
7001 '**in ** NOV%,X(NOV%),Y(NOV%),Z(NOV%),NOL%,LIN%(2,NOL%),
           R(4,4),PPD
7009 'move ACTUAL points to their OBSERVED positions (XX,YY,ZZ).
7010 FOR I%=1 TO NOV%
7020 XX=R(1,1)*X(I%)+R(1,2)*Y(I%)+R(1,3)*Z(I%)+R(1,4)
7030 YY=R(2,1)*X(I%)+R(2,2)*Y(I%)+R(2,3)*Z(I%)+R(2,4)
7040 ZZ=R(3,1)*X(I%)+R(3,2)*Y(I%)+R(3,3)*Z(I%)+R(3,4)
7049 'store perspective projections in arrays XD and YD.
7050 XD(I%)=XX*PPD/ZZ : YD(I%)=YY*PPD/ZZ
7060 NEXT I%
7069 'draw the lines.
7070 FOR I%=1 TO NOL%
7080 L1%=LIN%(1,I%) : L2%=LIN%(2,I%)
7090 XPT=XD(L1%) : YPT=YD(L1%) : GOSUB 9500 'moveto
7100 XPT=XD(L2%) : YPT=YD(L2%) : GOSUB 9400 'lineto
7110 NEXT I%
7120 RETURN
```

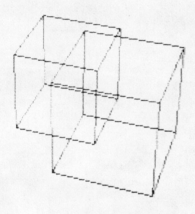

Figure 11.4

in front of a television screen and that the perspective view plane is identified with the plane of the television screen. Normally the observer is sitting at a distance that is about three times the height of the screen from the terminal. In the scale of our mapping from the real-world to the graphics area of pixels, this is a distance 3 *VERT (the value we used above). If we choose PPD to be greater than this value it is as though we are creating a *close up*, and if PPD is less than 3 *VERT we get the smaller image of a *long shot*. You will have noticed that perspective pictures are independent of the screen size, that is the absolute values of HORIZ and VERT are irrelevant, only their relative values matter, therefore in perspective pictures we shall always take HORIZ = 1: you can change the main program accordingly.

Example 11.4
We now draw a perspective hidden surface view of a stack of cubes (listing 11.2). Note how the vertical edges appear jagged. This is always the case in true perspective views because of the concept of vanishing points: compare with the rectangular bar blocks of listing 6.4, where the three-dimensional effect is a cheat! Figure 11.5 was drawn with mode 1, HORIZ = 1, (EX, EY, EZ) = (20, 10, 40) and (DX, DY, DZ) = (4, 1, 0). To demonstrate that the picture is independent of the screen size try the same picture with HORIZ = 40.

Figure 11.5

Clipping
Theoretically, objects may be positioned throughout space, even behind the eye, although we consider only points with positive z-coordinates in the OBSERVED position. Even so, some of these points go outside the cone of vision and become invisible. In fact, part of the cone of vision is outside the screen area (we can after all see the outside of the graphics area). We are left with a subset of the

Listing 11.2

```
100 'scene3 / stack of 27 cubes ( hidden lines removed )
110 GOSUB 9700 'start
120 DIM X(8),Y(8),Z(8),XD(8),YD(8)
130 DIM A(4,4),B(4,4),R(4,4),Q(4,4)
140 GOSUB 9300 'idR3
150 GOSUB 8200 'look3
160 PPD=3*VERT
169 'store Q : the ACTUAL to OBSERVED matrix.
170 FOR I%=1 TO 4 : FOR J%=1 TO 4
180 Q(I%,J%)=R(I%,J%)
190 NEXT J% : NEXT I%
200 GOSUB 60000 'colour monitor
210 XMOVE=HORIZ/2 : YMOVE=VERT/2
220 GOSUB 9600 'setorigin
229 'loop through the different placings of the cubes.
230 FOR ZV=-16 TO -4 STEP 6
240 FOR YV=-6 TO 6 STEP 6
250 FOR XV=-6 TO 6 STEP 6
259 'move cube to its ACTUAL position.
260 GOSUB 9300 'idR3
270 TX=XV : TY=YV : TZ=ZV : GOSUB 9000 'tran3
279 'then to its OBSERVED position.
280 GOSUB 9100 'mult3
290 FOR I%=1 TO 4 : FOR J%=1 TO 4
300 A(I%,J%)=Q(I%,J%)
310 NEXT J% : NEXT I%
320 GOSUB 9100 'mult3
329 'draw visible faces of each cube.
330 GOSUB 6500 'cube
340 NEXT XV : NEXT YV : NEXT ZV
350 GOSUB 60100 'monochrome monitor
360 END

6500 'cube : perspective hidden surfaces.
6501 '**in ** PPD,R(4,4)
6510 DATA 1,1,1, 1,1,-1, 1,-1,-1, 1,-1,1,
      -1,1,1, -1,1,-1, -1,-1,-1, -1,-1,1
6520 DATA 1,2,3,4, 5,8,7,6, 1,5,6,2, 2,6,7,3, 3,7,8,4, 4,8,5,1
6530 RESTORE 6510 : DIM XC(4),YC(4)
6539 'position the vertices.
6540 FOR J%=1 TO 8
6550 READ XX,YY,ZZ
6560 X(J%)=R(1,1)*XX+R(1,2)*YY+R(1,3)*ZZ+R(1,4)
6570 Y(J%)=R(2,1)*XX+R(2,2)*YY+R(2,3)*ZZ+R(2,4)
6580 Z(J%)=R(3,1)*XX+R(3,2)*YY+R(3,3)*ZZ+R(3,4)
6589 'place perspective projection of vertices in arrays XD and YD.
6590 XD(J%)=PPD*X(J%)/Z(J%)
6600 YD(J%)=PPD*Y(J%)/Z(J%)
6610 NEXT J%
6620 FOR J%=1 TO 6
6629 'read facet data and check orientation.
6630 READ F1%,F2%,F3%,F4%
6640 DX1=XD(F2%)-XD(F1%) : DY1=YD(F2%)-YD(F1%)
6650 DX2=XD(F3%)-XD(F2%) : DY2=YD(F3%)-YD(F2%)
6659 'if anticlockwise then draw the facet.
6660 IF DX1*DY2-DX2*DY1 < 0 THEN GOTO 6730
6670 NC%=4 : COLFAC%=1 : FOREGROUND%=2
6680 XC(1)=XD(F1%) : YC(1)=YD(F1%)
6690 XC(2)=XD(F2%) : YC(2)=YD(F2%)
6700 XC(3)=XD(F3%) : YC(3)=YD(F3%)
6710 XC(4)=XD(F4%) : YC(4)=YD(F4%)
6720 GOSUB 4000 'filler
6730 NEXT J%
6740 ERASE XC,YC
6750 RETURN
```

cone of vision — the *pyramid of vision*. Thus all points outside this pyramid, that is those whose perspective transformation take them off the screen, must be ignored. This is conveniently done for us on the IBM PC; however you should note that this is not necessarily true on other computers. In fact we further limit scenes so that all vertices in the OBSERVED position will have positive z-values, that is all objects must lie in front of the eye (although not necessarily inside the cone of vision). This will avoid a peculiar property of our perspective projection, namely points that lie behind the eye appear on the screen. If you run the above program (the stack of cubes) and vary the values of (EX, EY, EZ), for example (0.9, 0, 0), while all the other values stay the same, then the eye may be in among the cubes and the picture will go haywire or even fail. Also see project XVII in chapter 14.

Exercise 11.3
Experiment with perspective views of all types of wire figures, such as bodies of revolution or regular solids. Consider cases where an object is drawn within the construction routine, that is the values of XD and YD must now be calculated here and not in the 'drawit' routine. Change the program that drew the jet of figure 9.3 so that you get a perspective view, and note that the further the eye gets from the plane the smaller it appears — a phenomenon that does not occur with the orthographic projection.

Exercise 11.4
Write a hidden line algorithm for a single convex body by using the ideas of listing 11.2.

Exercise 11.5
Write a program that draws a perspective view of a mathematical surface that is similar to the one given in chapter 10. The method will be exactly equivalent to listing 10.8, with the exception that you must work with the XD/YD values rather than the X/Y arrays.

These hidden surface and line algorithms are perfectly adequate for specially defined single objects. We extend these ideas in chapter 12 where we consider the more general case of a number of objects that are scattered arbitrarily about space. But first we look at stereoscopic projections which enable us to get true three-dimensional images from the IBM PC.

Stereoscopic Views

Perspective views are all very well but unfortunately (or fortunately!) we have two eyes. Each eye should have its own perspective view, which will differ slightly from that of the other eye. This is the means by which we appreciate the three-dimensional quality of our world. We use this concept to produce a stereoscopic view of space, namely we produce a perspective view for each eye. This leads to a problem. We cannot simply draw two such projections because the left eye will see not only the view created for it, but also that made for the right eye, and vice versa. To stop this confusion we must ensure that each eye sees its own view, but only its view. This is achieved by using a pair of stereoscopic spectacles: a pair of transparent plastic sheets, one magenta (left eye) and one cyan or light blue (right eye). Most stereoscopic spectacles are not magenta and cyan, but are in fact red and blue. This is not a problem. The wavelengths of red and magenta, and blue and cyan are so close that the red/blue spectacles can be used on the pictures created by listing 11.3. In this way the left eye cannot see magenta lines because they appear to be the same colour as the white background (that is, both are tinted magenta) but cyan lines appear black. Similarly for the right eye which cannot see cyan lines, but magenta lines look black. So the computer must make two line drawings of a scene: one in cyan for the left eye, and one in magenta for the right eye. The brain will merge the two black images into one and the cyan and magenta background into white, to give a three-dimensional effect.

So we wish to devise a method of producing the stereoscopic projection of a general point $P \equiv (x, y, z)$, that is two points $PL \equiv (x_l, y_l)$ for the left eye and $PR \equiv (x_r, y_r)$ for the right eye, in the coordinate system of the perspective view plane (see figure 11.6). We sensibly choose the same view plane for both eyes. We shall assume that the origin is between the eyes, that space is in the OBSERVED position, and that the direction of view for each eye (the straight-ahead ray) is parallel to the z-axis. The eyes have coordinates $(-e, 0, 0)$, left, and $(e, 0, 0)$, right: in the program that follows, e is given by variable ED, which is normally about 0.2 * VERT. Again the perspective view plane is a distance d (variable PPD) from the origin. In order to find PL we move space by $(e, 0, 0)$ so that P becomes $(x + e, y, z)$ and the perspective transform of this point for the left eye is $((x + e) \times d/z, y \times d/z)$, which when we return space to its original position becomes $((x + e) \times d/z - e, y \times d/z)$. Similarly, the right-eye transformation produces $PR \equiv ((x - e) \times d/z + e, y \times d/z)$. Listing 11.3 is a 'drawit' routine which draws a stereoscopic view of a wire object with NOV% vertices and NOL% lines stored in the usual way. Figure 11.7 shows a grey-scale picture of such a stereoscopic view of the two cubes of figure 9.2 by using 'lib0', 'lib1', 'lib3' and listings 9.5 (line 140 adjusted for PPD) and 9.6. It has mode 1, palette 1, HORIZ = 16, (EX, EY, EZ) = (10, 20, 30) and (DX, DY, DZ) = (0, 0, 0).

For the best stereoscopic views it is best to make the view plane cut the object being viewed, that is make $\sqrt{(EX^2 + EY^2 + EZ^2)} = PPD$ (= 3 * VERT). Therefore in the case of stereoscopic views we cannot keep HORIZ and VERT fixed, since for the best projections VERT (and hence HORIZ) depends on (EX, EY, EZ).

Exercise 11.6

Draw stereoscopic views of all the objects drawn previously, including the jet
and bodies of revolution.

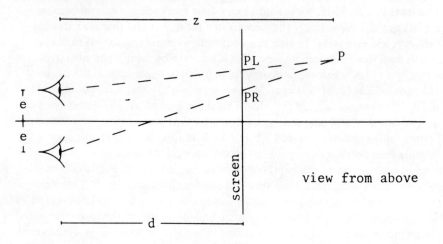

Figure 11.6

Listing 11.3

```
7000 'drawit / stereoscopic
7001 '**in ** NOV%,X(NOV%),Y(NOV%),Z(NOV%),NOL%,LIN%(2,NOL%),
            PPD,R(4,4)
7008 'use stereoscopic glasses with red over left eye and blue
      over right. The background should be white, so the image
      must be drawn in MODE 1, Palette 1.
7009 'The image for the left eye must be drawn in cyan (colour 1)
      and the right eye in magenta (colour 2) to get a good
      stereoscopic effect.
7010 FOREGROUND%=1 : ED=VERT*.2 : DIM SKREEN%(8002)
7019 '(XTL,YTL) and (XBR,YBR) are the world coordinates of the
      top left and bottom right of the screen respectively.
7020 XTL=PMAP(0,2) : YTL=PMAP(0,3)
7030 XBR=PMAP(319,2) : YBR=PMAP(199,3)
7039 'first left eye and then right.
7040 FOR J%=1 TO 2
7050 LINE (XTL,YTL)-(XBR,YBR),3,BF
7060 FOR I%=1 TO NOV%
7069 'vertices in OBSERVED position.
7070 XX=R(1,1)*X(I%)+R(1,2)*Y(I%)+R(1,3)*Z(I%)+R(1,4)
7080 YY=R(2,1)*X(I%)+R(2,2)*Y(I%)+R(2,3)*Z(I%)+R(2,4)
7090 ZZ=R(3,1)*X(I%)+R(3,2)*Y(I%)+R(3,3)*Z(I%)+R(3,4)
7099 'stereoscopic projection.
7100 XD(I%)=(XX+ED)*PPD/ZZ-ED : YD(I%)=YY*PPD/ZZ
7110 NEXT I%
7119 'draw the object.
7120 FOR I%=1 TO NOL%
7130 L1%=LIN%(1,I%) : L2%=LIN%(2,I%)
7140 XPT=XD(L1%) : YPT=YD(L1%) : GOSUB 9500 'moveto
7150 XPT=XD(L2%) : YPT=YD(L2%) : GOSUB 9400 'lineto
7160 NEXT I%
7169 'now use other eye.
7170 ED=-ED : FOREGROUND%=2
```

```
7180 IF J%=1 THEN GET (XTL,YTL)-(XBR,YBR),SKREEN% : CLS
              ELSE PUT (XTL,YTL),SKREEN%,AND
7190 NEXT J%
7200 ERASE SKREEN%
7210 RETURN
```

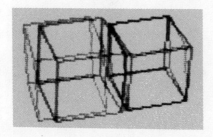

Figure 11.7

Exercise 11.7

Produce stereoscopic hidden line pictures of convex bodies. Now you must not colour in the facets, just draw the visible edges of the object, once in cyan for the left eye, and once in magenta for the right eye.

Exercise 11.8

Use the animation technique of listing 10.6 (the rotating sphere) to create a stereoscopic movie of a cube rotating about a central vertical axis, and viewed from any position.

Complete Programs

All the programs below need 'lib0', 'lib1' and 'lib3' MERGEd with them. Run the programs in MODE% = 1 with PALETTE% = 1, BACKGROUND% = FOREGROUND% = 0 and PAPER% = 3.

  I. Listings 9.5 ('scene3') and MERGE in listings 9.6 ('cube') and 11.1 ('drawit'). The 'scene3' routine must be adjusted for perspective thus:

       140 NOV% = 0: NOL% = 0: PPD = 3 * VERT

Data required: HORIZ and repeated values for (EX, EY, EZ) and (DX, DY, DZ). Try 1, (5, 15, 10) and (0, 0, 0): (1, 2, 20) and (0, 0, 1).

II. Listing 11.2 ('scene3' etc. for the stack of cubes). Data required: HORIZ, (EX, EY, EZ) and (DX, DY, DZ). Try 1, (20, 30, 40) and (0, 0, −6).

III. Listing 9.5 ('scene3') and MERGE in listings 9.6 ('cube') and 11.3 ('drawit': stereoscopic). Adjust line 140 as in I above. Data required: HORIZ, (EX, EY, EZ) and (DX, DY, DZ). Try 16, (10, 20, 30) and (0, 0, 0).

12 A General-Purpose Hidden Surface and Hidden Line Algorithm

There are many different types of hidden line and/or surface algorithm. One variety has a rectangular array that represents the totality of pixels on the screen. We imagine rays of light that leave the eye through each of the pixels on the screen. These rays naturally pass through objects in our scene and we can note the coordinates of these points of intersection. The array will hold the 'z-coordinate' (initially infinity) of the nearest point of intersection. So we build up a picture by adding new objects, finding where the rays cut the object, and changing the array values (and the pixel colour on the screen) whenever the latest point of intersection is nearer the eye than the corresponding value stored in the array. This technique (*ray tracing*) is very useful if we wish to shade-in areas in subtly differing tones of a given colour. It does, however, have enormous storage requirements and needs a very powerful computer, well beyond the capacity of microcomputers. Because we must work with only four colours and have limited storage we give another general algorithm which works on the 'back to front' principle mentioned earlier.

As in previous chapters, we assume that objects are set up by the 'scene3' routine; however we now insist that the NOV% vertices in the scene are stored in the X, Y, and Z arrays. Their perspective projections on to the view plane are stored in arrays XD and YD. The NOF% convex facets are stored as a list of vertex indices (a maximum of six) in array FACET%, and the number of edges on any facet is placed in array SIZE%. Non-convex facets can be constructed out of convex facets.

We assume that all objects are closed. They need not be convex but each must be closed and its surface must be composed of convex facets which are stored in anticlockwise orientation. Thus it is impossible to see the under-side of any facet; that is, when projected on to the view plane we see only facets that maintain their anticlockwise orientation. Strictly speaking, this means that we cannot draw planar objects. If these are required for a particular scene then we avoid the problem by storing each facet of a planar object twice — once clockwise and once anticlockwise — so whatever the position of the eye, on perspective projection we shall see one and only one occurrence of the facet. This restriction was imposed to speed up the hidden surface algorithm. This is very necessary because we are now approaching the limits of the processing power of the IBM PC.

Nevertheless, we think it is important to study general hidden line/surface algorithms for educational reasons. It is essential for anyone with more than a passing interest in computer graphics to understand the problems implicit in drawing views of three-dimensional objects with the hidden lines/surfaces suppressed. The procedure given in listings 12.1 and 12.2 is such a hidden surface algorithm, which can be transferred to larger machines where it will run with ease. If you get the opportunity to use more powerful computers it will be very instructive to run these programs on them.

In order to produce a hidden surface picture of a scene that is stored in the OBSERVED position, each facet on the objects in the scene must be compared with every other facet in order to discover whether their projections overlap on the view plane. Because of the above restrictions we need compare only the visible facets, that is those that when projected keep their anticlockwise orientation. If they do overlap we then need to find which facet lies in front and which behind. Once this information is compiled we can work from the back of the scene to the front to get a correct hidden surface picture. We do have another limitation: we assume that it is impossible for a facet to be simultaneously in front of and behind another facet (that is facets do not intersect one another except at their edges) and we cannot have situations where facet A is in front of (>) facet B > facet C etc. > facet A.

Our algorithm for discovering whether two facets (I% and J% from our database) do overlap when projected on to the view plane is given in routine 'overlap' in listing 12.1, a variation of listing 3.6. The method depends on the concept of *inside* and *outside* developed in chapter 3. We place the x-coordinate and y-coordinate of the vertices of facet I% in arrays XF(1, . .) and YF(1, . .) respectively. We then take one line from facet J% and cut off all parts of the facet that lie on the negative side of the line: the resulting polygon is placed in arrays XF(2, . .) and YF(2, . .). We then take the next line and compare it with these values and store the resulting polygon in XF(1, . .) and YF(1, . .) etc. After all the lines from facet J% have been used then we are left with the polygon that is common to both projected facets. If at any time this polygon becomes empty we know that the projected facets do not overlap and so we leave the routine setting OVER% = 0.

If the facets do overlap then OVER% = 1 and we draw a line from the eye to intersect a point inside the common polygon on the view plane and find the intersections with facets I% and J%: the point we choose is the median of the first three points on the polygon. Comparing the z-coordinates of the respective intersections enables us to discover which of I% and J% is in FRONT% and which is at the BACK%.

Listing 12.1

```
5000  'overlap
5001  '**in ** XD,YD,SIZE%,FACET%,FA%,FB%
5002  '**out** OVER%,FRONT%,BACK%
5008  'the NA% vertices of facet FA% and the NB% vertices
       of facet FB% are found from array FACET%.
```

```
          Polygons stored in anticlockwise orientation.
5009  ´check if the view of facets FA% and FB% overlap.
          OVER% is set to 1 if they do, and to 0 if they do not.
5010  P1%=1 : NA%=SIZE%(FA%) : NB%=SIZE%(FB%) : NF%=NA%
5020  DIM XF(2,NA%+NB%),YF(2,NA%+NB%)
5029  ´place projected view of facet FA% in the arrays
          XF(1,...) and YF(1,...).
5030  FOR K%=1 TO NA%
5040  V%=FACET%(K%,FA%) : XF(1,K%)=XD(V%) : YF(1,K%)=YD(V%)
5050  NEXT K%
5059  ´use each edge line of facet FB% to slice off part of
          the polygon stored in XF,YF.
          Line joins point (X1,Y1) to (X2,Y2).
5060  V1%=FACET%(NB%,FB%) : X1=XD(V1%) : Y1=YD(V1%)
5070  FOR K%=1 TO NB%
5080  V2%=FACET%(K%,FB%) : X2=XD(V2%) : Y2=YD(V2%)
5089  ´the line is  CA.y+CB.x+CC=0 .
5090  CA=X2-X1 : CB=Y1-Y2 : CC=-X1*CB-Y1*CA
5099  ´go round the NF% vertices in XF,YF. If positive relative
          to the line then add point to new XF,YF set. If negative
          then ignore.
5100  P2%=3-P1% : XI1=XF(P1%,NF%) : YI1=YF(P1%,NF%)
5110  VAL1=CA*YI1+CB*XI1+CC : A1=ABS(VAL1) : NC%=0
5120  IF A1<.000001 THEN S1%=0 ELSE S1%=SGN(VAL1)

5130  FOR M%=1 TO NF%
5140  XI2=XF(P1%,M%) : YI2=YF(P1%,M%)
5150  VAL2=CA*YI2+CB*XI2+CC : A2=ABS(VAL2)
5160  IF A2<.000001 THEN S2%=0 ELSE S2%=SGN(VAL2)
5170  IF S1%>=0 THEN NC%=NC%+1 : XF(P2%,NC%)=XI1 : YF(P2%,NC%)=YI1 :
                         IF S1%=0 THEN GOTO 5210
5180  IF S1%=S2% OR S2%=0 THEN GOTO 5210
5189  ´if there is an intersection then also add to new XF,YF arrays.
5190  MU=A1 : UM=A2 : DENOM=A1+A2 : NC%=NC%+1
5200  XF(P2%,NC%)=(UM*XI1+MU*XI2)/DENOM :
          YF(P2%,NC%)=(UM*YI1+MU*YI2)/DENOM
5210  VAL1=VAL2 : S1%=S2% : A1=A2 : XI1=XI2 : YI1=YI2
5220  NEXT M%
5229  ´if facets do not overlap then OVER%=0.
5230  IF NC%<3 THEN OVER%=0 : GOTO 5440
5240  NF%=NC% : P1%=P2% : X1=X2 : Y1=Y2
5250  NEXT K%
5259  ´find (XMID,YMID) common to both projected facets.
5260  XMID=(XF(P1%,1)+XF(P1%,2)+XF(P1%,3))/3
5270  YMID=(YF(P1%,1)+YF(P1%,2)+YF(P1%,3))/3
5279  ´MU1 is the distance of the eye from that point
          on facet FA% which is projected into (XMID,YMID).
5280  V1%=FACET%(1,FA%) : V2%=FACET%(2,FA%) : V3%=FACET%(3,FA%)
5290  DX1=X(V1%)-X(V2%) : DX3=X(V3%)-X(V2%)
5300  DY1=Y(V1%)-Y(V2%) : DY3=Y(V3%)-Y(V2%)
5310  DZ1=Z(V1%)-Z(V2%) : DZ3=Z(V3%)-Z(V2%)
5320  A=DY1*DZ3-DY3*DZ1 : B=DZ1*DX3-DZ3*DX1 : C=DX1*DY3-DX3*DY1
5330  D=A*X(V1%)+B*Y(V1%)+C*Z(V1%)
5340  MU1=D/(A*XMID+B*YMID+C*PPD)
5349  ´MU2 is the distance of the eye from that point
          on facet FB which is projected into (XMID,YMID).
5350  V1%=FACET%(1,FB%) : V2%=FACET%(2,FB%) : V3%=FACET%(3,FB%)
5360  DX1=X(V1%)-X(V2%) : DX3=X(V3%)-X(V2%)
5370  DY1=Y(V1%)-Y(V2%) : DY3=Y(V3%)-Y(V2%)
5380  DZ1=Z(V1%)-Z(V2%) : DZ3=Z(V3%)-Z(V2%)
5390  A=DY1*DZ3-DY3*DZ1 : B=DZ1*DX3-DZ3*DX1 : C=DX1*DY3-DX3*DY1
5400  D=A*X(V1%)+B*Y(V1%)+C*Z(V1%)
5410  MU2=D/(A*XMID+B*YMID+C*PPD)
5419  ´if MU1>MU2 then facet FB% is closer to the eye, that is
          facet FB% is in front of facet FA%. Similarly if MU1<MU2.
5420  OVER%=1
5430  IF MU1>MU2 THEN FRONT%=FB% : BACK%=FA%
                         ELSE FRONT%=FA% : BACK%=FB%
5440  ERASE XF,YF
5450  RETURN
```

The next step is to work out how to use this information to produce the final picture. This is achieved in listing 12.2, which contains the routines 'hidden', 'topsort', 'push' and 'pop'. The method is to compare each visible facet with every other and to produce a *network* of information about the relative positions of the facets (in front or behind). For each visible facet (I% say) the idea is to set up a *linked list* (LIS%(I%)) that contains the indices of all facets that lie in front of it, and the array G%(I%) will contain the number of facets that facet I% obscures. Array G% is also used initially to denote if the facet is clockwise and invisible (G%(I%) = −1), or anticlockwise and visible (G%(I%) = 0).

We then create a *stack* on to which we initially 'push' any facet that does not obscure any other (that is, whose G% value is zero). Then one at a time we 'pop' a facet off the stack and draw it on the screen. Once the facet is drawn, we go down the linked list for that facet and decrement the G% counts for each facet in the list. If the G% count for any facet becomes zero then the number of that facet is pushed on to the stack. Eventually this method, called *topological sorting* (the 'topsort' routine), gives the correct order in which facets may be drawn to give the true back to front hidden surface view.

The linked lists and the stack are implemented by using a method known as a *HEAP*. HEAP% and POYNT% are arrays of integers whose values are the *information* section and a *pointer* of the HEAP, respectively. Initially the heap contains zero information and POYNT% points to the next pair of array locations. There is a variable called FREE% which denotes the next available location in the heap. Whenever store is required for a linked list or a stack (which is itself a linked list) the FREE% location in HEAP% is made available, and the value of FREE% changed. A *garbage collector* is built into this system so that whenever a location is no longer needed it is reallocated to the FREE% list. The stack can only become empty when all the facets have been drawn because of our restriction that facets cannot be simultaneously in front of and behind one another. See Knuth (1973), or Horowitz and Sahni (1976) for a formal description of linked lists, stacks and topological sorting.

Because we cannot be sure of the size of the HEAP% and POYNT% arrays, they must be input into the program. As a rough guide the heap size is best set at about three times the number of facets. If you underestimate this array requirement then the program will fail. You can always run it again with larger values! The execution of such routines is necessarily slow when you consider the number of comparisons that have to be made, so we print out information about the facet being compared to show the program is working.

Listing 12.2

```
3000 'create the background : load from disk
3010 DEF SEG=&HB800
3020 BLOAD "B:BACKGRND.PIC",0
3030 RETURN

7000 ' general hidden line algorithm
```

```
7001 '**in ** NOF%,FACET%,XD,YD,HORIZ,VERT
7009 'setup data structure arrays.
7010 INPUT "Size of heap ",HSIZ%
7018 'HEAP%(I%) and POYNT%(I%) are the storage and pointer
     locations available for the construction of linked lists.
7019 'LIS%(I%) points to a list of indices of facets
     that lie in front of facet I%.
7020 DIM G%(NOF%),LIS%(NOF%),HEAP%(HSIZ%),POYNT%(HSIZ%)
7029 'FREE% points to a list of free storage locations
     available in the HEAP% (and POYNT%) arrays.
     NVIS% is the number of anticlockwise (visible?) facets.
7030 FREE%=1 : NVIS%=0
7039 'initialise the POYNT% pointers for the linked lists.
     Initially all the storage in HEAP% is FREE%.
7040 FOR I%=1 TO HSIZ%
7050 POYNT%(I%)=I%+1
7060 NEXT I%
7069 'orientate the projected facets :-
     G%(I%)=-1 means projected facet I% is clockwise
     G%(I%)=0 means it is anticlockwise (visible?).
7070 FOR I%=1 TO NOF%
7080 I1%=FACET%(1,I%) : X1=XD(I1%) : Y1=YD(I1%)
7090 I2%=FACET%(2,I%) : X2=XD(I2%) : Y2=YD(I2%)
7100 I3%=FACET%(3,I%) : X3=XD(I3%) : Y3=YD(I3%)
7110 DX1=X2-X1 : DY1=Y2-Y1
7120 DX2=X3-X2 : DY2=Y3-Y2
7130 IF DX1*DY2-DX2*DY1>0 THEN G%(I%)=0 : NVIS%=NVIS%+1 : LIS%(I%)=0
        ELSE G%(I%)=-1
7140 NEXT I%
7149 'compare visible facets : FA% with FB%.
     G%(FA%) will now hold the number of facets not already
     drawn  that will lie behind facet FA%.
7150 FOR FA%=1 TO NOF%-1
7160 PRINT " considering facet ";FA%
7170 IF G%(FA%)=-1 THEN GOTO 7260
7180 FOR FB%=FA%+1 TO NOF%
7190 IF G%(FB%)=-1 THEN GOTO 7250
7200 GOSUB 5000 'overlap
7209 'if facets overlap i.e. facet FRONT% in front of facet BACK%
     then increment G%(FRONT%), and add FRONT% to the list of
     facets in front of facet BACK%. Adjust the HEAP%.
7210 IF OVER%=0 THEN GOTO 7250
7220 G%(FRONT%)=G%(FRONT%)+1 : NFREE%=POYNT%(FREE%)
7230 HEAP%(FREE%)=FRONT% : POYNT%(FREE%)=LIS%(BACK%)
7240 LIS%(BACK%)=FREE% : FREE%=NFREE%
7250 NEXT FB%
7260 NEXT FA%
7270 GOSUB 60000 'colour monitor
7280 XMOVE=HORIZ/2 : YMOVE=VERT/2
7290 GOSUB 9600 'setorigin
7299 'if required enter routine to draw background.
7300 GOSUB 3000 'background
7309 'topologically sort the network of linked lists.
7310 GOSUB 7500 'topological sorting
7320 GOSUB 60100 'monochrome monitor
7330 RETURN


7500 'topological sorting
7501 '**in ** NOF%,FACET%,SIZE%,COL%,G%,NVIS%,XD,YD
7510 STACK%=0 : DIM XC(6),YC(6)
7519 'create a stack. Push on it all facets F% that have
     no facets behind them i.e. G%(F%)=0 .
7520 FOR F%=1 TO NOF%
7530 IF G%(F%)=0 THEN VALIN%=F% : GOSUB 8000 'push
7540 NEXT F%
7549 'find an order for drawing all the visible facets
     so that hidden sections are obliterated. Draw
     facets that have no undrawn facets behind them.
```

```
7550 FOR F%=1 TO NVIS%
7559 'pop a facet which has no undrawn facet behind it.
7560 GOSUB 8100 'pop
7569 'if no facet available there is an error in the data.
7570 IF VALOUT%=0 THEN PRINT "network has a cycle" : STOP
7579 'draw the facet.
7580 NC%=SIZE%(VALOUT%) : COLFAC%=COL%(VALOUT%)
7590 FOR I%=1 TO NC%
7600 V%=FACET%(I%,VALOUT%) : XC(I%)=XD(V%) : YC(I%)=YD(V%)
7610 NEXT I%
7620 GOSUB 4000 'filler
7629 'after the facet is drawn, adjust the values of array G%.
     Use the list LIS% to find facets in front of last facet drawn.
     Now G%(F%) holds the number of undrawn facets behind facet F%.
7630 PT%=LIS%(VALOUT%)
7640 IF PT%=0 GOTO 7700
7650 F2%=HEAP%(PT%)
7660 G%(F2%)=G%(F2%)-1
7669 'if facet F2% has no undrawn facet behind it, push it on stack.
7670 IF G%(F2%)=0 THEN VALIN%=F2% : GOSUB 8000 'push
7680 PT%=POYNT%(PT%)
7690 GOTO 7640
7700 NEXT F%
7709 'topological sort complete.
7710 ERASE XC,YC
7720 RETURN

8000 'push
8001 '**in ** VALIN%,FREE%,STACK%,POYNT%,HEAP%
8002 '**out** FREE%,STACK%,POYNT%,HEAP%
8009 'FREE% is first available HEAP% location.
     push value VALIN% onto the stack at this location.
     Then the pointer FREE% must be updated.
8010 NF%=FREE% : FREE%=POYNT%(FREE%)
8020 HEAP%(NF%)=VALIN% : POYNT%(NF%)=STACK% : STACK%=NF%
8030 RETURN

8100 'pop
8101 '**in ** FREE%,STACK%,POYNT%,HEAP%
8102 '**out** VALOUT%,FREE%,STACK%,POYNT%,HEAP%
8109 'pop value VALOUT% from top of stack.
     Make this location FREE% for future use.
8110 NF%=STACK% : VALOUT%=HEAP%(NF%)
8120 STACK%=POYNT%(NF%)
8130 POYNT%(NF%)=FREE% : FREE%=NF%
8140 RETURN
```

Note that a call to a 'background' routine is included in the 'hidden' routine. The background could be a complex construction subprogram, or a BLOAD of a previously constructed picture (for example, "B:BACKGROUND.PIC" as in listing 12.2), or even a trivial clearing of the screen in PAPER% colour.

Example 12.1
We can now draw a hidden line, perspective view of the scene that we first saw in figure 9.2: one of the two cubes shown in figure 12.1. Note that the 'background' is one of the pictures produced in chapter 1. The scene has HORIZ = 1, and is viewed from (15, 10, 5) to (0, 0, 0).

Figure 12.1

The complete program uses 'lib0', 'lib1', 'lib3', 'overlap' (listing 12.1) and 'hidden' etc. (listing 12.2) together with the 'scene3', 'cube' and 'background' routines given in listing 12.3. This last version of 'cube' means that we have considered all the array methods of constructing an object, that is, stored/not stored and lines/facets. We have deliberately used the cube over and over again in the diagrams because it is such a simple object and because it is easy to understand its various constructions; therefore it does not complicate the discussion of the **general principles of three-dimensional graphics.** Now is the time to introduce complexity into the objects: provided that you understand the limitations of **the algorithms, you will find that** the ideas we have discussed are equally valid.

Exercise 12.1
Construct hidden surface scenes that are composed of cubes, tetrahedra, pyramids, octahedra and icosahedra. Introduce new backgrounds and write your own procedures for an octahedron, icosahedron, rhombic dodecahedron etc. (see Coxeter, 1974).

Example 12.2
By now you will have realised that hidden surface algorithms are very slow programs — we have to make a large number of comparisons. This means that we are

Listing 12.3

```
100 'scene3 / two cubes stored
110 GOSUB 9700 'start
120 DIM X(16),Y(16),Z(16),XD(16),YD(16)
130 DIM FACET%(4,12),COL%(12),SIZE%(12)
140 DIM A(4,4),B(4,4),R(4,4),Q(4,4)
149 'create the scene.
150 NOV%=0 : NOF%=0 : PPD=3*VERT
160 GOSUB 9300 'idR3
170 GOSUB 8200 'look3
180 GOSUB 6500 'cube
190 FOR I%=1 TO 4 : FOR J%=1 TO 4
200 Q(I%,J%)=R(I%,J%)
210 NEXT J% : NEXT I%
220 GOSUB 9300 'idR3
230 TX=3 : TY=1.5 : TZ=2 : GOSUB 9000 'tran3
240 GOSUB 9100 'mult3
250 FOR I%=1 TO 4 : FOR J%=1 TO 4
260 A(I%,J%)=Q(I%,J%)
270 NEXT J% : NEXT I%
280 GOSUB 9100 'mult3
290 GOSUB 6500 'cube
299 'draw a view with hidden surfaces not visible.
300 GOSUB 7000 'hidden
310 END

6500 'cube / add OBSERVED position to data base
6501 '**in ** R(4,4),PPD
6510 DATA 1,2,3,4, 5,8,7,6, 1,5,6,2, 2,6,7,3, 3,7,8,4, 4,8,5,1
6520 DATA 1,1,1, 1,1,-1, 1,-1,-1, 1,-1,1,
         -1,1,1, -1,1,-1, -1,-1,-1, -1,-1,1
6530 RESTORE 6510
6540 FOR I%=1 TO 6
6550 READ F1%,F2%,F3%,F4% : NOF%=NOF%+1
6560 FACET%(1,NOF%)=F1%+NOV% : FACET%(2,NOF%)=F2%+NOV%
6565 FACET%(3,NOF%)=F3%+NOV% : FACET%(4,NOF%)=F4%+NOV%
6566 COL%(NOF%)=1 : SIZE%(NOF%)=4
6570 NEXT I%
6580 FOR I%=1 TO 8
6590 READ XX,YY,ZZ : NOV%=NOV%+1
6600 X(NOV%)=R(1,1)*XX+R(1,2)*YY+R(1,3)*ZZ+R(1,4)
6610 Y(NOV%)=R(2,1)*XX+R(2,2)*YY+R(2,3)*ZZ+R(2,4)
6620 Z(NOV%)=R(3,1)*XX+R(3,2)*YY+R(3,3)*ZZ+R(3,4)
6621 XD(NOV%)=X(NOV%)*PPD/Z(NOV%)
6622 YD(NOV%)=Y(NOV%)*PPD/Z(NOV%)
6630 NEXT I%
6640 RETURN
```

rather limited in the scope of objects we can draw. Nevertheless it is very good practice, and if you have the opportunity to use larger machines you will see that the above algorithm will work on these also, but much faster. We give examples of two three-dimensional star-shaped objects in listing 12.4 (both require a parameter A which changes the elongation of the spikes) as well as a 'scene3' routine. These two 'star' routines are based on the tetrahedron and cube. Figure 12.2 was drawn with HORIZ = 1, and viewed from (35, 20, 25) towards (0, 0, 0).

Listing 12.4

```
100 'scene3 / two stars stored
110 GOSUB 9700 'start
120 DIM X(22),Y(22),Z(22),XD(22),YD(22)
130 DIM FACET%(4,36),COL%(36),SIZE%(36)
140 DIM A(4,4),B(4,4),R(4,4),Q(4,4)
150 NOV%=0 : NOF%=0 : PPD=3*VERT
160 GOSUB 9300 'idR3
170 GOSUB 8200 'look3
179 'create star 1.
180 A=6 : GOSUB 6000 'star1
189 'store ACTUAL to OBSERVED matrix.
190 FOR I%=1 TO 4 : FOR J%=1 TO 4
200 Q(I%,J%)=R(I%,J%)
210 NEXT J% : NEXT I%
219 'create star 2.
220 GOSUB 9300 'idR3
230 TX=5 : TY=5 : TZ=5 : GOSUB 9000 'tran3
240 GOSUB 9100 'mult3
249 'recall ACTUAL to OBSERVED matrix.
250 FOR I%=1 TO 4 : FOR J%=1 TO 4
260 A(I%,J%)=Q(I%,J%)
270 NEXT J% : NEXT I%
280 GOSUB 9100 'mult3
290 A=4 : GOSUB 6500 'star2
300 GOSUB 7000 'hidden
310 END


6000 'star 1 / add to data base
6001 '**in ** A,R(4,4),PPD,NOV%,NOF%
6002 '**out** NOV%,X(NOV%),Y(NOV%),Z(NOV%),XD(NOV%),YD(NOV%),
             NOF%,FACET%(?,NOF%),SIZE%(NOF%),COL%(NOF%)
6010 DATA 1,2,9, 2,3,9, 3,4,9, 4,1,9, 6,5,10, 5,8,10, 8,7,10, 7,6,10,
          2,1,11, 1,5,11, 5,6,11, 6,2,11, 4,3,12, 3,7,12, 7,8,12, 8,4,12,
          1,4,13, 4,8,13, 8,5,13, 5,1,13, 3,2,14, 2,6,14, 6,7,14, 7,3,14
6020 DATA 1,1,1, 1,1,-1, 1,-1,-1, 1,-1,1, -1,1,1, -1,1,-1, -1,-1,-1,
          -1,-1,1, 2,0,0, -2,0,0, 0,2,0, 0,-2,0, 0,0,2, 0,0,-2
6030 RESTORE 6010
6039 'create facets.
6040 FOR I%=1 TO 24
6050 READ F1%,F2%,F3% : NOF%=NOF%+1
6060 FACET%(1,NOF%)=F1%+NOV% : FACET%(2,NOF%)=F2%+NOV%
6070 FACET%(3,NOF%)=F3%+NOV%
6080 COL%(NOF%)=1 : SIZE%(NOF%)=3
6090 NEXT I%
6099 ' Create vertices.
6100 FOR I%=1 TO 14
6110 READ XX,YY,ZZ : NOV%=NOV%+1
6120 IF ABS(XX)>1 THEN XX=SGN(XX)*A
6130 IF ABS(YY)>1 THEN YY=SGN(YY)*A
6140 IF ABS(ZZ)>1 THEN ZZ=SGN(ZZ)*A
6150 X(NOV%)=R(1,1)*XX+R(1,2)*YY+R(1,3)*ZZ+R(1,4)
6160 Y(NOV%)=R(2,1)*XX+R(2,2)*YY+R(2,3)*ZZ+R(2,4)
6170 Z(NOV%)=R(3,1)*XX+R(3,2)*YY+R(3,3)*ZZ+R(3,4)
6180 XD(NOV%)=X(NOV%)*PPD/Z(NOV%)
6190 YD(NOV%)=Y(NOV%)*PPD/Z(NOV%)
6200 NEXT I%
6210 RETURN


6500 'star 2 / add to data base
6501 '**in ** A,R(4,4),PPD,NOV%,NOF%
6502 '**out** NOV%,X(NOV%),Y(NOV%),Z(NOV%),XD(NOV%),YD(NOV%),
             NOF%,FACET%(?,NOF%),SIZE%(NOF%),COL%(NOF%)
6510 DATA 2,1,8, 3,2,8, 1,3,8, 1,2,7, 4,1,7, 2,4,7,
          2,3,5, 4,2,5, 3,4,5, 3,1,6, 4,3,6, 1,4,6
6520 DATA 1,1,1, 1,-1,-1, -1,1,-1, -1,-1,1,
          -2,-2,-2, -2,2,2, 2,-2,2, 2,2,-2
```

```
6530 RESTORE 6510
6539 'create facets.
6540 FOR I%=1 TO 12
6550 READ F1%,F2%,F3% : NOF%=NOF%+1
6560 FACET%(1,NOF%)=F1%+NOV% : FACET%(2,NOF%)=F2%+NOV%
6570 FACET%(3,NOF%)=F3%+NOV%
6580 COL%(NOF%)=2 : SIZE%(NOF%)=3
6590 NEXT I%
6599 'create vertices.
6600 FOR I%=1 TO 8
6610 READ XX,YY,ZZ : NOV%=NOV%+1
6620 IF ABS(XX)>1 THEN XX=SGN(XX)*A
6630 IF ABS(YY)>1 THEN YY=SGN(YY)*A
6640 IF ABS(ZZ)>1 THEN ZZ=SGN(ZZ)*A
6650 X(NOV%)=R(1,1)*XX+R(1,2)*YY+R(1,3)*ZZ+R(1,4)
6660 Y(NOV%)=R(2,1)*XX+R(2,2)*YY+R(2,3)*ZZ+R(2,4)
6670 Z(NOV%)=R(3,1)*XX+R(3,2)*YY+R(3,3)*ZZ+R(3,4)
6680 XD(NOV%)=X(NOV%)*PPD/Z(NOV%)
6690 YD(NOV%)=Y(NOV%)*PPD/Z(NOV%)
6700 NEXT I%
6710 RETURN
```

Figure 12.2

Exercise 12.2

The program in listing 10.1 checks that the order of the vertices of a triangular
facet is anticlockwise. The program was devised for use with convex bodies
that contain the origin. Extend it so that it can cope with the most general case,
that is specify the position of the observer and the coordinates of a point inside
the object (not necessarily the origin) so that this point and the observer lie on
opposite sides of the infinite plane that contains the facet. Use this program to
check the above star-shaped objects (in fact for these figures the origin could
act as the inside point).

Then produce your own star-shaped objects that are based on an octahedron, cuboctahedron, icosahedron or dodecahedron. Always check the order of the vertices in your facets. You can produce stars that are based on very simple bodies of revolution, and we need not use only symmetrical objects! It is for these non-symmetrical shapes that you really need the extended version of listing 10.1. Provided that you stay within the restrictions mentioned, then listings 12.1 and 12.2 will draw any shape.

Example 12.3
We now give the procedures (listing 12.5) needed to set up and draw a much more complex picture (figure 12.3) which contains 120 facets (about 60 will be visible at any one time). It is viewed from (10, 20, 30) towards (0, 0, 0) and will take quite a time to draw. So be patient!

Figure 12.3

Exercise 12.3
Use the hidden surface program to construct complex pictures such as a car, camera, machine tools etc. Then enter the stored picture into the diagram labelling routine of chapter 6 to tidy up the final picture. For example, figure 12.4 is a view of a racing car, modified in this way. The outside of each wheel was defined as a combination of hexagons, each containing two radial edges. All radial lines were subsequently deleted by the interactive labelling program.

Now you have read (and understood) chapters 7 to 12 you will have found that we have reached the limits of three-dimensional graphics on the IBM PC. You must have access to larger computers if you wish to go further in your study of this type of computer graphics. Then you must study the techniques of using data

Figure 12.4

structures and extend the very simple applications given in this chapter. If you use
certain structured languages, Pascal for example, you will find that it is not essential
to build up your own HEAP% and POYNT%, such structures are implicit to the
language. This should enable you to use complex data structures for storing useful information about scenes. For example, a complete scene can be regarded
as a linked list of pointers, each of which refers to a linked list of information
about the facets on a particular type of object. The facets themselves can be
stored as lists of vertices! A seemingly complex idea, but one that makes the use
of fixed-size arrays obsolete. Certain context relationships between objects may
be stored implicitly in the lists. When you have grasped these ideas you can go on
to the complicated graphics algorithms which include methods for animating,
colouring, patching, shading, shadows and mirror reflections. You will find the
books by Horowitz and Sahni (1976) and Knuth (1973) invaluable for the study
of data structures. You should read Newman and Sproull (1979), Foley and van
Dam (1982) and Harrington (1983) for the really complex three-dimensional
graphics methods.

Listing 12.5

```
100 ´scene3 / hollow cube
110 GOSUB 9700 ´start
120 DIM X(160),Y(160),Z(160),XD(160),YD(160)
130 DIM FACET%(4,120),COL%(120),SIZE%(120)
140 DIM XQ(8),YQ(8),ZQ(8)
150 DIM A(4,4),B(4,4),R(4,4),Q(4,4)
160 DATA   1,1,1,   1,1,-1,   1,-1,-1,   1,-1,1,
          -1,1,1,  -1,1,-1,  -1,-1,-1,  -1,-1,1
170 RESTORE 160
179 ´READ coordinates of simple cube.
180 FOR M%=1 TO 8
190 READ XQ(M%),YQ(M%),ZQ(M%)
```

```
200 NEXT M%
210 NOV%=0 : NOF%=0 : PPD=3*VERT
219 'move corners into ACTUAL position.
220 FOR M%=1 TO 8
230 GOSUB 9300 'idR3
240 TX=4*XQ(M%) : TY=4*YQ(M%) : TZ=4*ZQ(M%)
250 GOSUB 9000 'tran3
260 GOSUB 9100 'mult3
270 LH=1 : HT=1 : WH=1 : IC%=2 : GOSUB 6500 'rect
280 NEXT M%
289 'move spars into ACTUAL position.
290 FOR M%=1 TO 4
300 GOSUB 9300 'idR3
310 TX=0 : TY=4*YQ(M%) : TZ=4*ZQ(M%)
320 GOSUB 9000 'tran3
330 GOSUB 9100 'mult3
340 LH=3 : HT=1 : WH=1 : IC%=1 : GOSUB 6500 'rect
350 GOSUB 9300 'idR3
360 TX=4*ZQ(M%) : TY=0 : TZ=4*YQ(M%)
370 GOSUB 9000 'tran3
380 GOSUB 9100 'mult3
390 LH=1 : HT=3 : WH=1 : IC%=1 : GOSUB 6500 'rect
400 GOSUB 9300 'idR3
410 TX=4*YQ(M%) : TY=4*ZQ(M%) : TZ=0
420 GOSUB 9000 'tran3
430 GOSUB 9100 'mult3
440 LH=1 : HT=1 : WH=3 : IC%=1 : GOSUB 6500 'rect
450 NEXT M%
459 'move complete object into OBSERVED position.
460 GOSUB 9300 'idR3
470 GOSUB 8200 'look3
480 FOR M%=1 TO NOV%
490 XX=X(M%) : YY=Y(M%) : ZZ=Z(M%)
500 X(M%)=R(1,1)*XX+R(1,2)*YY+R(1,3)*ZZ+R(1,4)
510 Y(M%)=R(2,1)*XX+R(2,2)*YY+R(2,3)*ZZ+R(2,4)
520 Z(M%)=R(3,1)*XX+R(3,2)*YY+R(3,3)*ZZ+R(3,4)
530 XD(M%)=X(M%)*PPD/Z(M%)
540 YD(M%)=Y(M%)*PPD/Z(M%)
550 NEXT M%
560 GOSUB 7000 'hidden
570 END


6500 'rectangular block
6501 '**in ** LH,HT,WH,IC%,R(4,4),NOV%,NOF%
6502 '**out** NOV%,X(NOV%),Y(NOV%),Z(NO%V),
            NOF%,FACET%(?,NOF%),SIZE%(NOF%),COL%(NOF%)
6510 DATA 1,2,3,4, 2,1,5,6, 6,5,8,7, 7,8,4,3, 2,6,7,3, 5,1,4,8
6520 DATA 1,1,1,   1,1,-1,   1,-1,-1,   1,-1,1,
          -1,1,1,  -1,1,-1,  -1,-1,-1,  -1,-1,1
6530 RESTORE 6510
6540 FOR I%=1 TO 6
6550 READ F1%,F2%,F3%,F4% : NOF%=NOF%+1
6560 FACET%(1,NOF%)=F1%+NOV% : FACET%(2,NOF%)=F2%+NOV%
6570 FACET%(3,NOF%)=F3%+NOV% : FACET%(4,NOF%)=F4%+NOV%
6580 SIZE%(NOF%)=4 : COL%(NOF%)=IC%
6590 NEXT I%
6600 FOR I%=1 TO 8
6610 READ XX,YY,ZZ : NOV%=NOV%+1
6620 XX=XX*LH : YY=YY*HT : ZZ=ZZ*WH
6630 X(NOV%)=R(1,1)*XX+R(1,2)*YY+R(1,3)*ZZ+R(1,4)
6640 Y(NOV%)=R(2,1)*XX+R(2,2)*YY+R(2,3)*ZZ+R(2,4)
6650 Z(NOV%)=R(3,1)*XX+R(3,2)*YY+R(3,3)*ZZ+R(3,4)
6660 NEXT I%
6670 RETURN
```

Complete Programs

All the programs below need 'lib0', 'lib1' and 'lib3' as well as listings 12.1 ('overlap'), 12.2 ('background', 'hidden', 'topsort', 'push' and 'pop') MERGEd with them. Run the programs in MODE% = 1 with PALETTE% = 1, BACKGROUND% = FOREGROUND% = 0 and PAPER% = 3.

  I. Listing 12.3 ('scene3', 'cube'). Data required: HORIZ, (EX, EY, EZ), (DX, DY, DZ), size of HEAP. Try 1, (20, 5, 10), (0, 0, 0), 40.
 II. Listing 12.4 ('scene3', 'star1' etc.). Data required: HORIZ, (EX, EY, EZ) and (DX, DY, DZ), HEAP count. Try 1, (40, 30, 20), (0, 0, 0), 200.
III. Listing 12.5 ('scene3', 'box' etc.). Data required: HORIZ, (EX, EY, EZ) and (DX, DY, DZ), HEAP count. Try 1, (30, 20, 10), (0, 0, 0), 300.

13 Advanced Techniques for Programming the Text-Only mode

This chapter returns to the text-only mode (mode 0) for the first time since chapter 1. Having reached the limits of graphics modes in BASICA, the study of computer graphics in this book is completed with a demonstration of some sophisticated manipulations of text displays.

The text screen on the IBM PC uses the same memory buffer as the graphics screen (locations &H00 to &H4000 of the memory segment starting at &HB8000: DEF SEG = &HB800). It consists of 25 rows of 40 or 80 columns (depending on the WIDTH setting). Each of these 1000 (= 40 * 25) or 2000 (= 80 * 25) individual character positions on the screen requires two locations in memory — one to hold the ASCII code of the character at that position, and the second to hold colour information. The eight bits in a byte allow any of the 256 ASCII codes (0 to 255) to be stored; the colour information, however, needs more explanation. The 8 bits of colour information are divided into three groups. The bottom four bits, bits 0, 1, 2 and 3, hold the foreground colour (allowing 2^4 = 16 possible colours). The next three bits, bits 4, 5 and 6, hold the background colour (allowing 2^3 = 8 possible colours). The top bit, bit 7 holds the blinking (or flashing) information, 1 for blinking, 0 for not flashing. Therefore a WIDTH 40 screen requires 2000 memory locations and a WIDTH 80 screen needs 4000 locations.

This information can be accessed in BASIC with the SCREEN function (note: a SCREEN *function* and not the SCREEN statement which is altogether different: see below). This function is used in the following format:

v = SCREEN (row, column[,z]).

If no value for z is included or it is zero, then the function returns v as the ASCII code of the character displayed at the specified row and column on the screen. If z is non-zero then v is the colour information in the coded form above. It can be decoded thus:

foreground colour = v MOD 16
background colour = ((v-foreground) MOD 128)/16
if v ≥ 128 then blinking else not

The character and colours are usually placed on the screen by first setting the colours with a COLOR command, then LOCAT(E)ing a position on the screen and finally PRINTing a character at that position.

Obviously the information regarding a given row and column can be PEEKed from or POKEd into the location in the screen buffer, provided that location is known. The screen buffer is a block of &H4000 = 16384 consecutive locations, and a text screen only requires 2000 (< 2048 = &H800) locations for WIDTH 40, and 4000 (< 4096 = &H1000) locations for WIDTH 80. In other words the screen buffer has space to hold 8 40-WIDTH screens (or pages) or 4 80-WIDTH pages. The ith of the 40-WIDTH pages (0 ≤ i ≤ 7) starts at offset i * &H800 of DEF SEG = &HB800. The ith of the 80-WIDTH pages (0 ≤ i ≤ 3) starts at offset i * &H1000 of the same memory segment. Thus the information about a character appearing at a given ROW% (1 to 25) and COLUMN% (1 to WYDTH%, WYDTH% = 40 or 80) on a given PAGE% (0 to 8 or 0 to 4) is found at offset locations LOC% (ASCII code) and LOC% + 1 (colour) of DEF SEG = &HB800, where

LOC% = PAGE% * &H800 * (WYDTH%/40) + (ROW%−1) * 2 * WYDTH% + (COLUMN%−1) * 2

The page can be set from within BASICA. Chapter 1 described the SCREEN statement, where

SCREEN 0, 1, active page, visible page

allows the user to PRINT on an active page, while viewing a visible page. Even when PRINT is not used, and all information is PEEKed from and POKEd into memory, the SCREEN statement is needed to make the required screen visible. When the active page entry is omitted from the SCREEN statement, it defaults to its previous value; if there is none then it defaults to page zero. The visible page defaults to the active page. Functions POS and CSRLIN can be used to access the cursor position on the visible page. There is only one cursor shared between the multiple pages. If you need to use different cursor positions when switching between pages, it is necessary to store a cursor position, using POS and CSRLIN, and then to LOCATE it back on the screen when required.

Care must be taken with scrolling. If a character is PRINTed in the rightmost column of rows 24 or 25, then rows 1 to 24 of the screen move upwards. Row 25 stays fixed. To avoid such a disturbance of the screen, the information can always be POKEd into the equivalent memory locations.

This is all you need to know about the text-only screen. There now follows a number of examples that demonstrate the power of the above apparently simple operations. Note that all these examples at some stage use a zero third-parameter of the LOCATE statement to suppress the flashing cursor. Listings 13.1, 13.2 and 13.3 all run in page 0, whereas listings 13.4 and 13.5 use multiple pages.

Example 13.1

This example may be run with WIDTH 40 or 80 and will describe two different types of animation that can be achieved with the text-only screen.

The first method uses the blinking colours. A rectangular edge of blinking solid character blocks (ASCII 219) is drawn around the screen. The colour of these blocks alternates between foreground red and background cyan, and foreground cyan and background red. The blinking creates an impression of the blocks moving either clockwise or anticlockwise around the edge (it depends on the observer). Note that blinking (binary 1), cyan background (logical 3 = binary 011) and red (logical 4 = binary 0100) foreground is defined by a colour information value 180 (binary 10110100 = 128 + 32 + 16 + 4). Similarly blinking red background, cyan foreground has colour value 195 (binary 11000011 = 128 + 64 + 2 + 1). Listing 13.1 finds the two memory locations of each of the edge positions around the page 0 screen and POKEs the character and correct alternate colour information into them. Of course, POK(E)ing the information around the edge of the screen means that scrolling caused by PRINTing in rows 24 and 25 is avoided.

The second method of animation is the standard PRINT technique used for animating text characters (for example, listing 5.6, also compare with the PUT animation of listing 1.17).

Listing 13.1

```
100 'two types of simple text animation.
110 KEY OFF : MODE%=0 : BORDER%=0
120 FOREGROUND%=1 : BACKGROUND%=0
130 GOSUB 60000   'colour monitor
139 'animation using blinking.
140 DEF SEG=&HB800 : COLOR%=180
150 BOTTOMROW%=2*24*WYDTH%
158 'alternate COLOR% between 180 and 195.
    Both >128 so both colours blinking.
159 '180 is red foreground, cyan background.
    195 is cyan foreground, red background.
160 FOR COLUMN%=0 TO WYDTH%-1
169 'fill top and bottom rows of screen.
    POKE solid character block (ascii 219) in character byte,
    and COLOR%  in colour byte, for each COLUMN% position.
170 COLOR%=375-COLOR%
180 POKE 2*COLUMN%,219 : POKE 2*COLUMN%+1,COLOR%
190 POKE BOTTOMROW%+2*COLUMN%,219 :
    POKE BOTTOMROW%+2*COLUMN%+1,COLOR%
200 NEXT COLUMN%
209 'fill leftmost and rightmost columns of screen.
210 FOR ROW%=1 TO 24
220 POKE 2*WYDTH%*ROW%,219 : POKE 2*WYDTH%*ROW%+1,COLOR%
230 COLOR%=375-COLOR%
240 POKE 2*WYDTH%*(ROW%+1)-2,219 : POKE 2*WYDTH%*(ROW%+1)-1,COLOR%
250 NEXT ROW%
259 'animation using PRINT.
    Character (ascii 2) to be drawn at (ROW%,COLUMN%).
260 ROW%=2 : COLUMN%=2
270 LOCATE ROW%,COLUMN%,0 : PRINT CHR$(2);
279 'ROWADD% and COLADD% are the horizontal and vertical
    increments made by the character with each move.
280 ROWADD%=1 : COLADD%=1
289 'PRINT animation loop. Store last position.
290 OLDROW%=ROW% : OLDCOL%=COLUMN%
299 'move to new position. If boundary is hit then change
    corresponding increment and make a SOUND.
300 ROW%=ROW%+ROWADD%
310 IF ROW%=24 OR ROW%=2 THEN ROWADD%=-ROWADD% : SOUND 400,1
320 COLUMN%=COLUMN%+COLADD%
330 IF COLUMN%=WYDTH%-1 OR COLUMN%=2
    THEN COLADD%=-COLADD% : SOUND 100,1
339 'blank out character in  old position.
340 LOCATE OLDROW%,OLDCOL%,0 : PRINT " ";
```

```
349 'draw character in new position.
350 LOCATE ROW%,COLUMN%,0 : PRINT CHR$(2);
359 'small delay
360 FOR I%=1 TO 100 : NEXT I%
370 GOTO 290
380 END
```

The next two examples are of simple video games. They are about the limit of complexity that can be achieved in interpreted BASICA. You can speed them up by deleting REMarks and unnecessary spaces as well as reducing the length of the variable identifiers. There are other methods for speeding things up; however, there is a limit to what can be achieved. Ultimately you will have to write in Assembly Language or get a compiler. These programs are nevertheless useful indicators of what is possible.

Example 13.2

A extension of PRINT animation is given in listing 13.2, the 'bat and ball' game (run with WIDTH 40). The basic idea is for a routine 'initialise' to create a background scene consisting of 126 musical notes (ASCII 14), a bat (three ASCII 178 characters in a vertical line), a ball (ASCII 2) and a score line (rows 24 and 25). Incidently the routine also initialises variable values. In the game a bat moves repeatedly under control of the keyboard while a ball bounces about the screen. The one-character step movements of both bat and ball are achieved in two separate routines 'move bat' and 'move ball'. The relative frequency of calls to these routines creates the relative velocities of the bat and ball. In the program given, the bat moves two vertical steps for every single diagonal step of the ball.

The ball moves in a manner similar to listing 13.1, bouncing off the edge of the screen. Since rows 24 and 25 are the score line, scrolling is not a problem. The SCREEN function is used to find what character would lie under the ball after its next move. If the function returns ASCII 14 then the ball will hit a musical note. In this case the ball is moved and over-writes the musical note, a SOUND is made and the score changes. If the ball hits the bat (that is, the SCREEN function returns the ASCII code 178), then instead of carrying on in the same direction, the ball rebounds diagonally.

The bat is moved up or down under control of the ↑ and ↓ cursor keys respectively. The IBM PC has a keyboard buffer, which means that up to 15 characters may be held at any one time, waiting for processing. This facility, which is useful in most text-editing processes, causes real problems in the game situation. The natural reaction when playing a game is to hold down a key. This fills the input buffer with an unknown number of directional characters (↑ or ↓). The game player may wish to change the direction of the bat instantaneously because of the situation on the screen, only to find that up to fifteen directional instructions must be obeyed first before a new direction, or even stopping the bat, can be achieved. All is not lost however, the answer is to flush the input buffer after each character has been INKEY$ed. This is achieved by the following code:

DEF SEG = 0: POKE 1050, PEEK(1052)

The animation of the three-character bat is created by PRINTing just two characters at each step. An ASCII 178 extends the bat in the direction of movement, and a blank (ASCII 32) deletes the now fourth character at the other end of the bat. Naturally, checks must be made for collisions between the bat and the edge of the playing area. The game terminates when a predetermined number of notes have been over-written.

Listing 13.2

```
100 'bat and ball game
110 GOSUB 1000 'initialise
119 'game loop. Draw bat twice as often as ball, so it
    moves at double the vertical speed.
120 GOSUB 2000 'move bat
130 GOSUB 3000 'move ball
140 GOSUB 2000 'move bat
150 COLOR ,1
160 LOCATE 25,5 : PRINT"total = ";TOTAL%;SPC(2);
170 LOCATE 25,22 : PRINT"TIME = ";TIME$;
180 GOTO 120
190 END

1000 'initialise
1002 '**out** TOTAL%,MIDBAT%,BROW%,BCOL%,RINC%,CINC%
1010 KEY OFF : CLS : RANDOMIZE
1020 MODE%=0 : BORDER%=4 : FOREGROUND%=0 : BACKGROUND%=3
1030 GOSUB 60000    'colour monitor
1040 IF WYDTH%<>40 THEN STOP
1049 'fill screen in cyan
1050 CLS
1059 'draw 21 by 6 block of "notes"
1060 TOTAL%=21*6 : COLOR ,2
1070 FOR ROW%=3 TO 23
1080 LOCATE ROW%,1,0 : PRINT STRING$(6,CHR$(14));
1090 NEXT ROW%
1099 'draw the bat
1100 MIDBAT%=12 : COLOR ,3
1110 LOCATE 12,8,0 : PRINT CHR$(178);
1120 LOCATE 13,8,0 : PRINT CHR$(178);
1130 LOCATE 14,8,0 : PRINT CHR$(178);
1139 'draw the ball, add 1 to BROW% to allow for scrolling.
1140 BROW%=3+INT(RND*20) : BCOL%=40
1149 'ball moves in increments RINC% and CINC%.
1150 RINC%=1 : CINC%=-1
1160 TIME$="00:00:00" : COLOR ,1
1169 'print out messages at bottom of screen,
     scrolling the screen in the process.
1170 TIME$="00:00:00" : COLOR ,1
1180 LOCATE 25,1 : PRINT"    total = ";TOTAL%;SPC(2);
1190 LOCATE 25,20 : PRINT"  TIME = ";TIME$;SPC(4);
1200 RETURN


2000 'move bat, present middle of bat is row MIDBAT%, column 8
2001 '**in ** MIDBAT%
2002 '**out** MIDBAT%
2010 COLOR ,3
2019 'input from keyboard.
2020 KB$=INKEY$
2029 'flush keyboard buffer.
2030 DEF SEG=0 : POKE 1050,PEEK(1052)
2036 IF LEN(KB$)<>2 THEN RETURN
```

```
2039  ´return if neither up nor down cursor is pressed.
2040  KB$=RIGHT$(KB$,1)
2050  IF ASC(KB$)=72 THEN GOTO 2120
2059  ´down cursor
2060  IF ASC(KB$)<>80 THEN RETURN
2069  ´if the bat is neither at the boundary nor hitting the ball,
      then move the bat down 1 row.
2070  IF MIDBAT%=22 OR SCREEN(MIDBAT%+2,8)=2 THEN RETURN
2080  LOCATE MIDBAT%-1,8,0 : PRINT " ";
2090  MIDBAT%=MIDBAT%+1
2100  LOCATE MIDBAT%+1,8,0 : PRINT CHR$(178);
2110  RETURN
2119  ´if the bat is neither at the boundary nor hitting the ball,
      then move the bat up 1 row.
2120  IF MIDBAT%=2 OR SCREEN(MIDBAT%-2,8)=2 THEN RETURN
2130  LOCATE MIDBAT%+1,8,0 : PRINT " ";
2140  MIDBAT%=MIDBAT%-1
2150  LOCATE MIDBAT%-1,8,0 : PRINT CHR$(178);
2160  RETURN

3000  ´move ball to new position {row BROW%,column BCOL%} from
      its previous position {row PROW%,column PCOL%}.
3001  ´**in ** BROW%,BCOL%,RINC%,CINC%,TOTAL%
3002  ´**out** BROW%,BCOL%,RINC%,CINC%,TOTAL%
3009  ´row increment RINC% and column increment CINC%
      previous row increment PRI%.
3010  PROW%=BROW% : PCOL%=BCOL% : PRI%=RINC%
3020  BROW%=BROW%+RINC% : BCOL%=BCOL%+CINC%
3029  ´make adjustments [ and sounds ] if ball hits boundary
3030  IF BROW%<1 OR BROW%>23
           THEN RINC%=-RINC% : BROW%=PROW% :
                BCOL%=BCOL%-CINC%*RND : SOUND 800,1
3040  IF BCOL%<1 OR BCOL%>40
           THEN CINC%=-CINC% : BCOL%=PCOL% :
                BROW%=BROW%-PRI%*RND : SOUND 900,1
3049  ´delete previous ball
3050  IF SCREEN(PROW%,PCOL%)<>178
           THEN LOCATE PROW%,PCOL%,0 : PRINT " ";
3059  ´check if ball hits bat
3060  IF SCREEN(BROW%,BCOL%)=178
           THEN CINC%=-CINC% : BCOL%=BCOL%+CINC% : BEEP
3069  ´check if ball hits "note" : end if < 40 "notes" remain
3070  IF SCREEN(BROW%,BCOL%)=14
           THEN SOUND 37+16*BROW%+BCOL%,2 : TOTAL%=TOTAL%-1 :
                IF TOTAL%<40 THEN GOSUB 4000 ´endit
3079  ´draw next ball
3080  LOCATE BROW%,BCOL%,0 : PRINT CHR$(2);
3090  RETURN

4000  ´endit routine : give final result
4010  CLS : COLOR 16,7
4020  LOCATE 11,15,0 : PRINT"GAME OVER";
4030  LOCATE 13,8,0 : PRINT"time taken :- ";TIME$;
4040  GOSUB 60100 ´monochrome monitor
4050  END
```

Exercise 13.1
Use a variation on listing 13.2 to construct a BREAKOUT game.

Example 13.3
Another type of animation is given in the 'muncher and catcher' game of listing 13.3. The screen is coloured cyan and three of its edges are filled in blue. A horizontal 'catcher' under keyboard control (with input buffer flushed) is defined

by three characters, from left to right ASCII 201, 205 and 187, and stored in variable CATCH$. This can be LOCATEd at the top of the screen (row 1, column LH%). A sequence of ten hearts (ASCII 3) and an ever-increasing number of munchers (ASCII 2) are drawn between columns 2 and 39 of row 24. Drawing two blue solid-character blocks LOCATEd at row 24 column 40 has the effect of scrolling the screen upward. Following this, the same solid character is POKEd into this same position. The combination of these two operations has the effect of moving the whole picture on the screen up one row, while leaving the blue edge intact. Repeated application of the method creates animation – the whole screen moving upwards. With each scroll, the catcher naturally disappears off the top of the screen. The catcher is under control of the keyboard cursors (←, →) and can be redrawn, either one position left, right or remaining in the same position to give the effect of it moving horizontally in the top row. SCREEN can be used to find if a heart or a muncher is in the centre of the three-character catcher. A heart increases the score, while a muncher terminates the game. The higher the score the greater number of munchers appear on the screen. Eventually the game must terminate. In the extreme case there will be a solid line of munchers moving up the screen.

Listing 13.3

```
100 'simple game utilising scrolling.
110 GOSUB 1000 'initialise
119 'game loop.
120 WHILE STILLINPLAY%
130 GOSUB 2000 'make a move
140 WEND
150 COLOR 7,0
160 GOSUB 60100 'monochrome monitor
170 END

1000 'initialise
1002 '*out** STILLINPLAY%,SKILL%.CATCH$,SCORE%
1010 CLS : SCORE%=0 : STILLINPLAY%=-1 : LH%=19
1020 INPUT"type skill factor 0 (hardest) to 100 (easy)",SKILL%
1029 'CATCH$ is the 3 character "catcher".
1030 CATCH$=CHR$(201)+CHR$(205)+CHR$(187)
1040 MODE%=0 : BORDER%=6 : FOREGROUND%=1 : BACKGROUND%=3
1050 GOSUB 60000 'colour monitor
1060 IF WYDTH%<>40 THEN STOP
1070 KEY OFF : DEF SEG=&HB800
1079 'draw blue line at the bottom of the screen.
1080 LOCATE 25,1 : PRINT STRING$(40,CHR$(219))
1089 'fill screen in cyan with blue edges.
     PRINT blue blocks at (24,40) and (25,1),
     scrolling will move these blocks up the screen.
1090 FOR I%=1 TO 25
1100 LOCATE 24,40,0 : PRINT CHR$(219);CHR$(219);
1110 NEXT I%
1119 'fill space left by scrolling.
1120 POKE 1919,16
1129 'print "GET SET" message
1130 LOCATE 11,19 : PRINT CATCH$;
1140 LOCATE 13,6,0 : COLOR 16,7 : PRINT "press any key to start game"
1150 COLOR 1,3
1160 LOCATE 15,19 : PRINT CATCH$;
1170 IF INKEY$="" THEN GOTO 1170
1179 'scroll off previous message & print SCORE%.
```

```
1180 FOR I%=1 TO 14
1190 LOCATE 24,40,0 : PRINT CHR$(219);CHR$(219);
1200 NEXT I%
1210 LOCATE 25,14 : COLOR 7,1
1220 PRINT "SCORE = ";SCORE%;
1230 RETURN


2000 'make a move
2001 '**in ** SCORE%,LH%,SKILL%,CATCH$
2002 '**out** SCORE%,LH%,STILLINPLAY%
2010 DIFFICULTY%=1+INT(SCORE%/16)
2019 'add 10 "hearts" to row 24.
2020 COLOR 4,3
2030 FOR I%=1 TO 10
2040 LOCATE 24,2+INT(RND*38) : PRINT CHR$(3);
2050 NEXT I%
2059 'add an ever increasing number of "munchers" to row 24.
2060 COLOR 0
2070 FOR I%=1 TO DIFFICULTY%
2080 LOCATE 24,2+INT(RND*38) : PRINT CHR$(2);
2090 NEXT I%
2099 'key in move of "heart-catcher" : left or right cursor.
2100 KB$=INKEY$
2109 'flush the input buffer.
2110 DEF SEG=0 : POKE 1050,PEEK(1052)
2120 IF LEN(KB$)<>2 THEN GOTO 2160
2129 'change left hand edge {LH%} of "catcher".
     also check if it hits edge of screen.
2130 KB%=ASC(RIGHT$(KB$,1))
2140 IF KB%=75 THEN IF LH%>2 THEN LH%=LH%-1
2150 IF KB%=77 THEN IF LH%<37 THEN LH%=LH%+1
2160 DEF SEG=&HB800
2169 'HIT% is the character [ASCII] caught after scrolling.
2170 HIT%=SCREEN(2,LH%+1)
2179 'scroll the screen.
2180 LOCATE 24,40,0 : COLOR 1
2190 PRINT CHR$(219);CHR$(219); : POKE 1919,16
2199 'draw "catcher".
2200 LOCATE 1,LH% : PRINT CATCH$;
2209 'a "heart" is caught : increase score.
2210 IF HIT%=3 THEN SCORE%=SCORE%+1 : SOUND 220+RND*1000,6 :
                        COLOR 4 : LOCATE 1,LH%+1 : PRINT CHR$(3);
2219 'a "muncher" is caught which proceeds to eat "catcher".
2220 IF HIT%=2 THEN STILLINPLAY%=0 : SOUND 4600,2 : SOUND 5000,6 :
                SOUND 37,8 : COLOR 0 : LOCATE 1,LH%+1 : PRINT CHR$(2);:
                COLOR 16,7 : LOCATE 13,15 : PRINT"GAME OVER";
2229 'print score.
2230 LOCATE 25,14 : COLOR 7,1
2239 'a "muncher" is caught which proceeds to eat "catcher".
2240 PRINT "SCORE = ";SCORE%;
2249 'delay .
2250 FOR I%=1 TO SKILL% : NEXT I%
2260 RETURN
```

Exercise 13.2

Use the scrolling animation method to produce an 'upside-down' Space Invaders game.

Example 13.4

Another form of animation is used in listings 13.4 and 13.5. Using WIDTH 40 means that there are 8 text-only pages available. These can be brought into view in quick succession using the SCREEN statement. If a sequence of pages has been carefully constructed, and is repeatedly brought to the screen in the same fixed order, then this method results in an extremely powerful animation technique.

Listing 13.4 creates seven pages, numbered 1 to 7. Each page is constructed in two stages. The first stage places nine concentric coloured rectangles on the screen, leaving a black area at the centre which is composed of 7 rows by 22 columns. The second stage writes a message in this central area. The first page has the rectangles coloured 1, 2, 3, 4, 5, 6, 7, 1, 2 from the outside towards the centre. The second page has colours 2, 3, 4, 5, 6, 7, 1, 2, 3 etc. When the pages are brought onto the screen in quick succession the coloured rectangles appear to be expanding and moving outwards. The message has seven lines, which are drawn in the seven rows of the central area in cyclic order. The page animation makes the message appear to scroll off the top of the central area and reappear at the bottom.

Listing 13.4

```
100 'animation using multiple TEXT SCREENs
110 KEY OFF : CLS
120 MODE%=0 : BORDER%=0 : FOREGROUND%=1 : BACKGROUND%=3
130 GOSUB 60000   'colour monitor
140 IF WYDTH%<>40 THEN GOTO 130
149 'screen buffer segment. Delete flashing cursor.
150 DEF SEG=&HB800 : LOCATE 1,1,0
159 'READ MAP% and MESSAGE$ arrays.
160 DIM MAP%(7),MESSAGE$(7)
169 'MAP%(1) to MAP%(7) contain the numbers 1 to 7 which are
       rotated 1 place left in the array with each new PAGE%.
       MAP%(0) always contains a zero.
170 FOR I%=0 TO 7 : READ MAP%(I%) : NEXT I%
180 DATA 0,1,2,3,4,5,6,7
189 'MESSAGE$(1) to MESSAGE$(7) holds 7 lines of text,
       MESSAGE(0) is not used.
190 FOR I%=0 TO 7 : READ MESSAGE$(I%) : NEXT I%
200 DATA "","","ADVANCED  GRAPHICS","    with the",
           "   I B M  P C ","", "          by",
           "    Ian O. ANGELL"
209 'consider PAGEs 1 to 7 in turn.
210 FOR PAGE%=1 TO 7
220 SCREEN,,PAGE%,PAGE%
229 'present PAGE% starts at offset PAGEADDRESS% of screen buffer.
230 PAGEADDRESS%=2048*PAGE%
239 'find ADDRESS% of COLUMN%, ROW% of PAGE%.
240 FOR COLUMN%=1 TO 40
250 FOR ROW%=1 TO 25
260 ADDRESS%=(40*(ROW%-1)+COLUMN%-1)*2+PAGEADDRESS%
269 'find MIN%, the distance of (ROW%,COLUMN%)
       from nearest screen edge.
270 MIN%=41-COLUMN%
280 IF MIN%>26-ROW% THEN MIN%=26-ROW%
290 IF MIN%>COLUMN% THEN MIN%=COLUMN%
300 IF MIN%>ROW% THEN MIN%=ROW%
309 'if MIN%>8 then character block (I%,J%) coloured black,
       else MAP%(MIN%) with 0<MIN%<8. The rotated values of MAP mean
       colours appear to move outwards in successive PAGEs.
310 IF MIN%>9 THEN MIN%=0 ELSE MIN%=(MIN%-1) MOD 7+1
319 'POKE a blank (ASCII 32) into ADDRESS%and the colour
       MAP%(MIN%) - moved 4 bits to the left - into ADDRESS%+1.
320 POKE ADDRESS%,32   : POKE ADDRESS%+1,MAP%(MIN%)*16
330 NEXT ROW%  : NEXT COLUMN%
339 'now PRINT the 7 messages, positioned using MAP% array, so
       that they appear to rotate upwards on successive PAGEs.
```

```
340 COLOR 7,0
350 FOR I%=1 TO 7
360 LOCATE 9+I%,12 : PRINT MESSAGE$(MAP%(I%))
370 NEXT I%
379 'rotate the values MAP%(1) to MAP%(7).
380 TEMP%=MAP%(1)
390 FOR I%=1 TO 6 : MAP%(I%)=MAP%(I%+1) : NEXT I%
400 MAP%(7)=TEMP%
410 NEXT PAGE%
419 'infinite animation loop.
420 WHILE 0=0
430 FOR I%=1 TO 7
440 SCREEN,,I%,I%
449 'small delay
450 FOR K%=1 TO 100 : NEXT K%
460 NEXT I%
470 WEND
480 END
```

A Text Screen Editor

It is not always convenient to construct a text screen picture with a program such
as listing 13.4. Particular combinations of characters mean that an interactive text
screen editor is far more suitable. Such a program is given in listing 13.5, and
should be used with WIDTH 40. Pages 1 to 7 are used to hold text pictures, and
page 0 contains a 'menu' and a variety of request prompts. The program is
structured in a manner similar to that of the programs of chapters 5 and 6. A
'supervisor' program awaits keyboard entry of character indicators and acts on
the input. The solutions to a number of tasks are programmed: a list of these tasks
and their character indicators is given below.

(1) "M" calls the routine that constructs a Menu in page 0 of all the available
    options and their indicators.
(2) "V" makes a page Visible. First page 0 becomes visible and a prompt asks
    for the number of the page that is to become visible. When this number is
    INKEY$ed by the program, that page becomes visible before control is
    returned to the 'supervisor'. The writing of prompts in this and other
    routines involves a change of text colours. It is essential therefore that the
    present working values of these colours are stored (in FOREGROUND%
    and BACKGROUND%) so they can be restored after the prompt has been
    printed.
(3) "C" Copies one page (A%) into another (the visible page VPAGE%), and
    finally returns to page 0 when the copy is complete.
(4) "S" Saves the 2000 locations of a given page (A%) onto disk. The name of
    the file is requested on page 0.
(5) "L" reLoads a previously saved page from disk. Again the name of the file
    is requested on page 0.
(6) "E" Erases a given page (VPAGE%) by filling it with the present BACK-
    GROUND% colour. The number of the page and a double check are
    requested on page 0.

(7) "W" switches the present blinking (Winking) state of the text FORE-GROUND% colour between steady and winking, or vice versa. Entry is made on the present active page, not necessarily page 0.

(8) "F" changes the text FOREGROUND% colour. A prompt is made on page 0, but experienced operators can make the entry while remaining in a non-zero visible page. This obviously speeds up operations, so avoiding the need to keep changing visible pages.

(9) "B" changes the BACKGROUND% colour in a similar way.

(10) "X" changes the present state of the text cursor, so switching between blinking visible and invisible or vice versa.

(11) The keyboard cursor keys ($\downarrow$, $\uparrow$, $\leftarrow$, $\rightarrow$) are used to move the text cursor around the screen: if the cursor is invisible it is sensible to make sure that it becomes visible by using "X". The cursor is organised so that, if it moves off the screen horizontally, then it reappears on the other side of the screen in the same row. Similarly if it moves off the screen vertically, it reappears in the same column but on the opposite edge.

(12) "A" initiates an Animation sequence of frames 1 to 7, exactly like listing 13.4.

(13) "Q" Quits the animation.

(14) The Home key terminates the program.

Now for the operations that do all the work of drawing characters on the text screen.

(15) "K" initiates the Keyboard input of text onto the screen, and by implication onto the present visible and active page. After "K" has been pressed, any character entered on the keyboard is drawn on the screen at the present cursor location in present FOREGROUND% and BACKGROUND% colours and winking state. After the character is drawn, the winking cursor moves one place to the right. The program is written with an extra routine to cope with the scrolling effect of column 40 in rows 24 and 25.

(16) The End key exits from character input. While in the keyboard mode, text need not be drawn in consecutive columns. The cursor is still activated, so characters can be drawn independently anywhere on the screen.

(17) "R" is a useful extra option, which takes the character under the present cursor position and Redraws it at the same position but in the present, possibly changed, FOREGROUND% and BACKGROUND% colours and winking state.

The program is extensively commented, with plenty of spaces and meaningful variable names. Readers should analyse the routines carefully to get not only a full understanding of this program, but also by implication a greater appreciation of the text screen capability of the IBM PC.

Listing 13.5

```
100 ´  TEXT SCREEN EDITOR
110 ON ERROR GOTO 200
120 MODE%=0 : BORDER%=6
130 FOREGROUND%=1 : BACKGROUND%=3
140 DIM NOSCOLL%(7)
150 FOR PAGE%=0 TO 7 : READ NOSCOLL%(PAGE%) : NEXT PAGE%
160 DATA 1918,3966,6014,8062,10110,12158,14206,16254
170 CURSROW%=1 : CURSCOL%=1 : CURSVIS%=1
180 VPAGE%=0 : CLS
190 GOSUB 60000 ´colour monitor
200 IF WYDTH%<>40 THEN GOTO 230
210 GOSUB 2000 ´layout of menu
220 GOSUB 1000 ´supervisor
230 COLOR 7,0
240 GOSUB 60100 ´monochrome monitor
250 END

1000 ´supervisor
1001 ´**in ** FOREGROUND%,BACKGROUND%,CURSROW%,CURSCOL%,CURSVIS%
1002 ´**out** FOREGROUND%,CURSVIS%
1009 ´keyboard input and supervisor loop.
1010 KB$=INKEY$ : IF KB$="" THEN GOTO 1010
1020 DEF SEG=0 : POKE 1050,PEEK(1052)
1030 KB%=ASC(RIGHT$(KB$,1))
1040 IF LEN(KB$)<>1 THEN IF KB%=71 THEN RETURN
                                 ELSE GOSUB 7000 : GOTO 1010
1050 IF KB%>96 THEN KB%=KB%-32 : KB$=CHR$(KB%)
1060 IF KB$="M" THEN GOSUB 2000 ´layout
1070 IF KB$="V" THEN GOSUB 4000 ´make visible
1080 IF KB$="C" THEN GOSUB 3000 ´copy page A% to page B%
1090 IF KB$="L" THEN GOSUB 3600 ´load page A% from disk
1100 IF KB$="S" THEN GOSUB 3400 ´save page A% on disk
1110 IF KB$="E" THEN GOSUB 3200 ´erase page A%
1120 IF KB$="W" THEN FOREGROUND%=(16+FOREGROUND%) MOD 32 :
                              COLOR FOREGROUND%,BACKGROUND%
1130 IF KB$="F" THEN GOSUB 5600 ´foreground change
1140 IF KB$="B" THEN GOSUB 5800 ´background change
1150 IF KB$="X" THEN CURSVIS%=1-CURSVIS% :
                         LOCATE CURSROW%,CURSCOL%,CURSVIS%
1160 IF KB$="K" THEN GOSUB 5000 ´print keyboard string
1170 IF KB$="A" THEN GOSUB 8000 ´animation
1180 IF KB$="R" THEN GOSUB 6000 ´replace colours
1190 GOTO 1010

2000 ´layout of menu
2002 ´**out** VPAGE%
2010 VPAGE%=0 : SCREEN 0,,0,0
2020 COLOR 0,7,6 : CLS
2030 LOCATE 5,3,0  : PRINT"M : supervisor Menu {this page}";
2040 LOCATE 6,3,0  : PRINT"V : make page A Visible";
2050 LOCATE 7,3,0  : PRINT"C : Copy page A to page B";
2070 LOCATE 8,3,0  : PRINT"L : Load page A from disk";
2080 LOCATE 9,3,0  : PRINT"S : Save page A on disk";
2090 LOCATE 10,3,0 : PRINT"E : Erase page A";
2100 LOCATE 11,3,0 : PRINT"R : replace colours of character";
2110 LOCATE 12,3,0 : PRINT"W : flip current Wink{flash}ing state";
2120 LOCATE 13,3,0 : PRINT"F : change current Foreground colour";
2130 LOCATE 14,3,0 : PRINT"B : change current Background colour";
2140 LOCATE 15,3,0 : PRINT"X : flip - visible/invisible cursor";
2150 LOCATE 16,3,0 : PRINT"K : start drawing Keyboard characters";
2160 LOCATE 17,3,0 : PRINT"End : End drawing characters";
2170 LOCATE 18,3,0 : PRINT CHR$(24);" : move cursor up";
2180 LOCATE 19,3,0 : PRINT CHR$(25);" : move cursor down";
2190 LOCATE 20,3,0 : PRINT CHR$(26);" : move cursor right";
2200 LOCATE 21,3,0 : PRINT CHR$(27);" : move cursor left";
2210 LOCATE 22,3,0 : PRINT"A : animation of frames 1 to 7";
```

```
2220 LOCATE 23,3,0 : PRINT"Q : quit animation";
2230 LOCATE 24,3,0 : PRINT"Home : Exit program";
2240 COLOR 16,7 : LOCATE 2,10,0
2250 PRINT"Type Operation Code";
2260 RETURN

2500 ´clear top 3 lines of page 0
2502 ´**out** VPAGE%
2510 SCREEN,,0,0 : VPAGE%=0
2520 COLOR 0,7 : LOCATE 1,1,0
2530 PRINT STRING$(120," ");
2540 RETURN

3000 ´copy page A% to page VPAGE%
3002 ´**out** VPAGE%
3010 SCREEN ,,0,0 : DEF SEG=&HB800
3020 COLOR 7,0 : LOCATE 1,1,0 : PRINT STRING$(120," ");
3030 LOCATE 2,1 : INPUT"Copying from Page ";A%
3040 LOCATE 2,22 : INPUT"to Page ";VPAGE%
3050 SCREEN ,,VPAGE%,VPAGE%
3060 ADDTO%=VPAGE%*2048
3070 FOR ADDFROM%=A%*2048 TO A%*2048+1999
3080 POKE ADDTO%,PEEK(ADDFROM%)
3090 ADDTO%=ADDTO%+1
3100 NEXT ADDFROM%
3110 SCREEN ,,0,0
3120 COLOR 7,0 : LOCATE 2,1,0 : PRINT STRING$(80," ");
3130 LOCATE 2,1,0 : PRINT"copying complete : next operation?"
3140 RETURN

3200 ´erase page
3201 ´**in ** FOREGROUND%,BACKGROUND%,CURSROW%,CURSCOL%,CURSVIS%
3202 ´**out** VPAGE%
3210 SCREEN ,,0,0
3220 COLOR 7,0 : LOCATE 1,1,0 : PRINT STRING$(120," ");
3230 LOCATE 2,1,0 : INPUT"Give the page to be erased ";VPAGE%
3240 LOCATE 3,1,0 : INPUT"Do you really mean that!: Y/N ";KB$
3250 IF KB$<>"y" AND KB$<>"Y" THEN GOSUB 2500 : RETURN
3260 SCREEN ,,VPAGE%,VPAGE%
3270 COLOR FOREGROUND%,BACKGROUND% : CLS
3280 LOCATE CURSROW%,CURSCOL%,CURSVIS%
3290 RETURN

3400 ´save page A% on disk
3410 SCREEN ,,0,0 : DEF SEG=&HB800
3420 COLOR 7,0 : LOCATE 1,1,0 : PRINT STRING$(120," ");
3430 LOCATE 2,1 : INPUT"Saving Page ";A%
3440 LOCATE 2,17 : INPUT"on file ";FILE$
3450 BSAVE FILE$,A%*2048,2000
3460 COLOR 7,0 : LOCATE 2,1,0 : PRINT STRING$(80," ");
3470 LOCATE 2,3,0 : PRINT"Saving complete : next operation?"
3480 RETURN

3600 ´load page A% from disk
3610 SCREEN ,,0,0 : DEF SEG=&HB800
3620 COLOR 7,0 : LOCATE 1,1,0 : PRINT STRING$(120," ");
3630 LOCATE 2,1 : INPUT"Loading Page ";A%
3640 LOCATE 2,17 : INPUT"from file ";FILE$
3650 SCREEN ,,A%,A%
3660 BLOAD FILE$,A%*2048
3670 SCREEN ,,0,0
3680 COLOR 7,0 : LOCATE 2,1,0 : PRINT STRING$(80," ");
3690 LOCATE 2,3,0 : PRINT"Loading complete : next operation?"
3700 RETURN

4000 ´make page visible
4001 ´**in ** FOREGROUND%,BACKGROUND%,CURSROW%,CURSCOL%,CURSVIS%
4002 ´**out** VPAGE%,CURSVIS%
4010 SCREEN ,,0,0
```

```
4020 COLOR 7,0 : LOCATE 1,1,0 : PRINT STRING$(120," ");
4030 LOCATE 2,1,0 : INPUT "Which page is to be visible?";VPAGE%
4040 IF VPAGE%<0 OR VPAGE%>7 THEN GOSUB 2500 : RETURN
4050 SCREEN ,,VPAGE%,VPAGE%
4060 CURSVIS%=1 : LOCATE CURSROW%,CURSCOL%,1
4070 COLOR FOREGROUND%,BACKGROUND%
4080 IF VPAGE%=0 THEN GOSUB 2000 ´screen menu
4090 RETURN

4500 ´INKEY$ input from keyboard of 1 or 2 digit number KB%
4502 ´**out** KB%
4509 ´first digit.
4510 KB$=INKEY$ : IF KB$="" THEN GOTO 4510
4520 KB1%=ASC(KB$)-48 : PRINT KB1%;
4530 IF KB1%<0 OR KB1%>9 THEN KB%=-1 : RETURN
4539 ´second digit : if RETURN pressed KB% just one digit.
4540 KB$=INKEY$ : IF KB$="" THEN GOTO 4540
4550 KB2%=ASC(KB$) : PRINT KB2%-48
4560 IF KB2%=13 THEN KB%=KB1% : RETURN
4570 IF KB2%<48 OR KB2%>57 THEN KB%=-1 : RETURN
4580 KB%=10*KB1%+KB2%-48
4590 RETURN

4700 ´INKEY$ input from keyboard of 1 digit number KB%
4702 ´**out** KB%
4709 ´first digit.
4710 KB$=INKEY$ : IF KB$="" THEN GOTO 4710
4720 KB%=ASC(KB$)-48 : PRINT KB%;
4730 IF KB%<0 OR KB%>9 THEN KB%=-1
4740 RETURN

5000 ´print string of characters
5001 ´**in ** FOREGROUND%,BACKGROUND%,VPAGE%
5010 IF VPAGE%=0 THEN RETURN
5020 COLOR FOREGROUND%,BACKGROUND%
5030 KB$=INKEY$ : IF KB$="" THEN GOTO 5030
5040 IF LEN(KB$)=1 THEN GOSUB 5200 : GOTO 5030
5050 KB$=RIGHT$(KB$,1): KB%=ASC(KB$)
5060 IF KB%=79 THEN RETURN
5070 GOSUB 7000 ´cursor move
5080 GOTO 5030

5200 ´print character on visible page
5201 ´**in ** CURSROW%,CURSCOL%,CURSVIS%,VPAGE%,KB$
5202 ´**out** CURSROW%,CURSCOL%
5210 IF VPAGE%=0 THEN RETURN
5220 LOCATE CURSROW%,CURSCOL%,CURSVIS%
5230 IF (CURSROW%=24 OR CURSROW%=25) AND CURSCOL%=40
     THEN GOSUB 5300 ELSE PRINT KB$;
5240 CURSCOL%=CURSCOL%+1
5250 IF CURSCOL%=41 THEN CURSCOL%=1
5260 LOCATE CURSROW%,CURSCOL%,CURSVIS%
5270 RETURN

5300 ´poke character onto page to avoid scrolling.
5301 ´**in ** FOREGROUND%,BACKGROUND%,VPAGE%,NOSCROLL%,CURSROW%,KB$
5310 ADDRESS%=NOSCROLL%(VPAGE%)
5320 IF CURSROW%=25 THEN ADDRESS%=ADDRESS%+80
5330 COL%=BACKGROUND%*16+(FOREGROUND% MOD 16)
5340 IF FOREGROUND%>15 THEN COL%=COL%+128
5350 DEF SEG=&HB800
5360 POKE ADDRESS%,ASC(KB$)
5370 POKE ADDRESS%+1,COL%
5380 RETURN

5600 ´change foreground colour
5601 ´**in ** FOREGROUND%,BACKGROUND%,VPAGE%,
               CURSROW%,CURSCOL%,CURSVIS%
5602 ´**out** FOREGROUND%
```

```
5610 SCREEN ,,0,VPAGE%
5620 COLOR 7,0 : LOCATE 1,1,0 : PRINT STRING$(120," ");
5630 LOCATE 2,1,0 : PRINT "New foreground colour ";
5640 GOSUB 4500 'INKEY$ 2-digit input from keyboard
5650 IF KB%<0 OR KB%>31 THEN GOSUB 2000 : RETURN
                          ELSE FOREGROUND%=KB%
5660 SCREEN ,,VPAGE%,VPAGE%
5670 COLOR FOREGROUND%,BACKGROUND%
5680 LOCATE CURSROW%,CURSCOL%,CURSVIS%
5690 IF VPAGE%=0 THEN GOSUB 2000 'menu layout
5700 RETURN


5800 'change background colour
5801 '**in ** FOREGROUND%,BACKGROUND%,VPAGE%,
               CURSROW%,CURSCOL%,CURSVIS%
5802 '**out** BACKGROUND%
5810 SCREEN ,,0,VPAGE%
5820 COLOR 7,0 : LOCATE 1,1,0 : PRINT STRING$(120," ");
5830 LOCATE 2,1,0 : PRINT "New background colour "
5840 GOSUB 4700 'INKEY$ input-digit from keyboard
5850 IF KB%<0 OR KB%>7 THEN GOSUB 2000 : RETURN
                         ELSE BACKGROUND%=KB%
5860 SCREEN ,,VPAGE%,VPAGE%
5870 COLOR FOREGROUND%,BACKGROUND%
5880 LOCATE CURSROW%,CURSCOL%,CURSVIS%
5890 IF VPAGE%=0 THEN GOSUB 2000 'menu layout
5900 RETURN

6000 'replace colours in character
6001 '**in ** CURSROW%,CURSCOL%
6010 CHARASC%=SCREEN(CURSROW%,CURSCOL%)
6020 KB$=CHR$(CHARASC%)
6030 GOSUB 5200 'print character
6040 RETURN

7000 'cursor move
7001 '**in ** CURSROW%,CURSCOL%,CURSVIZ%
7002 '**out** CURSROW%,CURSCOL%
7010 IF KB%=72 THEN CURSROW%=1+(CURSROW%+23) MOD 25 :
                    LOCATE CURSROW%,CURSCOL%,CURSVIS%
7020 IF KB%=80 THEN CURSROW%=1+CURSROW% MOD 25 :
                    LOCATE CURSROW%,CURSCOL%,CURSVIS%
7030 IF KB%=75 THEN CURSCOL%=1+(CURSCOL%+38) MOD 40 :
                    LOCATE CURSROW%,CURSCOL%,CURSVIS%
7040 IF KB%=77 THEN CURSCOL%=1+CURSCOL% MOD 40 :
                    LOCATE CURSROW%,CURSCOL%,CURSVIS%
7050 RETURN

8000 'animation
8002 '**out** CURVIS%
8010 LOCATE 1,1,0 : CURVIS%=1
8020 WHILE 0=0
8030 FOR PAGE%=1 TO 7
8040 SCREEN,,PAGE%,PAGE%
8049 'small delay
8050 FOR K%=1 TO 50 : NEXT K%
8060 KB$=INKEY$
8070 IF KB$="Q" OR KB$="q" THEN LOCATE 1,1,1 : RETURN
8080 NEXT PAGE%
8090 WEND
8100 RETURN
```

Exercise 13.3

Characters with ASCII code greater than 127 can be entered from the keyboard with the Alt(ernative) key used in conjunction with the numeric keypad. Use these characters, in particular codes 219 to 223, to construct animation text-scenes. For example, draw seven low-resolution pictures of a man, in seven stages of lifting a hat off his head. Then use the animation sequence of the editor program. It may take a long time to construct such scenes, but time can be saved by using the copying facility. Also note that partially completed pictures can always be stored on disk for later completion.

Exercise 13.4

Add extra options to the TEXT SCREEN EDITOR. For example, the various symmetry relationships seen in chapter 5, or invert colours (background with foreground – if legal) and so on.

Placing such explanatory text screen displays (perhaps animated) between graphic mode displays (such as bar-charts) for demonstration purposes adds that professional touch to the presentation of data. A complete slide-show stored on disk makes an impressive presentation.

Exercise 13.5

Write WIDTH 80 versions of the previous four programs.

This discussion of text screen manipulation brings to an end the theoretical part of the proceedings. The next chapter will set you a number of large-scale projects. It is time for you to implement the ideas that you have learned in this book on your IBM PC. Good luck!

Complete Programs

'lib0' must be MERGED with all the listings given below.

   I. Listing 13.1. Animation example. WIDTH required: 40 or 80.
   II. Listing 13.2 ('bat and ball' game). Program requires a seed for the random number generator (an integer between −32768 and 32767) and a WIDTH of 40. The bat is controlled by the up/down cursor keys (↑, ↓).
   III. Listing 13.3 ('catcher and muncher'). Program needs a skill factor between 0 and 100, and a WIDTH 40. Game starts after any key is pressed. The catcher is controlled by the left/right cursor keys (←, →).
   IV. Listing 13.4. Multiscreen animation. WIDTH 40 is the only data required.
   V. Listing 13.5. The TEXT SCREEN EDITOR. WIDTH 40. Numerous operational commands. See the Menu on the screen, or text, for details.

14 Projects

I. Use your IBM PC to draw a digital clock. Use the PIXEL BLOCK GENERA-TOR of chapter 5 to produce the special large blocks to represent all the digits as well as a colon to separate them in the display. Your clock can be made to keep correct time by using the internal clock of the PC (see the manual).

II. Make a program that tests the Morse Code proficiency of the user. The data for the program will be a paragraph of text, which the IBM PC should trans-late into Morse and then print out the dots and dashes, using either special user-defined characters or pixel blocks. It must also use SOUND to simulate the sound of Morse. Your program should have a variable rate of production of the code so that the speed of the test increases as the user gets more proficient. You could also produce a text-only mode version of the program.

III. Draw sets of special symbols, such as International Road Signs, the Flags of Nations, Company Logos. Your program should have routines that create any specific background (for example, the red triangles of the road signs) and then use your own special interactive routines or the labelling program of chapter 6 to finish off the foreground.

IV. Construct crossword puzzles on your colour monitor. Each square of the puzzle must be 16 pixels square (that is, 2 characters square). The four blocks will either be black (in which case nothing goes in the square), or white with the bottom left-hand corner holding the letter of a solution, and either the top two characters holding clue numbers (if any) or the top left character holding two 'narrow' digits. This allows space for a 20 by 12 puzzle.

You also have to place the clues on the screen. These can be printed on request in a viewport. Naturally the screen must be stored in an array so that it can be reset later. Solutions to the puzzle can be added by a 'cursor' method or by having a special input code, such as letter 'A' (across) or 'D' (down), followed by the number of the clue, followed by the solution. You can add messages to reject incorrect answers.

V. The BASIC manual has shown you how to use SOUND to create music(?). While SOUND is making the noises, you can draw the musical notation on the screen. You can construct the staves and then use special characters or pixel blocks to place quavers, minims etc. on the screen. The old Music Hall method of the 'bouncing ball' could be used to beat the time of the tune.

VI. Use the character blocks to draw mazes. Naturally your program must generate mazes with real solutions. You can give yourself time limits for getting through the maze. You can make the mazes dynamic; that is, they change as the game progresses. Add extra problems: pixel block man-eating monsters which roam the maze, holes that suddenly appear and can swallow you up, 'space warps' which can transfer you anywhere in the maze if you do not move fast enough.

VII. Extend the ideas of chapter 6. Draw your own special histograms, pie-charts and graphs. Make them dynamic by drawing a number of graphs on the same axes and then GETting them into memory and finally PUTting them back onto the screen under keyboard supervision. Generate whole sets of special characters. Draw solid data graphs by joining each point on the graph to the x-axis, or by tile-PAINTing under the graph. Extend the mathematical surface program (listing 10.8) to draw three-dimensional histograms. For every rectangle on the x/z grid there must now be one y-value. So for each such grid rectangle, starting at the back and working forward, you simply need to draw the rectangular block from the grid base up to this y-value.

VIII. Create patterns. Use PUT (XOR) with large numbers of random lines or polygons to create different moiré patterns. For example, draw two closely packed spirals in the graphics modes, one slightly off-centre, and see what patterns emerge.

Extend the ideas of the tessellated pattern program of chapter 5 to produce complex symmetrical patterns – any introductory book on crystallography (such as Phillips, 1956) will give you lots of ideas.

IX. Books on geometry (such as Coxeter, 1974) and crystallography (such as Phillips, 1956) will give you many ideas for three-dimensional objects. Extend into four dimensions – each vertex is simply a vector of four numbers and so requires 5 x 5 matrices for transformations. The simplest projection of a four-dimensional point is again the orthographic, where now two of the coordinates are ignored (as opposed to one, z, in three dimensions). There are many more complex projections. What are translation, scale and rotation in four dimensions?

X. A chessboard has already been created in chapter 5. There are many more possible board games: Draughts (or Checkers), Scrabble, Hangman, Ludo, Master Mind, or even construct a complete chess set. You can create a Compendium of Games. The IBM PC may simply act as the board, but it can also act as a referee. If you feel really adventurous it can even act as an opponent.

XI. Use combinations of preconstructed pixel blocks to display a deck of Playing Cards. These can be incorporated into a program to play Blackjack (or Pontoon) with the PC acting as both bank and opponent.

XII. You can draw certain types of brain-teasers on your monitor. For example, suppose you have nine squares, each divided into quarters down the diagonals. Each quarter will be PAINTed in one of four colours (numbered

1, 2, 3 or 4) and have a sign (+ or −). The number of colours available in a palette can be extended by tile-PAINTing. Hence a square may be represented as a sequence of four numbers corresponding to the four quarters taken clockwise around the centre. For example, they could be $(-1, -2, 1, 4)$, $(-1, 3, 4, -2)$, $(1, -4, -2, 3)$, $(1, 2, -3, -4)$, $(1, 3, -2, -4)$, $(1, 4, -3, -2)$, $(2, -3, -4, 3)$ and two occurrences of $(-1, -4, 3, 2)$. The problem is to place the nine squares in a three by three arrangement, so that if two quarters on neighbouring squares touch, then they must be of the same colour but of opposite sign. You can use the IBM PC to draw the squares as pixel blocks initially on the left side of the screen and a three by three grid of squares of the same size on the right. Then using a cursor you take squares from the left and place them in the grid, or replace them back to the left. Also write a recursive program which finds the two independent solutions of the above problem.

XIII. Another brain-teaser is the Seven Hexagons Problem. Each hexagon is broken into six equilateral triangles. These triangles are in six different colours (numbered 1 to 6) taken clockwise around the centre of the hexagon. For example, the seven hexagons could be $(1, 2, 3, 4, 5, 6)$, $(1, 5, 3, 2, 4, 6)$, $(1, 5, 6, 3, 2, 4)$, $(1, 3, 2, 5, 4, 6)$, $(1, 6, 5, 2, 4, 3)$, $(1, 2, 6, 5, 3, 4)$ and $(1, 5, 6, 4, 2, 3)$. The hexagons are to be placed on a table, one in the centre with each of the remaining six touching, edge to edge, one side of the central hexagon. The problem is to place the hexagons in such a way that, when two hexagons touch, the triangles on either side of the edge of contact have the same colour. Write an interactive graphics program to play this teaser, and also a recursive program solution.

XIV. Use the labelling package of chapter 6 to manipulate the mode 1 screen so that it produces an approximation to a photograph. The character generator is used to store 16 special characters. Each character (8 by 8 pixels) is divided into four 4 by 4 pixel blocks, each of which can be coloured either black or white. The sixteen characters are therefore all the possible black/white combinations within such a restriction. These characters will be placed on the screen in the text matrix of 40 by 25. Take any photograph of yourself and superimpose a grid of 80 by 50 on it. Each square in this grid corresponds to a four by four pixel block. For each grid square, decide whether it is mainly light or dark, and colour the corresponding quarter character accordingly (white or black). Four neighbouring blocks define a character which can be PRINTed on the screen to get the low-resolution photograph. This seems like a lot of work, but note that most of the picture will be a light background, so if a white background and black foreground are used, most of the squares need not be considered. You could draw two heads side by side on the screen.

XV. Write a PAC MAN type of video game in BASIC. This involves drawing five moving objects (PAC MAN and four ghosts) on the screen at a time, either as user-defined characters or pixel blocks. In order to make the game move faster, you will have to limit the number of ghosts that can move with each move of PAC MAN. The ghosts should find the quickest path towards PAC MAN when chasing him, and the best escape route when running away. Some compromise is necessary if the game is not to be too slow. The game layout is far too complicated for best solutions to be found in interpreted BASIC. For example, just move towards (or away from) PAC MAN if there is no wall in the way. Calculating position and collisions, and PRINTing, will be a time-consuming part of the game, so find efficient ways of coding these routines. Speed is the essence of a good video game, so perhaps machine code routines could be used in the most-used sections of the program.

XVI. Write a program that first prints a graphics menu of special symbols on some part of a graphics-mode screen. For example, use the stylised components for electronic circuits (resistors, capacitors etc.). These symbols should consist of combinations of lines and be stored as pixel blocks. Keep a copy of the screen in the same way so that the whole screen is buffered as in the diagram programs (chapter 6). Use a cursor to point at any menu-symbol and then drag a copy of it to a required position on the screen (exactly like the pixel block drag of the diagram labelling routine). Also add a facility for drawing connecting lines ('rubber-banding') and labelling with narrow numeric and special characters (such as Ω for ohms). You should also allow deletion of symbols inadvertently placed in the wrong position. Extra options could include saving and loading.

XVII. In all the perspective diagrams it is assumed that the objects lie totally in front of the eye. Change the programs so that they deal with the general case where vertices may lie anywhere in space, including behind the eye. See Newman and Sproull (1979), Foley and van Dam (1982) and Harrington (1983) concerning this concept of three-dimensional clipping.

Change the three-dimensional procedures so that they form an interactive program. Set up a complex scene (such as a group of houses) and use the menu technique to specify and change the observation point. You can change the observation point or a point on the straight-ahead ray by moving it a specified distance in the x, y or z directions.

XVIII. Produce stereoscopic hidden line views of three-dimensional objects. Now the facets must be coloured in background white and the edges in red or cyan. Remember that when you are drawing the facets for the second eye, they must not obliterate the lines drawn for the first eye.

XIX. Draw a Rubik's Cube or Rubik's Revenge. Enter the rotation details from the keyboard and redraw the cube in each new position. Again four colours in a palette are not enough: use tile-PAINT.

References and Further Reading

References

Cohn, P. M. (1961), *Solid Geometry*, Routledge and Kegan Paul, London
Coxeter, H. S. M. (1974), *Regular Polytopes*, Dover Publications, New York
Davenport, H. (1952), *The Higher Arithmetic*, Hutchinson, London
Finkbeiner, D. T. (1978), *Introduction to Matrices and Linear Transformations*,
   3rd edition, W. H. Freeman, San Francisco
Foley, J. D. and van Dam, A. (1982), *Fundamentals of Interactive Computer
   Graphics*, Addison-Wesley, Reading, Massachusetts
Harrington, S. (1983), *Computer Graphics: a Programming Approach*, McGraw-Hill,
   London
Horowitz, E. and Sahni, S. (1976), *Fundamentals of Data Structures*, Pitman,
   London
Knuth, D. (1973), *The Art of Computer Programming. Volume 1: Fundamental
   Algorithms*, 2nd edition (*Volume 2: Semi-numerical Algorithms*, 2nd edition
   1981. *Volume 3: Sorting and Searching*, 1972), Addison-Wesley, London
Liffick, B. W. (1979), *The BYTE book of Pascal*, Byte Publications, New Hampshire
Mandelbrot, B. B. (1977), *Fractals*, W. H. Freeman, San Francisco
McCrae, W. H. (1953), *Analytical Geometry of Three Dimensions*, Oliver and Boyd,
   London
Newman, W. M. and Sproull, R. F. (1979), *Principles of Interactive Computer
   Graphics*, McGraw-Hill, London
Phillips, F. C. (1956), *An Introduction to Crystallography*, 2nd edition, Longmans,
   London
Stroud, K. A. (1982), *Engineering Mathematics*, 2nd edition, Macmillan, London
Tolansky, S. (1964), *Optical Illusions*, Pergamon Press, New York

Further Reading

Read any periodical, magazine or journal that is relevant to computer graphics such
as *SIGGRAPH, CADCAM, CAD Journal* (and there are many, many others), and
the more advanced graphics textbooks (such as Newman and Sproull, 1979; Foley
and van Dam, 1982) as well as the general computer newspapers and monthly
magazines (such as *Byte, Personal Computer World, Practical Computing* etc.). It

does not matter if you do not immediately understand the more advanced articles: it is important to appreciate the flavour, excitement and achievement of the subject. Obtain the promotional and advertising literature of the major graphics companies (Tektronix, Imlac, A.E.D., Sigma, Hewlett-Packard, D.E.C. etc.), and get as much information as possible about graphics software packages. Keep an eye on the television usage of computer graphics, whether it be in science programmes, science-fiction melodramas or advertisements. Study video games and try to understand from the display how the characters are drawn and manipulated.

Appendix: Contents and Availability of Related Software

A companion double-sided diskette is available, which has been designed especially for use with this book. It is suitable for all DOS versions and contains all the program listings given in the book, as well as the four data files mentioned in the text:

NARROW.DAT PATTERN.DAT PIECES.DAT and ROTCHARS.DAT

The four library files 'lib0', 'lib1', 'lib2' and 'lib3' are stored as LIB0.BAS, LIB1.BAS, LIB2.BAS and LIB3.BAS respectively.

All the other listings are named in the format Li#j.BAS, where

i represents the chapter – that is, I (introduction) or an integer between 1 and 13 (chapter 14 has no listings!)

j represents the listing within a chapter. An integer gives the listing number. If listings are combined then an & is used to denote this combination.

For example, L1#2.BAS holds listing 1.2, while L9#5&6&7.BAS holds the combination of listings 9.5, 9.6 and 9.7.

All the program listings are stored in ASCII format, so they can be MERGED into other programs at will. Check the 'Complete Programs' section at the end of each chapter to see which listings must be combined to give the required programs, and also note the order in which the listings must be MERGED.

Availability

The double-sided diskette is available through all major bookshops, but in case of difficulty order direct from

Globe Book Services
Houndmills
Brunel Road
Basingstoke
Hampshire RG21 2XS

ISBN 0–333–38854–2

The diskette is priced at £21.50 (inclusive of VAT) in the United Kingdom.

Index

(In general, only the definitions of variable names appear in the index)

front 130, 172
FRONT% 222
functional notation, representation
 58–60, 64–9, 154–6
furthest 201

G 101, 109, 126
G% 224
gap 128, 130
GAP 128, 130
garbage (collector) 92, 177, 224
general point 45, 48, 50, 56, 64, 67,
 142–5, 150, 154, 159
geometry 252
GET 17, 19–21, 24, 101, 104, 109,
 115, 118, 126, 127, 198, 252
goblet xvi, 187
GRAFTABL 5, 92, 94, 117
graph paper 184
GRAPHICS 25, 117
graphics area, frame, rectangle, screen
 7, 13, 27, 29, 30, 33, 38, 53–6,
 198, 208, 213, 214, 248
graphics command, operation 2, 12,
 23–5
graphics definition language 14
graphics mode 5, 8, 15, 34, 92,
 250, 252, 254
graphics monitor *see* colour monitor,
 display
graphics pen 14
graphs xiv, 117, 134, 135, 252
green 3, 6, 33, 193
grey scale 139, 217
grid 2, 100–2, 108, 109, 111, 115,
 184, 204, 205, 252
GRIDX% 101
GRIDY% 101

H 118, 127, 128
hand-compile 1, 181
Hangman 252
hardware 1
hatch mark 135
hatching 66–9, 128
HCF% 45
heap 224
HEAP% 224
hearts 241
height 181, 183, 193
hexadecimal 11, 92, 93, 96
hexagon 177, 231, 253

hidden lines, surface xiv, 60, 63, 156,
 157, 170, 178, chapter 10, 219,
 chapter 12, 254
high byte xv
high intensity 3
high resolution xi, 2, 27
highest common factor 45
histogram *see* bar-chart
HOLD% 127
hole 15, 45, 65, 91
hollow 12, 233
Home key xvii, 122, 127, 245
HORIZ 29, 34, 35, 39, 42, 50, 53,
 56, 79, 81, 90
horizon 207
horizontal axis, scale 128, 130,
 131, 163
horizontal characters, label 96, 127
horizontal column, edge, line, row
 12, 19, 27, 29, 62, 113, 141, 186
horizontal set 186
house 80
hyperbola 42, 65

I 102
icosahedron 192, 193, 227, 231
identifier xiv, 70, 73, 238
identity matrix 71, 73, 78, 81, 83,
 159, 166, 171–3, 175, 178, 181
idiot proof 1
Illegal function call, error 17, 118
illumination vector 201
implicit data 85, 87, 189
in xv
in front 222, 224
INC% 122
increment 109, 122
index 30, 36, 84, 87, 159, 177
indicator 126, 128, 244
infinity 28, 48, 141
information section 224
INKEY$ 238, 244
INPUT 90
inside 60, 62, 65, 190, 191, 210,
 222, 230
INT 19, 29
integer code 189
integer name 19
intensity 3
interactive control, program 7, 100,
 117, 122, 126
International Road Signs 251

interpreter 1, 5, 25, 92, 94
interrupt vector 93
intersection 48, 51–4, 60, 61, 63, 66,
    68, 69, 135, 145–56, 205,
    221, 222
inverse matrix 71, 72, 76, 151, 153,
    164, 165
inverse transformation 76, 164
inverted colours 34, 96, 102, 109,
    128, 250
invisible 214, 224
IX 54
IY 54

Jackson Pollock 13
jaggedness 38, 214
jet 184, 216, 218
joystick 122
junction 189

K 146, 152, 245
key 127, 138, 238, 245, 249
KEY OFF 1
keyboard 25, 83, 100, 101, 103, 109,
    118, 119, 122, 126, 128, 238,
    240, 241, 244, 245, 249, 252
keyboard (input) buffer 238, 240
Kilobyte 2
Knights Tour 111

L 109, 118, 127, 149, 244
LABCOL% 96
labels xiv, 7, 96, 113, 115, 117, 118,
    121, 122, 126–9, 133–8, 181,
    231, 253, 254
LABEL$ 96
LABROW% 96
large-scale representation 108
layout 108
least significant 3, 12, 13
left 3, 8, 11, 14, 16, 73, 101, 128
left eye 217, 219
left-hand corner (bottom) 8, 12, 23,
    24, 27, 29, 115
left-hand corner (top) 27, 100, 108,
    109
left-handed axes, triad 141, 162, 163
length 8, 9, 48, 68, 181, 183, 193
level of recursion 110, 111
lib0 xvi, 1, 2, 4, 5, 13
lib1 xvi, 32, 53, 57, 61
lib2 91

lib3 xvi, 188
library file, routines xvi, 2, 181
lightpen 122, 128
limits, limitations 1, 15, 39, 42, 53,
    61, 73, 83, 184, 189, 199, 221,
    222, 227, 231, 235, 238
LIN% 78, 87, 177, 181
line 12, 14, 17, 23, 27, 28, 31, 34, 38,
    42, 48–64, 67–70, 76, 79, 82–4,
    87, 90, 122, 134, 141–7, 152–8,
    167, 170–3, 177, 181–7, 189,
    191, 197, 198, 204–11, 217,
    222, 227, 252
LINE 12, 13, 18, 30, 55, 108, 115,
    130, 137, 138, 140, 181
line of sight 171, 176
linear equations 159
linear transformation 70, 74, 159
linearly dependent 142
linked list 224, 232
LIS% 224
list 110, 221
LOAD xiv
LOC% 236
local variables 111
LOCATE 3, 4, 8, 235, 236, 241
locations 11–13, 80, 224, 235–7, 244
logical colour 6, 7, 11, 13, 16, 18, 21,
    37, 80, 87, 93, 102, 109, 111,
    115, 118, 122, 126, 127, 130,
    135, 139, 177, 192, 201, 237
logo 251
London 129, 131
long shot 213
low byte xv
low intensity 3
low resolution xi, 250
lower bound 135, 138
lower case xiv
Ludo 252

M 14, 109, 118, 126, 149, 244
machine code 1, 61
machine tools 231
machine-dependent 31
magenta 3, 6, 193, 217, 219
mainframe computer 2, 122
maintain the vertical 175, 178
major axis 40, 65, 85
major diagonal 110, 211
map, mapping 29, 32, 35, 90
mask 12

Where to Find Routines referred to in Text

Availability of Diskette

The double-sided diskette is available through all major bookshops, but in case of difficulty order direct from

Globe Book Services
Houndmills
Brunel Road
Basingstoke
Hampshire RG21 2XS

ISBN 0-333-38854-2

The diskette is priced at £21.50 (inclusive of VAT) in the United Kingdom. See appendix for further details.